The Handbook of
PRACTICAL PSYCHOLOGY

B. RICHARD BUGELSKI

Distinguished Professor of Psychology Emeritus

ANTHONY M. GRAZIANO

Professor of Psychology

State University of New York at Buffalo

PRENTICE-HALL, INC.

Englewood Cliffs, N.J. 07632

A SPECTRUM BOOK

Library of Congress Cataloging in Publication Data

Bugelski, Bergen Richard
    Handbook of practical psychology.

    (A Spectrum Book)
    Includes index.
      1. Psychology.   I. Graziano, Anthony M.,
1932-   joint author.   II. Title.
BF 121.B838   150   80-17677
ISBN 0-13-380600-6
ISBN 0-13-380592-1 (pbk.)

Editorial/production supervision and interior design by Suse L. Cioffi
Cover design by Honi Werner
Manufacturing buyer: Barbara A. Frick

10   9   8   7

Printed in the United States of America

for
Mary Beth
and
Amy, Lisa, and Michael

PRENTICE-HALL INTERNATIONAL, INC., *London*
PRENTICE-HALL OF AUSTRALIA PTY. LIMITED, *Sydney*
PRENTICE-HALL OF CANADA, LTD., *Toronto*
PRENTICE-HALL OF INDIA PRIVATE LIMITED, *New Delhi*
PRENTICE-HALL OF JAPAN, INC., *Tokyo*
PRENTICE-HALL OF SOUTHEAST ASIA PTE. LTD., *Singapore*
WHITEHALL BOOKS LIMITED, *Wellington, New Zealand*

PREFACE

In 1979, psychology celebrated its centennial as an academic pursuit. In that 100 years, the subject of psychology has developed along at least two tracks—one of the academic, experimental, laboratory, or scientific track, the other that of the clinic, the hospital, and the consulting room. A third, the business, or industrial, track might also be listed. We make bold to represent the two tracks of experimental and clinical psychology, although we cannot presume to be the nominees of the thousands of psychologists now at work. In all probability we are not the ideal choices, but we feel the need for such a work as this, and no one else seemed to want to volunteer for the job. The first author, B. R. Bugelski, has been engaged in laboratory and industrial research for the last forty years, largely concerned with problems of perception and learning. The second author, A. M. Graziano, has followed a career in clinical psychology since 1961 and has specialized in problems of child development and in psychotherapy.

Although clinicians and experimentalists have traditionally viewed each others' efforts with some skepticism, the present collaboration arose from a mutual respect and common interest in evaluating what psychology as a whole has contributed to the welfare of the citizens who have supported it for so long. What we have tried to do here is to distill the research findings that are reported in psychological journals and books that are unfamiliar to the general public into brief summaries of useful points expressed in clear terms. Obviously, we are not experts in all of the areas, and we have taken advantage of the vast amount of work reported by thousands of psychologists over the years. We have presented here only what amount to well-established findings such as might be found in general psychology texts. The difficulty with the general psychology texts is that they are designed for a different purpose and many of them, quite justifiably, do not discuss the items we have chosen to include, or, if they do, they treat them at a theoretical level. In our preparation, we consulted numerous texts and usually came away unsatisfied about finding a practical application of an item. It made us sympathetic to student complaints about the lack of relevance.

Obviously, we do not pretend to have covered every topic or to have handled each item to everyone's satisfaction. We will be grateful for suggestions about other topics and about improvements of our coverage.

In our preparation of this volume, we had the helpful criticism of our numerous colleagues at the State University of New York at Buffalo. Rather than list all of those who made helpful and critical suggestions, we prefer to thank them all and shoulder the responsibility for any errors of fact and unsound judgments. We cannot thank two of our staff enough, however, by such anonymous references. Dr. Ira Cohen, the department chairman, facilitated our work enormously by providing all the necessary encouragement and material aids; he even contributed the section on Temperament. The section on psychiatric commitment was written by Attorney Sheila Graziano. Ms. June Ackerman supervised the preparation of the manuscript through its various alterations and, with department staff, provided a test public for our presentations. Without her efficient control, the manuscript would still be in preparation.

We do not pretend to any originality or new discoveries, as this is not the kind of book in which to present such new information. This book is, indeed, not even our own in any particular or distinctive sense, since it tries to demonstrate what psychology itself has to offer. Presumably, any other psychologist could have prepared a similar volume simply by doing what we did—reading what other psychologists had reported over the years about the topics chosen.

Buffalo, New York
September 30, 1979

INTRODUCTION

During World War II, a Harvard psychologist, E. G. Boring, prepared a small volume he thought might help our armed forces personnel. He called it *Psychology for the Fighting Man.* In that book, he tried to present whatever material psychologists had some confidence in that might help soldiers handle some of the problems they faced in military service. His book dealt mainly with problems, ideas, and concepts related to perception and learning. Despite his best efforts, much of the material was not of great practical value because psychologists up to that time were primarily involved with theoretical issues. Even in the 1960s and 1970s, college students were demanding that their psychology courses be more relevant than they appeared to be to young people of college age. It was not easy to respond to their demands because much of what psychologists knew about was not of great interest to college age youngsters.

Since World War II, however, a great deal of information has been acquired—much of it negative, to be sure—about problems that do concern the average citizen, especially if he or she is a parent and is facing problems of child rearing. Many other issues of practical interest have also engaged the academic psychologist. Psychologists have been very active in the fields of psychotherapy, education, industry, social issues, and practically every form of human activity. The press and television have brought many issues to public attention that formerly were quietly ignored. Almost everyone has read in the newspapers and so-called family magazines about incest, homosexuality, drug abuse, marital problems, and sexual inadequacies. Much of the advice that appears in newspapers and the family magazines is competent and helpful, and people are becoming a great deal more sophisticated than they were in earlier times. The trouble with an account, such as one might read in a magazine or newspaper, is not its inadequacy as much as that what is read is quickly forgotten once the newspaper or magazine is thrown away. When an issue comes up on which someone might want advice, there is no handy source. In this book, we have tried to prepare brief discussions of the many kinds of problems people run into or which run into them at various times in their lives. We try to provide the professional advice newspaper readers are often urged to seek by the columnists they read.

Although the press and other media have been helpful in bringing applied psychological information to the people, they have also catered to the less sophisticated readers by exploiting their interests in various fringe areas that are frequently misidentified as being of a psychological nature. Thus, we have lurid tales of psychic phenomena, mysterious ladies who help police find victims of crimes, other mysterious Russian ladies who read through their fingers, columns on astrology, biorythms, and prophecies for the coming year by alleged psychics. The movies and television have not been loathe to picture multiple personalities, vampires, witches, demons, and their exorcism, along with a host of other kinds of psychological science fiction relating to drugs, crime, and psychotherapy. In this volume, we try to indicate the fallacies involved in such matters although, like the preacher who scolds the congregation about those who are not present, we may be addressing the wrong audience. People who believe in astrology or witchcraft are not likely to be reading this work. Perhaps parents might be able to use our presentations to prepare their children for the foibles of the news and entertainment media.

Our purpose in preparing this book was to serve all those citizens who have not had the opportunity to study psychology for many years, either in or out of college. Students in psychology courses might find in this work some of the relevance they might be seeking, but our interest has been in preparing a psychology for the citizen, the parent, and the person concerned with psychological problems—either ones of his own or ones of those close to him. We have not tried to deal with controversial matters or with theoretical issues of interest to a smaller audience of academicians. Our concern is to tell you only what you might want to know and not much more than that. Where our coverage of a topic appears brief, it is because the practical application of any knowledge related to that topic is small in scope, even though books have been written on the subject.

This, then, is not a book that should be read from cover to cover. Instead, it should be treated like a reference book, like a dictionary or encyclopedia, and topics should be looked up as they become of interest. The topics discussed are presented in alphabetical order for easy identification. If you do not know the technical term under which a topic might be discussed, check the index, where both technical and popular terminology are listed.

Some of our coverage of topics may appear negative. This is not because we take any delight in saying that something is not true or worthless. In many such matters, we would be pleased if the findings has been positive and of some possible value to the world. To tell a cancer patient that laetrile does not work may be disappointing, but it will at least save him some time and money. It would be much better, of course, if laetrile did work. Similarly, when we point out that some kind of promised psychotherapy is of no known value, we would much rather that it did work, but we prefer to ask people to face the facts as they are known today.

Although this book is designed to provide advice to people with problems, we try not to tell anyone what he or she should do in matters and affairs where psychology has no business taking sides. On moral and ethical matters, people will do what they feel is right, and we cannot tell people whether they should get married, have children, get divorced, or do many of the kinds of things people do. We can only hope to provide some guidelines about how some kinds of problems may be solved, at least as far as psychologists have determined the facts.

A

ABILITY AND CAPACITY   (See TEST-TRAIT FALLACY)

Words like *skill* and *ability* refer to present demonstrable operations. Words like *aptitude, talent, capacity,* and the like refer to some kind of *potential*, given certain conditions like training or equipment. It is assumed that one might have the aptitude but not the skill. An aptitude test for salesmanship, for example, might yield a high score for someone who has never sold anything; that same person might be a poor salesman if not properly trained and equipped or if he did not have other required characteristics. Talent and capacities, similarly, refer to some future potential that may never be realized. Words like *tendency* or *susceptibility* are rather circular and meaningless in that we can say that one might be susceptible to a cold but not catch it; if one does catch a cold, we can say he was susceptible, but the only basis for such a remark is that he did indeed catch the cold.

It is commonly assumed that aptitudes are inherited; one either has them or not. Such an assumption has no factual foundation except in such cases where some inherited defect may be present that incapacitates someone from some activity. One does not employ deaf piano tuners. Even in such cases, however, some kind of equipment might be devised to enable a person to do a task for which he seems unsuitable. Thus, a visual display of a sound wave could enable someone to adjust a tuning pin in order to produce a particular wave, and each key on a piano could be brought to a known pitch.

Aptitude tests are convenient for sorting out for what kinds of operations some might appear to have a head start over others. Suitable training, however, can overcome great weaknesses in test scores if the time and cost of training are not prohibitive. College admission officers prefer to accept those applicants who score well on tests because the expense of bringing applicants with lower scores up to a suitable level is beyond their control. The same attitude guides employers if they have suitable tests for new applicants. Even with aptitude, such factors as motivation, other interests, physical strength, and so on enter into decisions about what one might do with an aptitude. Many college drop-outs find the college experience meaningless, even though they could handle the academic work. Others are screened out and prevented from following careers in law or medicine because they do not score well on aptitude tests that are part of the admission requirements. Such tests may or may not have much to do with success in law or medicine, but they help the admissions committee to reduce the number of applicants. There are special schools and training texts that help test takers to improve their scores on such tests. Such pretest training does help a great deal in many cases and is available at an additional expense for the determined candidate.

The important point to consider is that aptitude is only one of the factors in controlling success. Without any aptitude, failure is, of course, likely, but with aptitude, there is no guarantee of success. The lack of aptitude can be remedied in some cases, depending on the reasons for the lack. A boy who has never played with a baseball is unlikely to make the team his first time out. The question might very well be:

Why is he going out now if he has never played before? Unless there were no baseballs in his prior environment, he obviously had no previous interest in baseball, and it might be just too late for all concerned for that person to begin now. The same reasoning holds for many occupations and activities. By and large, aptitudes and interests must be considered together, since both are necessary for any kind of progress.

ACCIDENTS AND ACCIDENT PRONENESS   (See CARELESSNESS)

An *accident* is normally thought of as an unexpected event. It presumably shouldn't have happened and would not have if the people involved had done something else. The very definition of accidents as unexpected events precludes doing much about them in advance. After an accident has happened and we discover how and why it happened, we may be able to arrange conditions to prevent that particular accident from happening again. If someone falls into a well, a cover can be put over the well so that no one else can fall in. Of course, if the cover makes the well unusable, we are faced with another problem, but no one will fall into a covered well. The point is that accident prevention calls for work and expenses with frequent undesirable accompaniments. What this amounts to is that people will continue to talk about accidents and accident prevention instead of doing something about accidents. They will put up signs asking people to be careful and will perform other such costless operations, but being careful is a meaningless expression, since one can attend only to what he is doing and not to something else, especially unexpected events or situations.

A person involved in an accident will often try to blame somebody else and otherwise justify his or her own behavior. When someone has had a number of accidents, we tend to reject his or her attempts to assign blame and assume that he or she is somehow responsible. People with more than their apparent share of accidents are sometimes called *accident prone,* with the implication that they are somehow inviting accidents and that their personalities need investigation rather than the accidents themselves. There is no evidence for any kind of accident-prone personality. If there are people around who have an unusual number of accidents, it may be just a statistical point. Some people have to have more than others if there is to be a statistical average. The people who do have the accidents may be working in more hazardous situations or may be improperly trained for the demands on them.

ACHIEVEMENT TESTS   (See INTELLIGENCE TESTS)

Achievement tests are not tests of intelligence or ability but rather tests of knowledge or accomplishment. Thus, a test of American History would normally test one's knowledge of the subject and not his capacity to learn it. Achievement tests, of course, assume some capacity to handle tests in general, and when a whole group of people is exposed to some material, as in a grade school course, the final results, in a way, reflect what they were able to get out of the exposure and might indirectly reflect upon the children's capacity. It is assumed that, all other things being equal, the brighter child will achieve more than the dull one. Some *aptitude tests* call for the solution of mathematical problems and for the use of language (proper grammar, spelling, compositional skills); such *ability* tests are then based on a certain amount of achievement. All *intelligence tests* call for some experience with language and some familiarity with objects in the real world. Thus, achievement and intelligence are supposed to be related, but the degree of that relationship is not known and cannot be specified. Children who speak only a foreign language cannot pass an intelligence test given in English with any distinction—they must first achieve a knowledge of English. Such children should be tested in their own languages where they have achieved some mastery.

In general, intelligence tests are built on the assumption that as a child grows and matures in a normal environment, he will encounter and learn about the kinds of items that appear on the test. If he does not handle the questions well, it can be argued that he has not achieved—that is, acquired—the proper background. Although we should not claim that there is a vicious circle in the achievement—intelligence testing situation, it is clear that there is a circle: Intelligent children are expected to achieve more, and such achievement suggests an underlying intelligence.

ADAPTATION, SENSORY ADJUSTMENTS

Psychologists in the early history of psychology were primarily concerned with sensory capacities, structures, and functions. They learned a great deal about the senses, much of which is now common knowledge. One question that has not been answered is this: Just how many senses are there? The common answer of five includes only vision, audition, taste, smell, and touch. A most important sense, kinesthesis, by which we know about the position of our limbs, is commonly overlooked. To all these senses we can probably add the senses of pain, balance, motion, and gravity (astronauts in outer space experience weightlessness). The commonly listed five senses, themselves, break down into various special senses, such as those for color, for rhythm, or perhaps for different kinds of smell and taste (some people cannot taste some substances that others can; others cannot smell certain odors). Perhaps we should add a temperature sense or senses. The sense of touch may break down into a whole variety of senses (tickle, itch, pricklyness, smoothness, roughness, clamminess, etc.).

Adaptaton. In all senses, we tend to get used to the prevailing stimulation and come to ignore any constant sources or surrounding stimulation. Thus, at a cocktail party, we can ignore the general hubbub and carry on a conversation with some person even though the noise level is alarming to someone just entering the room. Psychologists have, in recent years, paid much attention to *adaptation levels*. We are always at some stage or level of stimulation, and we get used to it; it becomes our standard for evaluating any changes. Thus, if we put a hand in a bowl of water (avoiding extremes), it will at first feel warm, cold, or tepid, but in a few minutes, if the temperature does not change, we will get used to it, adapt, or come to regard it as nonstimulating; it becomes the standard. Now any change will be measured against that standard. In a shower, originally hot water may no longer seem so hot, and so we adjust the control to get hotter water if we want to feel warmer.

Visual adaptation. Sometimes we begin to read late in the afternoon when the print is quite visible, and we read on into the late afternoon when a newcomer into the room is shocked to find us reading in what he or she might call the dark. We may be having no problem about the reading because our eyes have adjusted to the level of illumination present as far as print on white paper is concerned. If we tried to match colors or appreciate color detail at such a time, we might find ourselves surprisingly inept.

In the case of visual adaptation, we recognize that the eye is equipped with two kinds of visual sensors or sense organs: On the retina, there are tiny organs called rods and cones. The rods are specialized for seeing in dim light, whereas the cones are specialized for seeing in brighter light and for colors. The cones adapt out faster than do the rods, and so we cannot see colors well when the illumination drops, such as when afternoon changes into twilight or evening. At night, we cannot make out colors at all; hence the expression: "At night, all cats are grey." If you sit in the dark for about ten minutes, you will find that you will be able to see things much better than someone who walks into a dark room from a lighted one. Such improved vision is attributed to dark adaptation—you have adapted to the dark and are viewing things with your rods.

Other sensory adaptations—Olfaction.   Normally, if you smell some odor—for example, cabbage cooking in the kitchen—you will become adapted to the odor in about two minutes. In this case, adaptation means that you have lost the sensitivity for that particular odor. If someone now asks you to smell something that has none of the cabbage ingredients, you will smell it as you normally would. In short, olfactory adaptation is specific to the substances concerned. It could be dangerous for you to become adapted to something like the odor of some gas if you find that you don't smell it any more after a few minutes. The gas may not have disappeared, but your sensitivity to it has. If you go outside and breathe the air, you will recover your sensitivity quite quickly. People who work in odorous areas, such as hospitals or stockyards, seem to develop a rapid adaptation to the odors and claim that they do not notice them even when coming into the area from the outside.

Taste adaptation.   Just as we adapt to smells, we also adapt to tastes. The only tastes we have are sweet, sour, salt, and bitter. All other tastes are combinations of tastes and odors. If you hold your nose, you cannot tell the difference between an apple, a potato, or an onion by biting into a piece. The taste of fresh celery is mostly odor plus wetness, crunchiness, and other textural qualities. After we eat something sweet, coffee might taste more bitter than usual because we have adapted out the sweet sense. Different substances, then, will taste differently depending on what we have eaten just before. People should arrange their menus in accordance with the successive adaptations that will occur. Whether the classical arrangement of beginning with soup and fish is ideal may be a question for the gourmet to unravel. In drinking alcoholic beverages, one should note that the first drink will start an adaptation process for some of the ingredients and that these will adapt out so that the second drink and later ones will taste smoother or better, especially as one becomes more inebriated.

The concept of adaptation level has been extended by some psychologists beyond the sensory realm so that any level at which you are now operating in work, play, social activity, political and economic life, and so on becomes your standard, and changes are evaluated against that. Thus, a raise in pay will possibly bring you to a new adaptation level, and you need not feel at all satisfied.

ADDICTION   (See DRUG ADDICTION, ALCOHOLISM)

People take many addictive substances into their bodies, such as drugs, alcohol, and tobacco. To be addicted means that the person's body has developed a physiological craving or need for the substance over a period of time and that the person cannot get along without it. At first, before the person is fully addicted, he or she finds that using the drug, alcohol, or tobacco is somehow pleasant, helpful, makes him or her feel good, or accepted by some group, eases pain, or helps him or her to forget problems or worries. The person at this point does not think that there is any problem and often answers questions with, "I can stop any time I want."

But as one continues to use the substance, the body begins to adapt to it and to develop an increased physiological tolerance for it. The usual doses no longer have the same pleasant or intoxicating effects, and the person must take increasingly larger doses to obtain those pleasant effects. At this point, one is well on the way to full addiction. The body has become physiologically habituated to the substance, so that any attempt to stop taking it causes a severe physiological imbalance. The addict who tries to stop or who can no longer find or afford the substance suffers physiological and psychological discomfort, usually severe and sometimes life threatening, and a condition called withdrawal, which often produces severe withdrawal symptoms.

Addiction is a physiological condition, but it has important psychological and social consequences. Alcoholics or drug addicts can become so totally involved in serving the addiction that they severely neglect or harm other people, family, friends, and strangers. Two smokers in a family who feel the growing financial pinch of inflation or who have read that their smoking might have serious health effects on their children might nevertheless continue smoking and spend a thousand dollars a year on cigarettes. Other drugs are more costly, and addicts frequently must turn to crime to fund their habits.

Some drugs, such as marijuana, are not physiologically addictive, but a user might still find them pleasant, learn to crave them, and develop habitual use of the substance. These users become not physiologically addicted but psychologically dependent on the substance. Strong cravings and intense discomfort similar to withdrawal symptoms may be experienced if the user tries to stop the use. In either pattern, physiological addiction or psychological dependence, the substance used can be dangerous in many ways and can cause severe damage to the person physically, psychologically, and socially.

It is generally agreed that true physiological addiction does develop after taking harmful drugs such as alcohol, nicotine, heroin, and barbiturates for long periods of time. Many dangerous drugs are craved and used by people, but nicotine is the drug craved by the greatest number of people.

There is little that family or friends can do by themselves to help addicts through their patience, understanding, attempts to shield them and to hide their addiction, or by their criticism and punishment. Individual psychotherapy is of no known use in helping to cure addicts. The best advice is to seek professional help that will try to bring the addict through complete withdrawal under close medical super-vision. After that, psychological treatment to help the person stay off the addictive substance might be attempted. Many cities now have specialized alcohol, tobacco, and other drug-abuse agencies. Good places to find local information are your city or county health departments, public hospitals, medical clinics, or your own family doctor.

ADOLESCENCE

Adolescence is a much talked-about period of growing up. It is a major developmental bridge lasting several years, from childhood to adult maturity. The essence of this period is the sequence of major and often rapid changes that, to the adolescent, are simultaneously exciting, mystifying, expected and unexpected, desired and feared, and generally, it seems, demanding and difficult.

The adolescent is changing in several important respects. *Physiologically,* adoles-cence includes a growth spurt, major sexual changes and maturation, and a noticeable change in body proportions and lines. *Psychologically,* the adolescent is in all of the turmoil of rapid psychological change from dependency to independency; of changes in values, interests, and knowledge; of a growing awareness of new things in life; of new relationships among people; and of sexual growth and interest. There is a new and powerful, but still mixed, determination to become completely independent from his or her parents. Sociologically, adolescents comprise a large group in our population, a group with many of its own social values, beliefs, and pressures on its individual mem-bers. Adolescence is a period of rapid changes from the dependent status of a child to the sexually mature, social independence of adults.

Often adolescents are difficult for parents to understand, and conflict between the generations is very common. The adolescent caught up in all of the rapid changes is often demanding, irrational, moody, excitable, all of which are characteristic of people under conditions of rapid change. We sometimes forget that the parents, too, are in a period of change; usually they are moving into middle life, their children are nearly grown up, and their family lives will soon change in many ways. Like the adolescents, the parents in this period of change can also be excitable and change-able. It is no wonder that conflicts occur.

The responsibility for being understanding, patient, and helpful, however, clearly belongs to the parents because they, after all, are the more mature members of the family. Our best advice to parents of adolescents is keep calm; be patient; and do your best to help, support, and guide the adolescent to full, independent maturity. As diffi-cult as this period of child rearing might appear to be at times, it is an important and exciting period, and the parents can find a great deal of pleasure and regard for them-selves in carrying out their parenting responsibilities and guiding the adolescent to adulthood.

ADVERTISING   *(See PROPAGANDA)*

Advertising is propaganda for commercial purposes. It is designed to make money and to entice people to buy things they would not ordinarily buy—that is, to buy a particu-lar product instead of a similar or competitive one. Frequently, the nature of the product is not distinctive enough in its qualities or contents to invite attention to itself, and the advertiser commonly ignores the actual product and talks about or presents side issues or attractions. Thus, to sell a car, some screen personality is shown driving it, even though that person actually may own some other type of car. Attractive models are shown lounging in the vicinity of the car in various stages of dress or undress. Such efforts are designed to appeal to some positive emotion and to make the viewer feel good in relation to the product whereas the product itself is incidental. Advertisers typically use the standard propaganda techniques that are used by politicians and promoters of various causes. These techniques generally include the following:

1. Appeal to authority. Testimonials in one form or another are solicited or gathered. Some well-known figure is paid to lend his or her name or picture to a product even though he or she is not an authority in the area. Frequently, doctors, laboratories, or scientists are cited or referred to with appropriate gimmickry, such as white coats, test tubes, and so on—all designed to suggest that the weight of scientific opinion is on the side of the product. Mysterious ingredients are mentioned but not described.

2. Glittering generalities. Appeals are made in the name of God and country, patriotism, youth, health, success, motherhood, and other virtuous concepts or figures. Everything is new and improved, but no one says how. It is implied that the user of a product gains success in fields quite divorced from the product itself. The fact that some garment looks good on a slim model is taken to suggest that some aging and overweight consumer can also enjoy the attention the model receives.

3. Plain folks. Another common appeal is to old-fashioned values—to suggest that there is nothing fancy or unique, just good old-fashioned goodness, like Mother used to cook, or rough and ready, pioneer style, just like anybody else. This appeal is to attract those who do not succumb to the glittering generalities approach; in short, it is an effort to cover all bases.

4. The band-wagon. "Everybody's doing it, so don't get left behind" is the basis of this approach. The effort is made to demonstrate that people from all walks of life—rich and poor; minority groups; all political stripes, liberal and conservative—are getting into the act. Anybody and everybody is shown participating, and woe to him who is too late.

The trouble with advertising, as with propaganda, is that other advertisers or propagandists are also pushing their wares or personalities or programs, and the efforts of one are always diminished in their effect by the competition. The net effect perhaps results in no great advantage. There may be temporary shifts in effects as one new campaign gains momentary success. The others quickly copy, on the general grounds that nothing succeeds like success. If one kind of TV show is successful other networks quickly mount similar shows.

The educated consumer consults technical guides for his purchases and tries to ignore advertising. Unfortunately, there are very few educated consumers, and most people succumb to the pressures of advertising, which is relentlessly imposed upon an innocent and unprotected public. Of course, all of the expense of advertising is paid for by the public, so that it is assaulted twice.

Effect of advertising on children.   Because children are unable to discriminate between advertising and the rest of the material presented to them on television, they frequently ask for things that their parents are unable to afford or should not buy in any case. All kinds of presweetened foods that can cause tooth decay are demanded by children because the foods are associated with favorite characters. Similarly, toys that do not work, that break easily, or that are not as easily operated as the television ads suggest, are often demanded by children who do not need them and who might very well be better off without them.

ADVISING OTHERS

When people ask you for advice about some problem, you will normally ask for information about the situation. The advice seeker will tell you a story, and you might proceed on that basis to offer your most reasonable opinion. The trouble is that people rarely tell the truth, the whole truth, and nothing but the truth. There seems to be, for most people, some need to present themselves in the finest light and as the injured party. They rarely if ever tell the other side or sides of a story, even to their lawyers or doctors—and certainly not to newspaper advisors. Even in such newspaper columns where help is sought to get action out of a contractor or company that has allegedly failed in its responsibilities, the complainer tells only his or her side as he or she remembers it or as he or she chooses to present it. The news people then call the alleged culprits and frequently find that the complainer is also at fault, sometimes completely. There is little one can do about such situations, since they call for getting the other side of the story before any action can be taken. Frequently, marriage counselors have to interview couples together because interviewing either party to a dispute results in a one-sided tale that one person will not repeat in the presence of the other since he or she may be lying and knows that the story is a lie, which may be too uncomfortable to tell in the presence of the other. The best advice is probably not to give advice because, if action is taken and turns out badly, the advisor will then be blamed with a newly distorted story of what the advice amounted to. Advisors must be extremely careful in situations that cannot be controlled so that action initiated can be reversed. If there is no possibility of reversal, the advice should not be given, as in the case of taking a new job, giving up an old one, and, in effect, burning bridges behind one. Only situations that can be described as "try this and see if it works" lend themselves to advice, with the understanding that trying this will not in itself be harmful or irreversible.

AFTERIMAGES

If you look at the bright sun for a moment or if a flash bulb goes off directly in front of you, you will continue to see a round disc of light for some time after the exposure. Such persistence of vision is called a positive *afterimage*. If you turn on and immediately turn off a light in a dark room, you will be able to see the room for a short period in the dark. Such afterimages are of no great importance in daily life. A somewhat more important effect occurs if we look at some colored object for about thirty seconds (or a black or white object, for that matter). If we then look away toward a white painted wall or any surface, we will be likely to see a negative afterimage. The black object we looked at will appear as a white figure, and vice versa. Green objects will now appear as reddish or purplish forms; red objects will appear as green; blue as yellow, and vice versa. Actually, one does not have to stare at any colored object in order to experience the negative afterimage; even a second spent looking at a colored item will start the negative afterimage process, and if we turn away and look elsewhere, we may catch a momentary afterimage. Even as you look at a red piece of paper, you can notice that a purplish afterimage is developing around the edges. When two colors are adjacent to one another, the afterimages of each begin to affect the area where the two colors meet in a kind of contrast effect.

We mention these afterimages in order to indicate that they are normal products of vision and are created by photochemical reactions in the retina. There is nothing wrong with your vision if you see something that is not really there, as in the case of afterimages. If you do *not* get afterimages, there might be something wrong with your vision. Some people claim they do not get afterimages even after staring at some colored item for 30 seconds. They are probably somewhat fearful of accepting the notion that they are seeing something that is not there. Incidentally, the afterimage grows in size as the distance at which you project it increases. A postage stamp can look rather large (in a different color) if you look at a distant wall after examining the stamp.

ALCOHOLISM   *(See ADDICTION, DELIRIUM TREMENS, DRUG ABUSE)*

Alcoholics consume so much alcohol that mental and bodily health and social functioning are disturbed. Alcoholics lose control over their consumption, are unable to control how much or when they drink, and consume enough to disrupt their lives seriously.

The excessive drinker is at least psychologically dependent upon the alcohol, needing it to feel good or to get through the day. Long-term excessive use leads to true physiological addiction in which the body craves alcohol and cannot function effectively without it. In either case, psychological dependence or physiological addiction, the person has made alcohol use a major—and usually *the* major—part of his or her life.

Excessive drinking has many socially destructive effects—far more, for example, than marijuana use. Police statistics show that about 31% of all arrests are for public drunkenness; that 25,000 auto deaths a year are due to drinking; that homicide is an alcohol-related crime; and that suicide, parental child abuse, and severe family fights are often associated with alcohol use.

Alcohol, in any amount, is a drug that affects the central nervous system. It is a depressant, not a stimulant, and it numbs certain higher brain centers, those that help control a person's behavior. Because the control centers are numbed, the person feels freer, less inhibited, and often euphoric. Judgment, probem-solving ability, and normal social constraints decrease. With continued drinking, a person can lose more and more control over mental and physical functioning, have difficulty in coordination, such as in walking and talking, and, in severe drinking episodes, pass out completely.

Prolonged use of alcohol results in alcoholic addiction and in many serious physical illnesses, such as malnutrition, permanent memory loss, cirrhosis of the liver, heart failure, hypertension, and frontal lobe brain damage.

People on the way to becoming alcoholics seem to progress through stages that may take a few months or a few years. At first, they might be social drinkers enjoying the good times associated with drinking and only occasionally drinking heavily. Gradually, those heavy drinking episodes, still in the good-times context, become more frequent. In time, the heavy drinking continues, but the social aspect diminishes, and they begin to engage in more solitary bouts of drinking, not needing a party in order to start drinking. During this stage, heavy drinkers might express concern over the drinking and what it seems to be doing to them and their families, but it is clear that they have become dependent on it and cannot easily control it. In the final two stages, the drinkers lose all control over drinking and also lose interest in work, family, or other parts of life in general. Finally, when they become chronic, addicted alcoholics, they physiologically crave alcohol constantly, and nothing else is important.

The two major views of alcoholism are that it is a disease and that it is a set of destructive habits and a lack of self-control. The first view tends to excuse the alcoholic, saying that after all, he is sick and can't help it; the second view tends to hold the alcoholic fully responsible for all his or her acts, giving him or her no excuse for illness. Psychologists tend to favor the latter view, although it is not clear which of the two views leads to the most effective control approaches.

ALLERGIC DISORDERS   (See ASTHMA)

Some people are highly senstitive to certain chemicals, and they suffer from negative, uncomfortable, and sometimes seriously threatening bodily reactions. People can be sensitive or allergic to airborne substances, such as pollen or dust; to sunlight; to foods, such as egg yolk, chocolate, or oranges; to animal hair and dander; to bee venom; and so on. The body's heightened sensitivity produces reactions that, although characteristic for one person, can vary greatly between people. Some people, for example, characteristically respond with stomach problems; others with respiratory disorders, such as asthma; still others might respond dermatologically and break out in rashes. In some instances, the person may respond in all of those ways, although usually a person reacts more heavily in one way than in another.

Although psychological problems do not bring on the allergies, the allergies can create psychological problems. For example, the asthmatic child can become extremely frightened at the repeated attacks during which he has great trouble breathing. People with allergic skin rashes can become easily embarrassed and psychologically sensitive to their appearances and their normal social behaviors might be interfered with during those attacks. Allergies can be treated medically, and, when they are successfully controlled, whatever psychological issues might have been involved should disappear.

AMBIVALENCE

Very often, we can feel both positively and negatively about something or someone. We both like and dislike a person; we want the new stereo but do not want to pay the high price. At one moment, we are for something and a moment later, against it; we have *ambivalent* feelings.

Feeling ambivalent toward other people, including family members, and toward ourselves and our own action is a common, everyday occurrence. All of us have been ambivalent about many little things and often about major issues, such as changing one's job or moving to another city.

For some people, ambivalent feelings become a psychological problem. Conflicted, ambivalent emotions can grow to dominate a large part of their lives or to characterize a particular relationship, such as those between a wife and a husband, a parent and a child. If people cannot solve the ambivalence themselves, then professional help may be required. There is a good chance for the resolution of such feelings.

AMNESIA *(See MEMORY, RETROGRADE AMNESIA)*

Few of us are too concerned over the fact that we forget things about our own lives. We tend to accept such memory losses as natural aspects of aging or as the normal result of newer memories crowding out or interfering with older memories. In some rare cases, however, some people have a severe loss of memory for events in their own lives, including their names, addresses, or ages; sometimes they do not even recognize family or friends. *Amnesia* is the term used for such severe loss of memory.

In some cases, amnesia is due to actual brain damage that has occurred through illness or injury. Psychologists believe that in such cases there has been an actual loss of some of the information stored in the brain because of the damage to brain cells. The information that had been stored as memories is thought to be truly lost and is no longer available to the person.

In some cases, however, amnesia occurs in people for whom there is no known organic brain damage or nervous system disorder. Psychologists believe that in such cases, the stored information has not been truly lost from memory but that the person, for a variety of reasons, keeps his or her attention away from those memories. thus appearing to have lost them. There is a good deal of evidence for this view. Many amnesiacs, for example, regain the lost memories when they are hypnotized, and many will spontaneously recover their memories. Because hypnotism seems to be a special case of heightened willingness to cooperate and to carry out suggestions and instructions, it appears that the amnesiac will, under certain conditions, agree to cooperate and recall his or her lost memories, with the understanding that the recall is only temporary. Such cases of spontaneous memory recovery and recall only under hypnosis give support to the psychologists' belief that the memories have not been lost but rather were, in some manner, blocked from attention and recall.

The amnesiac's loss of memory is always selective. That is, although he or she might not remember his or her name, age, address, or occupation or recognize family and friends, he or she will still typically remember how to read, speak, use a vending machine, drive a car, order and pay for a restaurant meal, and so on. What the amnesiac forgets is *personal* experiences, not general learning experiences. Further, he or she typically appears quite normal in all other respects.

What is it that is selectively forgotten? Psychologists cannot readily carry out experiments with amnesiacs, but they can draw conclusions from the many clinical case histories that have been studied. In general, psychologists agree that the amnesiac forgets those things that are too distressing to remember. Typically, the amensiac has been under considerable pressure of one kind or another—often pressures that are quite ordinary for other people. But as a way to deal with the pressures, he or she forgets and then does not have to deal with them. In some very rare cases, the forgetting is extreme, and the person, forgetting all his or her identity, wanders away from home and creates a whole new life for him- or herself. The idea of escape from pressures seems quite clear in such cases.

ANESTHESIA   *(See HYSTERIA, MALINGERING)*

The general meaning of the word *anesthesia* is a loss of sensation or feeling in parts of the body without general loss of consciousness. In dentistry and surgery, local anesthesia is frequently used to numb only the small portion of the body that is to be treated, while the patient remains conscious.

A more specialized meaning in psychiatry and psychology is the loss of feeling or sensation reported by hysterical or conversion reaction patients. In those cases, the person may complain of having no feeling in some part of the body. Called *hysterical anesthesia,* this loss of feeling has no organic cause. The person has developed an apparent physical complaint as a way of reducing psychological anxieties, that is, by developing a physical symptom on which attention can be focused and drawn away from emotional or psychological concerns. The hysteric can gain attention, sympathy, and support from family members and medical professionals and can soon become convinced that there is a real physical disorder. It is then, of course, up to the doctors and not the hysteric to understand and treat the condition. By becoming firmly convinced of the reality of their illnesses, hysterics can both turn away from their other problems and, at the same time, put all the responsibility for improvement on other people.

It is important in these cases that medical examination carefully rule out any physical causes and complications before relying upon any psychological treatments. It should be remembered, too, that although no physical illness is present, the person is not deliberately faking or malingering. Rather, these persons have thoroughly convinced themselves that they have true physical ailments that need medical attention.

ANGER, FRUSTRATION, EMOTION   *(See FRUSTRATION, RESPONSIBILITY)*

Anger was one of Watson's three innate emotions, along with fear and love. Watson identified anger in a baby with the behavior that follows holding a baby's arms and legs together so that the limbs cannot move. Watson should have extended his view to include any interference with freedom of movement. Watson considered such thwarting of bodily movement the natural stimulus for anger and thought that all subsequent angry states would have to be conditioned to other stimuli that might accompany thwarting. The adult who displays any anger would then be responding to some stimulus that could in some ways be considered to be thwarting to his or her bodily freedom or to his or her freedom to move about. The argument might have some plausibility if we think of the common anger shown by motorists in a traffic jam: tooting horns, yelling, even banging into other cars. Here, there is a definite thwarting of freedom to move. We can easily transfer the argument to other fields where physical motion may not be the actual concern. Whenever we are thwarted in any of our desires or expectations, we may experience some kind of emotional disturbance. Frequently enough, the emotional disturbance takes the form of striking out, yelling, or otherwise expending energy beyond what others who have not been frustrated might think is called for. We must note that some people do not react in an aggressive way when they are frustrated, but we can assume that they are emotionally disturbed if the frustration did indeed occur. How we believe and/or look may vary with the situation, and people do not always react in the way we might think they should when we know the situation. When the situation can be called a frustrating one and there is aggressive or hostile behavior, we call the reaction one of anger. If the hostility is hidden in some way, then the observer may be frustrated, since he or she may not understand the failure of hostility to emerge.

On the adult human level, we normally get adjusted to physical frustrations, such as bad weather for our planned picnics, illness in the family that requires some postponement of other activities, and the like. Some people even adjust to traffic jams and read magazines or papers until the delay is over. Most of our anger reactions involve other people who prevent or delay the fulfillment of our wishes or plans. Probably the biggest single factor in our angers is our tendency to blame someone else for our difficulties—the someone else may really be responsible, in one sense, for our frustration—but, as far as psychologists are concerned, no one really deserves to be blamed for anything he or she does: He or she could not help doing what he or she did; he or she had to do it because of the way he or she is, a product of a certain heredity and environment. In our culture, the belief in personal responsibility is responsible for most of the anger and misery that we undergo or encounter. A person who recognizes that someone who has frustrated him or her is not really able to behave otherwise might subdue his or her own hostility, just as he or she has learned to tolerate the weather or other physical obstacles. The auto driver who has someone in front of him or her jam on the brakes unexpectedly or swerve into his or her path is prone to react with curses and other expressions of hostility. He or she does not normally react in the same way if he or she sees a policeman up the street waving traffic along past an accident. The driver is just as delayed in passing the accident as he or she might have been by some driver, but he or she accepts the accident; he or she does not, however, accept the indolent and incompetent driver who causes him or her to adjust his or her own driving. If we can learn to regard other drivers as no more responsible for their behavior than dogs, ducks, or trees that fall onto the road, we can reduce our anger periods in the driving siuation, and by applying the same approach to any other situation, we can reduce our angers to some occasional and mild expressions that will help to make us look not only more human but also charitable or poised.

The point is that there is no point in being angry at someone. It is said that anger adds strength and that we might hit such a person harder when we are angry, but the other side of the story is that anger also makes us lose our coordination and that we may not hit him at all, although the effort may be mighty. Professional boxers who survive and prosper do not get angry in the ring. They know that they are working at their art and that anger may spoil their effort. Although there may be a place in our social lives for righteous indignation, there is still no justification for blaming somebody for anything he or she does. We can and should show our displeasure over some unacceptable action. It is often important to let others know how strongly we feel about some matters. If we do not display anger, they may assume that we are unconcerned. Some psychologists think that it is good to blow off steam on occasion. There is no research support for this catharsis view, although it has a kind of intuitive validity. In any case, the action we take should be directed at the actions of others, not at the others themselves. This is especially important in dealing with children whose actions might be described as wrong, bad, or stupid, but the children themselves should not be labeled. Obviously, we cannot merely accept or endorse undesirable behavior, and a display of anger (real or put on) may be useful on occasion. If possible, however, undesirable behavior of others should be anticipated, prevented, or eliminated by some more efficient means. A display of anger is most likely to generate anger or fear in the person we are trying to control. Husbands and wives can end up hating each other over what began as a trivial incident through a succession of insults or recriminations and the reactions to these.

ANIMAL NATURE OF MAN

When we say about someone, "He's an animal," we usually mean it in a derogatory sense, as if some people were not animals, whereas others behave in ways that are lower, poorer, or less desirable than we might like. When we are in a calmer mood, we might recognize that humans, too, are animals in that we share various characteristics of living beings, but we usually add that we are higher animals—if not the highest, whatever that might be. The notion that humans and animals are somehow alike and at the same time different was forcefully presented by René Descartes (1596-1650), who first proposed that animals were really physical machines that behaved the way they did because they were so constructed. He believed that behavior was largely a matter of hydraulic energy. If you stepped on a dog's tail, certain liquids (animal spirits) would move along tubular nerves to various other places where the additional liquid would force some other devices (muscles) to operate. The dog would emit a yip because air was forced through its lungs, but the dog would not have felt anything because it had no structures or mechanisms for feelings of any kind. From Descartes' point of view, if you cut an animal apart, it would not suffer any pain (regardless of how it howled or screamed) since it was no different, in principle, from taking apart a machine by loosening various bolts and screws. Man, however, said Descartes, had a soul, and this distinguished him from animals. Man's behavior was just as mechanical as that of the dog, but it could be directed by the soul, and the soul could also sense the stimuli that impinged upon it. This view of man as possessing both body and soul or mind, a doctrine known as dualism, has come down to us as a kind of obvious truth, although it had not been commonly held before Descartes.

In 1859, Charles Darwin provoked a still lively controversy by suggesting that man was descended from animals by an evolutionary process he described as *natural selection* through variations among individuals. The more fit members of a species survived long enough to have progeny. Characteristics of the more fit were passed on to their offspring. Steps in evolution might be large or small, but nowhere was there any evidence for any qualitative difference in the evolutionary line, so that if animals had no souls or minds, there did not appear to be any way in which men could have them either.

At the present time, most biologists and psychologists have accepted the Darwinian point of view and regard man as only another kind of animal who has various strengths and weaknesses compared with other species. The special characteristics that distinguish man are his erect posture, the forward placement of his eyes, his opposable thumb that makes the hand much more efficient for some kinds of functions, and, most important, his ability to speak and use language. The latter ability enables man to pass on information from one generation to the next, and, with the invention of writing, man has extended this ability to accumulate experience over centuries. Man is still regarded, as Descartes suggested, as a machine—a very complicated and delicate machine, one that shows the unusual capacity for growth and change, both through natural factors (heredity) and through learning. No other machines appear to share this changeable feature of growth; they merely decay through rust or wear out through activity; man can also grow through activity, as in body-building exercises.

Computer technologists are foremost in making analogies between men and machines. Some computer experts spend their time developing models to display *artificial intelligence* (AI). Computers are programmed not only to solve problems but to recognize symbols (stimuli) and make appropriate adjustments through the manipulation of other equipment fitted with motors and so on. The strongest support for a computer analogue is the fact that the nervous system of animals does share the computer's basic operating procedure: Nerves, like switches, are either in an off or on state; that is, nervous impulses discharge in terms of pulses that can be described as being on or off at any particular moment. Only the complexity of the human brain, with something like 12 billion nerve cell units that have an apparently infinite capacity for connections with each other, makes the computer look simple, however large and involved its wiring may be. The present position of psychologists can be stated as follows: Man is a complex animal, sharing many of the behavior patterns of other animals; he is not necessarily higher or lower, but he is different and will probably become more different as the centuries go on.

ANIMAL TRICKS

All kinds of animals have been trained to perform various tricks. Pet owners who wish to teach their pets to perform some stunts, either for entertainment or for some useful purpose bringing in the newspaper, must recognize a number of points. First, make sure that some animal of the same kind has been known to perform a particular stunt. There is no point in trying to teach someone something he or she cannot do easily. Some animals can learn some stunts only with great difficulty and considerable effort on the part of the trainer. No one has ever seen a polar bear sign his or her name, and it would be rather difficult to achieve this if anyone had the time and patience. Teaching cats is somewhat more difficult than teaching dogs, or, at least, more stringent measures are involved. Assuming that some dog, for example, has been known to lie down and roll over on command, it should be possible to teach any dog to do so. The problem is to get the dog to want to do so. The physical act itself is something the dog has probably done many times before in the absence of any command. Such a stunt, however, is easily learned even when all the training rules are violated at one time or another. All that is required for this and most tricks is to use a suitable reward—for example, a desired food, dog candy, perhaps, and to use it when the animal wants it. In laboratories, rats, pigeons, and dogs are fed only meagerly for a few days in order to make them lean and hungry before anyone tries to use them in learning studies. At home, one can plan on teaching the pet dog a new trick just before a daily feeding time, when the animal is moderately hungry. Some pets eat all the time anyway, and as long as they are interested in the food, you are ready for business. You can start to shape up the pet by showing it the food and making it follow it with its nose. You lower the food just out of reach and make the animal lower itself to the floor as it follows the food. With the dog on the floor, you move the food in a circular path around the dog's head, and the head will follow the food, with the rest of the body twisting in accommodation. With or without a bit of a shove, the body will flop over. At this point, the food is given to the dog while you say, "Roll over." With a few repetitions, you can add the "Lie down" as the dog is settling down to follow the descent of the food. After about ten such trials, the dog should be fairly good at the stunt without the trainer having to get down on his or her knees. While the dog is eating the food, the trainer pats the dog, saying, "Good dog," so that the words become sufficient satisfiers when there is no food to give the dog and when the stunt is called for.

Along similar lines, any trick known to be possible can be taught to any animal. The general procedure is called *shaping,* a term that B. F. Skinner applied to a process such as the following: Whatever the desired response, you prepare yourself with some desired reward and prepare the animal to desire it—by making him hungry, for example. The reward should be one that can be provided in small amounts so that the animal will remain interested over a number of trials. At the first stage of training, you wait for the animal to make some move of the desired nature or in the desired direction. As soon as it does so, you provide a bit of the reward. If you wanted the animal to pull a chain to flush a toilet, for example, you would stand around in the vicinity of the animal and wait for the animal to at least look at the chain or in its general direction. After a few rewarding looks, you would wait longer and keep waiting until the animal made a head turn or took a step toward the chain. You would immediately reward such a next step. After rewarding a few head turns or steps, you would wait some more until the dog was definitely moving toward the chain. After a step or two, you would reward this phase or stage of the shaping. With progressive steps, you would wait and reward only those movements that brought the animal closer and closer to the chain. Eventually, the animal would be close enough to touch the chain. You would wait until that happened and reward the animal. After that, you would wait until the animal got its mouth in the vicinity of the chain, and finally you would wait until the chain was bitten or grasped before providing the reward. The last stage would be waiting until the biting or grasping resulted in a tug that would achieve the desired result. Note that you are not concerned with whether the dog knows what it is doing or not. You merely reward closer and closer approximations to what you want.

In order to make the rewards work, it is best to establish some kind of signal related to the reward. A wire clicker, finger snap, or other noise can be associated with the food by pairing a noise and a piece of food in some preliminary training so that the dog can be rewarded immediately (by the snap) upon making an appropriate move. In this fashion, many animals have been trained to perform what look like marvelous tricks, but in all cases a situation is arranged wherein the animal can do something natural that results in some equipment working in some way to produce an illusion of the animal's capacity. A chicken can be made to look as if it is playing baseball by reinforcing it for pecking at home plate on a miniature field. The peck releases a ball, and the chicken pecks at some point that operates a swiveling bat that hits the ball.

The only trick to training animals is to pay them off for doing what you want them to do, but you must know the separate and serial steps involved in the total act and move approximately from step 1 to step 2 and so on for as many steps as it takes to complete the operation.

ANIMISM

Anima refers to soul or spirit and, in general, to life. *Animism* refers to the practice of attributing life to inanimate objects or forms of energy. Thus, primitive people have been known to attribute various life characteristics to mountains, trees, rivers, stones, and the like. Modern civilized people who talk to their plants reflect a similar orientation. The fact that plants and trees are alive in a biological sense does not justify endowing them with various other powers or characteristics. Because roses and stones have no auditory receptors, it cannot matter much what we say to them. Of course, plants do react to various kinds of energy, especially that from the sun and the wind, but such reactions are presumably the ordinary reactions to physical, not psychological forces.

ANOREXIA NERVOSA—Loss of Appetite   *(See EATING DISORDERS IN CHILDREN, SYSTEMATIC DESENSITIZATION)*

Judy, a 14-year-old girl, had been so intent upon losing weight that she imposed a strict diet on herself and dropped from 115 to 70 pounds in just over six months. After the first ten pounds' loss, Judy and her parents were pleased at the good results of the girl's diet, although the parents had some misgivings because they had thought her diet was too severe right from the beginning. But Judy was not concerned. She continued losing weight, passed the healthy goal of 100 pounds, and continued to drop. Her eating habits deteriorated, and her nutrition balance was clearly far out of order. The parents grew alarmed, but Judy was very pleased with herself and kept right on losing weight. During all of this period, she continued what was an already heavy schedule of physical activity in high school, clubs, dance classes, and so on. The thinner and bonier she became, the more concerned her parents grew and the more pleased with herself Judy became. She was immune, it seemed, to reason, discussion, pleadings to eat more, arguments, and outright orders by her parents. In fact, the more pressure they put on her, the less she seemed to eat; but when they left her alone and put no pressure on her at all, she just kept losing weight anyway. No matter what the parents did, Judy grew thinner and thinner. Where the parents saw only a thin, frail, little body, Judy saw in her mirror a lithe, attractive figure. She could not seem to understand that she had gone far beyond the limits of good health.

The problems eventually reached the point where Judy had to be hospitalized and fed intravenously in order to get some nutrition. But even faced with the hospital treatment, she continued to maintain that she was not at all skinny and did not have to eat more. She did eat more and brought her weight up a little, but it almost seemed as if she were doing so just to get out of the hospital.

Anorexia nervosa, which is what Judy's refusal to eat is called, is actually a severe loss of appetite due to emotional rather than to organic reasons. It is quite a rare condition. But teenage girls, at about the start of puberty, seem to make up a large proportion of the cases. In some instances, the poor eating becomes chronic over a long term, and the person actually dies from the disorder.

The factors that give rise to anorexia nervosa are not yet known. In fact, although psychological treatment of anorexia nervosa has been conducted for a long time, systematic psychological research has been carried out only in the past ten or fifteen years. The most recent data are all tentative, and they suggest that, unlike obesity, genetic factors in anorexia may not be too important. Rather, at this point in the research, family and personal psychological factors seem to be the most important. Another suggestion of recent research is that the anorexic may not be so much lacking in appetite—as the term anorexia suggests—but, rather, extremely phobic about being obese. Some short-term treatment success has been reported by systematic desensitization of the patient's phobia of obesity.

When anorexia nervosa is suspected—and it is difficult to miss it when it occurs—medical treatment should be sought immediately to deal with any imminent health hazards. Along with that, behavior therapy is recommended for short-term or immediate improvement in eating behavior. But of equal importance—and this is an area where we have little information—long-term treatment should be provided to maintain the improvements and to prevent relapses. The type of treatment best for such long-term cases is not yet known.

ANOXIA

Anoxia is a condition where the level of oxygen supplied to the brain has been lowered. It can come about if oxygen is simply not available in adequate amounts, as is the case in high-flying airplanes that either do not have pressured systems or have pressure systems that fail. On high mountains, over 10,000 feet, the oxygen level becomes lower than at lesser heights. In general, altitudes over 12,000 feet have inadequate oxygen available, and people climbing to such levels need to carry oxygen supplies. Victims of drowning or other suffocation situations also suffer oxygen loss. If they are revived in time to survive, their postrecovery lives may not be worth living if they have been deprived of oxygen for over five minutes, since serious irreversible changes will occur in the brain. Even shorter periods may result in drastic mental impairment. In so-called oxygen chambers, researchers can lower the atmospheric pressure and the effective oxygen levels gradually and observe the effects on experimental subjects. The decrease in oxygen will result in a giddiness, a euphoria, and an inability to concentrate and to make coordinated movements. Problem-solving ability will decrease, and the subjects can pass out happily, never knowing that anything ever went wrong. Pilots of airplanes usually have oxygen-chamber experience to acquaint them with the dangers of flying too high without oxygen available.

ANXIETY   *(See FEAR)*

The term *anxiety* is one of the most widely used of psychological terms by both professionals and lay people. We often apply the term anxiety to describe ourselves; therapists use it to describe their clients and try to explain their behavior; psychologists create tests to measure it; pharmacologists develop new drugs to try to get rid of anxiety; and sociologists have even called this century the age of anxiety. Many personality theorists and therapists have identified anxiety as the central, most important factor in cases of psychological disorders.

Despite differences in details, there is a traditional agreement on the general meaning of the term. It refers to an aroused state, a feeling of upset or disquiet, often accompanied by vague expectations of some negative event about to occur. Anxiety is a feeling of upset, unease, and some foreboding fear all mixed together, with a physiological arousal that is similar—and perhaps identical—to the arousal involved in the reaction of fear. As in fears, this arousal includes increased heart rate and breathing.

The experience of anxiety might range from mild, so-called normal levels to extreme intensity, where the person's normal functioning is disrupted. We all have our own ideas of how the extremely anxious person acts—rapid movements, fumbling, smoking, pacing incessantly, and so on—such behaviors indicate a very aroused person. At whatever intensity it may be, the anxiety experience can be momentary or last for very long periods of time. When extreme anxiety continues for very long periods, the person can become physically and mentally exhausted and unable to function normally.

Although anxiety at extreme intensity and/or for prolonged periods certainly often poses severe problems, it is not always bad or abnormal. According to many psychologists, anxiety is a normal condition and, depending upon how the person deals with it, may be a valuable experience. Anxiety, in this view, might be just enough arousal for the person to get the job done. Anxiety at normal levels is thus seen as a normal part of responding to difficult or stressful demands, and it may be usefully arousing. If it is a normal part of human functioning, then the somewhat prevalent idea that people should be free of all anxiety is wrong. Everyone experiences anxiety at many times in his or her life. It is important not to view it as necessarily a sign of serious problems. Only when the anxiety becomes very hard to control, causes real disruption in the person's life, or continues at either high intensity or for prolonged periods should we begin to consider the experience abnormal.

APHASIA

If a person suffers a wound or other trauma, such as a stroke on the left side of his brain, he may suffer a variety of kinds of paralyses, depending on the location of the trauma. If the trauma occurs in or near Broca's area (just above the ear and forward of the ear), he or she may find that he or she has difficulty in speech; there is nothing wrong with his or her vocal apparatus except that it cannot be made to function properly, and the person may be completely mute, even though he or she understands everything he or she hears and can write verbal responses. In severe cases, he or she may appear not to understand any verbal message. Such a person is said to have *anterior aphasia*. His or her speech, if speech is at all possible, will consist of stammered hesitations, seemingly endless searches for words, and a retrieval difficulty, even though he or she may give quick and normal responses in a free association test. He or she may also have difficulty with syntax and grammar and have problems in identifying common objects, but he or she will generally come up with a related response—he or she might, for example, call a knife a spoon, a book a paper, and so on. To some extent, we all do that in our normal conversation, especially when we are momentarily flustered; at such times, our friends often may supply us with words. Victims of anterior aphasia may recover completely if the trauma is not severe or extensive and, especilly, if they are young at the time. Some of us suffer a mild form of aphasia that can only be detected by special testing of language use and comprehension.

Posterior aphasia can occur if the trauma occurs on the left side of the brain but farther back, past the location of the ear. Such aphasia does not interfere with speech as far as speech production is concerned, but the production itself is essentially meaningless. It sounds like speech, with proper pronounciation and normal structure, but the person keeps talking without saying anything sensible. If aphasia is a language disorder, the posterior aphasic seems to be using the language for some other function than its normal one; there is nothing improper about his or her words or individual sentences except that they do not communicate any meaning or message. In short, posterior aphasia is a disturbance of the thought process in which the victim is unaware of his or her problem (he or she may be quite happy and sociable, although sometimes somewhat paranoid), whereas the anterior aphasic is unhappily conscious of his or her problem. There is no available treatment except to wait and hope for the aphasic to recover, if possible.

ASSERTIVENESS TRAINING   (See BEHAVIOR THERAPY)

Assertiveness training is one of the methods used in behavior therapy. It is usually applied with clients who are too inhibited, anxious, or frightened to express or act on their emotions or to act in terms of how they really feel in some social situations. For example, a person at work might know that the boss gives him or her a disproportionate amount of work—in essence, taking undue advantage—because the worker never protests. But the person finds it impossible to do anything but comply meekly, no matter how he or she really feels about it. In assertiveness training, the therapist helps the client to learn how to express and to act upon the real feelings in such situations and to do so in a manner that results in success in that situation.

The assertiveness training sessions involve direct instructions and rehearsals in how to act and what to say in those common situations where other people usually take advantage of the client. The client, after sufficient rehearsal with the therapist, waits for some frequently occurring situation, such as that of the overdemanding boss, and then begins to try out his or her newly learned skills in that real situation. Obviously, the power relationships must be taken into account. One may not want to lose a job or a friend, for example, just to enjoy speaking up. At first, the client is instructed to try out the new techniques only in the less complicated, easier situations and, as he or she gains practice and assurance, gradually move on to more difficult situations.

Theoretically, a person's anxiety in troublesome situations will decrease as one continues to experience success in practicing assertiveness and how to stand up for one's own rights.

ASTHMA   (See ANXIETY, ALLERGIC REACTION)

Asthma, a respiratory disorder, is the most prevalent of chronic diseases of childhood. It is also an adult disorder, but about 60% of all cases occur in youngsters under age 17. Children are affected seriously enough so that asthma accounts for about 25% of the total of all school absences. Although asthma is basically a medical problem, there are psychological aspects in its control.

Parents whose children have experienced asthma recognize the condition by the pronounced wheezing that comes from the chest as the child tries to pull air through restricted air passages. The child's respiratory system is highly sensitive to chemicals, some foods, or temperature extremes, and the air passages become very narrow, causing difficulty in breathing. The characteristic wheezing is the sound of air going through the restricted passages.

Asthma can begin very suddenly at any time in a child's life. The attacks may be frequent or only occasional, lasting for minutes or hours. For children whose asthma began before age 13, some 70% improve in adolescence and young adulthood. Many, however, do not and must remain on controlling medication throughout their lives. Although not usually fatal, there are some deaths (1.5 per thousand) due to asthma.

An asthmatic attack can be extremely frightening for a child who is struggling, with great difficulty, to breathe, and children become highly anxious and sometimes depressed, often thinking that they are going to die during an attack. The extreme anxiety can escalate into panic in both the child and the parent. With modern medications, asthma can be controlled, but asthma must not be taken lightly.

About thirty or forty years ago, many psychiatrists and psychologists believed asthma to be a psychosomatic illness, that is, one caused by the child's psychological problems. Those professionals made the error of seeing the extreme anxiety of asthmatic children as somehow *causing* the disorder. Today, particularly in light of modern knowledge about allergies, asthma is no longer thought of as psychosomatic. Rather, the psychological distress is properly seen as an understandable *reaction* to the frightening breathing difficulty.

However, because the attacks can create so much anxiety, and because asthmatic children can thus become generally anxious, frightened, and very sensitive to psychological demands, it is important that parents and children learn how to control both the asthmatic attacks and the resulting anxiety and fear.

Parents with asthmatic children should do the following:

1. Learn with a physician's help to treat or obtain emergency treatment for asthmatic attacks.
2. Learn what the child's sensitivities are—dust, pollen, mold, foods, and so on. Do this through consultation with an allergist.
3. Control or eliminate those attack-inducing substances from the child's environment: his room, toys, blankets, rugs, and the like.
4. Teach the child what foods, drinks, and other things to avoid and how to control attacks once they start.
5. If the child is old enough, teach the child how to relax and avoid panic.

ASTROLOGY   (See PALMISTRY)

Millions of people in the United States and around the world believe that their lives are in some ways controlled by the positions of various planets, stars, or constellations. They subscribe to astrology magazines and consult astrologers who plot their horoscopes, relating the time of birth to the present positions of specific celestial bodies. The astrologers advise their clients about the wisdom of some action. The advice might even be good if it is not based on any beliefs about the influence of the stars on our daily lives. There is no scientific evidence to support the belief that the heavenly bodies have any influence over human bodies. Whether you are a Virgo or a Scorpio is probably the least important fact in your existence, except to another believer.

The attraction of astrology for some people probably derives from ancient efforts of early astronomers to understand the movements of the stars and planets. Names of humans or gods were attached to various constellations of stars and added an anthropomorphic feature to the skies. Some discoveries about sun spots, the influence of the moon on the tides, eclipses, and so on added to the notion that the earth and its inhabitants might be influenced by the stars and planets. Various religious views added more mystification, and the ancient priest-astronomer-astrologer came to be an important person, since he would be the only one qualified to intercede between man and the heavens and to predict his destiny.

ATTENTION   (See HUMAN FACTORS, MEDITATION)

Although everyone talks abut *attention,* no one can define it precisely. We are attentive when we are focusing in on something, reacting to one stiumulus or set of stimuli, and ignoring everything else that is going on around us. A sudden bolt of lightning or thunder clap immediately commands our attention. If we try to attend to more than one thing at a time, our efficiency drops strikingly. One cannot really read and watch television at the same time. Both activities will suffer. One can, of course, divide his or her attention, and many operations can be performed automatically, as when we drive a car and carry on a conservation at the same time. If the traffic gets sticky, however, the conversation must suffer.

In studying attention, psychologists have tried to determine how much a person can observe in one instant, how many items can be remembered after one hearing, and how brief a stimulus must be in order to be apprehended. If a card with a random arrangement of dots is flashed before your eyes, you will be able to report accurately that there were five, six, or even seven dots. If there are more than seven dots, you are not likely to be correct, and your score drops precipitously with higher numbers. Psychologists have generalized that there is a magic number of seven that limits our grasp. Telephone numbers of seven digits are readily remembered, especially if they are grouped, as is the usual case, in units of three and four. Thus, it is easy to remember 689-9307, although you might have trouble with 6,899,307, especially if you do not know that there will be seven numbers coming. During World War II, servicemen were trained by the flash system to recognize aircraft, ships, tanks, and so on with exposures as short as a tenth or a fiftieth of a second. At such short exposures, too short for eye movements or counting, they could also report accurately up to about seven items if they were all the same and were ungrouped in any way. Grouping helps considerably, and one could report twenty items if they consisted of five squares formed by four corner dots.

If one tries to concentrate his or her attention on some small object, he or she cannot look at and see it clearly for more than thirty seconds or so. It tends to disappear. One cannot concentrate on a word and repeat it over and over without its losing its meaning. Our attention is limited by time, number, and speed of presentation. It is also limited by our set, or relative preparation for looking. If we see an accident or a holdup and are called on to report what we saw, the chances are that we will not be very accurate if we were not expecting it to happen, and, even then, if the situation is emotionally packed, we will be relatively unreliable. The usual remark will be, "It all happened so fast!" Even when we are prepared to make an obervation, our desire to see some particular thing (or our reluctance to see something) can affect our accuracy.

Any kind of observational activity is a function of how keyed up or toned up we are. Some people require more background stimulation in order to be able to work effectively. Teenagers sometimes cannot study if it is too quiet around them and insist on radio or record music. They may do better under such conditions than in complete silence. If such is the case, parents should not interfere.

The problem in connection with attention is that there are occupations, (e.g., piloting a plane, scanning radar scopes) where there are too many things to do at once, too many instruments or other signaling devices, or too much noise—that is, background stimulation that resembles the items of interest. Some of these problems can be solved by technological advances, automation of some activities, arranging instrument displays so that they all read out in some simplified way (e.g., all arrows point up when everything is in good order), and by special, emphatic signals to indicate that something is wrong. Such devices do not always work. A pilot executing a difficult landing maneuver may not hear a loud horn signaling him that his wheels have not been lowered. The basic truth about attention is that we can really pay attention to one thing at a time.

ATTITUDES AND OPINIONS   *(See TEST-TRAIT FALLACY)*

When we want to predict what someone else might do, we sometimes try to find out what his or her *attitude* toward this or that might be. The implication of such a search is that the person involved has some predisposition to respond in some particular way regarding some issue. If we knew how he or she habitually responded, we might not worry about his or her attitude or even raise the question and might merely assume that he or she would react as he or she has done before. Social and personality psychologists hope that by finding out about attitudes, they can save themselves the trouble of checking out the life history of an individual in whose behavior they are interested. They think of attitudes as they do about personality traits, as something a person possesses, carries around with him or her, or as something that characterizes the person. Usually they define an attitude as everything a person thinks and feels about objects, persons, or issues. More behavioristic psychologists argue that worrying over attitudes is not profitable and that a better prediction can be made by knowing the life history or at least the history of reinforcement in some situation. They think that attitudes are unnecessary third parties in the stimulus-response formula, with the attitude being aroused by the stimulus and then controlling the response, and they see no point to a concern over attitudes if the correlation between stimulus and response is sufficiently high to predict the response.

Sometimes attitudes are described as having an action factor, as determining the behavior. A person with a negative attitude toward nuclear energy might join picketing groups, write letters to Congress, and so on. One must raise the question as to whether anything more is known about a person when we also know that he or she has a negative attitude toward nuclear energy than when we see him or her at a protest march. Ordinarily, when attitudes are measured (by rating scales, questionnaires), the person being measured is in no position to take action about anything, and we assume from the test results that he or she is then predisposed or has tendencies to act in certain ways. Because he or she may not actually act in any way, the measurement of the attitude may be quite meaningless.

A distinction is often drawn between attitudes and opinions. An *opinion* is an expression in some form, usually verbal, that is supposed to express the attitude. If someone slaps some other person, we also have an expression, an opinion, that we assume spells out some attitude. When we ask, "What is your opinion about ____?", we are inquiring about someone's attitude. He or she may lie, of course, and we will not have learned much, if anything. Assuming that an opinion is a verbal expression of an attitude, we can, of course, acquire some information about a person's thoughts and feelings about an issue, and, assuming the truth of the response, we might venture to predict how he or she might behave. Republicans normally do not vote for Democrats, for example, and if someone endorses a Republican candidate, we can assume that he or she would like us to vote for this candidate and that he or she will also do so. Our assumption may not be justified if we do not know a good deal more about the opinion stater.

What we should recognize is that people have had histories of good and bad experiences with all manner of objects, people, and issues and that such experiences have altered them in ways that will make them react to new instances in positive or negative ways, in minor or major degrees. To say that they also have attitudes may not be very helpful, except when we do not have time to find out about their histories. We then attempt to get at their attitudes as a kind of shorthand way of assessing the probabilities of their reactions and find that sometimes questioning them may be of assistance: If truthful answers are given, we may find useful correlations with behavior. What we want to avoid is the notion that a person carries attitudes around with him or her. Attitudes, like habits, are not agencies that initiate behavior on their own. We can certainly recognize that in any given situation a person will be thinking and feeling in some way, whether he or she acts positively, negatively, or in some neutral fashion. For some purposes, it might be useful to know what he or she felt and thought, whether or not he or she acted. We would then know something about his or her attitude and might take it into account for future predictions.

AUDITORY PROBLEMS   *(See DEAFNESS)*

In some ways, it is easier to discover that children might be suffering from some hearing loss than from visual defects. If children do not respond to speech when not facing the speaker, one can suspect a problem. As with visual problems, there are physicians who are specialists in problems involving hearing, and they should obviously be consulted. Our concern here is more with the appreciation of how hearing losses are measured. Typically, an *audiometer* is used to score a listener's hearing range; that is, how low pitched and how high-pitched a tone one can hear and at what intensity or loudness a tone must be presented to be heard. A person might be able to hear a particular tone if it is loud enough, but that might be too loud for other people. Most people do not appreciate that they hear best in their early years, childhood, and adolescence. As the years go on, many people begin to lose the higher tones, and the quality of what they hear (the overtones, higher multiples) is frequently missing for those over fifty. It is comparable to the loss of visual acuity that strikes most people in their forties and fifties when they get reading glasses. Instead of adding hearing aids, however, we grumble that other people now mumble instead of speaking clearly.

Audiometer scores or readings are given in decibels, a measure unfamiliar to most people. A *deci*bel is one tenth of a bel, and that simplifies the problem a bit. All that we need to know is what a bel is. A bel, named after Alexander Graham Bell, the inventor of the telephone, is a logarithm (to the base 10) of the ratio of two numbers. Logarithms are simple code numbers for other numbers. Thus, we can let a number like 1 stand for 10, 2 for 100, 3 for 1,000, and so on. If we now have a ratio like $\frac{100}{10}$ or 10, since the logarithm of 10 is 1, we would have 1 bel or 10 decibels. In measuring sound, the divisor in the ratio is taken as .0002 dynes (a measure of pressure that also appears to be the lowest pressure that could make a sound audible for normal hearing). Thus, any sound source can be compared to .0002 dynes, and the resulting ratio can be translated into a logarithm. If the ratio turns out to be, say, 1,000, then we would have 3 bels or 30 decibels. Forty decibels is about the level of sound that one hears in a quiet office. Normal conversation goes on at about 60 decibels. Ninety decibels is like the sound of jet airplanes at about 500 feet above and is about the loudest sound anyone might care to hear. Sound becomes painful at about 120 decibels. Prolonged exposure to high decibel sounds damages the ear drum and may damage the internal hearing structures in the inner ear.

After taking an audiometer test, one can see a graphical display of his or her hearing capacity showing how loud (in decibels) a variety of pure tones can be heard along the range from 16 vibrations or cycles per second to 20,000 cycles per second (the cycles are frequently described as Hertz after Heinrich Hertz, a physicist working in electromagnetics). The graph is compared with an average of people who have normal hearing, and weakness of hearing can be recognized as deviations from the normal curve. As with vision, no one is likely to fall on the normal curve at all points, and so we all have some degree of abnormality in hearing. Extreme hearing loss calls for specialized treatment; lesser weaknesses may be helped by hearing aids or may simply be lived with.

B

BED-WETTNG—ENURESIS   (See TOILET TRAINING)

All children wet their diapers, pants, and beds. The resultant cleanup work becomes irritating to mothers who would have a little more freedom if they did not have to take the appropriate actions. Very few people at age 21 wet their pants or beds. When they get much older, they will again wet their pants and beds and maybe require diapers again. The point, of course, is that if you have children, you might best resign yourself to some work and not worry about what you have done wrong in the training process. In all probability, the child is not trying to revenge himself against you. It is best to forget any fanciful psychological interpretations and consider the probability that the child is a heavy sleeper with a small but developing bladder. It is also too comfortable in bed, and it may be dark in the bedroom, so that getting up and going to the toilet is not inviting. If the child can be wakened as soon as urination starts and forced to get out of bed, the problem will soon be eliminated. Special mattress pads have been designed to set off alarm clocks when the pad is moistened, and these can be obtained inexpensively at many department stores. They work. Psychological treatment is probably useless and unnecessary.

BEHAVIORISM

At one time, psychologists tended to associate themselves in schools or groups with various points of view toward what they called their subject matter. In 1913, John B. Watson introduced a point of view that he labeled *behaviorism*. From this point of view, the only proper subject matter of psychology was behavior that could be observed by others. Essentially, man was to be studied like any other animal species.

Whatever might be believed to be occurring inside the man, other than glandular secretions or minor muscular contractions, would or should be of no interest to psychologists, since it was unobservable and could not be measured or checked by others. So-called mental functions or operations were thus excluded by definition of the subject matter. The fact that man talks was taken to indicate that man could engage in another kind of behavior—namely, verbal behavior. Words could be recorded or observed and taken into account on their own, not necessarily as indicative of anything beyond themselves. Thinking, according to Watson, was a special kind of behavior —a matter of talking to yourself—but, because of social training, the speech in thinking is conducted without lip movement, in most cases, and with minimal contractions of vocal musculature of the tongue, larynx, and so on. Because such internal speech could not be easily observed, it was referred to as implicit behavior, but it was still behavior, nevertheless. The Watsonian view was adopted in large measure by many American psychologists because it had a kind of scientific flavor with its promise of objective measurement, and it was a more or less dominant approach in psychology up to the 1960s, when a kind of reaction against behaviorism arose in the development of new viewpoints, such as cognitive psychology, which does concern itself more with what goes on under the scalp. The practice of external observation and measurement that Watson promoted has remained a standard operating procedure for most psychologists.

BEHAVIOR MODIFICATION: BEHAVIOR THERAPY
(See CONDITIONING, MODELING, SYSTEMATIC DESENSITIZATION)

Since the 1920s, psychotherapy as practiced in the United States has been dominated by ideas generally associated with psychoanalysis. The major idea in that model is that psychological problems—neuroses, psychoses, fears, bedwetting, stealing, depression, and so on—are all caused by some very complex, unconscious processes that are all going on inside a person without the person's awareness. Psychoanalytic treatment was aimed at getting through to clear up those hidden internal conflicts and needs.

An alternative model, *behavior modification,* also developed in the 1920s but did not become important until the 1960s. In this view, people's psychological problems are not so much driven from inside but, rather, are maladaptive habits and misunderstandings that people have *learned.* They might also have failed to learn adaptive behavior. Thus, in behavior therapy, some combination of learning maladaptive behavior and failing to learn adaptive behavior is seen as the person's major problem. Treatment in behavior therapy is aimed at teaching adaptive behavior. An 8-year-old, for example, who wets the bed is not seen as doing so to express unconscious needs or to aggress against the parents; rather, the behavior therapist views the child as having failed to learn how to wake up when the bladder is full. Behavior therapy would aim at simple training rather than complex analysis.

Behavior therapy focuses on teaching and training people to learn more adaptive behavior. It has grown rapidly in the past twenty years and is now one of the major therapy approaches in the United States. Many therapeutic techniques are included in behavior therapy and are applied to different kinds of psychological problems.

At present, there are two major divisions or schools using the behavioral approach, with many offshoots and variations. One school follows a conditioning model with heavy reliance on relaxation and desensitization. The other major school follows a reinforcement of desired behavior approach. The former school likes to be identified by the label of *behavior therapy*, whereas the latter favors a label of *behavior modification*.

BEHAVIOR MODIFICATION: TOKEN SYSTEMS   *(See REWARDS)*

One of the most basic psychological ideas in behavior modification is that providing rewards helps to strengthen behavior, whereas withholding or taking away rewards tends to weaken behavior. This is a generally accepted idea in our society, and all of us use it in a variety of ways—not always effectively—every day. In behavior modification, the use of rewards is very precise and systematic in order to strengthen or weaken specifically identified behaviors.

There are three basic steps in any behavior modification program: (1) The undesirable behavior is defined precisely and a count of its occurrence is made over a suitable time period—for example, a week or two; (2) rewards are introduced for desirable behavior, and a record is kept of the improvement, if any; (3) the rewards are withdrawn to see if the undesirable behavior returns—this is done to make sure that it is the reward system and not some other factor that is responsible. Once the usefulness of the rewards is established, the rewards are reinstituted. With careful manipulation, the number of rewards can be reduced and even eliminated if the new behavior now brings its own rewards.

In behavior modification, we apply rewards to increase or strengthen desirable behavior, and the rewards can take many forms depending upon what is valuable or rewarding for the particular persons being rewarded. For example, parents can reward a child for going to bed quickly and cooperatively, without his or her usual fuss, by reading to the child in bed for fifteen minutes or so; a teacher gives gold stars or high marks; an employer might reward with a raise or a bonus; an audience rewards the singer with applause; all of us can reward each other with a well-timed smile, a "thank you", or a nice compliment; we can even reward ourselves in a variety of ways by a vacation or other treat. Rewards, in many forms for different people, when used properly, are powerful incentives for continuing in the behavior that led to the reward.

Token Systems.   One particular system for rewards used in behavior modification is the *token system* or, when very complex, the *token economy*. Essentially, this is a very carefully designed behavior modification system to increase desirable behavior and weaken undesirable behavior. For example, children who are underachieving in school can agree to cooperate in a token system run by the teacher, whereby the students are rewarded immediately with small cardboard tokens for doing good academic work. Simply completing an assignment might be worth one token, an 80% paper might be rewarded 2 tokens, and a 90% paper might be worth 5, whereas a 100% paper might bring 10 tokens. It is important to grade the papers immediately when the students complete them and to assign the tokens immediately upon grading. The idea, of course, is that the children will now begin to work hard to complete each class assignment and to do better and better work.

But once the children earn their tokens, what can they do with them? The children are allowed to spend their tokens to buy a variety of things, such as fifteen minutes of free time, an extra recess, a good letter or note sent to the parents by the teacher, a party for the class, and so on. Using that system, the teacher would not scold or punish the children for *not* doing their work but would emphasize praising and rewarding with tokens for *doing* the work and *doing it well*. The system of specified behavior (academic behavior), of token rewards given immediately, and the back-up reinforcers that can be bought with the earned tokens constitute a token system or token economy.

Some token systems have been very complete token economies for an entire psychiatric ward. In those systems, patients who for years have been inactive or withdrawn or shown bizarre behavior have gradually become more active and responsive in the token economy. They gradually learn that they can earn a wide variety of luxuries, activities, attention, and so on by behaving in increasingly normal ways.

Although token systems in the classroom are fairly easily managed and are a good deal of fun for both teacher and children, the more complex token economies in psychiatric wards require a great deal of effort, record keeping, monitoring, and constant correction of and by the staff. They are difficult to operate in those settings and, unfortunately, often fail because it is much easier to continue running the ward the way it has always been run than it is to maintain an entire positive reward system.

BIOFEEDBACK

The feedback in *biofeedback* refers to some source of information about what is going on in the body. If you count your pulse, the count is a kind of biofeedback. Similarly, when your blood pressure is being taken, the sphygmomanometer provides some numbers. When your bladder is full, you feel the pressure, but you have no numerical count. When your breathing rate rises or falls, this can be measured by a pneumograph if you are in a position to have one strapped around you. With recent electronic developments, it is possible to measure a variety of bodily activities of people who are suitably hooked up or wired, and astronauts in space can have their blood pressure, heart rates, and other bodily functions monitored in space through radio signals. It is possible to translate the activity of various parts of the body into signals other than numbers. A heart rate increase could be made to sound a tone, raise the pitch of a tone, or increase the brightness of a light. If your brain waves in some range—for example, alpha waves—appear or disappear, this can also be made to start or stop a tone or light while the brain waves are being recorded.

The availability of such means of displaying information about your body's status has been the subject of much laboratory study and popular exploitation. A person can be suitably wired to display his pulse or alpha waves at a tone of a certain pitch. He can then be asked to change the pitch either upward or downward. If he can succeed in doing so, he demonstrates that he has some control over such bodily functions. These functions are not ordinarily under voluntary control, and we do not go about raising or lowering our blood pressure at will, although the pressure does change from moment to moment, to some extent. Clinical practitioners have become interested in trying to get people to learn to control some of the bodily functions that may have serious medical consequences—for example, high blood pressure or migraine headaches. The underlying assumption is that most internal physiological functions are, in principle, like the functions of urination and excretion that we all learn to control in childhood and that it should therefore be possible to control such things as sweating, flushing, peristalsis, blood pressure, pulse, and possibly various glandular functions by suitable training.

For some time in the 1960s, various highly positive reports were published by researchers who claimed that they had trained rats and people to control a whole range and variety of functions. More recent reports are far less promising or optimistic, and any claims of positive results should be weighted very critically. It is true that people can make their alpha waves come and go rather easily by opening or closing their eyes, tensing up or relaxing, day dreaming or trying to visualize various problem situations. There does not appear to be much value in controlling alpha waves, however, since their presence indicates a kind of state of relaxation in which one is not productively engaged in any meaningful enterprise. If one has an increase in blood pressure when he gets angry, there might be some point to the increase, and advice about not getting angry might be foolish if the person should be angry. In any case, it is not likely that anyone engaged in any routine daily activity will be moving about with some kind of electronic monitoring devices attached to his body. At the same time, if one is busy with life in a real world, he cannot be paying any attention to his pulse. It is presumably for this reason that we have evolved so that our autonomic nervous systems take care of ordinary life functions while we go about the business of living or earning one. It may be possible some time in the future to discover how one can reduce or relieve the muscular tensions that might bring about migraine headaches. When one has such a headache, he or she is probably incapacitated for anything else anyhow, and he or she might as well be trying to ease his pain. Although biofeedback may have a promising future, at present it has not developed to the point where anyone can use it effectively, especially when going about the business of normal living.

BIORHYTHMS

Over the millions of years of evolution, humans, plants, and animals have adapted to various annual, seasonal, and daily changes in the amount of daylight and in daily and seasonal temperature changes. The rising and setting of the sun forced us, before the invention of artificial sources of light, to be active in the daytime and to sleep at night. In man, there seems to be what is called a *circadian rhythm* (circa—around; dies—day) of somewhere in the range of 24-27 hours so that, roughly, we get to feel sleepy about the same time of night and rise about the same time in the morning. Some scientists, living in caves, with no clocks by which to measure time, have found that periods as long as six months do not alter this cycle to any marked degree, although the 24-hour cycle is not any fixed period for any particular individual. When we travel abroad across time zones, we need a period of adjustment to the new time schedules observed by people in the new zones: We get sleepy at the wrong times and hungry when other people are not accustomed to eating. The condition is called *jet lag* and affects different people differently, some experiencing hardly any trouble. The regularity of one's behavior in respect to time has given support to the notion that we all have internal clocks that control our activity and that there appear to be neural centers that do control such things as blood cell counts (low in the morning), body temperature (low at night), and activity.

The biological rhythms are more noticeable among some animals. Rats, for example, are nocturnal creatures and display most of their activity at night. When given access to an activity wheel, they will run for longer periods at night than in the daytime, even though they live in lighted quarters and could not know whether it was day or night. Sexual activity in rats follows a 4-day cycle in females, so that they are low in receptivity on one day but high on others; in human females, the 28-day cycle of menstruation is another instance of a biorhythm.

Because of habit, circumstances of employment, or perhaps for some as yet unknown biological reason, some people appear to be most efficient or effective at certain hours of the day. Some cannot get started in the morning and prefer to work at night. People who work swing shifts sometimes have difficulties adjusting their sleep schedules to the morning or afternoon hours. There are, of course, many reasons why someone might not feel like sleeping in the afternoon and through the regular dinner hour. How much importance should be attached to people's preference for the hours in which they feel they are most effective cannot be assessed at present. Newspaper columns about biorhythms for any particular day are sheer nonsense on a par with their astrological predictions. At the present time, there is no scientific support for any statements about biorhythms and individual behavior on any given day. Such columns may help sell newspapers, but they only lead to greater confusion for the people confused enough to read them.

BIOSOCIAL THEORY   *(See INSTINCT)*

Since the 1970s, some biologists and ethologists have been studying the social life of insects, birds, and some mammals from the viewpoint of sociology. They observe the apparent organization of activities, division of labor, or classes into which members can be divided, such as queen, drone, worker, and so on, in order to determine if any useful conclusions might be drawn about human society. Some sociobiologists, such as E. O. Wilson of Harvard, have been particularly interested in patterns of behavior they can identify as *aggression* or *altruism* to determine if those response patterns have an evolutionary and, therefore, a hereditary base and if they might also be identified as human heredity characteristics. In sociobiological contexts, altruism is identified with the observation that some individuals in a species appear to sacrifice themselves so that the rest of the group can survive. Although the observations of sociobiologists are interesting to psychologists, the latter are more inclined to emphasize environmental influence over behavior and have not taken kindly to the suggestions of sociobiologists. Most psychologists are still inclined to attribute both aggression and altruism to training and not heredity and will tend to ignore the sociobiologists until they present more convincing evidence.

BIRTH TRAUMA

Birth trauma is a psychoanalytic concept proposed by Freud and later expanded by other psychoanalysts. In essence, the idea is that birth itself is a sudden and disruptive change from the warmth and safety of the womb to the cold, noise, glare, and danger of the outside world. For all infants, according to the analysts, this is a physiologically upsetting situation, or a *trauma*. Freud proposed that this trauma creates the beginning or basic prototype for all later anxiety and anxiety disorders. In some cases, psychoanalysts will trace the current adult problems of a client all the way back to the supposed birth trauma.

Like most of the psychoanalytic ideas—all of which came out of the 1800s—the birth trauma hypothesis cannot be scientifically tested. Although no one would deny that birth may be a physiological shock, psychologists today find no use for the concept in their therapeutic or research work. Only the remaining few orthodox psychoanalysts give it any credence at all. The birth trauma remains an interesting idea still believed in by some psychologists, but not taken seriously by most.

BLINDNESS AND DEAFNESS

We can partially appreciate the problems of the blind by merely closing our eyes and trying to get about in our own homes. The inability to see, like the inability to hear or to feel our own bodies, is catastrophic as far as getting along in life is concerned. Like deafness, blindness may have many causes, and again, like deafness, it can occur in various degrees and at various stages in life. To be born blind means to live in a very different world from that of those who suffer blindness later in life because of accidents or other trauma.

Many blind people are able to make reasonable adjustments and even achieve some success at higher occupations because they do have the facility for language that the deaf do not enjoy. The blind can learn to read and write with a grammatical language, something pretty much beyond the ability of the deaf. Language is the major factor in any kind of successful learning, and even if it is limited to Braille, it enables the blind to operate in terms of literature and abstract ideas.

Psychologists are not of much help in dealing with the blind. One factor of some importance, however, should be considered with the blind, just as it should be considered with people suffering from any other affliction—that is, the handicapped person may be under the influence of one of two kinds of faith: He may believe that his affliction is a punishment from God and that prayer or other kinds of religious activities may bring about a miraculous cure, or he may believe that modern science and modern medicine will make great strides in the almost immediate future and provide him with a cure. In either case, the faith may prevent any personal effort to improve his condition. Why bother to learn Braille if one will be able to see tomorrow? Some handicapped people keep looking for special doctors who are alleged to have had marvelous successes in similar cases, and these pesons may spend fortunes in their searches. It is of basic importance to have an appropriate assessment of the nature of the blindness, deafness, or other handicap and, after appropriate consultation with two or three recognized experts in the field, try to determine what actual hope there may be. If there are no grounds for faith in a medical cure, the blind person must be counseled into making the best of his handicap. In the case of the blind, many successful practitioners in law, medicine, and other fields can be presented as examples, and, assuming a basic intellectual capacity, an appropriate training program can be instituted.

The blind do enjoy a great advantage over the deaf, if that is some consolation. They can listen to records, radio, and even television and make some sense of that is going on. For the deaf, a television story becomes a succession of pictures where very little makes sense. Some cartoons can be followed, but even these employ a lot of sound effects in order to make their points. If you turn off the sound on a television program and watch the pictures, you will get some insight into the problems of the deaf.

In the cases of both the blind and the deaf, if the affliction occurs after the childhood years, the previous history of language in the case of the deaf and of the visual experience in the case of the blind can be of major benefit in serving as a source of imagery and memories.

BLIND SPOTS   *(See VISION)*

We sometimes use the expression *blind spot* to refer to someone's inability to see some defect in his or her friends or loved ones, but the fact is that we all have real blind spots in each of our two eyes. At the point on the retina where the optic nerve joins the eye, there are no visual cells (rods and cones) that can be stimulated by light, and consequently any object in our visual fields that reflects light onto these portions of the retina will not be seen. Those are the blind spots. Normally, we do not notice this gap or hole in our visual fields because the blind spots are not located on corresponding points of the two retinas, and what we do not see with one eye will be seen by the other. If one eye is bandaged or vision is lost through accident or disease, we might miss observing objects to the side of whatever we are looking at. Unless we move our good eye about, we will actually have a blind spot in our vision. Such a spot will increase in size with the distance of the object, so that if we are looking straight ahead down a road, we might not see something as large as a truck or a barn somewhat to the side of the road. People with only one good eye do drive cars and have been known to fly airplanes successfully. They can function if they move the eye about, but there is always some danger that they might miss seeing something to the side.

THE BRAIN AND THE NERVOUS SYSTEM
(See BIOFEEDBACK, BRAIN WAVES)

The nervous system can be thought of as a railroad or telephone network. It is a system in that all of the parts are connected with a central location, the brain, with arrivals and departures of nervous impulses from the central location to and from all parts of the body. The nervous impulses are electrical and chemical discharges, and they travel along nerves, which are collections of nerve fibers, which in turn are extensions of neural cells or neurons. The neurons consist of a central nucleus with extensions called dendrites and axons. The combination of a nerve cell and its extensions makes up a nerve fiber which can be short or long, like a section of track. Each fiber connects with one or more other fibers via a short gap called a synapse. A neural impulse crosses over the synapse, although the exact nature of the transmission is not fully known. If your toe is touched, a neural impulse is generated that will move up your leg, into your spinal cord, and up to your brain in a short period of time. Impulses can travel as fast as 100 yards per second on some fibers. Generally, they are slower than that; the nerve impulse does not travel with the speed of light. When the impulse reaches the spinal cord, it may generate or stimulate an impulse in a motor nerve going back to the toe and the toe may twitch or move or the foot may be withdrawn, depending upon many situational and stimulus factors. There is a kind of one-way traffic in the nervous system, since the impulses always travel along the axons and cross over to dendrites of another neuron, where they activate the nucleus and pass on over the axon of that neuron to the dendrites of the next, and so on. You can think of each neuron as a short piece of wire, track, or tubing with functional connections at both ends. Note that the connections are functional, not actual permanent physical connections.

The central nervous system.   The brain and the spinal cord are usually described as the *central nervous system.* The brain consists of about three to four pounds of matter, cells, fibers, liquids, blood vessels and various kinds of supportive, nonneural material. The brain contains some 12 billion neurons, or gray cells, with their fibers, or white matter, arranged in two hemispheres connected via a mass of fiber tissue called the corpus callosum. The two hemispheres give rise to the fibers that make up the spinal cord, which is encased in the spinal column or backbone. Through openings in the backbone, some 32 pairs of spinal nerves emerge, connecting the various parts of the body to the brain. The spinal nerves consist of a sensory component and a motor component: The former brings impulses from sense areas; the latter carrying impulses out to the muscles.

The cerebellum.   At the rear and below the two hemispheres is another body of nervous tissue called the *cerebellum* whose function it is to maintain motor coordination and balance. The rest of the brain is generally referred to as the cerebrum or the cerebral hemispheres.

Cerebral functional localization.   Exploration of the brain by electrical stimulation and by inference from tumors, wounds, strokes, and other traumatic episodes has resulted in some knowledge of more or less specific functions of parts of the *cerebrum.* The very front of the brain (the frontal lobes) is not well explored, and little is known of what goes on there. Some people have had extensive damage to the frontal lobes with no apparent permanent loss of any functions. The sides of the brain (temporal lobes) appear to be related to hearing. The back of the brain (occipital lobes) has been fairly carefully mapped for visual functions. Motor and bodily sensory functions appear to be localized along a deep fissure separating the frontal lobes from the rest of the cerebral hemispheres. Language functions normally appear to be localized in the left cerebral hemisphere, whereas appreciation of shapes and visual forms normally appears to be a function of the right cerebral hemisphere.

The brain is curiously organized in that the normal expectations one might have are generally reversed. We might expect vision to be localized up front, but it is actually localized at the rear of the brain. Functions of the toes are organized at the top of the brain, with a kind of reversal from foot to head: The functions of the upper part of the body are localized in the lower portions of the brain. The left hemisphere sends its impulses down the right side of the spinal cord, so that the bodily functions of the right side are represented on the left side of the brain and vice versa. A person who suffers a stroke on the left side may find his or her right side paralyzed and/or anesthetized. Because functions of speech and language are localized on the left side, a stroke or injury there might result in an inability to speak or process language, whereas the left side of the body might be unimpaired.

Below the cerebral cortex lies the so-called old brain, which contains many centers where impulses are generated that result in thirst, hunger, sex-related activities, and their opposites. Temperature control is also automatically organized in the old brain.

The autonomic nervous system. The internal bodily functions of the various glands and visceral organs are rather automatically controlled by what is called the *autonomic nervous system*. This consists of nerves arising from masses of cell bodies called *ganglia* that lie outside the spinal cord but are connected to the cord. From these ganglia, nerve fibers run to the heart, liver, kidneys, stomach, intestines, and other internal organs. The fibers are usually described in terms of their location, with the upper (cranial) and lower (sacral) fibers and their ganglia comprising what is called the *parasympathetic system,* whereas those in the middle are described as the *sympathetic system.* The sympathetic system is sometimes called the emergency system and seems to operate in emotional flight or fight situations when ordinary routine patterns of circulation, breathing, and digestion are upset or inhibited and when more energy (blood and blood sugar) is needed by the muscles. The parasympathetic system operates to keep the body on an even smooth course in nonemergency situations.

The autonomic nervous system is sometimes considered an involuntary system, in that it does not call for any attention—we do not direct our breathing—we just breathe; our hearts keep ticking away without any concern on our part. Even if we try to affect any of our internal functions, we are usually unable to do much without activating the external muscles of the arms and chest, over which we do have some control. We do achieve some mastery over our bladders and rectums, but we can do little about our heart rates by just thinking about them. There is also some partial control over sex organs, in that ejaculation (sympathetic nervous system) and erection (parasympathetic nervous system) are subject to some management.

BRAINSTORMING

Brainstorming is a specialized procedure for trying to solve problems by group efforts. It is based on the assumption that one person, facing a problem, may not be able to come up with a solution because the next step toward a solution does not occur to him or her at the moment and may never occur to him or her because of some kind of block in his or her thinking. Frequently, people in a problem situation tend to go around in circles and just miss a solution, even though they are quite capable of handling the problem. In a group with a common problem, each person can speak up and offer his or her suggestion, however useless it may be; another person in the group, stimulated by the first offering, may think of something better or find some flaw; a third person can then bring up something else that occurred to him or her in the context of the previous suggestions. Such a process of offering solutions and flaw-finding can go on until the problem is solved or declared insoluble.

In typical training sessions, a problem, such as how many uses can be found for a broom? or what can be done with an old shoe besides throwing it away? might be posed. An enormous amount of enthusiastic activity can be generated, and a large number of suggestions can be developed as one person expands on a previous suggestion. This is called hitch-hiking or piggy-back-riding. What is suggested in brainstorming sessions is that everyone let him- or herself go and not be inhibited. Any suggestion at all may prompt someone else to think of something that he or she would not ordinarily think of. The procedure of brainstorming is presumed to be one kind of creative thinking operation.

In our social history, there is no evidence that any problems of importance have been solved in such group efforts. Experimentally minded psychologists have argued that a number of people working alone on certain problems can come up with as many solutions as the group of equal number could develop if the suggestions of individuals are added together. Also, individuals working alone can solve more soluble problems than the group can, given some fixed number to solve in a given time. Such experimental tests may or may not be relevant. Certainly, the basic proposition that one idea can lead to another in someone else's head is correct. For many problems, however, specialized knowledge is required, and just any group of random people might come up with only impractical ideas; this, in turn, suggests that for technical problems, the group should consist of technical people who have the necessary backgrounds; they might help each other.

BRAINWASHING

From the time of the Korean War, we have been accustomed to reading about some mysterious process the newspapers call *brainwashing*. At first, it was regarded as some unique procedure devised by wily orientals until it was recalled that during the Soviet purge trials under Stalin, many stalwart Bolshevik leaders confessed to crimes they could not possibly have committed and that a Catholic cardinal even confessed to unlikely actions to his Communist judges. One does not have to be a Communist or an oriental to be credited with the capacity for brainwashing someone else.

All we have to support the theory of brainwashing is that someone now acts in a way that he or she did not before and in which he or she could not reasonably have been expected to act unless something unusual happened to him or her. This much is true, and something unusual has happened to victims of so-called brainwashing. One thing that did not happen was that nothing was done to their brains in any direct way. The term is an obvious misnomer. Although nothing has been done to the brain of victims, usually plenty has been done to their bodies, including starvation, beating, rape, isolation, prevention of sleep, endless interrogation, and, commonly, rewards for acting along lines indicated by the captors. Under such conditions of physical abuse, alternated with pleasant and sympathetic treatment, along with the obvious example of superior strength, authority, and power of the captors, at least some people go along with their captors, join with them in abusing other victims, and otherwise identify with former foes. It is not a new phenomenon in world history, and there have been many accounts of prisoners who become trusties in prisons or concentration camps and outdo their captors in inflicting misery and abuse on their former fellows.

Perhaps the strangest feature of so-called brainwashing is that some victims develop fondness, even love, for former abusers. This may be the result of abusers occasionally granting favors to the abused at times when they are desperately in need of such favors, such as a sip of water to someone dying of thirst. Different people, of course, stand up to their captors at different times, depending upon how they have been brainwashed before. If someone has a great deal to lose by allying himself with his or her captors, he or she may resist for a long time. People with little education, no assets, and no previous history of success in their original environments can be more easily convinced that joining their captors might be appropriate behavior. A strong identification with one's nation, religion, family, friends, and so on can help resistance, but, given enough abuse alternated with favorable treatment, nearly everyone can quite probably be brought around, especially if convinced that his or her cause is lost, that the enemy will surely win, and that there is no hope for any rescue.

Brainwashing is not a scientific application of any special psychological techniques and can be successfully practiced by virtually primitive people who have never heard of psychology. It is basically a physical abuse technique in which a victim is deprived of health and vigor by people who do not care whether the victim lives or dies and who treat the victim like some lesser form of life, which he or she eventually comes to believe to be the case.

BRAIN WAVES   *(See BIOFEEDBACK, THE BRAIN AND THE NERVOUS SYSTEM)*

When suitable electrodes are attached to the scalp and connected to amplifiers, electrical activity in the brain can be detected, amplified, and recorded by activating pens on moving paper. The activity can appear to occur in the form of waves, and a picture of such waves is known as an *electroencephalogram,* or EEG. The frequencies and amplitudes of the waves can be measured, and the characteristics of the wave activity can then be analyzed in terms of the locations of the electrodes. If many electrodes are attached to the scalp, activity can be recorded from many regions at the same time. An expert with long experience at examining the kinds of waves that are normally observed can sometimes detect abnormalities of activity in specific areas and can then diagnose the possible existence of a tumor or other abnormality. People working with EEGs find it convenient to classify waves as fast or slow and with large spikes or small ones. When a wave seems to have cycles of 8-12 per second, the name alpha wave is used as a description. Faster, smaller waves are known as beta waves. Slow, large-spiked waves are called delta waves. The alpha waves are more often prominent when the subject is resting quietly with eyes closed and is not especially concerned over any problems. If he opens his eyes, the alpha wave may disappear, in the sense that the activity from that pen now speeds up and gets smaller in range. Closing the eyes may restore the alpha wave. Delta waves are picked up when the subject is asleep. The disappearance of delta waves is an indication that the subject is about to waken.

Brain wave monitoring.   Subjects can be connected to an EEG device so that when they are showing a run of alpha waves, a low tone sounds; if the alpha waves drop out, the tone stops. If the subject is asked to try to keep the tone on, he can do so after some practice. This a type of biofeedback procedure (see Biofeedback) and indicates that we can, if we want to, get to the stage where we can control some of our brain waves. Because alpha waves represent a kind of vegetative state where we are not engaged in any serious thinking activity and where our minds are more or less blank (not strictly the case, since there are other waves that can be recorded at the same time), there is no great purpose being served in such mastery. Some people identify such alpha states with altered states of consciousness that they have somehow come to admire and desire. We can only wish them luck.

BREAST-FEEDING AND BOTTLE-FEEDING

Most American babies are bottle-fed rather than breast-fed. Since the late 1960s, however, there seems to have been an increase in the number of new mothers intending to breast-feed their infants. By 1977, the estimated percentage who planned to breast-feed had risen to more than 38%.

Public health authorities agree that breast-feeding is generally preferable to the use of bottles and formulae, pointing to the close physical experiences that are shared by mother and child during nursing. This physical closeness, many psychologists believe, is an important part of the child's experiences. One potential problem with breast-feeding is that drugs taken by the mother, including alcohol and nicotine, are ingested by the baby through the milk. Nursing mothers, then, should be particularly careful about their drug intake, including even prescription medicines.

In many cases, the mother cannot breast-feed or chooses not to for other reasons. Psychologists believe that bottle-fed infants can be just as secure and physically close to the mothers as the breast-fed infants. What seems important is the mother's affectionate, patient, and gentle behavior toward the baby, regardless of whether breast or bottle is used. It is not wise to prop up a bottle in the crib and leave the baby to himself or herself, as a variety of problems can result, not the least of which is the lack of the mother-child relationship.

BRIBERY   *(See REWARDS)*

Many parents frown on what they consider bribery because the term smacks of corruption. Because of the illegal aspects of bribery in business and politics, there is an aura of corruption about any kind of bribery, and some parents object to using bribing tactics in bringing up their children, hoping that somehow or other children will do the right thing because it is right in itself. Such hopes are delusions, according to most psychologists who endorse a reinforcement principle. We behave the way we do because of what amounts to self-interest. If something brings us pleasure and satisfaction or makes us feel better, we will do it or continue to do it. If it brings us pain, fear, or anxiety, we will stop doing it or refrain from it in the future. This is an ancient principle, that of hedonism, a pleasure-pain principle, the carrot and stick operation.

Obviously, parents should not promise rewards for illicit or illegal behavior. That would be corrupt. But there is nothing illegal about eating spinach: It may not be attractive to the child, but it is not illegal, and if a parent wants a child to eat spinach, it might be necessary to offer ice cream as an antidote a little later. The offer of ice cream is not different in principle to offering tokens in a token economy or money as salary or wages at the end of a week's work.

We are constantly engaging in reinforcing or rewarding other people for doing what we want them to do. We laugh at their jokes if we want to hear more. We smile in greeting if we want their continued friendship; we reinforce others in thousands of ways in our attempts to influence their behavior toward us. As long as our reinforcements are not calculated to encourage illegal, immoral, or unethical acts, we are merely reinforcing, not bribing. Parents should not hesitate to reward desired behaviors, nor should they hesitate to offer rewards in exchange for good behavior. It is probably the only way they will ever get it. The difficulty, of course, is with the amount of the reward, its frequency, and its timing. If a child learns that he or she can manipulate his or her parents, then the child is bribing the parents by his or her good behavior. The rewards should be in some proportion to the situational demands. They should be skipped on occasion, and the child may learn to find other satisfactions from the behavior. A child who does not want to learn to swim might be persuaded to do so by various rewards. Later on, the child may find sufficient pleasure in swimming to make the rewards unnecessary. Some children even learn to like spinach and reward themselves by eating it.

C

CARELESSNESS

Among the most common words parents employ are "Be careful," as they admonish their children about crossing streets, eating, playing, sports, and a thousand other activities. The words have virtually no value and only indicate that the parents are concerned. Being careless amounts to doing *this* instead of *that*—that is, someone fails to do what we want him or her to do and does something else instead, if he or she does anything. No one can be careful in the sense of being able to attend to more than one thing at a time. A careful surgeon might not notice that the operating room is on fire. A driver watching the car in front of him or her may not notice a car alongside or behind. A child intent on getting a piece of cake may not notice the glass of milk at his or her elbow. When some accident occurs, we blame the culprit for carelessness. He or she actually may have been careful about something else.

There is no such thing as a trait of carelessness that operates to create troubles, accidents, and so on. There are only faulty or undesirable ways of going about some task, and if there are many factors involved in any one task, the amount of training that goes into effective behavior can be enormous. We illustrate with such a matter as crossing streets. If children are not taught specifically to look in both directions before crossing, there may be a tragedy. It does no good to tell children such things; they must be put into the situation and specifically instructed. The same kind of training of "do this, do not do that" must be spelled out, demonstrated, and tested in all kinds of situations that might involve undesirable consequences. Telling someone to be careful may result in his or her thinking of being careful, whatever that might mean, while he or she proceeds to endanger himself.

CASE STUDIES

Many self-help books are based on someone's familiarity with cases of individuals who behaved in some way or who had certain problems. Case studies are intensive, longitudinal studies of individuals, even though the individual might be a small town or a foreign culture. By their nature, case studies are not controlled scientific experiments and can *prove nothing*. They can be very helpful in suggesting leads or ideas, but 10,000 cases will prove nothing about the next case that comes up. In this volume, we will not deal with case studies except to illustrate some particular kind of symptom or syndrome. Science depends on controlled observation—that is, basically, a setup where various factors can be introduced to determine their effects while a constant or controlled situation is maintained for comparison in which the changes are not introduced. It is impossible, for example, to determine whether a particular president was a good one or a bad one. Somebody else might have done a better or worse job in that time and under those circumstances, but we can never know for sure.

CATHARSIS   (See ASSERTIVENESS TRAINING)

Psychiatrist Joseph Breuer developed the *cathartic method* in psychotherapy in the late nineteenth century. Breuer hypnotized his patients and then had them talk about and, in a sense, re-experience their early traumas and anxieties. By re-experiencing them, the patient supposedly released the emotional pressure that had built up inside and thus would presumably begin to feel and function better. Sigmund Freud gained some of his early training from Breuer, including the use of the cathartic method. In time, Freud decided that hypnosis was not necessary, but what seemed important was to encourage patients to talk freely about their feelings and ideas. He termed his non-hypnotic method *"free association,"* and it became a major procedure in psychoanalysis.

Although all of us have probably experienced some relief after venting or expressing our emotions, the cathartic method did not prove to be an effective therapy technique for solving long-standing emotional problems. It is generally a good idea to recognize and to express our feelings at low or normal levels rather than to try to vent or release them at high intensities.

The original basis for catharsis as a therapy stems from Aristotle, who suggested that watching tragedies on the stage enabled those in the audience to expunge their emotional conflicts to some degree. Watching our team win helps rid us of some hostilities and aggressive impulses, according to modern ethologists like Lorenz. One might worry about the fans of the losing side. We must also note that expressing our feelings may create more problems than are solved. In any case, catharsis is no longer a major goal of therapists, who are more concerned about developing positive adaptive patterns of behavior.

CHARACTER   *(See PERSONALITY)*

Character is frequently confused with personality. We have defined *personality* as an individual's difference from anyone else, and so everyone has a personality in that he is unique, barring some features of identical twins, in structure and some consistent behavior patterns. Character is a social or cultural distinction in that, in any society, certain behavior patterns carry value judgments. It is considered proper, for example, in the United States, that people be truthful, that they be faithful in marital relations, that they keep their words, that they be dependable, and so on. The white Protestant work ethic is usually held up as the model for the citizenry. If you do work hard, save your money, love your mother, and observe the Boy Scout and other laws, you will be regarded as having a good character; on the other hand, if you get drunk, abuse drugs, lie, steal, cheat, and bet on horses, you might be called a bad character. Potential employers ask for character references as well as some comments on personality. In our culture, the word integrity has a high value; if it can be said of someone that he or she possesses integrity, it is possibly the highest praise. We should note that in various gangs and subcultures an entirely different set of behavior patterns might be covered by the term *integrity,* where it also might be valued highly. In general, character is a moralistic term, whereas personality is more inclusive. Some film personalities, for example, might lead rather profligate lives and still be admired or at least not censured for their escapades. Their personalities might be considered attractive, whereas their characters might be deplored.

CHILD ABUSE

Child abuse is a crime of violence against children committed by parents or other adults who are responsible for the child's welfare. The problem in the United States is severe, with an estimated tens of thousands of child abuse and neglect victims each year, reaching extremes in which American children are starved, beaten, mutilated, tortured, or murdered by their supposed protectors. In New York City alone, some ten thousand cases of suspected child neglect and/or abuse are reported every year. It is not known how many cases throughout the country are kept secret and never reported to the authorities.

Professionals make a distinction between child neglect and child abuse. Child neglect is the failure to provide adequately for the proper care of children, such as in cases of poor nutrition or health care. Child abuse, usually more severe, is the direct injury of children, usually by their own parents or other adult caretakers. Both neglect and abuse can be extreme, and in either case, the child suffers.

Over the years, physicians and emergency room attendants have learned a great deal about the kinds of injuries suffered by abused children and the medical treatments needed. But little is known about the personal or psychological aspects of the abused child and the abusing parents. Medical and social agencies and the police and local governments are all involved, but none know how to deal adequately with this growing problem.

Over the past decade, a few facts have become clear. First, the abusing parent is not limited to any particular economic or ethnic group, as was once thought. Abusing parents are found at all levels of society, from comfortably expensive suburban homes to poverty-level families. Some common characteristics of the abusing parents are their unrealistic expectations that children, even infants, should do something for the parents—that is, make them happy or make them feel fulfilled. When these parents find out that raising children means constant responsibility and work on their part, they become angry, enraged, and punitive. Another characteristic is the parents' belief that spanking and other physical punishment of children for discipline is acceptable. Often the child-abusing parent begins with acceptable levels of spanking, which, with added frustration and rage, escalate over weeks, months, or years to severe abuse. Very often, only one child in the family is the target for abuse. Perhaps one of the most consistent findings is that child-abusing parents were themselves neglected or abused by their own parents. They seem to carry on the child-abuse tradition.

Abusing parents usually know that they are abusing their children, but many claim that they can't help it; they become enraged and lose control and feel badly afterwards. But they are afraid to seek professional help because, after all, they are breaking the law.

What should parents do if they know that they are abusing their child or suspect that they might lose control when they punish a child? What should any adult do—a wife or husband, a neighbor, a relative or a friend—when they know that child abuse is going on in a family? Our advice is this: (1) Your major concern must be for the safety of the child. Remember that a child is in pain and might be severely injured or killed if nothing is done about it. (2) As difficult as it may be, you must report it to the authorities. If it is a crisis situation, call the police. The police will act quickly to protect the child. A social agency might take months before anything is done. (3) If it is not an immediate crisis situation, call the local hospital, a child welfare agency, a mental health association, or your own family doctor or pediatrician. Tell them the problem and indicate that you need professional help right away. If you cooperate and honestly seek help, professionals will also cooperate with you and try to help you. The police need be involved only when the person has not sought or received help and when the abuse has gone to extremes.

If you are concerned, as a citizen, about child abuse in your own city or town, you should try to get the authorities and professionals to provide both emergency and long-term medical, psychological, and social services. Throughout all of this, the safety and welfare of the child must be the foremost concern.

CHILD ADVOCACY

Some current writers and historical investigators believe that Western culture has not always recognized childhood as a distinct phase of life that is significantly different from adulthood. In medieval times, children were thought to be little men and were treated much like adults, with little or no special attention, toys, games, or education.

On the other hand, many so-called primitive people apparently did give special recognition to childhood.

In the 1600s in Western Europe and England, upper-class families began to recognize childhood as a different phase of life with its own particular characteristics, and children began to be valued for their more endearing qualities of innocence and enthusiasm. Since then, there has continued a tradition of adult control over children, tempered somewhat by a recognition of the children's special needs and characteristics. We no longer buy and sell them, but we do have special laws governing their behavior, prohibiting them from owning and controlling substantial property; compelling them to attend school; allowing then no legal right to challenge, for example, a medical doctor who, at the request of the parents, can commit children up to age 14 to institutions; and so on.

Because of such special laws and the general lack of legal rights and control over their own lives, children are seen by many concerned adults as truly oppressed humans, denied the rights granted to most adults. In recent years, we have seen the voting age and age of consent for a variety of contractual and social agreements dropped from age 21 to age 18, and there is some pressure to reduce it further for some activities. It seems, then, that our concept of childhood continues to evolve and will undoubtedly be very different in two or three generations.

At present, there are many people trying to improve the conditions and rights of younger people. They are advocates for the rights of young people, and a whole social-legal area of child advocacy is developing. In 1971, the National Center for Child Advocacy was established in Washington, D.C. Various local children's agencies, school boards, or social service departments can provide more current information.

CHILDHOOD AUTISM

Childhood autism is a rare condition that affects about five out of 100,000 children, or an estimated 5,000 children in the United States at present. Psychologists agree on the three most important characteristics that help to diagnose autistic children: (1) They are loners to an extreme degree and often fight or scream if someone, even a parent, tries to play with or talk to them. (2) Autistic children have severe language problems. As infants, they do not babble very much; they have trouble even learning to use simple gestures to communicate, and 50% of such children never learn to talk at all. Those who do learn to speak do so in a very limited, distorted manner, with much echoing and parroting, with seemingly endless repetitions of phrases, and with confusions of the words "you" and "I." (3) Autistic children insist on sameness in their lives and become extremely upset when their routines are interrupted. There are other common but not universal characteristics, too: Many autistic children scream and have violent tantrums when frustrated; strange gestures and bizarre facial expressions are frequent; some show brief flashes of special abilities, such as doing picture puzzles very well or memorizing long phrases, songs, or television commercials. Unfortunately, these flashes of ability never seem to develop any further. In general, the development, particularly of language and social skills, is slow.

Until about fifteen years ago, there was a great deal of misinformation about autistic children and their parents. For example, it was thought by some that autism was caused by unloving, cold, and rejecting parents; that individual psychotherapy, such as could be provided by psychiatrists or psychologists, for one or two hours a week was useful; that the parents were disturbed and therefore needed psychotherapy themselves; that the occasional flashes of ability indicated a touch of genius.

Our best knowledge at present is that childhood autism is probably due to genetic or biochemical problems or to brain damage; that individual psychotherapy for the children is probably a waste of money and the parents' time; that, at present, there is no known cure for childhood autism. However, very carefully detailed special education and behavior modification programs can help the children to learn some language use, to interact more with others, and to control much of their bizarre and aggressive behavior. Some autistic children do learn to read and write and to progress even into high school academic levels.

Our best advice to parents of autistic children is:

1. Demand that your school system provide a special program for autistic children, one focused on language training, on social skill training, and, lastly, on academics. Federal law now mandates that schools must provide education for *all* children.

2. Keep active and informed about the school's program and staff, and don't hesitate to help them, criticize them, and make demands of them. Try also to get help from your county or state mental health department. Cooperate with other parents of autistic children.

3. Try to get training yourself in how to teach autistic children at home. A *good* school program will include heavy emphasis on parent training. In general, do all you can to educate and train the children in special programs and at home for as long as possible.

4. Maintain good, regular medical and dental examinations and make sure that your child is receiving a well-balanced diet.

5. Remember that the most effective treatment currently available for autistic children is a combination of special education and behavior modification programming in special group settings. This requires a social agency, such as a school, and cannot be provided by individual, private psychotherapists.

CHILDREN'S GAMES

Children spend a great deal of their time playing in a variety of activities; traditional games, spontaneous, made-up games of make-believe and acting adult roles. In recent generations, we have seen more emphasis on adult control over the children's games through commercially available board games and electronic TV games as well as through adult-organized and adult-controlled games and other activities for children, such as the various Little League teams.

Children gain a great deal in their play; exercising their muscles as well as their imaginations. They practice and learn motor and visual coordination, and they can gradually learn what many of their own limits are in relation to the game's demands and in comparison with other children.

In addition to the physical aspects of exercise in games, children also practice and learn about other people, and about the social and physical world. To a great extent, they also practice adult roles that they will carry out years later. When children play house, school, going to work, and so on, they are at least partly trying on adult roles. Psychologists also believe that there is a safety valve funtion in games, so that children can safely express the anger and aggression they may feel against parents, siblings, or authorities in general—feelings that they cannot easily express in most other situations.

Although many children's games still include traditional activities, and although the same fourth-grade jokes seem to be told in each recent generation, some things have changed. In some ways, children's games may be more restricted now than they were one or two generations ago, constrained now by the control imposed by commercial promotions and other adult management operations. In addition, television watching has taken up a great deal of the time children used to devote to active play. Nowadays, too, the range of play for girls has increased considerably, as they not only continue to play traditional girls' games but are now increasingly active in what were formerly limited to boys' activities. On the other hand, boys, according to some researchers, may have become somewhat more restricted than before in terms of their boy-appropriate behavior. In other words, it is not clear that the growing world of girls' play has been matched by any growth of the scope of boys' play.

It is important for parents to realize that children's play activities and games are important and to recognize, too, that increased television watching, increased commercial control over children's activities, and increased adult-organized and adult-controlled activities may be depriving our children of some important creative and expressive child-determined experiences.

CHILDREN'S SLEEP DISORDERS

Children's rituals of delaying bedtime as long as possible by requesting another drink of water or a story, by complaining of a stomachache, and so on are among the most familiar scenes in family life. Such delaying tactics are not sleep problems or disorders unless they involve repeated conflicts between parents and child at each bedtime. If this is the case, then the parents have probably mismanaged and helped to escalate the normal, common, delaying tactics into open nightly conflict. The parents should take a good look at their own behavior and try to see what they are doing that both stimulates and reinforces the child's delays.

In general, if bedtime is a problem, it may be helpful to do the following: (1) Have a definite bedtime set and not let it vary too much; (2) avoid highly exciting games, TV, or other activities shortly before bedtime; (3) be calm and patient yourself and communicate this to your child; (4) praise and reward children for going to bed well and for staying in bed all night without interruptions, except for going to the bathroom; (5) set limits—that is, once in bed, the child might be read to for five or ten minutes, but once the lights are out, there will be no drink of water, and so on—and firmly maintain the limits.

Sometimes children have difficulties falling asleep, not because they want to delay it but because they are very excited, perhaps scared, not feeling well, or because they have been sent to bed too early. Some parents who plan to go out for the evening convey a sense of tension that children not used to babysitters quickly pick up.

More serious than the normal delays or the occasional difficulty in falling asleep is *interrupted sleep*—that is, the child's sleep is frequently disrupted during the night by nightmares, night terrors, sleepwalking, bed-wetting (enuresis), or bowel movements during sleep (encopresis).

Nightmares and *night terrors* are two different phenomena, both involving frightening experiences during sleep. Nightmares are fairly common. They are dreams, and, like most dreams, they occur during the last two or three hours of sleep. Night terrors are rare. They are *not* dreams, since they occur during the first two hours of sleep, which is commonly a dreamless period. It is also the period of *deepest* sleep during the night.

The child usually awakens easily from a nightmare, may call the parents, and still seems afraid when awake. The child can describe and discuss the bad dream and, after being reassured and calmed, can usually go back to sleep without much trouble. The entire nightmare experience usually lasts only one or two minutes, although sometimes children will remain awake a long time afterwards, discussing the dream. Nightmares are usually remembered by the child.

Night terrors are far more distressing, for parents as well as for children. During the night terror, the child is deeply asleep, but he or she might be sitting up in bed with his or her eyes wide open, crying, calling for help, or talking incoherently—all giving clear indications that he or she is terrified of something. The child often perspires and moves or looks around, seemingly looking at frightening things in his or her room. He or she does not recognize his or her parents, and they cannot wake him or her or calm him or her down during the attack. The entire reaction might last as long as twenty minutes, but it is usually less. During a night terror attack, all the parents can do is protect the child and see that he or she is not injured by running into something or falling out of bed. After the attack is over, the child becomes calm and usually sleeps well for the rest of the night. Unlike nightmares, the night terror experience is not remembered by the child. The night terror is a phenomenon of the deepest sleep phase, whereas the nightmare occurs during the lighter sleep or dreaming phase.

No one knows what causes nightmares or night terrors nor how to treat them. The most hopeful information for parents is that both tend to disappear as the child grows older. In some cases, night terrors have been reduced with the drug, valium. But giving behavior-control drugs to children must be done with great care and constant monitoring and should be used only in the more extreme or long-duration cases.

Sleepwalking (somnambulism), like night terrors, occurs during deep sleep, and the child has no memory of it later. There is no fright involved in sleepwalking except when it is associated with the pattern of night terrors. Sleepwalking children must be watched because they can injure themselves by walking into things, out of windows, or falling over objects or down stairs. It is difficult to waken the child, and when the episode is over, the child usually sleeps well. It is probably best to guide the child gently back to bed and prevent any injury.

The causes of sleepwalking are not known, nor is there any particularly effective treatment. Drug therapy is as ineffective as psychotherapy. With time, somnambulism, like nightmares and night terrors, disappears.

Enuresis and Encopresis.   Beyond age 2 or 3, most children are no longer having involuntary bowel movements during sleep; beyond about age 3 or 4, almost all children are dry at night. Enuresis and encopresis, involuntary wetting and soiling in bed or in clothing, are problems after the age of three or four years. Prior to that, the child's continued accidents, although unpleasant for the parent—almost always for the mother—are within normal developmental limits.

If a child persists in wetting the bed beyond about age 4, it means that special training is needed. In general, as with all our adult interactions with children, our approach should be calm and helpful rather than angry, anxious, and punitive. The best available training is through use of a simple battery-operated device that was developed by psychologists O.H. and W.M. Mowrer in the 1930s. It sounds a buzzer when the child wets the bed, waking the child, and, in a fairly brief time, teaches him to wake up when his bladder is full. These devices can be purchased in many department stores (e.g., Sears) for about $25.00.

Continued involuntary defecation (encopresis) is a rare condition, occurring mostly with retarded children. However, some normal intelligence children also take a long time to train, but it is rarely found after age 7. Calmness, patience, and specific training using positive reinforcement for not soiling has been helpful. For the most part, parents must continue the training, being as helpful and supportive as they can. Both enuresis and encopresis decrease with age, but in some cases they will not entirely disappear without special training attempts.

CLASSIFICATION OF MENTAL DISORDERS

Several classification systems for diagnosing mental disorders have been developed. The standard system used by nearly all mental health professionals is described in the *Diagnostic and Statistical Manual, II* (1965) developed by the American Psychiatric Association and the World Health Organization. This manual provides a worldwide standard classification system. A revised version (DSM III) has been published in 1980.

The DSM III proposes seventeen major categories, each of which includes many subcategories. It should be noted that categorizing a person by diagnostic type does nothing to help that person. The diagnostic system is useful primarily for research and for clinical record-keeping purposes. The categories are as follows:

1. *Organic mental disorders* include mental problems associated with organic brain disorders, such as senile dementia, intoxication, brain damage, or addiction to drugs, such as heroin.
2. *Substance use disorders* include people who abuse and/or are psychologically dependent upon drugs that are ordinarily nonaddictive.

3. *Schizophrenic disorders* are severe, psychotic disorders in which there are major disorders of thinking, emotions, behavior, and poor personal and social adjustment.

4. *Paranoid disorders* are characterized by delusions, usually delusions of persecution or grandeur. These delusions are orderly (systematized) and strongly held.

5. *Schizoaffective disorders* describe a variety of disorders in which the person shows disturbance in both thinking processes and in mood or affect.

6. *Affective disorders* include disorders in which there are severe mood changes, such as in both acute and chronic manic and depressive disorders.

7. *Psychoses* include the psychoses that are not already included in other special categories.

8. *Anxiety disorders,* in the older classification system (DSM II), were called neuroses. In the present system, anxiety disorders are those problems in which there is strong anxiety, such as phobias, panic states, and generalized anxiety.

9. *Factitious disorder* include those people who present psychological and/or physical symptoms that are not real. Rather, the symptoms are created by and are under the voluntary control of the person.

10. *Somatoform disorders* present symptoms of physical disorder, such as partial paralysis, but there are no known organic reasons for the symptoms. The assumption is that the physiological symptoms are produced by psychological causes.

11. *Dissociative disorders* include problems such as amnesia and fugue states.

12. *Personality disorders* are disturbances that appear to be largely free of anxiety, psychological conflicts, or thinking disorders. The person behaves habitually in ways that cause or continue personal problems and/or conflicts with society—for example, antisocial personality, compulsive personality, and the like.

13. *Psychosexual disorders* include sexual inadequacies, perversions, and gender identity problems. It should be noted that homosexuality, considered a mental disorder in the 1968 diagnostic system, is no longer considered a disorder and does not appear in this classification system.

14. *Disorders usually arising in childhood or adolescence* comprise a large grouping of psychological disorders of childhood and adolescence. The category includes mental retardation, childhood autism, conduct disorders, and eating disorders.

15. *Reactive disorders* are psychological disorders brought on by sudden stress from outside sources. These could include psychological reactions to physical injuries, such as those sustained in accidents, or a major crisis, such as the loss of one's home in a fire, and so on.

16. *Disorders of impulse control* include problems such as uncontrollable gambling, fire-setting, stealing, and so on.

17. *Other disorders* comprise a category for nonpsychotic disorders not already included in other categories.

CLIENT-CENTERED THERAPY

Client-centered therapy was developed by psychologist Carl Rogers through the 1940s and 1950s, and it became a major alternative to traditional psychoanalytically oriented therapy. It is a verbal therapy, in that it consists of reports by a client to a sympathetic therapist. It does not involve drugs or any activities on the part of the client. The therapist makes no recommendations and leaves all decisions to the client. Similar to the older psychoanalytical model, the client-centered therapist meets with clients and carries on verbal interaction with them in an attempt to help the clients recognize, clarify, and understand their own emotions and previous hidden problems and confusions. Client-centered therapy was formerly called nondirective therapy because the therapist did not direct the course of the client's responses. The client was free to talk about anything at all or not to talk at all if he or she chose to remain silent. The therapist tried to reflect the client's feelings by adopting an empathetic attitude. It was believed by Rogers that such reflections, or mirroring, would clarify the client's problems.

Unlike psychoanalysis, client-centered therapy assumes that each client, given the right conditions of human acceptance and complete or unconditional positive regard on the part of the therapist, is *by nature* capable of understanding and solving his or her own problems. Thus the client-centered therapist attempts to create those conditions in the therapy situation that will allow the client's natural processes of growth toward what is called self-actualization.

Many client-centered therapists claim that the therapeutic experience is helpful in changing a person's thinking and self-understanding. However, as with other verbal therapies, such as psychoanalysis, there is very little scientific evidence that clients actually improve their real *behavior* as a result of the therapy.

Carl Rogers is an important person in the psychotherapy field. Almost single-handedly, insisting upon the necessity of studying therapy processes, he challenged the traditional psychoanalytic air of secrecy and mysticism and attempted an evaluation of what went on in therapy.

THE CLINICAL FALLACY   (See CASE STUDIES, ASTHMA, CHILDHOOD AUTISM)

Professionals, such as psychologists, psychiatrists, social workers, special educators, and so on, must be alert in order to avoid making the so-called *clinical fallacy*. Three examples are the beliefs that enuresis and asthma in children are caused by serious emotional problems and that childhood autism is caused by cold, aloof, rejecting mothers. Subsequent research has failed to support these hypotheses, but many professionals still accept them. Asthma, one of the most prevalent chronic diseases of childhood, is still described in many textbooks as a psychophysiological disorder.

How the clinical fallacy occurs is easy to see: Essentially, professionals work with special groups of people, clinical samples that have been highly selected on the basis of some disorders. The professionals might observe some strikingly constant factors, perhaps in all of the cases, and then conclude that those factors are causally related to the disorder. For example, among the first few cases of childhood autism studied in the 1940s, there was a strikingly high proportion of well-educated parents who appeared to be objective about their children's disorder. This led to the hypothesis that the objectivity and intellectual approach was tantamount to emotional coldness and aloofness and that this, in turn, might be a cause of autism. The professionals who made those early observations later rejected that hypothesis in light of accumulating evidence that the parents of autistic children seem pretty much like everyone else. Their first small sample had been clinically biased.

Therapists might rightly report that in all cases of childhood enuresis they have treated in thirty years of practice, the child's constant bed-wetting was brought about by his or her severe anxieties and/or disturbed child-parent relationships. The clinical fallacy is committed when the therapists, impressed with the constancy of the finding, then generalize from their limited clinical sample and conclude that the cause of childhood enuresis is severe emotional problems. The important implication of believing this clinical fallacy is that we would then expect, and probably look for, severe emotional problems in all enuretic children and that we would then be biased toward treating them all as somehow emotionally disturbed, to the exclusion of other probable causes.

It has been estimated that some 10 to 15% of children show emotional or psychological problems that are severe enough to warrant professional help. If we were to examine psychologically all children who are enuretic, we would probably find that 10 to 15% of them, just like the percentage of the general population, have such emotional problems. When those children from the 10 to 15% of enuretic children who have problems are taken to professionals, what the therapist sees are severe emotional problems in *all* of the cases—that is, the therapist sees a selected clinical sample.

Another factor that leads to the clinical fallacy is interpreting a relationship among variables as a *cause-effect* relationship. An enuretic child might very well become embarrassed, anxious, and defensive about his or her bed-wetting. An asthmatic child will almost certainly develop fear and anxiety about asthmatic attacks. In these instances, the psychological factors of fear, anxiety, and so on are very normal accompaniments of the disorder—reactions *to* and not necessarily causes *of* the disorders.

What is important here for parents to know is that children who are asthmatic or enuretic or, for that matter, those who may be having problems in school or who show specific fears, such as severe fear of the dark, are not necessarily suffering from some generalized psychological or emotional problems or disturbance. In some cases, they might be, but more than likely, they are showing problems around one very specific issue or situation. Attempts to help these children, then, would probably best be in the form of problem-solving attempts aimed at the specific situations rather than any attempts at generalized psychotherapy.

Many reliably effective specific treatments have been developed for specific problems, such as children's phobias, temper tantrums, bed-wetting, severe noncompliance, inattention in school, hyperactivity, and so on. These approaches often involve retraining the parents as well as the child.

In some cases, a more generalized psychotherapy approach with the child might very well be indicated, but we would suspect that these would be the exceptions and not the rules. The general rule we would recommend to parents who seek professional help for their children is this: Seek help that is problem-specific, that will teach both child and parents new skills in solving these specific issues.

COLIC

Many parents know about an infant's colic, a problem that arises in the first few weeks of the child's life. The infant with colic cries loudly and persistently, kicks his legs, tenses up, behaves as if he is having acute abdominal cramps, and is obviously in pain and discomfort. The distraught parents, particularly since this happens most often with the first child, find that they cannot calm or soothe the infant, and, try what they may, they have to wait until the spasm has passed and the child calms down.

The infant is clearly in great physical distress, and that is difficult for any parent to accept. But parents should be reassured that colic poses no lasting threat or danger and that it is a temporary condition, usually ending by about five months of age. The two major problems with colic are the following: (1) The immediate problem is the pain suffered by the child. There is little the parent can do directly to relieve this pain. The parents should see that the child is otherwise comfortable and should do all they can to soothe and gently reassure the suffering child. (2) The potentially most serious and permanently damaging problem in colic is the way the parents react to it. It is easy for parents to become upset, frustrated, and even angry at the infant's incessantly noxious screaming. When the parent loses patience under these conditions and becomes punitive toward the child or feels heavy guilt over the inability to help, then the parent-child relationship is in danger. The parents must keep themselves as calm and patient as possible, for the sake not only of the infant but of the future parent-child relationship. After all, the infant is in real pain and is not crying because of being spoiled or out of basic meanness. The colicky infant needs love, support, comforting, and lots of loving patience, and he or she has only the parents to depend upon for that.

Colic does not seem to be related to types or temperature of food or to swallowing too much air, although both of those might cause temporary distress. Colic might be related to the child's general level of reactivity or sensitivity, or, as several psychological studies suggest, it might be related to the mother's level of anxiety. Women who were more anxious during pregnancy seem to have a higher incidence of colicky children. In any event, the best advice for parents of colicky children is as follows: (1) Have the child carefully examined by a pediatrician in order to make sure that no other condition is responsible for the distress. (2) If colic is diagnosed, be calm, patient, and loving and resign yourself to several months of the child's turmoil, knowing that it will improve. (3) Do all you can to soothe and make the child as comfortable as possible in all other respects. Never, under any circumstances, blame or punish the infant, who is already in great distress.

COLLECTIVE UNCONSCIOUS   *(See UNCONSCIOUS)*

Carl Jung, a psychoanalyst initially trained by Freud, eventually broke away from Freud's influence and developed a variety of ideas of his own. The *collective unconscious* is one of Jung's concepts. Jung believed that part of everyone's unconscious is inherited and shared by all persons. He used it to "explain" the observation that many myths and symbols seem to be shared by cultures that are greatly separated by time and distance and that seemingly had little or no contact with each other.

The *collective unconscious* is an idea with little evidence to support it. It serves mainly as a theoretical point, a speculation, and it has neither practical value nor supporting evidence. Few modern psychologists take the notion of *collective unconscious* very seriously.

COLORBLINDNESS   *(See COLOR VISION)*

Some people do not see the world in the same way as does the majority. What looks colored to most of us may look drab, brownish, or grayish to those we call colorblind. Actually, no one has perfect color vision in the sense that he or she can discriminate all of the possible hues that vary with the wave lengths of light. Such wave lengths are measured in millimicrons, or $m\mu$ (millionths of a meter). Objects reflecting wave lengths around 400 $m\mu$ are seen as blue; longer waves are seen as green, yellow, orange, and red at about 700 $m\mu$. No one sees the 300 different hues that variations in single $m\mu$ would produce, so that we are all somewhat color weak, and those weaker than others are called colorblind. Mostly the weakness, when there is one, is with red and greens. These appear more or less brown to the colorblind. Yellow and blue blindness is rare. The weakness affects men more than women, is transmitted genetically through the mother, and is thus a sex-linked characteristic. There are no cures for the difficulty, and the colorblind need only know that others see the world differently. For most ordinary functions, they have no problem, although where color matching is of importance, the colorblind will have difficulties. For the most part, they can adjust to their limitations and get along perfectly well. Their visual experiences may be just as satisfying as those of normal color vision, and they do not need any sympathy or pity. The only point of importance is not to place reliance on their color judgments, since these may not correspond with those of the majority of people.

COLOR VISION

Everything that we see we see because of reflected light. A light source, usually the sun when we are out of doors, illuminates the world around us, and the reflections from various objects stimulate the retinas of our eyes, where a photochemical reaction occurs that, in turn, generates neural currents in the optic nerve. The photochemical reaction involves the breaking down of substances in the cell structure of the retina, which contains two kinds of specialized cells that look like tiny rods and cones and are called by these terms. The rods break down chemically when the reflected light is primarily white; the cones are affected by reflected light that is colored—that is, light that consists of one or more kinds of wave lengths that make up the spectrum of visible light. Light—that is, radiant energy—consists of waves that are measured in millimicrons, or millionths of meters. If the light affecting the eye is in the neighborhood of 600 millimicrons, you will see red; down at the 470 to 460 level, you will see blue or violet. Below 390, there are invisible rays—the ultraviolet (beyond the violet)—and above 600, there are the infrared rays that can burn but cannot be seen. Still longer waves become heat waves and radio waves. The spectrum of visible light provides the color hues of violet, blue, green, yellow, orange, and red. Note that there are no such pure hues as brown or purple. Such colors are produced by mixing pigments, not lights. Brown is a mixture of orange and black. Pure white light is made up of all of the colors, and black is the absence of color, as far as visual light rays go.

Color attributes. When psychologists speak of color, they talk about three features of color: hue, brightness, and saturation. Hue has been mentioned above. Brightness is a kind of intensity measure that is based upon the nearness to black or white. A bright color reflects more light energy. The third factor, saturation, describes the purity of the color—that is, its freedom from mixtures of white. Thus, pink is not a spectral color but consists of a mixture of white and red. We do not have separate names for all the different wave lengths that can be seen in the spectrum. A wide band of wave lengths will be called by the same name, e.g., red. But there are many different reds and many different yellows, blues, and so on. There are actually a great many hues; some claim as many as 150 different discriminable hues. Similarly, there are many degrees of brightness and saturation, so that there are literally thousands of discriminable colors. If someone calls something red, it is only one of hundreds of reds that could be produced by suitable changes in wave length, brightness, and saturation. This is why the knitter has so much trouble matching yarn if the original purchase was not enough for a job. Likewise, trying to match paints becomes virtually impossible if one does not acquire all of the needed amount from the same batch. It will be rare for two people to agree on a color match unless the samples came from the same dye lot. A person deciding to paint a room has literally thousands of choices if he or she is interested in mixing various hues and adding a little white or black. He or she will find that a little black goes a long way toward changing a color.

Color mixing. Most people are familiar with mixing water colors to get new colors. They find that mixing blue and yellow will produce green. This is true, but instead of adding blue to yellow, what the mixer is doing is subtracting hues, in that blue paint really amounts to a substance that absorb all hues except blue and green, which it reflects. Yellow paint absorbs all hues except yellow and green. Thus, the yellow will absorb the blue, leaving green; and the blue will absorb the yellow, leaving green, and one has green paint as a created product. If one mixes *light* instead of paint, there will be a different result. Try projecting a slide of red and a slide of green onto a screen with two projectors. Intersect the two images, and you will see an area of yellow. Now yellow has become the created novelty. If you similarly project yellow and blue instead of green, you will get nothing, since the two hues will absorb each other, leaving a black area. Visual scientists and engineers engaged in producing color film, television in color, or other color phenomena work with red, green, and blue lights to produce all the colors anyone desires by suitable mixtures. The artist will continue to call his red, yellow, and blue paints primaries, but the light-mixing visual technologist will call red, blue, and green the primary colors. All of the thousands of colors are then mixtures of hues, brightness, and saturation. In mixing paint, if a color is produced by adding some white, it is *tinted;* if black is added, the color is *shaded.* Pink is a tint of red. One should not say, "I like that shade of pink." There can be no such color.

COMMITMENT: PSYCHIATRIC   (See INSANITY)

Psychiatric commitment is a legal process in which a person is placed in a mental institution and held there with or without his or her consent. The person is judged to be incompetent or a danger to self or to others. Reasons for commitment include conditions such as alcoholism, drug addiction, mental retardation, psychosis, threats of or attempts at suicide, or any other state that indicates that the person cannot obtain, guard, or use the necessities of life (i.e., food, clothing, or shelter) or cannot guard life itself without help. Being a danger to others may range from committing criminal acts, such as assault or murder, to committing social nuisances, such as frightening the neighborhood children by talking excitedly to oneself. These are vague standards, and they are generally left to a psychiatric expert to define to a judge.

A person may be committed by his or her own request to a court or directly to a mental health facility. In such a *voluntary commitment,* the individual may sign him- or herself in and out at any time after a brief administrative wait. If during the stay the facility staff believe that the voluntary commitment should be of longer duration than the patient wants, the staff must go through a formal *involuntary* commitment procedure in order to keep the person in the facility. Children under the age of fourteen who are committed by their parents are considered to be voluntary commitments, even though the child might object strenuously. Because it is considered to be a voluntary act, the child may be committed directly, without any court hearing. They may not sign themselves out, although their parents may. Thus, children under fourteen may be legally committed and held against their will in a psychiatric hospital, but legally it is considered to be a voluntary act. A medical doctor may decide that the child is well enough to be released and discharge the child against the parents' wishes.

Involuntary commitment may be made only by request or petition to a court. The petition may be signed by a relative; a close friend; a public agency, such as a city or county social service department; or by law enforcement personnel, such as the police, a district attorney, a defense attorney, or even a judge. A preliminary hearing is held, at which time a judge will receive testimony or sworn affidavits in court from all concerned. Generally, depending upon state law, two psychiatrists must state that the individual is a danger to him- or herself or to others. The individual has the right to legal representation, and it must be provided free if he or she cannot afford a private attorney. The judge makes a determination based on a preponderance of the evidence on whether to commit the person for *observation.* The burden of supplying the evidence falls on the person or agency seeking the commitment. The person who is being judged need do nothing to prove his or her nondangerousness. But, unlike a criminal trial, this civil procedure does not require proof beyond a reasonable doubt, and since the initial commitment is only to allow the experts to make an evaluation, the tendency is to commit for observation. In addition, many judges feel that the psychiatric opinion in the preliminary hearing outweighs any other evidence presented. If, however, the judge decides that the individual is able to control or care for him- or herself, then the person will be allowed to return to the community or back into police custody if he or she has broken the law.

The preliminary commitment usually lasts 72 hours, depending upon state law, during which time the individual is observed, tested, and evaluated. This evaluation is within the context of an involuntary incarceration with other persons who have been judged to behave in an abnormal manner. The court will have another hearing to decide if further commitment is desirable. It is not always a requirement that the individual committed be present at the second hearing, but since the judge is reviewing evaluations from the mental health facility, the lawyer representing the person should be present in order to contest the expert opinion, if necessary.

If the judge decides that the person should be committed, the individual will be placed in an appropriate facility, such as a state, county, federal, or private hospital. There will be a periodic review of the patient's progress by the mental health staff and the court. These reviews might be careful and frequent or perfunctory and infrequent, depending upon state law, the professional conscience of the reviewers, and the degree to which the patient knows and is able to exercise his or her rights to review. Most disoriented or otherwise incompetent patients are not aware of their rights to legal representation and have virtually no way to obtain a lawyer without outside help.

The institution where the person is committed must be one that will provide treatment to overcome the emotional disturbance that resulted in the personal or social danger. The Supreme Court has said that treatment *must* be provided, or the individual *must* be released. Although there is no legal right to treatment, there is a legal right to release for the involuntarily committed. This high court decision has resulted in a massive release of patients from facilities run by various state and local governments. Unfortunately, the community does not necessarily provide treatment for those in need of mental health support.

Occasionally, when a person has been accused of a crime, he or she may be judged incompetent and committed for observation or committed for treatment. A judge may ask, on his or her own, or by prosecution or defense request, to have an evaluation in order to determine if the individual is competent to stand trial. If an individual cannot now knowingly participate in his or her own defense to a criminal charge, whether or not he or she knew what he or she was doing at the time the crime was committed, he or she cannot stand trial. Such an individual may be committed until he or she is able to understand the nature of the proceedings against him or her or until a set proportion (usually two-thirds) of any possible prison sentence for the particular crime has passed. Thus, even though the person may not have been guilty of the crime, he or she can still be committed without a trial and for reasons that may be insufficient to commit under other circumstances. If the person, after the mandatory commitment time has passed (two-thirds of a criminal sentence), is then evaluated as a danger to him- or herself or others, he or she may be recommitted at a new hearing.

A person who pleads not guilty by reason of insanity to a crime will have a full trial, at which time it must be shown that the defendant did not know the nature and consequences of his or her actions or that he or she did not know that such conduct is wrong—that is, he or she did not know what he or she was doing when he or she did it. When insanity is raised as a defense, the prosecution must disprove it beyond a reasonable doubt, in most states. If the defendant is found not guilty by reason of insanity, he or she is committed to a psychiatric facility for evaluation. This is a civil commitment, since the person is *not guilty* and is not a criminal, no matter how heinous the act. The individual is then subject to all the standard rules of commitment. If the person is now evaluated as competent and is not a current danger to him- or herself or to others, he or she must be released. If the person is evaluated as needing treatment, he or she will be kept in custody until improved enough for release. Generally, court supervision of the periodic re-evaluations and release of such not-guilty-by-reason-of-insanity individuals has become increasingly strict. Many laws and mental health associations have recommended the elimination of this type of verdict, substituting conviction and then treatment within a penal facility.

COMMUNITY MENTAL HEALTH

Beginning in 1963, Congress passed legislation to develop community mental health approaches. Before that, mental health agencies had provided various forms of medical or psychological treatment or, simply, hospitalization for individuals who sought services. The new community mental health approaches are based on a public health model in which the health needs of an entire community—such as a section of a city or an entire county—are carefully studied. Efforts are made to have an organized, central approach, including a good referral system; to predict community needs and to have services available when needed; to work actively for the *prevention* of mental disorders as well as to provide the more traditional emphasis on treatment. In providing treatment, the community mental health approach attempts to use the resources of already existing community groups, such as the YMCA, religious agencies, schools, and so on, rather than relying solely on hospitals, clinics, and private practitioners.

The community mental health approach includes a heavy emphasis on public education about prevention and normal stress situations and on how to get information on obtaining services when needed. Information can be obtained by contacting the local mental health association or the city, county or state mental health department.

CONDITIONED EMOTIONAL RESPONSE   *(See CONDITIONING)*

The *conditional emotional response* (CER) has come to mean, technically, the reaction of an animal that has been shocked (hurt and frightened) in a confined space in the presence of some signal, such as a tone or light. If the animal is in a small box where it has been trained to press a pedal for food, it is possible to shock the animal as it is pressing the pedal just after sounding a tone. After a few such pairings of shock and tone, the animal that previously has been pressing the pedal for food in a vigorous manner will now stop pressing whenever the tone comes on. It will tend to huddle and otherwise indicate fear. The CER can then be used to measure the strength of the pedal-pressing habit or to otherwise control the behavior of the animal.

Actually, the CER is a kind of prototype of any emotional conditioning. If any emotion is evoked by some stimulus, positive or negative, in the presence of some conditioning stimulus, the occurrence of the conditioned stimulus (CS) later on can bring about the emotion involved to some degree. On the positive side, for example, if a rat is pressing a pedal to get food, the food comes into the box via a tube and is accompanied by some mechanical noises as the apparatus that supplies the food is operating. The animal soon learns to respond to the sounds of the dispenser as if they were food, and it can be assumed that some positive emotional reaction is generated, first by the food and later on by the noises that accompanied food.

Conditioned emotional responses, both positive and negative, underlie our approach and avoidance of various situations and, in effect, guide our behavior. When we are doing something that is proceeding smoothly, we may not look emotional, but the underlying satisfaction is a response to the stimuli generated by our own movements and by the external signs of our success. If things are not going smoothly, we begin to react negatively, and the stimuli associated with unpleasant consequences guide us to avoid the actions that generate them.

CONDITIONING

Ivan Pavlov first described what have come to be known as *conditioned reflexes*. What Pavlov did was to start with a stable reflex, such as salivating to food in the mouth, and present some other stimulus just before the food appeared. After a few trials, about nine, the new stimulus would be followed by salivation even if no food appeared. Most people have heard of Pavlov and tend to think of him as ringing bells in order to make dogs salivate. Pavlov was not interested in dogs or salivation. He was interested in how one stimulus could be substituted for another, not only with dogs but with people. In short, Pavlov was trying to find a physiological base for the association of stimuli with each other and with behavior. In order to be able to communicate with others about his work with clarity, Pavlov chose to define several terms that are involved in conditioning in this way:

1. An unconditioned response is a natural response to some stimulus that usually or commonly elicits it, as a tap on the knee elicits a knee jerk. In this case, the tap on the knee is called an *unconditioned* stimulus, because there are no serious constraints or exceptions. The stimulus does not depend on a lot of special conditions being set up to do its work.

2. A conditioned stimulus is one that does not ordinarily produce the response that follows the unconditioned stimulus. Thus, a bell will not normally make a dog salivate. Only when the bell is presented under special conditions will the dog come to respond to the bell as he or she would to food. Among these conditions are the following: the dog should be hungry; the bell should precede the food by about five seconds; the bell should accompany the food frequently; the bell must not be so loud that it disturbs the dog, but it must be loud enough to generate a response. Pavlov called this a curiosity reflex—in other words, the dog must notice the bell. Under these conditions, the bell will eventually evoke a salivary response before the food appears.

3. A response given to the conditioned stimulus that is similar to the response given to the unconditioned stimulus is called a conditioned response. According to Pavlov, one stimulus has taken over the function of another: There has been a substitution of stimuli, and that, according to Pavlov, is how we learn most of what we do.

CONFORMITY

We usually do what the Romans do when in Rome; that is, we conform to common customs and mores; if we did not, there would be no customs or mores. Conforming is often the easiest way out: It saves explanations and endless other difficulties. We may resent regimentation and discipline and being told to dress in certain ways, but, left to ourselves, we will proceed to do as others are doing. Experimental studies indicate that if as few as two or three people will respond in a similar way, we will tend to follow along, even in ridiculous situations like matching lengths of lines. If two or three prior judgments are made by others who pick out the same wrong line, we will pick out the same line even if we know it is different. To do otherwise will put us in a situation of disagreeing with the majority, and we do not want to take that step in nonserious matters. Adolescents, despite their typical revolt against parents, will conform to their peers, and a whole generation has grown up wearing jeans, beards, and long hair. When the adolescents go job-hunting, they put on the strange garment called a suit, put on a tie, and begin to conform to the world of the grey flannel suit. Conforming is a kind of cooperation that is easier and usually more comfortable for all. To rock the boat might involve getting wet, and it is better, generally, to sit quietly like everyone else. On the other hand, if everyone else is rioting, we are likely to get into that act, too. Often, conformity in behavior masks a variety of personal beliefs. People who have strong negative attitudes toward others who differ in race or religion might very well behave rather decently toward the objects of their prejudice; similarly, people may act in a prejudiced manner even if they personally feel no animosity but do not want their friends to think them peculiar or treacherous.

William James called habit the "great fly-wheel of society." He might better have considered conformity to be such a fly-wheel that keeps society operating on a more or less balanced level. We expect other people to behave in certain common ways, and they usually do. Driving automobiles would be impossible if drivers did not conform, stop at red signals, keep on their own side of the road, and so on. Rebels and revolutionists are nonconformists until they become the dominant power, at which time they expect conformity to the new rules from the former majority, whereas former conformers may now become the rebels and reformers.

CONSCIOUSNESS AND ALTERED STATES OF CONSCIOUSNESS
(See UNCONSCIOUS)

In the 1970s, a great deal of print was devoted to descriptions of altered states of consciousness. The trouble with such descriptions is that they tell us nothing and leave us unsatisfied, perhaps feeling a little stupid, because we do not understand what seems to be written in plain English. The difficulty stems from the fact that no one knows what consciousness itself is supposed to be. Psychologists have been unable to describe consciousness in any meaningful terms beyond suggesting that consciousness is some kind of state in which we are not unconscious. The latter term seems a little more descriptive. When a person is anaesthetized on the operating table, we can say that he or she is unconscious in that he or she does not seem to feel pain or to hear or see anything and that he or she does not talk in any coherent fashion, although some patients do talk. If a person is asleep, has fainted, or has been knocked out by a blow or by some drug, we can also call him or her unconscious. Some psychologists use the term *awareness* as an alternate to consciousness and mean by awareness that someone can describe what is going on around him or her in some satisfactory manner. We are conscious, with such a definition, if we react appropriately to stimuli that we are supposed to notice. We are, of course, unconscious of any stimuli that we did not observe, in the sense that we could have mentioned or described them if we did notice them.

People who talk about altered states of consciousness accept a normal waking state as one kind of consciousness; sleeping is supposed to be another state or level of consciousness. Although it appears to be one of unconsciousness, a third state, that of dreaming, is also cited, making three states altogether. Now, if during the waking state, one can arrive at some state that is different from ordinary awareness, it would represent a fourth or altered state of consciousness. Transcendental meditators concentrating on a mantra claim that they can break through into this fourth state when, although still awake and able to notice sounds and visual objects, they arrive at what amounts to a blank mind. Such a condition is claimed to be restful, vitalizing, and invigorating. Meditators claim that they feel better and are more efficient after they emerge from a twenty-minute period of such relaxed quietude. There is no evidence that the thousands of meditators who have achieved altered states of consciousness in the last ten years have achieved anything else. Their claims to greater creativity, deeper insights, better personalities, and so on have not been objectively established. One cannot deny that they might feel that they have become better persons, and if they have, it might be well for them. They have not, however, contributed to our appreciation of the nature of consciousness, which still remains as much of a mystery as it was before people began talking about altered states. We know that people are altered in their ways of thinking and reacting by various drugs, Yoga exercises, taking naps, and taking up new religions. Sensory deprivation and hypnosis will also alter our consciousness in that we might perform in ways that we normally would not. We also know that placebos (sugar pills) will also affect some people's behavior, symptoms, or feelings, but none of these operations or agencies have helped us understand consciousness itself. We may have learned more about consciousness from studies of split brains than from any other source. We know that the right half of the brain can carry on a variety of operations that we normally attribute to some kind of consciousness but that people with split brains cannot tell us what is going on in the right halves of their brains or what they are experiencing, whereas they can do so about activities controlled by the left side of the brain. The only difference between the two halves of the brain appears to be in whether we can describe (awareness) what we see or what we are doing. If that turns out to be the only difference, then consciousness will amount to being in a state where we can talk about our perceptions and activities; all other conditions will have to be altered states, altered to the point where we cannot describe what we sense or perceive. Talking about altered states of consciousness as if such states were desirable may be a gross distortion.

CONSERVATION ABILITY IN CHILDREN

One of the important contributions of psychologist Jean Piaget is the concept of *conservation* ability in children. Conservation, in its psychological sense, refers to the ability to recognize that the substance, weight, and volume of anything remains constant even when its shape is changed. For example, a child is shown two balls of clay of equal size and shape. One ball is then flattened, as the child watches, into a large, flat pancake or rolled out into a worm shape. The child is said to be able to conserve substance if he recognizes that the amount of clay is the same in the two objects, despite the major change in shape.

Children develop their abilities to conserve in sequences and in age stages. Until about age 6, most children do not conserve; at above age 6 or 7, they begin to show conservation of substance; weight conservation begins around age 9 or 10, and conservation of volume at about age 11 or 12. When conservation ability is fully developed, the child is able to recognize that substance, weight, and volume remain the same despite shape changes. The 12-year-old can demonstrate conservation by changing a substance back and fourth from one shape to another, such as clay from a ball to a worm and back again, or a fixed amount of liquid from a short, wide glass to a tall, thin one, and understand that they are still the same.

Conservation ability is thought to be critical in the child's growing understanding of the world, of physical relationships, and of using abstract concepts. Training and schooling can affect conservation ability, and children in different cultures achieve conservation ability at slightly different ages. In any culture, when children have good play experience, such as playing with water or pouring water from one container into another, they learn conservation; when they play with clay, rolling a fixed amount into different shapes and feeling the weight as it remains the same, and so on, they are probably learning, through play, about conservation and other aspects of the world.

CONSTITUTIONAL TYPES   *(See TEMPERAMENT)*

Much folklore and some science deals with the relationship of body type and behavior or, if not behavior, temperament. Shakespeare has Caesar say, "Give me about me men that are fat; yon Cassius has a lean and hungry look." Clearly, Shakespeare had some notions about fat and skinny politicians, if not about people in general. In the 1950s, W. H. Sheldon, at Harvard, photographed thousands of Harvard students (front, side, and rear) in the nude. All photos were taken from a fixed position against a screen that could provide numerical measures of the height and breadth of various parts of the body. Sheldon then developed various breadth to height ratios and came up with a range of scores that could describe different body types. In practice, Sheldon preferred to rate the body types on three different 7-point scales. The first scale described what Sheldon called the *endomorph* and emphasized the inner embryonic tissue that develops into the digestive system. Roughly, endomorphy corresponds to fatness, roundness, or what was formerly called pyknic type of body. The second scale was called one of *mesomorphy* and emphasized tissues that give rise to muscles and bones. Mesomorphs were formerly called athletic. The third scale, the *ectomorphy,* was based on cells that develop into skin and nervous system. The ectomorph label refers to the tall and thin kind of person that children might call skinny. Sheldon observed and interviewed many of his subjects and arrived at conclusions about the temperaments that he thought were associated or correlated with body types. From his own interpretations, endomorphs could be judged as *viscerotonic* and would be inclined to enjoy food, rest, relaxation, and company. The viscerotonic thus corresponds to the popular notion that fat people are jolly. In fact, many fat people are miserable in our weight-conscious culture. The athletic or mesomorph type—somatonic, according to Sheldon —would be aggressive, risk-taking, excitable, and not concerned with creature comforts. The ectomorph would be a *cerebrotonic,* a defensive, nervous, introverted kind of person not given to social life, quick to tire, perhaps an oversensitive person.

Sheldon's characterizations were criticized as reflecting only his opinions in a situation where he made both the measurements and the judgments about temperament. Independent measures of temperament as described by Sheldon have not been done, and tests of body type and personality traits seldom show any relationships. When temperament questionnaires based on Sheldon's suggestions are used, there are some agreements, but not at the levels that scientists might require for serious conviction. Studies using Sheldon's measures on juvenile delinquents indicated that the athletic types (mesomorphic adolescents) were more likely to get attention from the police than the other two types; we must be quick to point out, however, that not all mesomorphs are likely to turn out to be delinquent and that some endomorphs and ectomorphs do, although at lower frequencies.

Personality psychologists have not been kind to a body type interpretation of temperament, although the work of S. Diamond suggests some agreement on the kinds of basic temperaments that might divide people. Diamond lists such temperaments as the needs to affiliate, to aggress, and to avoid others. These might correspond to viscerotonia, somatonia, and cerebrotonia. What Sheldon has contributed is the notion that there may be some constitutional, presumably hereditary, factors to be taken into account in our psychological interpretations of behavior. It may well be that some of us are born to be skinny; we can eat like a horse and not gain weight; others seem to put on pounds by just looking at food. Once we have our bodies started off in some general shape or form, we may very well become the targets of assaults or the butts of jokes; we may be proficient in sports or impossibly awkward and thus develop a whole collection of behavior patterns in order to defend ourselves while we make our way through life. The conclusions about body type are by no means final and await further research.

COPING *(See LEARNED HELPLESSNESS)*

Throughout our lives, we are challenged in many small and large ways, and we must, in some way, respond in order to meet the demand or challenge efficiently. When we succeed and respond adaptively to those demands or challenges, we are said to be coping with them. How well or successfully we cope with life's demands—and those demands are made of all of us—depends on many current and past factors, one of the most important factors being our past experiences in learning how to cope with a variety of normal demands. Children begin learning how to cope fairly early in life and, given good support, patient guidance by parents, and normal experiences, should mature into successfully coping adults. Children should be encouraged to solve their own problems without adult interference and help. Assistance should be offered only when failure is probable. Parents frequently are too impatient or in a hurry to get on with their own interests to watch and guide a coping process. The child can learn to cope or learn to be helpless if improperly trained.

CROWD BEHAVIOR

People as individuals may behave in one way. Joined together with others, their behavior might be quite unpredictable, depending upon the reasons for the joining. In a theatre, there might be several hundred people seated close to one another. Such an audience is not really a group—it it merely an aggregate of individuals who happen to be in the same limited place. They may have very little in common and may have quite different reasons for being there. Similarly, a class of students at a lecture is a group of a sort, but, again, the common interest might be limited. If some common motivation is aroused, the behavior of the group may take on quite different characteristics, depending upon that motivation. Should a fire break out in a theatre, the people may become a collection of individuals, each striving to save his own neck, regardless of the others. The motivation here may be common in that each one has the same desire, but it is not the same kind of motivation that a spell-binding orator might arouse by asking for some unified action in some direction. When each member is working toward the same objective, an objective that he or she cannot attain alone, we can begin to talk about a mob or a crowd. At one time, it was believed that a crowd was characterized by something called the group mind, that, somehow, all the individuals were coalesced into one body, and that all thought alike. We recognize, of course, that the crowd has no nervous system and no group mind but that the individuals in such a crowd, as individuals, have approximately the same motivations or goals. A lynch mob bent on destroying someone still consists of individuals, some of whom try to incite the others, who may be somewhat hesitant. Individuals who are drawn together for some common goal may help to identify themselves with a large mass by shouting the same slogans in unison, singing the same songs, interlocking arms, or lying down in the streets. The individuals involved might well refrain from any such actions if they are alone, but the presence of others may encourage individuals to engage in acts that they would perhaps like to perform alone but lack the courage to do so. They may not want to be identified, and the group provides the security of anonymity; the group also provides the necessary manpower if it is a matter of physical strength. When groups engage in physical assaults, violence, wanton damage, and vandalism, they are not doing anything other than what the members would like to do as individuals but which would be too dangerous to do alone.

CRUELTY

Civilized life is based on a hope, and that is about all it is, that people will not attack each other, hurt one another deliberately, or otherwise violate the Golden Rule. To the extent that there is some civilized life, there has been some modest support for the hope. In some cultures, there is a certain level of peace and serenity, but the history of mankind has been somewhat less than promising insofar as a general adoption of the Golden Rule is concerned. There has probably never been a time in human history when some kind of war, for example, has not been taking place. At any given time, somewhere on the globe, people were killing one another in declared or undeclared wars. War is, of course, an obvious example of mass cruelty, with thousands and, in some cases, millions of people being slaughtered. Man's inhumanity to man is notorious. Crimes of assault and battery, rape, homicide at various levels—in fact, any crimes—are examples of cruelty by someone to someone. Although we are all aware of crime and are concerned about its rates, it is of some comfort to recognize that most people are not criminals and that although jails are overcrowded, this could mean only that the jails are too small or that there are not enough of them. People, in general, are in no great danger of being victims of a crime if one thinks in percentage terms.

We sometimes delude ourselves that advances have been made in comparison to more ancient times when slaves were treated like animals and worse, when kings were beheaded, and when heretics were pulled apart by horses or on the rack. The extermination of millions of people by gas in World War II should remind us that so-called advanced civilizations have not made much progress toward the humane treatment of humans.

Those of us who think that we have acquired something more than a thin veneer of civilization might be surprised to learn that, given the appropriate circumstances, we too could maim and kill others and even feel justified in doing so. The obvious example is that of war, when we somehow accept the notion that it is necessary to follow orders and to do what we are told to do, even though it might result, as in the case of bombing by aircraft, in the destruction of an entire city with thousands of residents. We drop the bombs because it is our job. Or we burn out a village with little or no compunction about the people in that village. In times of peace, we also follow orders as part of our job, with little or no thought about the consequences of our acts. It is not only such matters as foreclosing mortgages on poor widows that we should consider. Almost any act of ours can have a disastrous consequence for someone else. A complaint to a business manager may result in the discharge of an employee who might have had his own side of the story to tell. Experimentally, it has been shown by Stanley Milgram that people will administer what they think are strong electric shocks to other people merely because they are told to do so by a scientist engaged in a study of learning. Very few people question the wisdom of the procedure and refuse to participate, even though they are not paid highly for the activity. Most of us are also dishonest in one way or another, and acts of dishonesty are cruel to others. Failure to return money, for example, when we are given too much change may hurt some clerk, who must make up for the loss.

Our capacity for cruelty appears to be so universal as to make it believable that it is quite natural for people to seek advantage over others in a competitive world or a competitive situation. Most of us eventually manage to behave in more peaceful or less aggressive manners, but it does not take much more than a scratch on our new car's fender to bring out the ogre in us. Writers who prefer to believe that man is not aggressive by nature blame all aggression on environmental and educational factors, but it is the experience of most parents that children must be trained and tamed in order to be peaceful and not selfish. The training and taming procedure works to various degrees and sometimes produces martyrs, saints, and people who will not step on an ant or slap a mosquito. These same people, however, will burn a living widow along with her dead husband (the Hindu practice of suttee, not illegal) in their kindness or have a dozen or more children in the hope that the survivors will take care of them in their old age while the rest die of malnutrition or lack of medical care. For anyone to believe that he or she is not cruel, it may be a revealing exercise to count the number of people he or she hurt in any one day or week, counting not only the acts of physical violence but the effect of his or her operations on the lives of those with whom he or she has dealt.

CRUELTY IN CHILDREN

The cruelty of children to one another is notorious; even siblings deny each other access to toys and privileges. Some children bully smaller children, robbing them, pushing them, and otherwise making their lives miserable. Most parents observe that other people's children can be very cruel to their children. Their own children's behavior, however, is excused on the grounds of age, provocation, accident, and the like. We should be careful to examine the charge of cruelty. There is probably no such thing as cruelty itself. The cruel or aggressive child is not expressing a mean streak. He or she is doing what appears to be natural in a given situation. If someone acts aggressively toward a child, who cowers and shrinks instead of also being aggressive, we are inclined to pin another label on him: He's a coward or has a yellow streak. There are probably no such things as mean or yellow streaks; there are only behavior patterns that are either natural or are modified in some ways by learning, example, and experience. Children can be trained to be either more or less aggressive than they might ordinarily turn out to be if left to themselves. What is difficult is to determine the appropriate kinds of behaviors for unanticipated situations. Despite the urgings of some religions, one cannot always turn the other cheek. Parents do have a difficult time trying to teach the manly art of self-defense to boys and ladylike behavior to girls. Perhaps the best training would be one where children are taught not to hurt anyone else and to use force merely to prevent injury to themselves; this, of course, is not easy.

To teach children appropriate defense tactics is a problem that society simply has not faced, and it might well be a matter for the schools as part of their physical training programs. Training in judo might be appropriate for all children. There are probably no simple solutions, and psychological advice cannot help the victims of aggressions. It might be possible to train bullies to make their strength and their aggressive activities socially useful, and parents of children who are accused of cruelty might be able to encourage their children to be helpful, following the usual advice given in behavior modification or habit change techniques.

CRYING

Crying is normally associated with babies, but strong men have been known to shed tears on occasion. With babies, crying is the only vocal means of expression for some discomfort that frequently cannot be identified. Parents speculate about colic, gas, and other internal disturbances that are occasionally verified by a burp. Frequently, no known cause is determined, and the baby still cries. Parents then assume that the baby is crying for attention. Attention may be the last thing the baby wants. It may need something, but the nature of that something is not always determinable. If a baby is picked up and does not cease crying until the holder stands and walks around, it is difficult to argue that attenion was the baby's goal, and it is equally difficult to argue that the baby wants to look around the room a few hundred times. If the crying baby stops crying when walked around the room, there might not be any great cause for alarm, although obviously the upright posture and the tight hold may be doing something for the baby that is not understood.

In general, if a baby is not cold, wet, hungry, or in pain—as far as can be ascertained—and it still cries, then picking up the baby (if this stops the crying) is the recommended operation. People who have babies also have a responsibility. The baby has no responsibilities of any kind, including that of keeping quiet. It is true that if a baby is allowed to cry until it stops, it will learn to be quiet. Some people favor this procedure of what is called extinction and are even proud of their success with the procedure, even though it might take eight solid hours of crying before a determined baby stops. Sooner or later, the baby has to be picked up to be fed or changed, and the extinction procedure is weakened by such necessary attentions. For a baby to learn to stop crying or to learn not to cry deprives it of the only means it has of revealing stress or troubles. A baby that learns not to cry may be in for a hard time in life later on. After babies start talking is time enough to learn to be a man.

Crying is a normal function of the autonomic nervous system in times of stress. Usually, the stress is involved in fears that come about from losses of security, status, prized possessions, or prized people, along with the stress of pain, which brings tears to one's eyes. There appears to be a conditioned component to crying such that adults will cry while witnessing a tear-jerker movie or even imagining some sad events or other emotion-arousing activities. Social practices approve or sanction crying at funerals, weddings, or other joyous occasions, such as the coming home of soldiers, long lost sons, and so on. Other social controls are imposed on men, particularly, that suggest that crying is somehow unmanly and improper. Crying is out of order when there is something to be done besides sitting around and feeling sad, and active people do not cry, whereas inactive ones may do so with propriety. Pallbearers characteristically maintain a firm grip on themselves as well as on the casket. They have other things to think about. Crying is a natural reaction surrounded by social custom and personal experiences. It is probably the best way of communicating and works best when words fail. Although in our culture, crying is allegedly a woman's weapon or wile, a man who can shed tears can win his way much more effectively because he is supposed to cry only under the greatest provocation to tears.

CULTURAL DEPRIVATION

The term *cultural deprivation* is usually applied to residents of inner cities or ghettos where different kinds of subgroups of the larger surrounding culture reside. The expression is not an accurate one, since every subgroup or minority has its own culture that may, in fact, be richer and more satisfying than the culture of the dominant or majority group. What is usually meant is that some slum residents do not participate in the activities of the surrounding population, in many cases because they cannot, whether they wanted to or not, either because of financial limitations or because of other restrictions. Poor people do not attend philharmonic concerts or visit art museums in great numbers. They do not subscribe to daily newspapers and popular magazines, often because they cannot read well enough. They do not have many books in their homes, and they may even speak a different language from that of the majority group. Their culture is, of course, different, if not deprived, and this may prevent the subgroup from making meaningful progress in terms of majority customs and practices. Minority group children drop out of school earlier than do the children of the majority. The lack of education adds another difference to the culture.

Being brought up in one environment does not prepare one for life in another, and the longer one remains in the original environment, the more difficult it will be to make any transition, since the cultural differences will be magnified. To talk about cultural deprivation is misleading, if not arrogant, since it implies that the values of the subgroup culture are of little importance. Presumably, a more positive approach would be one of recognizing cultural differences and identifying the needs of various groups and then developing means of increasing opportunities for all groups to meet such needs. The problems of a multicultural society are not easy to handle because of prejudices on all sides as well as because of the costs of improving the standards of living of the economically deprived. To add to the difficulty, we have the problem that some people want solutions immediately and propose solutions that create even more problems.

CULTURE-FREE TESTS

When one group of subjects is found superior to another group of subjects on some kind of test, usually an intelligence test, the group with lower scores can always claim that the test was unfair, that it was constructed in order to favor the superior group. The point can be appreciated if some French children score lower than English children on a test given in English. During World War I, the American army administered tests to recruits and, in general, found that recent immigrants from some parts of Europe and American blacks scored poorly on a group written test, the Army Alpha. When the recruits were tested on a nonwritten test, the Army Beta Test, the immigrants improved their standards somewhat but still showed up as inferior to native-born Americans. Such factors as knowledge of English, education, previous experience with tests, and general background (occupation, social class) were ignored in evaluating the results, and the conclusion was drawn that some national and racial groups were inferior to others. American whites of English and Nordic origin felt smugly superior. The tests had confirmed their prejudices. It is, of course, possible to construct tests on which American whites of English and Nordic ancestry will score poorly, whereas Australian bushmen will excel. Clearly, the language of the test, the form of instruction, and the kind of subject matter tested is of primary importance if one is to test people of different languages and backgrounds and if one is concerned over some impossible to answer question, such as, Are Japanese brighter than Greeks? Consider the problems one would encounter before even trying to construct a test to measure their relative brightness. The subjects to be tested would have to have come from the same social classes, have had the same educational backgrounds, have had equal exposure to the same subject matters, been told the same stories, have played the same games, and so on. If any factor could be found that was not the same in the two backgrounds, any test differences could be attributed to that factor. Instead of equating such backgrounds, test makers have tried to find questions to include in the tests where the background would not matter. Such questions might be found for some groups, but to take an extreme situation, the probability is that few if any equally fair questions, and probably not enough to make up a test, could be found to ask children from Eskimo and African jungle areas.

Culture-free tests simply do not exist. Any claim for such tests would be rejected by any groups that scored poorly and, in all probability, by the test makers themselves, if they found any sizeable group differences, because test makers usually assume that the average score on any test should be the same for the standardizing groups. If the average scores are not the same, they will suspect that the group was not randomly selected in the first place. Users of tests will interpret group differences along the lines of their prejudices and their fondness for environmental or hereditary influences. The field of interpretation is left wide open to parents, teachers, test makers, and test users, with the resulting state of chaos in which we find the testing movement today.

CURIOSITY   (See TEST-TRAIT FALLACY)

Although we all know that "curiosity killed the cat," that is about all that we do know about curiosity. We see children take toys apart and call them inquisitive or curious instead of destructive—if they are our children. Obviously, curiosity is a desirable trait if there actually is something that could be so labeled. Children are always asking, "Why, mommy?", but we do not know why they are asking except possibly to get attention, to ask for reassurance, or to attempt to master their worlds. The probability is that everyone is curious about some things and indifferent to others. Actually, it is impossible to be interested in everything, and we all become interested in things that we can manage and control, within some reasonable limits. To say that cats are curious is merely to recognize that they are "stimulus bound" and not to endow them with some desires for intellectual mastery. With children and adults, curiosity amounts to interest, which, in turn, comes from some measures of success. Boys who cannot hit a baseball lose interest in playing that game and turn to stamp collecting or basketball. Interests, concentration, and curiosity are merely terms for describing the behaviors we exhibit toward certain stimuli. The pathologist is concerned about the cause of death; the funeral director might care less. He or she is interested in a satisfactory (to him or her) disposal of the remains. Whether we spend our nights looking at stars through telescopes or at the movies is a function of our histories and, largely, of the history of our successes. We usually become less and less curious about things that we do not find rewarding. We cannot expect every child to be interested in everything around him. Like any other learned pattern, curiosity can also be increased by suitable programming. Boys can be made interested in baking cakes and bread if suitable models—for example, their fathers—show an interest and enlist the boys' help. Curiously enough, curiosity involves an element of challenge, threat, or danger of occasional failure. A string of successes will lead to boredom. Some unexpected lack of success may whet the appetite for pursuit of some happier result. The broad range of human occupations and hobbies allows all of us to be reasonably good at something as well as the opportunity to ask, "What does he see in that?"

To assume a trait of curiosity in a child merely because he or she asks questions is to overlook the ease with which such curiosity is terminated. The real question is what lies behind the child's questions. It is not likely to be some mysterious curiosity that provokes such questions.

D

DAYDREAMING

Probably everyone is familiar with daydreaming, since we all engage in it. Daydreaming is usually contrasted to serious, logical, and controlled thinking, as in problem solving. In daydreaming, we may also be problem solving, but the solution takes the form of wish-fulfillment: We imagine a problem solved without the trouble of going through the necessary action and overcoming the obstacles toward our goals. We usually think of daydreams as a complete waste of time, although they might have goals that someone else, if not we ourselves, can make practical. The term *daydream* is really a misnomer because it suggests a similarity to dreaming while asleep, which is usually incoherent and jumbled, with no objective. In daydreaming, we may and usually do have an objective; we merely ignore the obstacles that lie in the path. Daydreams are concerned with ends, not means. Daydreams occur during idle moments or when we are unconcerned about the activity around us, as when children daydream in school. Their daydreams may be about out-of-school activities and involve various kinds of successes that are usually unattainable. They might, of course, even daydream about academic success. Because nothing is usually done to achieve the ends involved, daydreams can be considered a waste of time by the action-minded. They can, of course, be the inspiration of some future action. Quite possibly, some inventions or accomplishments, such as the airplane, the telephone, and so on, are the results of daydreams. The early explorers of the earth, and now, those of outer space, had their imagined fantasies about what they would find.

Although there may be children and adults who daydream excessively, the requirements of daily chores and activities usually force a stop to fantasizing and require a facing of reality. When children are apparently daydreaming, the adult observer might inquire into the content of the dream and discuss the worthiness of the goals and perhaps the nature of the obstacles and how they might be overcome. Sometimes, as in military or other prisons, a prisoner can plan and build detailed structures in his daydreams and keep himself from greater stresses. There is no harm in daydreaming if one has nothing better to do, and there will always be such periods in everyone's life. The point, of course, is to confine the daydreams to such periods. They can be the sources of great achievements in art and in the solution of real world problems. It is what we daydream about that matters.

DEAFNESS   (See AUDITORY PROBLEMS)

We associate *deafness* with an inability to hear, but we all suffer such inability compared to other animals. Dogs, for example, can hear sound waves too high in pitch for humans to notice. Children, on the average, hear much better than do adults, and as we begin to lose our auditory acuity, we find that we need to adjust radios to higher volumes, that we must watch the speakers on television shows (lip reading, to some degree), and that we ask people to repeat what they just said. People who work in noisy environs or where some particular kinds of sounds occur at some intensity and with regularity will develop lacunae or gaps in their hearing range. So-called boilermaker's disease is a deafness for certain sounds. Although old people are often present at symphony concerts, just what they hear is debatable. Trained musicians do not have to hear every sound they produce (Beethoven could compose after he became deaf); but the feedback of the sound does normally control the performance, and if the feedback is missing, the performance may be poor. Many people cannot hear themselves as well as others hear them and may sing badly. We refer to them as having tin ears.

Most deaf people can respond to some sounds, especially if they are very loud; they prefer to consider themselves as having a hearing weakness or disability. In some cases, such disabilities can be remedied to some extent by hearing aids, although many people are defensive about wearing hearing aids, even though they may wear glasses without any concern at all. In a way, it is possible to hide deafness by appearing to ignore the sounds about one. Perhaps it eases some anxieties if one can hide a handicap.

If one is deaf or hard of hearing, as the people with auditory weaknesses prefer to consider themselves, it makes a great difference as to when one became so. If a person is born deaf, he or she never enters the world of sound as normal people know it, and the normal person cannot begin to comprehend the nature of the deaf person's world. It is a world where communication becomes extremely difficult, and an enormous burden of learning and training is involved before the deaf person can begin to make any serious contacts with the workaday world, earn a living, and participate in some kind of social life. The social life is commonly restricted to others who are deaf and who have learned the difficult arts of communication with those who cannot hear.

The world of the deaf child is radically different from that of the hearing child. No one sings to him or her or tells him or her stories. There is no point in talking to him or her, and he or she has no opportunity to learn what goes on around him or her except through vision. Although parents can cuddle and nurture deaf children, they cannot make use of the marvelous tool of language that distinguishes people from other creatures. Learning to communicate becomes the most difficult problem, and educators of the deaf are still insecure and unsettled about how to conduct the language training of deaf children.

The teachers of the deaf are divided into those who favor the use of the *American Sign Language (Ameslan)* and those who favor what are called *oral methods.* The oral method involves teaching a deaf child to sound words by imitating lip and jaw movements. Visual displays of voice records can also be used to help a child to produce vocalizations. The mechanically acquired speech is rarely satisfactory, but it obviously helps. On the receiving side, the oral speech methods require lip reading, which enables the efficient reader to catch about one-third of the message he might be trying to observe.

In what is considered a more total method, Ameslan is added to the oral method, if it is not used exclusively. Ameslan enables the deaf to communicate among themselves and with their teachers, but very few normal hearing people ever learn the sign language unless they are closely related to the deaf person, such as parents. Still, the sign language exposes the child to the fact of language and to the meaning of communication, and he can begin to learn written language as an added operation. Ameslan has no formal grammar, and written English is just not someting into which one can translate Ameslan. It has to be learned painfully, with the complications of cases, moods, tenses, and so on. Children born deaf do not often make serious academic progress, but they can acquire various meaningful skills where sound is not important. Some people progress to a college level of education, usually attending Gallaudet College in Washington, D.C. before they seek other higher level academic exposure. Those who have achieved high levels of education despite their deafness are eager to point out that communication among the deaf is not just a simplified pidgin English; rather, it can be a highly complex language with all the shadings of meanings found in English. Nevertheless, to a hearing person, it is truly a foreign language.

DEFENSE MECHANISMS   *(See REPRESSION, RATIONALIZATION)*

The concept of *defense mechanisms* is part of those current personality theories and psychotherapy procedures that are related to psychoanalysis. Essentially, the concept of defense mechanisms holds that people develop a variety of unconscious strategies to defend themselves *against themselves.* All people, according to the psychoanalysts, have basic, innate drives that operate within us and impel or motivate our behavior. Because they are unconscious, we are not aware of them or their effects. Sometimes the drives are inappropriate or unacceptable, and they cause us to feel anxiety. For example, a person might feel strong hatred or jealousy of a brother, sister, or other family member. But because we are taught that it is wrong to dislike those who are close to us, the person may *repress* the hatred, push it out of consciousness. The feelings of hatred are still there but are now unconscious, and, as such, they continue to cause feelings of anxiety. Instead of repression, some people might develop a different mechanism, one of turning the feelings of hatred around, and come to believe that they love a sibling but that the sibling hates *them.* Another strategy is to deal with the unacceptable feelings of hatred by acting in the opposite manner—that is, behaving in an excessively loving way toward the family member. Such a mechanism is called *reaction formation.* In any event, in all of such instances of defense mechanisms, a person's initial hatred is not really reduced, only hidden, changed, or redirected. The assumption of the analyst is that the hatred is really still there, unconsciously, and that it is impelling the person to maintain the defensive strategies.

Other examples would be the male who feels sexually inadequate and weak and, in order to deny it to himself, behaves as a great, strong he-man, the macho male. A more common, everyday example of a defensive strategy is that of the convenient memory, as when we forget something unpleasant that we were supposed to do that day.

All of us, according to the analysts, develop defense mechanisms as a normal part of our functioning. It is only when the defensive strategies take a great deal of our psychological energy and hide a large portion of ourselves from ourselves that they become a problem.

It is certainly true that people develop a variety of behavioral and thinking strategies in order to defend themselves against threats, and few psychologists would argue against this idea. However, many, and perhaps most, modern psychologists no longer accept the psychoanalysts' version of the nature and operation of our defensive strategies. The major difficulty with the psychoanalytic concept is that it is so interpretive that, in any application to a real person, it is virtually impossible to test and validate the interpretations under controlled conditions.

DELIRIUM TREMENS   (See ALCOHOLISM, HALLUCINATION)

Some severe alcoholics experience acute periods of delusions and hallucinations, such as seeing, hearing, or even feeling animals, distorted rooms, scenes, and grotesque faces fading in and out, coming at them, and so on. Although some people sometimes find some humor in the alcoholics' supposed visions of pink elephants, the state of *delirium tremens* is no joking matter. When it happens, the alcoholic suffers an extremely disturbing, frightening experience. Anxiety is high, at panic levels; wild and frightening ideas crowd in upon the alcoholic, such as vivid thoughts that things, people, animals, or monsters are after him to torment, hurt, or murder him; his mental state becomes panicked, incoherent, and confused, all within the powerful context of threat, danger, and intense fear. The hallucinations, or visions, are extremely vivid images of snakes, spiders, rats, or other small animals crawling over one, biting and eating parts of one's body. During this acute and frightening episode, the person may shake with uncontrollable tremors, fall to the floor, plead for help, fight with anyone nearby, shout incoherently, and so on. All in all, it is an extremely vivid, acute, frightening experience, not only for the alcoholic but also for anyone witnessing it, such as family or friends.

After the first or even the first few such experiences, the alcoholic almost always swears off alcohol, promising with some fervor that he or she has learned his or her lesson and will never, ever go through that again. Unfortunately, the experience is a lesson wasted, and the new resolve is short lived—in almost all cases, the alcoholic is soon back to drinking again.

Delirium tremens, or D.T.'s, are an indication of severe, advanced alcoholism, where bodily and mental processes are temporarily but very powerfully disturbed. The person in the acute episode must be carefully watched and cared for, even restrained, so as not to injure others or suffer personal injury. The alcoholic in a D.T. condition can be relieved temporarily by taking in alcohol, but this is only an emergency treatment. Medical treatment and detoxification—that is, medically supervised drying-out—is about the only thing that can be done for a more permanent cure.

DEMONOLOGY AND WITCH HUNTING

Grossly bizarre behavior has been observed in people at least since the beginning of recorded history. Confused thinking, babbling, strange or meaningless talking, grotesque or peculiar stereotyped actions, strange ideas, withdrawal, confusion, wild, manic behavior, and the like were all well described more than three thousand years ago. Such obviously different behavior needed explanation, and people have, all through history, developed ideas and theories about what causes such behaviors. The explanations, whether magical, religious or scientific, were and are always in accordance with the prevailing beliefs of society. Today, in keeping with our scientific and technological age, our explanations of bizarre behavior are based on scientific psychology and biology. In the Middle Ages, when people believed literally in the existence of demons, witches, ghosts, the devil, and so on, they explained bizarre behavior as being caused by some evil demon or spirit that had invaded and taken over a person's body. The demon supposedly controlled the person and made him act in the observed bizarre or dangerous ways.

Demonology dates back far earlier than the Middle Ages, and it certainly did not end there, but it seems to have reached its most powerful levels from about 1200 through about 1400. During that time, church people and, later, judges and civil authorities sought to detect and rout the devil and other demons that had taken over human bodies and were causing diseases and other catastrophes to occur. Some people were thought to have made a pact with the devil. They were called witches, and they, too, were hunted down. The witch hunters ranged all over Western Europe and England, seeking to uncover the devil and stamp out evil.

The witch hunters' procedure was to identify people who might be possessed by demons and to test or try them. Then, through various exorcisms that amounted to sheer physical torture, they attempted to drive out the demon or bring the witch or wizard (male) to recant and break her or his bond with the devil. Finally, in many cases, they killed the person. Most of the estimated thousands who were publicly tortured and killed were powerless and friendless members of society, such as old women who lived alone. The witch hunters and judges, interestingly, could legally divide up whatever property the tortured and executed witch or wizard left.

The basic ideas in demonology are that powerful forces are inside the human body; that these forces directly cause the body to commit the bizarre acts; that the behavior itself, although troublesome, is not the real problem; that the real problems are the inner forces that cause the disturbed behavior; and that in order to help the person we must get through to those inner forces and somehow weaken them or drive them out.

The legacy of demonology is clearly seen in modern psychoanalysis, in which the therapist tries to understand and change the internal conditions or forces that supposedly cause the observed behavioral problems.

In modern usage, witch hunting has taken on a political meaning. A witch hunt, today, is the activity of a person or a group, such as that of Senator Joe McCarthy in his 1950s campaign to uncover communists in the United States government. Like the earlier witch hunters, our modern day witch hunters cause a great deal of human destruction before they are finally stopped.

DEPRESSION   (See BEHAVIOR THERAPY,
ELECTROCONVULSIVE SHOCK TREATMENT)

Most of us have depression. Our mood is dejected, gloomy; we seem to lose motivation to do anything, we feel like just staying home; we feel that most things are unimportant and that trying to change anything is useless. Under some stress conditions, such as the death of a loved one, we feel intense grief and become thoroughly dejected. The first thing to know about *depression* is that this deeply disheartened mood is a normal and common reaction that has been experienced to some degree by virtually every adult. Depression usually occurs as one of our reactions to severe loss, such as death in the family; loss of one's home or business in a fire or through financial setbacks; loss of prestige or lack of success, as in the case of an actor whose play has failed or of a student who has failed in school. Frequently, depression is experienced at the end of a highly stimulating and successful achievement or period. The American astronaut, Edwin Aldrin, after all of the excitement and activity of going to the moon, is reported to have experienced periods of depression when it was all over—in a sense, the splash-down was also a come-down. Many ex-champions feel a strong sense of loss with the crowning of a new champion. No one enjoys being replaced.

Normal depression is self-limiting; that is, in time it dissipates, the person recovers and is soon back to normal moods and activity. Any of us might for years feel a tinge of sadness when we think of a parent or other person close to us who has died, but the acutely depressed mood will have resolved itself.

But when depresssion is extremely acute, deep, and/or long-lasting and is not clearly attributable to external conditions, such as real loss, then it is not a normal human depressive experience, but a psychological problem. It is widespread, with an estimated eight million Americans who suffer from abnormal depression. The problem is even more serious because one out of every two hundred persons with depressive illness (i.e., not the normal depressive reaction) will die by suicide.

One of the current major theories of depression, the *learned helplessness* model, has been developed by psychologist M. E. P. Seligman. That view holds that people who are under severe threat or punishment by adverse events over a long period of time eventually give up, since they come to believe that nothing they can do will alter or improve the conditions—that is, they learn to become helpless.

Depression can be treated successfully in a number of ways. *Electroconvulsive treatment,* or ECT, is widely used by psychiatrists for depressed patients. However, there is considerable controversy—not over its effectiveness in reducing depressive behavior but over its possible negative side effects, which may include brain damage and memory loss. ECT should be used only with extreme caution, perhaps only when all else has failed. Certainly it should never be used with children.

More recently, antidepressant drugs have been used, sometimes in conjunction with tranquilizers, to reduce anxiety and to lift the depressed mood. Antidepressive drug therapy might eventually replace some of the psychiatrists' reliance upon ECT.

Although ECT and drug therapy are effective in altering the depressed patient's mood, it is also important to deal with the psychological issues that brought it about in the first place. Unless the psychological treatment is effective, the ECT and drug therapy gains may be lost very quickly. Both psychoanalytic and behavior therapies are used in the treatment of depressive patients. Unfortunately, there is virtually no systematic evidence that psychoanalytic therapy is useful for depressed patients.

More systematic research has been carried out in the use of various behavior therapies, including systematic desensitization, to reduce the anxiety associated with depression. The evidence to date suggests that several different behavioral methods used in combination may be most effective. But it should be emphasized that none of the psychological treatments is as effective in reducing depression as the somatic (ECT and drug) therapies. The somatic treatments, however, do not necessarily last. The best treatments available today may thus be a combination of drug therapy and behavior therapy.

DETERRENCE   *(See PUNISHMENT)*

Some psychologists, perhaps because they are guided by humane principles, support the idea that the only way to change anyone is to reward him or her for doing what is desirable. Punishing undesirable behavior is said to be useless: If it seems to work, that is only temporary, and any permanent change requires the rewarding of different behavior. For this reason, these psychologists argue that punishing anyone by imprisonment, fines, or any other means is idle and useless. The data on which such claims rest are found in experiments where rats are shocked mildly and briefly. Other research using strong and long shocks points to a quite different conclusion: that punishment does stop the punished behavior. Criminologists and other social scientists frequently cite the alleged fact that in old England, when pickpockets were publicly hanged, there were more pockets picked than on any other occasion. There are never any data supplied about how many pockets were picked on hanging and nonhanging days. We can put this story away with other myths. Anyone who sees a police car in his rearview mirror while driving knows full well that the very sight of a police officer is a deterrent to illegal behavior. The trouble with the deterrence doesn't work hypothesis is that the punishment usually given is not long and strong enough. A millionaire will not be deterred by a $5.00 fine, nor will a car thief be deterred by being put on probation for unauthorized use of a motor vehicle. If he were properly called a car thief and sentenced to twenty solid years in jail, he would have a decided effect on other potential or active thieves. The fact is that the system of justice is fairly humane, and most malefactors do not go to jail, especially if they have competent lawyers. Even so, there is relatively little crime if one considers the total population figures. Probably fewer than 1% of the people commit serious crimes meriting any kind of judicial treatment. In short, most people do not commit crimes; they may be deterred. In many cases (and the number cannot be established easily), people behave themselves because of fear of arrest or hell, depending upon their upbringing.

DEVELOPMENTAL STAGES   *(See READINESS, HEREDITY,*
EARLY EXPERIENCE, LEARNING, ABILITY, MATURITY)

Poets, playwrights, philosophers, and psychologists have all considered the problem of growth and development as one of the key questions relating to human nature. What do we grow out of? Do we have to learn to do certain things, or do they just come naturally? Is some peculiar or undesirable behavior pattern just a phase? Numerous investigators have looked into the general problem of maturation and have emerged with various theories, depending on their special interests, but none of the theories can spell out the course of development of any individual child. What can be suggested is a kind of *developmental sequence,* in that some stages or kinds of behavior emerge after, and only after, certain other stages. Thus, walking normally follows a stage of crawling; once a child has begun to walk, he or she will rarely *begin* to crawl. When a particular child will walk cannot be predicted with any great precision in terms of weeks or even months, although the average healthy child will walk in about a year.

The areas of development that have interested various theorists fall into the following classes: motor development, psychosexual development, and intellectual development. In all three types of theories, it is assumed that human nature or hereditary factors exercise a dominant role and determine, more or less rigidly, the sequence of stages.

Motor development studies range all over the field of physical activities, from turning the head, sitting up, standing, crawling, walking, talking, picking up small items with the fingers, sleep patterns, and sucking to roller skating. As mentioned earlier, the course of the emergence of any such activity and its decline are individual matters, and what any child should be doing at any specific age cannot be stated with precision, although certain limits might be indicated.

Freud introduced a developmental sequence of his own without any formal investigations of children such as those that have been done in the area of motor development. He assumed, to begin with, a *narcissistic* period in which a child first goes through an *oral* stage where gratification is gained through sucking, examining things with the mouth, and eating. This phase lasts about a year and is followed by an *anal* stage where the child obtains gratification from urination and excretion or by withholding waste products; in another year, at about age 3, the child, if a boy, goes through a *phallic* stage, becoming interested in the penis, its absence in girls, and, generally, gaining pleasure in genital stimulation. Following this narcissistic period is a *latency period* where sexual concerns appear to diminish as the Oedipus complex begins to be resolved and ego development proceeds. With puberty, there is a return to a genital stage, which continues on through adolescence and adulthood. Freud believed that a child could be *fixated* at one stage or another in line with his emphasis on the importance of traumatic experience in childhood. The Freudian stages do not have any strong support from formal research but appear to be reasonable deductions from casual observation. What is missing is any evidence about the associated fixation hypothesis, which is a basic psychoanalytic explanation of adult disturbances.

The area of intellectual development has been dominated by the writings of Jean Piaget, the Swiss psychologist-biologist. Again, no specific dates can be assigned for any child, but certain expectancies are laid down for the average child. Piaget views intellectual growth as passing through three stages. The first stage is the *sensorimotor stage,* in which the child begins to deal with objects in the external world and starts forming simple concepts of size, shape, and motion; he or she differentiates between him- or herself—that is, his or her own sensations—and the external world. In the second stage, the *preconceptual* stage, the child learns to discriminate between objects, but only as separate objects and not as members of classes. Each object has its own identity and is not related to other objects of the same nature. This stage lasts approximately from age 2 to age 4. From ages 4 or 5 to age 7, the child enters the *intuitive thought* stage, wherein the child begins to make comparisons between objects but does not take surrounding conditions into account: He or she cannot recognize, for example, that amounts of water do not change as they are poured into larger or smaller containers—the amounts will look bigger or smaller to the child who responds directly to uncorrected perceptions. In the next stage, *concrete operations,* at ages 7 to 11, the child begins to organize his or her world; he or she can count objects, arrange them in order, ignore variations in classifying items—a small ball is nevertheless a ball, for example, and the child can operate systematically and make use of some symbolic reasoning. In the last stage, beginning at about age 12, the child enters the stage of *formal operations* and can deal with symbols abstractly; he or she no longer needs to have physical objects before him or her and can reason his or her way through problems logically. In this stage, he or she can deal with abstractions and concepts, such as identity and oppositeness, and he or she can state propositions and deal with theoretical ideas. Obviously, the various stages merge in different combinations with different children and are helped or retarded by various kinds of experience undergone by the developing child.

The various kinds of developmental theories are not of much help to the concerned parents of an individual and particular child. They see their own child in the context of other children of about the same age and find their child ahead of or behind other children in various skills, toilet training, temper tantrums, or what not, and are constantly wondering about their possible mistakes in child rearing. Parents of boys will argue that girls, after all, do develop faster, especially if their boys appear somewhat slow in walking or talking; they will speculate about their family trees for hereditary explanations of good points and look for causes of undesirable traits in the environments—schools, companions, the unfeeling world. The only practical course for a parent is to accept his or her own children for what they are and do the best for them without pushing and without invidious comparisons with other children. Some attention might be paid to signs that a child is ready for some activity or that he or she is equally ready to drop it. A problem arises in that children may be able to perform some activity, if rather poorly, at some early age; often, parents then *rush* the child into expensive lessons and practice sessions that could be much more effective at a later age. There is always the question of special gifts or talents that might die for lack of support. In such cases, the child will probably lead the way. In general, the children of the world do grow up—in spite of their parents—and move from one phase of activities to another. The wise parents note the phases and encourage appropriate moves at appropriate times.

DISCIPLINE

When most people talk about *discipline* or about disciplining children, they are usually thinking in terms of punishment used to maintain order, to teach unruly children to be more obedient. The words *discipline, obedience,* and *punishment* are often linked together in common usage. In effect, people commonly think of discipline as ways in which adults punish children in order to reduce their bad or undesirable behavior.

To use discipline primarily as a synonym for punishment is to distort its major meaning, for discipline is not limited to reducing bad behavior. Even more appropriately, it means ways of increasing and stabilizing good or desired behavior. The dictionary defines the major meanings of discipline as "teaching," "learning," "instruction," "a subject that is taught," "a field of study," "training." Thus the preferred meaning of discipline—at least with children—is to teach, to instruct, to train, and to help children learn.

Given this meaning, the question about disciplining children changes from the common idea, "How can we best punish children in order to reduce their undesirable behavior and make them obedient?" to "How can we best teach children to learn desirable behavior?"

In general, the best ways to teach children are to clearly know *what* it is you want them to learn; provide a good model in your own behavior; give them all of the support and help they need, and, as they learn, praise and reward them. Sometimes, parents might think that mild punishment is useful. But it is not necessary, and certainly punishment should not be equated with discipline.

DISCRIMINATED STIMULI   *(See CONDITIONING)*

We do not react to all the energy changes (stimuli) that occur around us. Rats, cats, and dogs may stop at every shadow or minor creak, whereas humans may carry on in some activity, such as reading in the library, in the midst of much surrounding activity. A machinist at his lathe may ignore the poundings of trip hammers, the sounds of other machinery, and so on. The casual visitor may wonder how anyone can work in such surroundings. Professor Donald O. Hebb of McGill University described rats and other animals as *stimulus bound.* Man is much more capable of ignoring his environment and responding only to certain changes in his environment. He learns that not everything that happens around him is important.

Professor B. F. Skinner chose to call those stimuli to which we do react when they occur *discriminated stimuli* and used the notation of S^D to identify them. As we walk along the street, we may pass hundreds of people, but if an acquaintance happens to appear, we greet him with a "Hello." We did not say "Hello" to anyone else. Clearly, the acquaintance is different from all of the others who passed. According to Skinner, if we are reinforced (rewarded) in the presence of and only in the presence of a particular stimulus for doing something, that stimulus will acquire a form of control over our behavior so that, in its presence, we are likely to make the previous rewarded response and, in its absence, refrain from doing so. In the laboratory, this is demonstrated by allowing a rat to press a little lever that results in a bit of food entering the box containing the rat. If a light is turned on and the rat presses, the food will appear. If the light is off, there will be no food after the press. After some trials, the rat will press when the light is on and refrain from pressing in the dark. The light has become an S^D. The control is not always perfect, and mistakes are made, just as we make mistakes in identifying people sometimes. We usually go to the door when the doorbell rings and not to the telephone. Door bells and telephone bells are discriminated stimuli. Note that in such cases we have also made discriminated responses. We learn to do certain things to certain stimuli, although there can be some confusion here as well. Sometimes we learn a variety of equivalent responses or variations. We might say, "How are you" or "Hi" instead of "Hello." Such responses have also been discriminated and represent different histories of reinforcement.

DIVORCE—EFFECTS ON CHILDREN

Divorce is now occurring in one out of every three first marriages, and, according to recent data, the rate is now approaching one in two. In 1970, more than six million children were affected by their parents' divorce, and the number per year now is even greater.

What are the effects of divorce? It is generally known that a marriage breakup is a series of shocks for all of the people involved, adults as well as children. The amicable divorce between reasonable people who remain good friends, who feel no strong negative results, and who impose no problems on their children is a myth. In reality, the feelings of inadequacy, failure, self-doubt, disappointment, anger, and hatred are strong and often overpowering.

Children react differently to their parents' divorce, depending upon the children's ages and the intensity and duration of conflicts prior to the breakup, but all children react with some degree of distress. Children of divorce often feel somehow vaguely responsible for their family's breakup, and they may be frightened because they do not know what worse may yet occur to them. The first two years after the divorce seem to be the most difficult for children: They frequently lose interest in schoolwork; they may become hostile, aggressive, depressed, and, in some cases, even suicidal. Many physical symptoms of stress often appear in the children, such as irritability, insomnia, loss of appetite, and skin disorders.

For the children, the divorce has broken up the family, disrupted their lives, and caused great anxieties about the future as well as the present. The children in divorce suffer, perhaps more than the parents.

Research suggests that after about two years a new balance or equilibrium develops, and the acute distress of the children earlier in the divorce process is lessened. They learn to adjust and to carry on their lives. In many cases, where the marriage was marked by very severe conflicts for a long time, the children seem psychologically better off some two years after the divorce than they were just prior to or shortly after the breakup. Even when the eventual resolution is good, the process is a painful one for the child.

In divorce, the parents devote a great deal of time and money to fight each other through the economic issues of ownership, alimony, child custody, and various rights and privileges, but they typically devote little time or effort to softening the emotional impact on the children. Lawyers, who are very involved in the details of divorce, have little understanding of these emotional issues and generally do not seem competent to counsel parents on how best to help their children to cope and adjust to the situation.

It is not too clear how children can be helped by their preoccupied, battling parents, whatever the parental good intentions may be. Some psychologists believe that the most important help the parents can give is to reassure the children that they are not responsible for the divorce. It has been suggested that parents help children to adjust by establishing and maintaining regular routines in the home, by not forcing the children to take sides in the adult dispute, and by not even suggesting such participation. It might be helpful to find another adult who might in some way help to fill the gap left by the parent who has gone away.

However carefully and amicably the parents might try to carry out the divorce, there is probably no way they can avoid a negative impact upon the children. It becomes important, then, for parents in the divorce process to take special efforts to minimize the children's distress as best they can. It requires active concern and work on the parents' part.

DOUBLE BIND   (See SCHIZOPHRENIA)

When a child is given inconsistent and contradictory messages, he or she is in a *double bind*. It is a very common occurrence for a parent to scold an adolescent for not behaving maturely, not acting his or her age, or not taking some expected responsibility. The parental complaint of not acting maturely can be made about many things. The child is then bound, in a sense, by the parent's clear message to act more maturely, more in keeping with his or her age.

The double-bind problem, however, occurs when a contradictory, equally binding message is also given. For example, the same parent, on another occasion, and perhaps the same day, might complain that the adolescent has again overstepped the limits, made some decision, or done something he or she is too young and inexperienced to do. "You can't have your own car. You're only a kid. You're not responsible enough." The adolescent is thus criticized both for failure to assume more adult responsibility and for trying to assume it. That is the double bind; no matter which way the adolescents behave, they are criticized. They are damned if they do and damned if they don't.

Double-bind messages between parents and children are probably fairly common and, for most people, are yet another of those many inconsistencies in life that we must somehow learn to deal with as we grow up. At times, especially over issues of independence, double-bind messages can create confusion, conflict, and quarrels between parents and children. But, by and large, they do not appear to be a particularly damaging set of events. The adolescents must just live a few more years before they are on their own. At that time, the double-bind messages are taken more casually.

About twenty years ago, some psychologists hypothesized that double-bind messages, particularly those involving love and acceptance, were an important part of the family experiences of schizophrenics. Possibly, they thought, the double-bind between mother and son was particularly important in causing the schizophrenic reaction of the son. Subsequent research, however, has not supported the hypothesis that double-bind messages are important causal factors in schizophrenia.

As noted above, the double-bind message is a common annoyance, a poor communication. It does often cause at least temporary anxiety or conflict, but it does not appear to be particularly important in the development of severe psychological problems. Life for adolescents and their parents would be easier without the double-bind messages, and it is wise for all parents to assume the responsibility to try to recognize and minimize such conflicting messages of their own.

DOWN'S SYNDROME, OR MONGOLISM

Affecting approximately one in every 660 births, *Down's syndrome,* or *Mongolism,* accounts for 10% of all retarded children with I.Q.s ranging downwards from about 50. These children have clear physical characteristics, such as slanted eyes (accounting for the early label, Mongolism): a wide, round face with flat features; stubby fingers; and, often, a tongue that is deeply fissured.

Down's syndrome children can be clearly identified at or shortly after birth. The parents can be alerted and proper training prepared. The condition cannot be reversed, but these children can be raised at home and taught a great deal through special education programs such as are available in nearly all urban areas. Among the retarded, Down's syndrome children seem in particular to do best at home, where there is love, good attention, and care, rather than in an institution. They can be highly affectionate children and, under good conditions, can learn a fair amount of self-care and can even learn to carry out relatively simple jobs as adults.

The condition is caused by an extra chromosome; that is, the Down's syndrome child has 47 chromosomes instead of the usual 46. The mother's age at the birth of the child seems to be an important factor, and the chances of having a Down's syndrome child increases from one in 1,500 for a mother in her twenties to one in 65 for a mother over age 45. Recently, ways of testing the amniotic fluid in the womb during pregnancy have been developed, and the presence of a Down's syndrome fetus can be determined. When a pregnant woman is over age 40, many obstetricians will have this test routinely performed.

DREAMS   *(See SLEEP)*

For thousands of years, people have tried to ascribe meanings to dreams. All sorts of interpretations of dreams have been offered, from Joseph in Egypt to Freud in Vienna, and all sorts of folklore have developed around the subject. Only recently have we discovered some actual facts about dreams, and the main conclusion that appears to be justified is that dreams do not mean anything except that the sleeper has shifted from a stage of relatively deep sleep to a lighter form where he or she is almost but not quite awake. When we are asleep, our brain waves vary from large slow waves to faster and smaller ones. Sleep seems to occur in periods of about 90 minutes, where we pass from drowsiness to deeper sleep to a more restless period and then start the cycle over. In the lighter phase of sleep, our eyes appear to move back and forth under the closed lids, and in these periods of rapid eye moment (REM), we appear to get our dreaming done. People awakened during periods of REM will report dreaming; being awakened at other times does not result in as many dream reports. The content reported by the awakened dreamer does not make any particular sense, even though he or she might later report a more coherent story. It appears that dreams usually revolve around events that have recently occurred, but there is no orderly sequence, although there may be some stretches that more or less follow some order. What is occurring during a dream is that the person is thinking, but his or her thinking is not under any restraints, normal controls, or critical evaluation. Dreams do not tell us about the future. At best, they might tell us a little about the past. Sometimes, dreamers will talk in their sleep and can be questioned, with some reasonable answers being supplied. Nearly everybody dreams, regardless of what they say, since there are periods of REM about every 90 minutes. The probability is that if you fall asleep for a short nap, under an hour, you will not dream during that period. Even if you do, however, there is, as of now, no reason to take any action on the basis of any dream you might have.

DRIVES   *(See MOTIVATION, ANXIETY)*

People are always asking the question, "Why?"—why someone does this or does that. The search for an answer to such questions led some psychologists to assume that people are born with certain biological needs that must be satisfied if they are to survive. Actually the term *need* is an abstraction and has never been defined except in a circular fashion. We see someone eating and assume that he or she has a need for food. Now it is true that if one does not eat, he or she will die, but that does not mean that he or she needs food: All that we know is that without food there will be certain changes in his or her blood stream and body cells and that after about seven days the person will no longer have any other concerns. A person does not need food anymore than an automobile needs gas. Without gas, the car will not run, and without food, a person will not do much running either—but neither needs anything.

If we ask ourselves what conditions must be met for a person to survive, we can list such things as oxygen, food, liquids, suitable temperatures, sleep, and some exercise. Note that we do not list sexual intercourse, since people can survive without it, even though the race cannot. What we have mentioned are conditions that lead to changes in the physical organism with the passage of time. Thus, if one eats, the digestive process will transform the food into various chemicals that will maintain or create new conditions or operations within the body. When our bladders are full, we will have a bodily or tissue condition that we do not have when our bladders are empty. With some bodily conditions, there will be stimulation of organic sense organs that inform us, usually not too well, that something should be done to change those conditions. Thus, with the full bladder, we will look for a convenient place to relieve the condition, if we are civilized adults. The stimulation from such bodily or tissue conditions has come to be called *drive stimulation,* and, again, a *drive* has been assumed to underlie the stimulation. Thus we frequently hear about hunger drives, thirst drives, sex drives, and the like. Actually there are only bodily changes with accompanying stimuli, some of which we can recognize. We might, for example, have a starch shortage in our bodily chemistry and find out about it only after a spaghetti dinner is found to taste unusually good. We can even say, on occasion, "My, I needed that," and, in some cases, we might be right.

Experiments on rats and children indicate that when they are placed on diets that are self-selected, they might, over a rather long period, come to eat just about what is good for them (note that we do not say what they need). Self-selection is not to be trusted too far, however, as any child will eat more chocolate than is good for him or her, and the teenagers' diet of cokes and hamburgers is not recommended by any nutritionist. The point, however, is that sometimes we know what our bodily conditions call for and sometimes we do not and that we may even think that we need something when there is no particular biological condition to adjust.

The introduction of sex into the need and drive category is perhaps the most erroneous inclusion. As far as anyone knows, no one needs sexual intercourse with a partner of either sex in order to survive. Female rats go through a cycle of changes in their reproductive organs that make them receptive to male rats every four days or so. Other female animals go into heat at various seasonal periods. Again, this does not prove that they need anything. The males of all animals, at least mammalian species, seem to be in heat at any and all times, but this only means that, given a receptive partner, they can respond with sexual activity; but such responses are largely conditioned or acquired and do not represent needs. To say that a male is highly sexed means only that he spends more time at sexual activity than do other males (or talks more about it) and not that he has a stronger than normal sex drive. It is true that the sex glands in both males and females produce secretions that are related to sexual activity and that the menstrual cycle in human females is marked by periods of greater and less receptivity, but sexual arousal in humans is more a learned and social business than a matter of satisfying biological drives.

From the biological appreciation of bodily or tissue changes, psychologists have tried to bridge the gap to social motivations, with limited success. We hear of drives for power, money madness, achievement motivation, and any number of nonbiologically founded drives or motives. We must recognize that these are not matters of heredity or biology and that they are learned patterns of operating in this world, presumably based on whatever kinds of successes we have managed to enjoy. Professor B. F. Skinner has suggested that the kinds of rewards we will work for are related to the things that we have been deprived of. Deprivation, of course, implies that we had previously developed a liking, desire, or use for such things, but the term may be useful in avoiding the problems we meet when we talk about needs and drives.

In order to explain much of human motivation, some psychologists have suggested that emotional arousal can function in the same way as other biological changes and serve to control or guide—certainly, influence—our behavior. Thus, if fear is considered as a biological state that is somehow related to some behavior patterns, such as fleeing or fighting, we would increase the number of drives or needs to include freedom from fear. Other emotions, such as hate, anger, love, relief, and disappointment, could similarly be related to certain behavior patterns. If any of these emotions is conditioned to some more or less unnatural stimuli, we could then behave in some fearful fashion, say, in the presence of a baseball, a lollypop, or whatever the conditioning stimulus had been. When a conditioned fear is aroused, we are said to be in a state of anxiety, but anxiety, like sex, needs external stimulation to come into being; it is not a biological drive or need in the same sense as the alleged need for oxygen. Because anxiety is frequently provoked in most of us by many situations or stimuli, we can go along with philosophers like Thoreau who told us, "The mass of men lead lives of quiet desperation" or with others who call this the Age of Anxiety and agree that much of our behavior is attributable to fear, in one form or another. This is not to say, however, that anyone has a fear drive in the same sense in which other drives are supposed to be characterized by periodic changes in bodily tissue conditions.

DRUG ABUSE: THE DRUG CULTURE   (See DRUG ADDICTION, DRUG USE DURING PREGNANCY)

The drug culture is a phrase used to label a set of behaviors and beliefs that place a high value on the use of various drugs for making people feel good or better or for helping to generate interesting emotional experiences. The phrase generates pictures of a minority of young people who drop out of normal society. They devote a great deal of their time to drug experiences, become knowledgeable about the subjective effects of various drugs and their availability, and, overall, live lives vastly different from the rest of society.

The drug culture, however, might not describe only a minority of people, but all of us. It is clear that the reliance upon drugs is not limited to a minority of young people. The most common drugs used by Americans in order to feel better are alcohol, nicotine, and caffein. Although up to ten million Americans are alcohol abusers, another 100 million, virtually our entire adult population, use the drug moderately, as an accepted kind of drug use.

Nicotine, a stimulant obtained from tobacco, is regularly used by about 75 million of us. Caffein is our most widely used stimulant and is obtained from coffee, tea, chocolate, and cola drinks.

Americans also use vast quantities of tranquilizers to calm down, sedatives to sleep, and stimulants to keep awake. Our American dependence on drugs is phenomenal, and it keeps our pharmaceutical industry very happy indeed. The entire American culture seems to be a drug culture. With drug use so thoroughly widespread and accepted by normal society, it is no wonder that young people, observing the adults' drug dependency, have developed their own particular favorites among drugs.

DRUG ABUSE: TREATMENT

There is little room for optimism about the success of treatment for drug abuse. In general, the treatment is far more difficult and far less effective with addicts—those using drugs that result in physiological addiction, such as narcotics (morphine and heroin) and the barbiturates. There is slightly more optimism for those taking drugs that do not result in physiological addiction, such as amphetamines (uppers, including cocaine) and the hallucinogens—LSD and marijuana. Treatment of any drug abuse, however, is a poor risk in general.

Psychological counseling or therapy alone is of no demonstrated use for those on physiologically addictive drugs. These addicts must be withdrawn under very carefully supervised medical control. After the physiological withdrawal has been achieved, psychological treatment may be attempted to help the people remain off the drugs in the future. But even after withdrawal and with psychological treatment, only about 15% of those treated remain off drugs. The others die or return to drugs.

A synthetic drug, methadone, has been used to treat addicts. Methadone is similar to heroin in its pleasurable effects and is just as addictive. Its advantage is that it does not produce heroin's psychological problems: it is also a legal drug under control of the clinic. The idea is to get the addicts to switch off heroin to methadone supplied by the clinic and thus get them out of the illegal drug market. It is hoped this will end the addict's criminal behavior to obtain money for heroin. Psychological counseling is supposedly part of the methadone treatment.

Methadone has generally not been an effective treatment. There is growing evidence of physical problems, such as liver damage, with long-term methadone use. Babies born to women on methadone can be born addicted themselves, as are many babies born to heroin addicts. Further, there has developed an illegal traffic in methadone itself, thus undermining one of the program's expected strengths.

Society has spent a great deal of time and money in attempts to treat addicts; but at present, we have no effective treatment methods. We can help addicts to withdraw, but we cannot yet help them to remain off the drugs. Virtually all addicts either die addicted or they temporarily withdraw, sometimes with the help of a treatment program, only to return soon to the active habit.

Psychological treatment of those using amphetamines (uppers) and hallucinogens (LSD and marijuana) is somewhat more hopeful, particularly in specialized behavior modification group home programs. But even there, the success rate is disappointing.

Both drug addiction and dependence are extreme problems that, once developed, are very difficult to modify.

DRUG ADDICTION   *(See ADDICTION, DRUG ABUSE)*

Drug addiction includes alcohol and tobacco use as well as the abuse of prescription drugs, but in common practice, the term is usually applied to the illegal use of substances derived from opium. We usually think of drug addiction as a problem of teenagers and young adults, but it is hardly limited to those ages.

The addictive drugs include *sedatives,* or downers, that have the effect of slowing down the body and give the user some pleasant sense of peace and relaxation. Their calming effects are very powerfully reinforcing, and the user can quickly become psychologically dependent upon them. Downers include synthetic drugs, such as barbiturates, and organic narcotics, such as morphine, heroin, and codeine, which are all derivatives of opium. Another major group includes *stimulants,* or uppers, which speed up nervous activity and increase alertness and motor behavior. These uppers include the synthetic drug group, amphetamines, and an organic drug, *cocaine,* derived from the cocoa leaf. As with the sedatives, users can quickly develop psychological dependence on these drugs. In both cases, uppers and downers, physiological addiction, with all of its severe ill effects, is virtually certain with prolonged use.

Among the most tragic events associated with drug addiction and even with drug dependence are the changes seen by families in their teenagers who, unknown to the parents, may be on marijuana or other drugs. At first attributed to normal teenage moodiness and the desire for privacy and independence, the adolescent's behavior becomes increasingly more excessive and obvious. A personality change is frequently reported by the parents as the adolescent draws farther away from them, becoming more isolated, moody, and unresponsive. Typically, interest in school, job, friends, dating, and so on all decrease as the adolescent devotes more and more time away from home to activities and with friends the parents know little about. The general picture of addiction is played out, with the adolescent losing all interest in other aspects of life and eventually becoming seriously ill, arrested, or, in many cases, another death by overdose.

As with other addictions, psychological treatment, such as in individual psychotherapy by psychiatrists or psychologists, has no proven effectiveness. Some special group programs that begin with medical supervision over physical withdrawal from the drug and are then followed by psychological group treatment may be helpful. However, the chances for the full recovery of a true addict of any substance—tobacco, alcohol, or other drugs—is rare and difficult to achieve.

DRUG TREATMENT OF MENTAL DISORDERS
(See DRUG ABUSE)

Many psychiatrists use drug treatments alone or in conjunction with verbal psychotherapies. The drugs fall into three categories and are used for different purposes: (1) *tranquilizers,* to calm down anxious patients and to help keep them on an even emotional level; (2) *antidepressants,* to help elevate depressed moods; and (3) *special problem drugs,* including, for example, the stimulants, methadone, and antabuse.

Tranquilizers. The use of tranquilizers is a major part of psychiatry today. It includes mild tranquilizers, such as meprobamate, and familiar trade names, such as Miltown, Equanil, Librium, and Valium. These are prescribed for anxious people who are not severely mentally disturbed. They are often prescribed by general practitioners and are in very common use by adults in our heavily drug-oriented society.

More powerful tranquilizers, such as chlorpromazine, thioridazine, and trifluoperazine, often called antipsychotic drugs, are used to reduce extreme anxiety and to treat patients diagnosed as psychotic, schizophrenics in particular. Some 85% of the patients in mental hospitals are on major tranquilizers. Those tranquilizers seem effective for many psychotic patients in reducing their bizarre behavior and confused and confusing language. Patients who just 30 years ago would have been locked up or even put in straight jackets can now, with tranquilizers, have a far greater degree of freedom and varied, more normal, activity. These major tranquilizers serve an important and very useful function. Recently, however, there has been increased concern over the possible negative side effects of long-term use. Some patients develop uncontrollable hand and face tremors and lip and tongue movements. The use of major tranquilizers must be medically supervised with great care.

Antidepressants. Antidepressants (tricyclic drugs), as their name suggests, are used with depressed clients. The tricyclic drugs have been shown to be effective in elevating the mood of many, but not all, depressed patients who take the drug. Research currently continues trying to determine which depressed patients will respond best to this drug.

Many drugs are used in special problem areas. *Antabuse* has been used in the treatment of alcoholics. This drug causes unpleasant feelings, nausea, vomiting, and lowered blood pressure if the person begins to drink while he has the drug in him or her. Although antabuse is physiologically effective, it has not been possible to convince alcoholics to keep using the drug. All they have to do is to stop taking it, let it get out of their system, and then they can drink alcohol without the unpleasant reactions. Hence, as a treatment for alcoholism, it has had very little success.

Stimulant Drugs.   *Stimulants,* such as amphetamine, have been used (paradoxically) to reduce hyperactivity in children. There have been reasonably good overall results in slowing down children, but there are also clear dangers. For example, just before 1970, as many as 10% of the school children of Omaha were being put on drugs by physicians in order to calm the children down. The program turned out to be an over-use, not sufficiently discriminating, and too routinely applied. We must be extremely careful about using drugs to control the behavior of children.

Methadone, a synthetic drug much like heroin, is commonly used in the treatment and control of drug addicts, but generally with very poor results.

DRUG USE DURING PREGNANCY

Taking drugs during pregnancy—nicotine; alcohol; hard drugs, such as morphine, heroin and codeine; as well as certain hormones and other substances used as medication—threatens the health of the developing fetus. A higher rate of spontaneous abortion, sexual overdevelopment and reversal, and cervical cancer are suspected results of the use of some synthetic hormones during pregnancy. Smoking in pregnancy is associated with babies of lower birthweight, higher heart rate, a reduction of blood and oxygen supply to the fetus, poor nutrition, and, as suggested in a recent study, lower intelligence. Excessive alcohol use during pregnancy can result in the recently discovered *fetal alcohol* syndrome, which includes slowed fetal growth, babies who are of small size at birth and who apparently never catch up to normal-sized children, sub-normal intelligence, defects of the heart and within joints. Alcohol withdrawal symptoms can be observed in these infants after birth. Addictive drugs taken by the pregnant woman, such as codeine, heroin and morphine, can cause the fetus to become addicted, to show withdrawal symptoms at birth, and therefore to require treatment for the drug addiction. Even if the physiological addiction is immediately treated and eventually cured, these addicted infants show continued psychological effects. They appear to be less alert than normal children, less responsive to parental cuddling and affection, more irritable, and apt to cry more. All of these characteristics could have negative effects on the mother-child relationship.

Drug use by pregnant women is a serious threat to the lives and welfare of developing children.

DYSLEXIA   *(See MINIMAL BRAIN DYSFUNCTION, READING)*

Dyslexia is a fancy term to describe poor reading ability. It is not a disease or any specific disorder. It is better considered as a symptom. Some children may have poorer reading scores than some of their age group, and, relative to such peers, they may be called dyslexic, but that is of no help beyond permitting someone to use a scientific-sounding term. Actually, children differ in reading ability for many reasons, and the real problem is to discover the reason for any particular child's difficulty.

It is popularly thought that dyslexia refers to some mysterious defect that makes children see words backwards, upside down, or with letters interchanged. Such perceptual errors do appear to be common enough in children up to eight or nine years of age at some times, but most of us can read words that are distorted in such ways if we have to. The problem is rather more general. A child with a poor vocabulary and poor pronunciation with little or no grammatical training is going to have trouble reading. The English language, with its lack of precise phonetic transcription in written form, does not help. There are, however, dsylexic children in other countries where English is not the common language.

Some children with sense organ deficiencies or other physical handicaps and/or a slow development may also experience reading difficulties compared with their age groups. These represent, rather generally, a small proportion of the poor readers. When a child cannot read well, it is easy to blame the child and to speculate on the presence of some personal defect of a physiological nature. If none is obvious, one can always point to heredity. Actually, poor reading ability can be shown to run in families, although it might be difficult to trace the poor reading genes, just as it is difficult to trace poor intelligence genes. Sometimes a hasty diagnosis of *minimal brain dysfunction* is offered. Such diagnoses should be regarded cautiously, with a request for proof. Gibson and Levine, in their *Psychology of Reading,* suggest that dyslexia may be due either to external factors (emotional and cultural deprivations) or internal factors (physiological disturbances). In any particular case, the specific causes should be determined before corrective treatment is instituted.

E

EARLY EXPERIENCE

A considerable mythology has grown up around the early years of life. We have the folklore of "as the twig is bent" and various assertions of psychoanalysts, religious sects, educators, and so on. The fact is that very little is known of how important the early years actually are as far as irreversible changes are concerned. The Jesuits used to be cited as claiming that if they had control of a child until the age of 7, that child would forever remain true and faithful to the church. Such claims have never been supported in any controlled studies. Freud claimed that early experiences of a traumatic nature, for example, witnessing the primal scene—that is, sexual intercourse of the parents—could have devasting impacts on the personality. Again, the evidence is wanting. The difficulty stems from the fact that the early years are spent at home in the care of the mother, father, and siblings and that nobody records the nature of all of the experiences a child might have of either a positive or negative nature. Nor can we know how the child would have turned out with different experiences. What needs to be considered is that early experience might have different effects in different areas of behavior or personality. We have mentioned religion and sex, but there are other arenas of experience, notably in the nature of adjustments in learning and social attitudes—for example, reactions to strangers, skills in coping, fears, and the adjustments to them. We cannot just say that early experience is or is not important on future development; we must say in what regard it is important.

The problem of early experience has become a heated one in connection with such efforts as Head Start, where the environments of deprived children are considered inadequate for their intellectual development. The children are taken from their mothers and their homes and exposed to other, presumably more stimulating, environments and compared with children from middle-class homes in their adjustments to school later on. If the Head Start treatment does not appear to be effective, it is claimed that the children were taken away too late and that the operation should start at age 2 or at age 1 instead of age 3 or 4. The argument is plausible, but there are no controlled studies of what possible negative effects of other kinds might be developed by taking children away from their basic homes for some time each day. Any kind of child-care operation designed for working mothers has to face the same questions. There simply is no evidence that excellent day-care centers are either helpful or harmful regarding a child's future. Jerome Kagan, the Harvard psychologist, in his book *Infancy,* questions the common assumptions about the impact of early experience and suggests that development is *discontinuous*—that is, not necessarily dependent on previous stages of some kind and also reversible, that is, unfortunate circumstances and experiences need not have permanent effects. Although children in certain cultures may arrive at certain concepts earlier than children in others, the latter can catch up and overcome the effects of poor early environments. The evidence cited by Kagan is not altogether satisfactory, and psychologists cannot be said to be in position to appraise the future impact of current or early experience on a child.

What may be of some importance, although it is still not definitively established, is that children—infants—do learn in their early months, even though they are unable to demonstrate their learning. They see and hear some of what goes on, and if the environment is stimulating in terms of light and sound, they pick up perceptual information of many complex varieties that is later used in the learning of various skills and routines. Professor Hebb at McGill University considered this kind of early learning as basic for future adjustments, but it does not call for any special environments other than that parents show some interest in the care and comfort of their infants and engage in some kinds of interactions with them. Expensive toys are not required, since the children may learn more from the boxes and wrappings the toys come in than from the objects themselves. Certainly, talking to a baby is important for language development; it should, of course, be noted that the kind of talking is going to be important, as the child that hears only loose grammar, mispronunciations, foul language, and so on is not going to be a polished speaker of standard English as an adult.

EATING DISORDERS IN CHILDREN
(See ANOREXIA NERVOSA, OBESITY)

Proper nutrition is an important need for healthy child development, and we can understand why so many mothers become anxious when they think their child is not eating enough. The parental concern may be misplaced, however, for too often the mother is quite satisfied when the child eats a large quantity of food, but the emphasis should perhaps be on the variety and quality of what the child eats rather than on the amount. Traditionally, a fat child is considered healthy, but lately, that idea has been increasingly questioned.

When we consider eating disorders of children, then, the first problem to which we should direct our attention is not the child, but the parent; that is, *the parental responsibility for providing the child with good nutrition.* Are the parents providing a good, balanced diet, making certain that foods are not adulterated with questionable additives? Unfortunately, people generally know so little about nutrition and proper food preparation and storage that millions of American children are undernourished, and their parents are not even aware of it.

More traditionally, the major psychological eating disorders of children include Anorexia Nervosa, Bulimia, Pica, and Rumination.

Anorexia Nervosa.   The child, most frequently an adolescent girl, is terrified of gaining weight and behaves in grossly excessive ways in order to lose weight. These children diet themselves far below healthy weight and often must be hospitalized for emergency treatment. They do not understand their condition or even believe that they have a problem at all.

Bulimia.   Like anorexia, bulimia occurs in adults as well as in children and adolescents. Briefly, bulimia is binge-eating. Bulimic children or adolescents will eat great amounts of food, gorging themselves in short time periods, usually of less than two hours. They eventually stop, often out of sheer stomach discomfort. Adolescents suffering bulimia are well aware that they have a serious eating disorder, are afraid of the obvious loss of control of eating, and may even become depressed over their repeated failures to control it. They try, repeatedly, to control eating and to lose weight by going on severely restrictive crash diets, using medications to curb the appetite, and forcing themselves to vomit after a large binge. But they soon go on another binge, gain back all their weight, and again experience failure, anxiety, self-reproach, and depression.

Pica.   Infants put almost anything they can into their mouths. It is, in part, one way for them to explore the world, to find out what things are like, and to provide themselves with stimulation through the taste and feel of different substances. This behavior, completely normal in infants, is potentially dangerous where parents do not adequately supervise the home. Many cases occur in which little children are injured or killed because careless parents leave toxic or otherwise injurious substances or things within the child's reach.

Pica refers to an abnormal exaggeration of that normal mouthing—that is, the child persistently eats non-nutritional things, such as dirt (soil, sand), plaster, paint chips, hair, and the like. If the behavior persists for more than a month, then the diagnosis of pica is made. This is no accidental ingestion of inedible substances, as often happens with normal children; children with pica seem to prefer and actively to seek out these substances to eat, no matter how often they are corrected. The parents must be particularly careful to supervise these children. Sometimes children with pica are injured by what they eat. For example, lead poisoning occurs with the ingestion of lead-based plaster and paint; eating hair might lead to hair-ball tumors and subsequent intestinal blockage.

Pica is found most often in mentally retarded or psychotic children, often in economically poor homes with undereducated parents, but it is also found, at times, in children of average intelligence and higher social-class homes. Ordinarily, it disappears by age 5. Very little is known about its causes and treatment.

If parents see this behavior in a child aged 1-5 years, and if it persists for more than a month and appears to be more intense than mere accidental ingestion, they should bring it to their doctor's attention. Usually, a combination of more careful supervision and ensuring an adequate diet will minimize the problem.

Rumination. All infants throw up food at times, just because something doesn't agree with them. Such rumination is a natural and, in fact, a self-protective response. Some children, however, after a period of normal development, will begin to regurgitate their food and progressively show weight loss and poor health. When all physical reasons are ruled out, there may be a basic psychological problem involved. Rumination is frequent with retarded and psychotic children, but it also occurs in otherwise normal children. All efforts should be made to find physical causes and treatment, since the disorder is life-threatening. Changes in diet, calming down both child and parent at mealtimes, and feeding only small amounts several times a day might help. Probably most important is to reduce the tension and anxiety that the parents must feel every time they feed the child, knowing that vomiting will probably occur. In some instances, the feeding situation becomes highly emotional, with both child and parent extremely upset and the parent becoming punitive in force-feeding the child. If that situation prevails, it is probably best to have someone else feed the child while the parents learn how to control their own behavior better and to gain more child-feeding skills.

Overeating and Obesity. Many children develop overeating habits, largely because of the eating behaviors they learn from their parents. Children's diets should be carefully controlled by checking weight gains and/or losses. Pediatricians can specify appropriate foods and amounts that will prevent the accumulation of fat cells, now suspected to be important determinants of future obesity.

EIDETIC IMAGERY   *(See IMAGERY, SPEED READING)*

At one time, it was thought that children, or at least some of them, can and do have very good imagery, amounting, in the case of visual imagery, to something like a picture of some previously observed object or event. When children are able to give relatively precise descriptions of fairly complicated scenes or pictures, they are said to possess *eidetic imagery,* the *eid-* from Greek for idol, suggesting something substantial. Research has not confirmed the notion that children are especially good at describing previously observed stimuli any more than adults, although it was at one time popular among psychologists to believe that the capacity for having images decreased with growth and development as the use of language and symbols becomes more prominent. Nowadays, the acceptance of imagery as a common tool of thinking is far more prevalent than it was just a decade or so ago.

After the camera was invented, people with especially vivid imagery were described as having photographic minds, and wild stories were told of people who could glance at a page of print and report every word on the page. The highest probability is that no one can report more than seven words seen at a glance, and if anyone can do better, he or she probably has studied the page beforehand. A photographic mind would enable anyone to memorize the *Encyclopedia Britannica* as fast as he or she could turn the pages and would result in the most informed man or woman in the world. He or she obviously does not exist. The best that most of us can do is give only rough and fragmentary reports of what we see and what we image. We have no reason, however, to doubt that we, or animals in general, have images and that what we call our memory amounts to what imagery is evoked by questions or other stimuli.

ELECTROCONVULSIVE (ELECTROSHOCK) TREATMENT

Electroconvulsive or *electroshock treatment* (ECT) was developed in the late 1930s after a Budapest psychiatrist, Von Meduna, observed that schizophrenia was rare among people who suffered from epilepsy. In those few cases where schizophrenic patients were also epileptic, their schizophrenic symptoms seemed to subside following an epileptic seizure. Perhaps, he thought, the convulsions somehow controlled or reduced schizophrenia. Then, why not try to induce convulsions artificially in schizophrenic patients and see if their symptoms, like those of the epileptic-schizophrenics, disappeared? Meduna tried a variety of chemicals to induce convulsions. Among them, he tried metrazol, which not only made his patients highly fearful but apparently caused many deaths in the treatment. The use of metrazol to produce convulsions gradually dropped out.

In 1938, two Italian psychiatrists, Cerletti and Bini, developed the use of electric current to produce convulsions. The patient lies on a bed and is given muscle-relaxing drugs to reduce injury during convulsions. An electrode is placed on each side of the head, and an electric current of about 150 volts is passed through the brain for about one or two seconds. This causes immediate massive convulsions and unconsciouness. Nurses and aides hold the patient down. On awakening, the patient is disoriented for a period of minutes to hours and cannot remember anything about the shock and some period after it.

In the 1940s and 1950s, electroconvulsive treatment was a common approach in mental hospitals and even in psychiatrists' private offices. Mental patients, both adults and children, were being shocked in seemingly wholesale numbers as standard practice, some patients receiving hundreds of shocks over a period of years. Psychiatrists are not trained scientists, and those who used electroshock seemed to accept it uncritically, never testing to see if it really worked or if it caused negative side effects, such as damage to the brain.

In the 1950s, research data began to accumulate that showed that the shock treatment was not effective treatment for psychotics generally. It did have good effects on some seriously depressed adults, but not on mental patients generally. Further, the data suggested that continued use of many shock treatments for any one person could lead to brain damage. The earlier, wholesale use of electroshock had been a serious mistake.

Today, it is usually limited to use with depressed patients. When muscle-relaxant drugs are used to minimize injury, and when the number of treatments is kept low, then ECT does appear effective and safe for depressed patients. It is still not known why it seems to work.

One of the continuing controversies concerns the use of electroshock treatment with children. Some psychiatrists, both in private practice and in mental hospitals, use it to treat schizophrenic children. Psychiatrist Lauretta Bender recommends its use with psychotic children and believes it is particularly useful if the children are given electroshock *before age 7*. At this date, despite those clinical reports by Bender and a few others, there is not enough sound scientific evidence to warrant the continued use of so radical a treatment with children, and it should be stopped.

ERRORS   (See ACCIDENTS, HUMAN FACTORS)

"To err is human," said Alexander Pope. We all make mistakes every day, but most of them do not matter because the situation in which we make some small error is not itself important. Spilling a bit of sugar on the kitchen counter is a mistake, but hardly one to worry over. If someone always spills a little sugar, it might become irritating to him- or herself or others and constitute a problem. A mistake in driving a car that results in killing the driver is uncorrectable. Before we worry about errors and mistakes, we have to evaluate their frequency and importance.

Actually, we are always making some kind of mistake. It all depends on the criterion that is established. Suppose that we are shooting at a target. The bull's eye is in the center of the target, but it has a certain area, and one rarely hits the exact center—if he or she gets into the area at all. We accept a certain range or degree of variation as natural. No one is perfect at all times in everything. Depending then, on the criterion, we do not expect to duplicate any performance in exactly the same way.

When we examine the variations that we can now call *errors* or *deviations*, we find that they are of two kinds: constant and variable. Constant errors represent some kind of bias in performance. Going back to target-shooting as an example, if we always or most often hit to the left of the target center, we are showing a left bias, or a left constant error. If our shots go left, right, up, and down as far as the center is concerned, then we are making variable errors. Recognizing constant errors allows us to correct for the bias. In archery, for example, if the wind is from the right, we aim to the right of the target instead of at the target. The wind will carry our arrow to the target if we allow sufficiently for the wind. A golf slice or some other constant error like putting too strongly can also be corrected. There is little that can be done easily about variable errors, since each is due to a different reason or set of circumstances. In order to develop some improvement, each effort must be analyzed, and the conditions responsible for the error must be eliminated one by one.

EXTINCTION   (See CONDITIONING)

The boy who cried "wolf" illustrates the essence of *extinction*. The shepherds in the nearby field did not come after the boy had fooled them twice. Ivan Pavlov, the formulator of the theory of conditioning, noted that if he failed to provide food after a dog had been trained to salivate whenever a bell rang, the salivation would begin to decrease in quantity until it ceased entirely after a few bells unaccompanied by food. He called such a cessation of responding *extinction*. The term, however, does not mean that the response has been eliminated in the sense of never being able to occur again. The dog would salivate normally to any presentation of food and could be reconditioned quickly. All that extinction means, then, is that a particular response to a specific stimulus can be reduced to zero if no reinforcer is provided. In general, then, learned habits will decline in strength and frequency if they are not followed by reinforcement. Parents can expect various kinds of undesirable behavior to disappear if they make sure that the child does not get whatever the reinforcer for the behavior might be. A child who throws a temper tantrum, for example, presumably wants to get his or her way or some desirable outcome. If the parent leaves the room and lets the tantrum continue, the child will stop the action after perhaps six to nine tantrums. The trouble is that the parent may think the child could harm him- or herself (and he or she could), and so the parent gives in. Similarly with crying. It is difficult to leave a child crying in his or her crib if one is not sure that he or she is safe, that he or she is not suffering from some colic or other condition, and that he or she will not cry him- or herself into some exhaustion, with some other negative effects likely. Instead of using extinction exclusively, the parent could try *counter-conditioning*—that is, try to get the child to do something else that can be reinforced in the presence of the stimuli, circumstances, or conditions when the child is doing something undesirable. A crying child normally ceases crying when picked up. What is happening is that crying is extinguishing or being stopped by a counter-conditioning operation. The problem, of course, is to prevent the crying in the first place by introducing a distractor (a reinforcer) before the crying starts, if the child can be gotten to behave in some other way. Teachers are often told to ignore a disturbing pupil and anticipate the extinction of the behavior. The difficulty here is that the child may be reinforced by his or her classmates and strengthen the behavior while the patient teacher continued to ignore him or her. Counter-conditioning is not easy, and if even an occasional reinforcement slips in, the conditioning will be stronger than ever. The basic notion underlying extinction is that the behaver learns something else, but that something else should not be left to chance, as it may be worse than the original behavior. If a rude and impudent child is trying to get the teacher's attention and ordinary misbehavior does not succeed, he or she may try something far worse. It is easy enough to extinguish a dog's salivary response, since no one will get disturbed if a laboratory dog is temporarily without food. In order to extinguish behavior, one must have rather complete control and be aware of all the potential hazards and consequences. The use of extinction procedures, then, by parents, teachers, and other child caretakers, is ordinarily not a realistic, practical solution to problems.

EXTRASENSORY PERCEPTION (ESP)   *(See PARAPSYCHOLOGY)*

If you believe in ESP, you probably think there is something to astrology, UFOs, exorcism, and most of the other fantasies peddled by the press, television, and an uneducated superstitious culture, and probably nothing can be done for you. You will probably argue that there is no proof *against* these fictions and will be awed by clever tricksters who appear to bend spoons by merely looking at them. In the special case of ESP or so-called *extrasensory perception,* you should recognize that there is no proof for such claims as are advanced. Proof would require an experimental demonstration that similar results would not be obtained if ESP was withheld or not present; there is no way to keep ESP out of an experiment, as no one knows how to do so. It is therefore impossible to conduct a controlled experiment in ESP because a controlled experiment would include a condition where ESP was deliberately excluded.

Guessing cards is a matter of chance. Think how well you could do at poker if you could see someone's hole card! So far, no one has been found who has such an ability even part of the time, where, in a normal game, there is much information from other cards and the betting. Even if you suspect that a person is holding, say, a king, you cannot be sure which king it is unless all the other kings are exposed. When many thousands of people venture guesses, some of them can be correct merely by chance. They can be lucky for even a large number of trials, but sooner or later, they all revert to chance. No one has yet been found who can consistently report a set of cards at anything above chance frequencies. Some people do have runs of luck, but then they get runs of bad luck. Supporters of the nonsense will then claim that the individual *had* the ability but has now lost it or that it isn't working at the moment, especially if there are critical people about.

EYE-WITNESS TESTIMONY   *(See ILLUSIONS)*

"I saw it with my own eyes" is commonly taken to be proof or evidence of some event and is regarded in court as the best testimony. In many instances, it is the best kind of evidence if we can assume that the person making the statement is truthful and is not personally involved with the outcome or consequences of his or her report. Psychologists have frequently staged dramatic episodes in classrooms to demonstrate that the students will not be able to give very accurate accounts of what happened. Such studies, however, only demonstrate that when you are not prepared to observe something, and when that something happens quickly in the midst of a lot of confusion, or when many things are happening at once, you are unlikely to be able to give an accurate statement.

You can believe the evidence of your own eyes only when you are able to examine something relatively simple at leisure and when you are, in a sense, a trained observer; that is, when you have experience in examining similar samples of objects or events. An umpire calling a close play at first base in a baseball game may usually be trusted, although television instant replays have provided evidence that even umpires can be wrong, if the play is very close. Note that the umpire is trained to make such observations and that he is in a position to see what goes on; the event is relatively simple, and normally, there is no great amount of confusion. Note also that the interested parties (the players and managers involved) may have violent disagreements about the decision.

Before any weight can be placed on *eye-witness testimony,* then, one must be assured of the objectivity of the observer, his or her experience, his or her opportunity to observe, and the complexity of the event. Another factor to consider is the time since the observation, since it is unlikely that one will remember an event with great accuracy and detail as the time since the occurrence passes. People who expect to serve as witnesses should take notes and photographs, make drawings, and try to get corroboration of what they say if others were present. When questioned about an event, one should always ask for the privilege of describing the event without any questions being asked and sticking to that report. Almost any question can be a leading question, in that it might make one respond inaccurately. For example, if one is asked if a certain man wore a red tie, one might be inclined to believe that the man did at least wear a tie, perhaps of some other color, and an answer such as, "I don't remember the color" might make one appear untruthful if the man involved actually had no tie. Questions about speeds of automobiles or times of events should also be carefully considered, since it is unlikely that anyone can estimate speeds or times with any great accuracy. Very few people can judge such matters as the passage of thirty seconds or two minutes.

The simple fact about eye-witness testimony is that it is not very accurate with regard to the actual details of almost any situation. People will not describe a simple table in the same way, certainly not with the same words in the same order. Experienced society reporters can describe a bride's gown and veil with considerable accuracy but probably could not tell you what the groom was wearing. The ordinary wedding guest will know only that the bride wore white. We normally see what we look for and what we are trained to appreciate. Other details quickly become background. Any remarks about sizes, weights, distances, and locations are likely to be erroneous, since we are not likely to be very good at such judgments, and even when we measure a room for purposes of buying a rug, we should measure several times.

The same kinds of cautions must be considered in terms of what we hear with our own ears. If a tape recording is made of a conversation and it is then played back, nearly everyone will say, "Did I say that?" Certainly, the details of sentences will not be recalled with great accuracy. Over the telephone, one rarely hears all the words spoken by the other party to a conversation because of the telephone's own limitations with certain sounds, especially with "s," "b," "p," "v," and "f." One would be wise to refrain from insisting on what someone actually said on a telephone. If a conversation between several others is being reported, the likelihood of accurate testimony is seriously limited. The best testimony is that of motion pictures and tape recorders, if they can be arranged; the eyes and ears are only second best.

In considering testimony of any kind, one must not forget the problems of deliberate lying, pressures to conform, biases of many parties, the desire of the average person to appear knowledgeable and intelligent, suggestions on the part of interrogators, and the tendency to stick to statements one may have made without due consideration just to avoid appearing inconsistent. All of these factors, along with those brought out above, make it rather unlikely that we ever get the truth, the whole truth, and nothing but the truth.

F

FAITH HEALING

Readers of this book will be unlikely to have any faith in *faith healing,* and we will comment here only on the possibility that the reader may want to advise a nonreader. Although the medical world has not yet found all the remedies for all the illnesses that strike people, the scientific approach to evaluating cures is reasonably well developed, and appropriate agencies have been established to license the use of various drugs, as well as the people who administer them. Unless a healer has proper credentials from proper training establishments, one should always be wary of any promised cures. The appropriate standards of evidence should be imposed on evaluating any claims. Dependence on religious leaders in matters of health is misplaced loyalty. Responsible religious leaders do not endorse any nonprofessional healers, and when sick, they seek the help of standard medical people. The medical world is not ready to cure everybody of everything, and some diseases elude cures or therapy. In such cases, some people turn to any of a variety of quacks or cult leaders, self-pronounced agents of God, or claimants of special gifts whose chief interest appears to lie in gifts to themselves. Only the naive and deluded believe that the medical profession is trying to keep some miracle drug off the market: The profession is more likely engaged in trying to find such drugs or treatments. When a despondent person turns to religion for physical health, there is not much one can do for him or her. He or she can believe that faith can move mountains. Practical people recognize that explosives and power shovels are the usual means.

FATIGUE

Psychologists have been unable to define *fatigue.* The difficulty comes from the fact that when we work for some time, we find three kinds of changes: (1) A chemical change in the body (depletion of sugars and secretion of lactic acid, for example); (2) a drop in output per unit time—this is common but not universal; people can keep pushing themselves so that output remains steady for a while; (3) subjective feelings of discomfort, aches, and pains, along with feelings of boredom. The three different factors are not strongly correlated, so that a person can feel fine while his or her output drops markedly, or vice versa. He or she may be using up energy and still feel quite effective and show little or great drops in productivity. Studies in fatigue usually make use of the *work decrement* as one objective measure of how the work is progressing, quite without regard to feelings or physiology. The pattern of work decrement appears to differ from one individual to another. Some people (at some tasks) appear to be steady and regular workers; others seem sporadic, with fits and starts; some start out slowly and build up; others seem to give their all in a short period of work; and so on. The way one works, however, differs with the task, and knowing how someone works at something like shoveling snow or sawing wood tells us little or nothing about how he or she would work at wrapping Christmas packages. It appears that the task itself determines an individual's approach, but the individual will tend to work in the same way at the same task.

Normally, individuals tend to slow down, feel tired, and find the work unattractive long before they are exhausted; there appears to be a built-in protective system that warns us against overworking. If we do reach a point of relative exhaustion, we can recover quickly and produce about the same amount of work after a very short rest. This, however, may not be true for successive efforts beyond the first two. One problem people encounter is that they become accustomed to some pattern of activities over a period of time, and when they change to some other activity, they may overwork themselves beyond a rapid recovery. Thus, shoveling snow after seven or eight months of no snow activity may bring on a variety of difficulties with unused muscles. The obvious advice is not to work long at any new activity.

FEAR OF THE DARK (See LEARNED FEARS AND PHOBIAS)

No one is actually afraid of the dark; it is what might be in the dark that scares us. Most adults are not bothered with this kind of fear, although some prefer to stay out of unlighted cellars at night because of suspicions about animal or other kinds of intruders. Children are usually not afraid of the dark until after they have become reasonably acquainted with their daytime worlds, about the age of 4. At that age, they might begin to ask for night lights or manifest other concerns about the dark. According to Professor Hebb, the Canadian psychologist, the problem is not with the dark as such (many children will cover their heads and be in complete darkness) but rather with the semidark, such as commonly prevails. In the semidarkness, various familiar objects take on unusual shapes and appearances and lack color and detail, so that they appear to be rather novel forms with which one cannot deal appropriately. It is this novelty or unfamiliarity that induces the fear. In a darkened room, if one must go through it, obstacles cannot be perceived accurately or distinguished readily. One becomes incompetent in a situation that he or she normally handles easily. The fear of the dark is, in principle, no different from the fear of any unfamiliar object, animal, or situation. One is unprepared by experience to ignore or handle such objects or situations. The normal reaction is, therefore, one of puzzlement, insecurity, and, in some instances, fear. In the case of the dark, as with the problem of snakes or other unfamiliar animals, children are also influenced by parental activities, such as denying permission for children to go outside because it's dark and similar warnings about a dangerous world out there. A child can readily imagine a variety of animals or strange creatures in the unusual shapes he or she perceives in a darkened room.

The simple remedy of a night light, along with the assurance that parents or other responsible parties will be close by, is usually enough to overcome all but extreme instances. In the minority of children who become severely fearful of being alone at night and who remain so for a year or more, excellent results have been obtained through behavior modification approaches. Essentially, the child and parents must agree to cooperate and to try to help the child to become braver at night. Once they agree, then children are coached each night for two or three minutes on keeping themselves relaxed and quiet and then going to bed and remaining there without complaint. Generous reinforcement is given for every successful fearless night, and the child soon learns appropriate bedtime behavior. It is important, in such programs, that the parents also remain calm, reassuring, and highly rewarding when the child succeeds. The help of a child psychologist who employs behavior modification approaches is recommended.

FLOODING THERAPY   (See IMPLOSIVE THERAPY)

Flooding is a little-used behavior modification technique for the reduction of fears. Essentially, the person is brought into close contact with some particular fear stimulus, such as, for example, a dog or a snake, is not allowed to run away or otherwise avoid it, and is thus flooded with anxiety. After a period of time, the person becomes less anxious in the presence of the fear stimulus, and later repetitions of the flooding procedure further reduce the anxiety.

Some researchers believe that flooding procedures may work because of fatigue and response extinction processes. The research carried out to date suggests that flooding may be an effective fear-reduction technique, but it is difficult to manage because of the high anxiety it generates and must be carried out by a skilled therapist. One potential problem is that flooding actually escalates the fear and anxiety response before it reduces it. If the flooding procedure were incomplete for some reason, the person might be left at an even higher level of anxiety than before. There are also possible physical effects of being left in a high-fear situation for a time. Flooding should not be attempted outside of carefully controlled conditions, such as a hospital, and certainly should never be used with children.

A related technique, *implosive therapy,* also uses highly fearful stimuli from which a person cannot withdraw. Unlike the flooding procedures, implosive therapy adds a major element of imagination and fantasy in creating horrific scenes based on psychoanalytic themes in order to increase one's anxiety. The research suggests that flooding procedures are promising fear-reduction techniques, but implosive therapy does not have adequate data to support its effectiveness.

FRUSTRATION   (See ANGER)

Frustration refers either to a feeling—that is, an angry state wherein one feels incompetent to do something about some undesired state—or to the physical fact that one is prevented from doing what he or she wants. What one wants may be as simple as being left alone, although it also includes any other desires one may have, such as sailing to the South Seas or wanting to eat spaghetti instead of steak. Most research done on frustration involves the physical definition after it is established or assumed that someone wants something. It is difficult to do research on the feelings involved.

At one time, it was believed that whenever someone was frustrated, he or she would begin to show signs of aggressive behavior; thus, the formula: *frustration leads to aggression.* In general, the reverse way of putting this formula might be correct— that is, whenever one sees aggression, there may be a frustration situation involved. Frustration does not always lead to aggression, however, as many people do not become aggressive. Instead, they may resign themselves, submit, seek other satisfactions, or just become disappointed and depressed. To argue that such a depressive state is really a form of aggression is playing with the language in order to salvage a theory.

What are the causes of frustration? John B. Watson argued that we are born with three basic emotional patterns that are ready to be displayed upon proper stimulation. His three were fear, anger, and love. In the case of anger, Watson believed that the human being is so constituted that he or she resents, automatically, being restricted in his or her movements. Thus pinning the arms and legs of a child so that he or she cannot be moved should be frustrating and lead to some display of anger. This hypothesis is not supported in many cultures where children are swathed in wrappers of one kind or another for the first year of life and are hardly ever uncovered or able to move. In general, however, such bodily restriction is somewhat intolerable. From such infantile resentment of restriction of movement, it may be a great leap to other kinds of restriction where no physical force is involved, as when one does not receive some desired affectionate response from a loved one. In such instances, the frustration is generated by a failure to be embraced, for instance.

Most people learn to want many things they cannot have, and they, correspondingly, will experience a great deal of frustration. The obvious, though difficult, answer is to train children not to want what they cannot get. The opposite kind of training is more common, and children are encouraged to reach out for success in many ways that are really beyond their grasp. Not all of the students in a high school can play on the football team; most of them have to sit in the stands, if they go to the game at all. To teach someone that something is unattainable may not always work, and the only alternative appears to be to teach someone to do his or her best. Along with such training, there should be a program that results in teaching children that things do not always go right; that accidents happen; that people are late for appointments; and that you do not always get what you want, when you want it, if at all. Parents rarely go about a deliberate program of education for frustration tolerance. Instead, we seem to expect it to develop naturally, while at the same time we urge, prod, and otherwise encourage children to realize impossible dreams.

Failure to teach frustration tolerance means that one form or another of substitute response must be acquired, and this, too, should be the object of positive training, since abject submission or depression are not positive adjustments. The practice of introducing satisfactory alternatives must be deliberately established. Thus, it does no real good for someone to decide that his or her child will be a doctor, trapeze artist, or hotel manager. The appropriate training may not be available. Medical schools have a way of turning away thousands of applicants. The prospective doctor must also consider being a prospective biologist, chemist, pharmacist, dentist, and so on. A range of alternatives, one of which may be met successfully, must be arranged. The old proverb of all the eggs in one basket is testimony to folk wisdom in this situation. More folk wisdom, such as that of Robert Burns's "best laid plans" must be taken into account, since the consequences of frustration can be severe, depending upon the importance of goals. In general, one must teach children to want the attainable without becoming Pollyannish about it. This is difficult, at best, and explains the enormous amount of frustration we have about us in the area of crime and general misery and unhappiness.

G

GAMBLING

Gambling at cards, dice, or slot machines or betting on horses, sports events, and so on is a widespread form of recreation, addiction, business, and social activity. In some forms (bingo), it is sponsored by churches; in other forms (lotteries), it is sponsored by governments; and, in general, it is a fact of life. When one buys a raffle ticket on a turkey for the benefit of some organization, he or she is contributing to charity, but he or she is also gambling. Gambling is not a problem for anyone who can afford to lose, which is the eventual outcome for anyone who gambles where any part of the stakes are skimmed by the house, race track, or underworld manipulators. No one can win consistently in a game of chance, if that is all that is allowed to operate. Eventually, after thousands of plays, he or she will come out even—or close to it. When skill is involved, the more skillful players should win, and they usually do, especially if they play against people who think only chance is involved.

Some people, who cannot afford to gamble, persist in the activity to the point where it can be called an addiction. The reason for the persistence has been explained as an example of the powerful effect of occasional, even small rewards. The persistent gambler wins occasionally. The occasional win keeps him or her going until the next win, and so on. If one began betting on horses and never won, he or she would, hypothetically, give up quickly; but there are other factors to consider. If one bets on a horse to win and the horse comes in second, the gambler is almost rewarded—his or her horse almost won—and it is these almosts that keep the gambler at the betting windows. Sometimes, the gambler picks a horse but does not bet for some reason. If the horse wins, the gambler is again rewarded. If he or she decides that a horse cannot win, and it winds up last, again the gambler is rewarded. On top of all the almosts and near misses, the gambler may enjoy the excitement, the action, and the society of people with interests like his or her own, and he or she may get a lot of satisfactions that are not related to the gambling as such. Similarly, a group of men playing poker can enjoy each other's company, exchange jokes and gossip, and consider any small losses as entertainment expenses. People playing bingo can enjoy the social aspects, the feelings of being part of something, and take their losses with ease. It is only when the losses are unaffordable that the gambler becomes a troubled person who frequently makes trouble for others, such as his or her family. Some gamblers can be cured by more persistent study of the activity involved. For example, the newspaper people who pick winners at various tracks can be followed for a period of time, with the general finding that they lose money in spite of their expertise. An introduction to probability and statistics can also help if that is missing in the gambler's background. Such efforts are based on the notion that the gambler wants to quit rather than get even The latter assumption is much more probable, and there is actually little to be done about the addict. Demonstrations that all horse players die broke are not very convincing to anyone who even thought a particular horse might win and almost bet on him. The "I should have followed my hunch" phrase is perhaps the most potent factor operative in gambling, and, in retrospect, we always have enough appropriate hunches.

GENERALIZATION   (See CONDITIONING, EXTINCTION)

Ivan P. Pavlov, in studying conditioning, observed that the conditioned stimulus, once established, did not have to be exactly the same on later occasions in order to elicit the conditioned response. If a metronome beating at 60 beats per minute had been used as the conditioned stimulus, it would be possible to obtain conditioned responses from metronomes beating at 50 or 70 beats per minute. The greater the difference from the original stimulus, the lesser the response in quantity and speed. Pavlov attributed the similar reaction to similar stimuli to a process he called *generalization*. He assumed that similar stimuli would excite the brain in closely related locations.

In our daily lives, we rarely encounter stimuli that are exactly the same in all respects. We see things from different angles, in different lights, and in different positions. Yet we respond to them in about the same manner. In traffic, for example, we manage to avoid trucks and automobiles of all manner of shapes, sizes, and models. We do not have to learn to avoid each and every type separately. Generalization saves a lot of specific learning and is obviously a great boon. On the other hand, we can easily make a great many mistakes by generalization if a specific stimulus is important. If we run after a person who looks like a friend and tap him or her on the shoulder, we may be embarrassed if he or she turns out to be a stranger. Most of our misspellings are satisfying to us because the words look right enough, and so on. Many really serious errors can result from generalization, as when a pilot of an airplane pulls the wrong control device because it feels right and is in about the same location as the proper control unit.

Pavlov also called our attention to the *generalization of extinction* as another important conditioning principle. If we are not reinforced in the presence of some stimulus that was previously reinforced, we may fail to respond to similar stimuli as well. Such failure to respond may, on occasion, be costly. A young man turned down by some maiden who had strung him along may sour on all women or turn to some other type.

GENIUS   (See INTELLIGENCE AND THE I.Q.)

The term *genius* is loosely used to describe unusual people who are successful beyond normal expectations in any field. Thus, we have military and musical geniuses, financial wizards, or scientific innovators who develop new ways of looking at familiar phenomena. People of the stature of Copernicus, Galileo, DaVinci, Newton, Beethoven, Einstein, Darwin, and similar figures have been described as geniuses. There does not appear to be any common factor operating among the kinds of people who have earned the label. Commonly enough, the genius does not consistently succeed in producing new contributions, but in most cases one is enough. A person regarded as a genius at some period may be regarded as incompetent at some later period; the times have to be just right for some kinds of work to be accomplished, or a genius might go unrecognized. It is also important to note that the great achievers in any field were prepared by backgrounds of study and hard work before they made their contributions. Genius is not some kind of spirit that descends on an idler or ignoramus and allows him or her to create something of value.

In the testing area, people with high I.Q.'s have sometimes been labeled with the term genius if the I.Q. exceeds 140. On that basis, about 2 1/2% of the population, a distinct minority, might lay claim to the title. Psychologists have followed up the life histories of 1,000 children who scored at 140 or above on I.Q. tests and observed that, in general, the group of such children grew up to lead rather successful lives, most of them becoming professional people with apparently good adjustments in their careers. Out of the group of 1,000, no one has surfaced who has made any outstanding contribution to humanity in any area to the point where history books will mark the efforts. The genius category, as measured by I.Q., does not necessarily identify children with special gifts along mathematical, musical, or other lines. Some children do manifest unusual abilities at very early ages, reading books at the ages of 2 and 3 and mastering advanced mathematics by age 6 or 7. The discrepancy between their achievement levels along such lines and their physical and social development is obvious and should be taken into account, but there has been no meaningful study of how such problems should be handled. Children with unusual aptitudes do not usually hide such abilities, and the differences from their peers can make problems, although many cases appear to have no great difficulty.

Although some children do master college-level mathematics before they are 10 years of age and even enter college as whiz kids, their later contributions do not appear to be any more important than the contributions of those who take the usual time to earn their college and graduate school training.

Many important figures in history have had high I.Q.s, as estimated from their writings or achievements, but we cannot ascertain how many high I.Q. people never got into position to become figures in history. A high I.Q. and the label genius is not enough to guarantee achievement. Other variables must obviously play a great part in creative achievement. For example, a now trite but still apt comment is that "genius is 10% inspiration and 90% perspiration."

GESTALT PSYCHOLOGY   (See BEHAVIORISM)

About 1912, in Germany, Max Wertheimer, subsequently joined by Kurt Koffka and Wolfgang Kohler, developed a point of view about psychology that was directed against any attempts at the analysis of behavior or mental reactions into parts or components. They wanted to consider any human or animal activity in terms of its whole nature, and they believed that when some behavior pattern was broken down into segmented parts, the behavior itself was lost as a phenomenon or event. Their original emphasis was on perceptual experiments, from which they concluded that people, by nature, contribute to any perceptual experience by some processes like organization, forming wholes, seeing good or closed figures where only parts are presented, and so on. They argued, for example, that the whole is greater than the sum of its parts. A melody was more than a string of notes, since the same melody could be perceived regardless of how it was produced, by whistling, by a symphonic orchestra, or at different octaves. Their emphasis was on wholes as opposed to parts. In the area of thinking or problem solving, they argued that a problem was solved when the parts fell into place, as in a particular perceptual pattern with the parts in certain relationships to one another. Until a suitable pattern was perceived, the problem could not be solved. When the correct perception did occur, the person involved would experience something like an "aha!" feeling; he would have achieved insight. According to the Gestalt psychologists, problems are solved by insight unless they are artificial problems, such as mazes or other unlogical setups, and trial and error learning occurs only when nothing else works.

The *Gestalt* view was an attack on other approaches to psychology, such as that of behaviorism, and found much favor with people who regarded behaviorism as too mechanical and too disrespectful of the presumed higher capacities of man as opposed to animals. Some educators took the Gestalt view to heart and tried to teach by methods such as discovery, wherein children had to achieve insight for themselves. In teaching reading another application of Gestalt psychology was the look and say method. This approach was based on the notion that whole words are perceived as units and not in syllables, as supposed by those emphasizing phonics.

Gestalt psychology affected some changes in the total psychological picture, and some of its approaches were incorporated into common views. It lost impact with the death of the leaders and is no longer regarded as a specific school of psychology.

GRAPHOLOGY

Graphology is an art of reading personality features from samples of writing produced by some individual. It is not a science in any meaning of that word and is not to be confused with handwriting analysis aimed toward identifying an individual writer. Handwriting experts can often determine that a given message was in fact written by someone whose writing patterns they can study from other sources. Teachers can recognize many of their students by their scripts. Graphologists who make judgments about personality based on whether "t"s are crossed or "i"s dotted are entertaining themselves and others since the pattern of one's writing has not been related to any known personality variables. Of course, as with palmistry or any other examination of the features or products of a person, something can be learned from a writing sample—such things as grammar, spelling, punctuation, neatness, care, or relative sloppiness are obvious, unless someone has tried to mislead us by writing with his or her unpreferred hand or with some other attempt at disguise. The probability of any neatness or sloppiness in writing as reflecting similar features in other behavioral aspects is simply not known, and certainly no decisions about a person should be made on the basis of his or her handwriting. A nice, neat, skilled penmanship might be the product of a dedicated minister, a careful forger, or a blackmailer.

GRIEF   (See DEPRESSION)

Grief is a normal reaction of intense sadness, remorse, and a powerful sense of loss, usually following the death of a loved person. People have also been grief-stricken over the loss of pets that they had loved for many years. Psychologists view grief as part of mourning the loss, and it may be a necessary part of the process of finally accepting that the loved person is, indeed, gone. After a while, the intense or acute grief subsides, and most people return to their usual behaviors. Although no longer actually grieving, most of us will always feel a momentary sadness whenever we think of our loss. In some cases, the grieving continues far beyond normal limits of intensity and time, and an abnormal state or depression may result.

The ways in which we express grief are largely culturally determined. They vary from celebration that sends the deceased person off to the other world through the stoic, near silence or quiet mourning of some cultures to highly expressive grieving behavior. Individuals, too, react differently, and one person's quiet mourning in no way suggests less feeling or sense of loss than another mourner's more outward expression.

GROUP THERAPY

Group therapy approaches were used as early as 1903 but did not become a major form of therapy until after World War II. At that time, they became of interest to professionals largely because they seemed to promise a more efficient way than individual psychotherapy to provide therapeutic services to larger numbers of people—a need that became very apparent in the war years because of the sharp increase in military psychiatric casualties. The development of group therapy as one of the important variations of traditional verbal psychotherapy has continued, not because it may be more cost-efficient but because professionals found that the group approaches seemed to offer therapeutic advantages for some people. It has since become a major form of psychotherapy in its own right and is no longer considered a cheaper and less intensive form of individual psychotherapy.

Eight to fifteen clients with similar backgrounds or problems meet together for regular, usually weekly, meetings that are led by one or two therapist(s). The therapist's task is to use the social structure and characteristics of the group to promote each individual's active, verbal participation. Group members respond to each other's statements, point out similarities with their own lives or problems, give problem-solving suggestions, point out a person's annoying characteristics, and, in various other ways, with the group therapist's support, try to help each other to recognize and solve their own problems.

Of the basic rationales of group therapy, two appear to be most important. One is the idea that the group is a small representation of society, but a safe one, in which the therapist does not allow the group to become destructively hostile. It is assumed that group members will respond to each other in this fairly safe social setting in much the same way that people in the larger society would respond. Thus, group members can presumably safely learn some of the effects on other people of their problem behaviors and of their styles in approaching other people. It is hoped that in the group experience the members become more aware of the social factors that affect them—such as the reactions of other people—and that they learn more effective ways of interacting with others.

The other important idea is the expectation of all verbal psychotherapies, that discussion of one's problematic thinking, feeling, and behavior in a safe setting can lead to understanding or insight into the motivational reasons for the problems.

Bringing together those two basic ideas, group therapy bridges the gap between individual psychotherapy, with its intense focus on a single person's inferred motivational characteristics, and the newer community mental health approaches, with their emphases on external, social conditions that affect behavior.

The United States Veterans Administration's hospitals and clinics were among the leaders in developing the group therapy approaches. Their clients were almost all adult males with military service-connected psychiatric problems. In time, the group therapy approach was expanded in its applications and is now applied to a wide variety of client populations, including children, adolescents, juvenile delinquents, senior citizens, business executives, and many others. Many personal problems, such as alcoholism, obesity, hyperactivity, submissiveness and passivity, vocational skill issues, and many others, have been approached by bringing together people who share those issues into a regularly meeting therapy group.

Just as group therapy's client population has expanded, so, too, have its methods. Groups now meet weekly, or even daily, for one- or two-hour sessions; some groups meet in marathon sessions only once, for an entire nonstop weekend or an entire day. Some groups retain the same members for months or, sometimes, years, whereas other groups re-form after each marathon session.

Groups are no longer limited to the original, supportive, insight-oriented approaches based on psychoanalysis and client-centered therapy. Now there are behavior therapy groups that focus on skill training, relaxation training, systematic desensitization, and other behavior therapy methods. Some groups, the encounter-sensitivity groups, encourage unrestrained expressions of strong emotions—hate, rage, sex. The leaders maneuver their clients into hostile encounters with each other in which the members are encouraged to criticize and challenge one another. Some of these groups focus on rage release, whereas others actively seek to break down social barriers and personal defenses by encouraging physical touching and feeling among members and, in some, nudity during the sessions.

Research on the effectiveness of group therapy tells us that many people—not all—do seem to benefit. Changes do occur, and many clients report feeling better or understanding themselves better. There is evidence that traditional insight-oriented and behavior modification group therapy are more effective than individual therapy for hospitalized psychotics. The behavioral groups seem best validated by research, perhaps because their goals are more specific, such as training relaxation or assertion skills or reducing specific phobic behavior.

A word of caution must be mentioned about the more florid extremes of the encounter-sensitivity groups, which many psychologists believe are the doubtful fringes of group therapy. Some research indicates that such encounter groups, especially where the leader is aggressive and authoritarian, may create difficulties for the clients. The encounter may leave people more uncertain and upset than they were before beginning therapy. However dramatically appealing—perhaps titillating—the encounter approaches may seem, anyone considering joining such a group should be aware of those possible dangers. What the research suggests—and we often have to act on such suggestions—is that verbally oriented insight groups, such as psychoanalytic and client-centered groups, do appear effective for many clients. Behavior modification groups where goals are highly specified are also apparently effective. Encounter-sensitivity groups, particularly the more aggressive and authoritarian variations, are of doubtful positive effectiveness and may actually create more problems for many of the clients.

GUILT AND SHAME

The basis of many personal difficulties is the feeling of *guilt* that most of us know quite intimately on a subjective level but which is difficult to describe in any objective terms. The feeling of guilt occurs only in people who have been trained to follow some ethical-moral-religious principle or set of principles that they now believe they have violated in some way. Thus, if you have learned that it is evil or wrong to steal and you have stolen something, for whatever reasons, you can now feel guilt whenever you think about the moral code you have been taught and the act you have perpetrated. Similarly, if you have been brought up to believe that mothers and fathers should be loved, before you found out how mean, selfish, and cruel they might be, and you now even think about doing something that would make you appear, to yourself, that you were not showing the proper love and affection to a parent, you can feel guilt. Note that if you only consider how other people might regard you, the feeling is more properly considered one of *shame.* You are ashamed when you are concerned about others' opinions; you feel guilt when you consider your own opinion of yourself.

A person who has not been brought up with a moral code to guide him does not feel guilt when he breaks some moral or civil law. People who follow some gang or underworld morality might even brag about their thefts or muggings—even about kicking the old lady out of the house. Such people are described as sociopaths. Of course, if they break the code of the streets or of the gang, they can also feel guilty. Guilt is an irrational feeling. It is the result of a conflict between (1) emotional conditioning, usually in childhood, where no logic or rational argument was ever employed to instill the moral code, and (2) the current violation of the code in some degree, a violation that is also based on some emotional factor. There is no easy solution for the person who feels guilty. Had his or her moral training been more effective and rigorous, he or she would not have violated the code and would feel no guilt; he or she might occasionally feel tempted in some way, but if his or her moral code is strong, he or she does not violate the principles and thus avoids guilt. He or she may suffer in other ways but can also rationalize his or her resistance to temptation by glorying in his or her superior morality. If the moral training was weak, the guilt will not be of any serious strength and will give only occasional trouble. In Freudian interpretations, guilt is unconscious and manifests itself in neurotic symptoms. At present, there does not appear to be any serious acceptance of such matters as unconscious guilts or unconscious conflicts. The guilty person knows full well what is troubling him or her. Some therapists suggest that a guilty person should confess to the person he or she has injured and take the consequences, whatever they may be, since the consequences are probably easier to live with than the persistent guilt. Such a solution is not appealing to most transgressors of their codes. The Freudian solution was to free the ego from the superego, that is, recognize that the code was not necessarily the last word in how one should lead one's life. Such a rejection of moral values is not easy either, and, if it is adopted, leaves the person without his or her familiar anchors. There is probably no solution for guilt feelings that can be provided by therapists of any stripe. Parents might take care that their children are not forced into some kind of rigid adherence to extremely strict codes that call for more than ordinary sacrifices of the normal pleasures enjoyed by the mass of mankind. To make a child stay home all day on Sunday and pray would be regarded as rather outrageous at the present time, although it was a custom centuries ago. To bring up children without any moral codes is similarly outrageous, since they then become sociopaths.

H

HABIT   (See HABIT BREAKING)

Well-learned responses that are performed quite automatically in response to some stimulus, often unrecognized by the performer, are called *habits*. One might have the habit of biting one's nails or keeping a wallet in the left hip pocket. If one is advised in the latter case to keep one's wallet in the right breast jacket pocket one may still reach toward the left hip pocket when the wallet is needed. If you have to stop and think about anything, it is not a habit. One usually does not have to think about where to look to see the time on his or her wrist watch if one has a habit of wearing it on the left wrist. Sometimes a well-practiced habit appears to be so natural that it invites people to talk about it as if it were inborn, or instinctive. A skilled boxer avoiding a left jab does so by habit. He does not have time to think about where the punches are going to land. Most of us develop a whole variety of habits to handle our daily chores. We put a sock on the same foot first every morning, but we may not be able to tell which it was. Skilled typists cannot tell without stopping to move their fingers which finger is used to type "k" or "r." The typing has become a string of habits, too fast for thought but highly desirable for efficiency

Sometimes, habit is identified with undesirable behavior only. Bad habits are in their nature no different from good ones. They are learned in the same way.

HABIT BREAKING

We use the word *habit* to describe some frequently repeated behavior, usually one of somebody else, where the behavior seems pointless or useless—perhaps even harmful— as in the case of smoking or other narcotic habits. If we always wear our wrist watches on the left arm, we do not refer to this as a habit, since it appears to be useful. Right-handed people might bump their watches more frequently against obstacles because they normally reach with their right hands to manipulate things. The point is that, whatever the habit, the individual usually thinks that he or she gets some advantage from the way he or she does things. To break the habit, then, the advantages to the person must be taken into account. He or she will not want the habit broken if the advantages are valued.

We recognize that habits are response patterns to stimuli. The smoker reaches for a cigarette when the coffee is served but not during the soup. He or she does not smoke or even want to in church, in the theatre, in a courtroom, or in other places where no one usually smokes. Given the right circumstances, he or she will light up.

In order to break habits, then, we recognize that we might have to deal with a source of satisfaction—that is, the practicer must want to change his or her ways and give up the real or imagined benefits; he or she must be made aware of what he or she is doing, and we must take into account the stimuli or situations that have become associated with the practice. In general, it will not be easy, especially as we usually want the habit practicer to do the job him- or herself.

A number of techniques for habit breaking have been proposed by psychologists working from different points of view. We can review these and let the reader see which situation some technique might benefit.

Extinction.　If one can discover what rewards, gratification, or other satisfaction are derived from the habit, then it may be possible to prevent the habit from leading to such rewards and satisfactions. When a smoker has a cold, for instance, he or she gets no pleasure out of smoking and frequently smokes less, either in terms of fewer cigarettes or fewer puffs per cigarette. If the cigarettes a person had to smoke could be made of materials that brought no satisfaction, the smoker would give up. Many smokers have switched to brands with less tar and less nicotine, only to find themselves smoking more than before because the cigarettes are less satisfying. Because it is difficult to control a smoker's supply, this method cannot work effectively.

Extinction can work with such matters as a baby's crying, although it is not recommended here. If the baby cries, as some people think, to get attention, and you choose not to give him or her attention, he or she will eventually stop crying. It may take an hour or two or even eight, but if you can stand it, the crying habit will disappear. The baby won't cry for attention if it does not get it. Before you decide that a baby is crying to get attention, make sure that it is not sick, cold, wet, or hungry, that it has colic, or that a pin is sticking into its posterior. Of course, such making sure will provide attention. The extinction technique depends on depriving the subject of satisfaction from what he or she is doing. This is obviously difficult, and other techniques might be considered.

Reinforcement for something else.　If a child is wetting his pants beyond some desirable age—for example, three or four—it may be necessary to institute a reward program for the child to go to the bathroom and take care of his or her problem there. Again, this is not easy, but by disrobing the child and thus making it easy to detect a miss, the parent might be able to get the child to the bathroom in time and, upon completion of the function, confer upon the child some desirable food or object. In order to encourage multiple trips, the child should be given liquids to drink at above his or her usual rate during training sessions or days. The procedure cannot work if the rewards are inadequate to encourage the child to make bathroom visits or if they are not systematically presented. Note that in the reward training effort you are trying to control the situational stimuli that invite the undesirable response. In the case of pants wetting, the child may come to observe the same stimuli, along with the internal ones.

Prevention of the response. This is an obvious technique but one that may be cruel or oppressive or otherwise undesirable and, thus, not recommended. Clearly a child cannot suck his or her thumb if it is tied behind his or her back or is so heavily bandaged that he or she cannot get it into the mouth. He or she will suck the bandage, but this can be soaked in an unpleasant substance. Such heroic methods create other difficulties. The child cannot use his or her hands effectively for legitimate purposes. In some cases, prevention of response is the only efficient way of breaking some habits. If a wild horse is to be broken, it is safer to tie a load on his or her back that he or she cannot dislodge, and after he or she exhausts him- or herself fighting the load, he or she may be safe to be mounted by a rider. For the rider to attempt to break the horse may prove dangerous, and if the horse throws the rider successfully, he or she will only be harder to break by the next rider who attempts it.

Practicing the habit. When a person does something that can be repeated as often as desired, it may prove effective to make him or her perform the response when he or she does not happen to want to or care to. Thus, if the thumbsucker takes his or her thumb out of the mouth, put it back again—and keep doing this until sick and tired of it. He or she may resent it and you, but may stop sucking if you are systematic and businesslike as well as dedicated to the problem. You probably are not, and so this method may not work. If the problem is one where the repetition is not harmful or otherwise difficult, the method has merit. For example, if a person consistently makes a particular error in typing, such as typing "hte" for "the," if the person sits down at the typewriter and types "hte" 1,000 times, saying to him- or herself, "This is not the way to type the," the habit will probably be broken. The method is called *negative practice* and can be used where the subjects seem to be unaware of when or why they are doing something. The procedure calls attention to the stimuli involved, which makes them recognizable so that prevention action can be taken. If a person smokes a pack of cigarettes in one sitting, lighting each from the butt of the previous one, he or she will get so sick of smoking that he or she will not want to smoke again, at least for a while. A repetition at that point might rid him or her of the habit. This is not a recommended procedure, since there could be harmful effects, and other methods might be more advisable in such a habit.

Tapering off. This is not usually recommended, but there is no great reason not to follow the practice of extending the period between practices of a habit until the period is indefinite. Tapering off is a long-term process, however, and works only if the person is really and seriously interested in breaking the habit. In the case of smoking, for example, a locked cigarette case that opens automatically after some set time period—for example, a half-hour—can work effectively to reduce the total number of cigarettes smokes per day, and the individual may find that he or she can extend the period to 45 minutes or an hour after a few days. Eventually, he or she can cut the number of cigarettes smoked to zero. The method has worked for many people, but it is based on the point made in the introduction that the person must be motivated to give up the pleasures of smoking. The fact that smoking is related to disease has convinced many people to give up, and many of these used the tapering off method. If one has no fear of cancer or heart disease, and, indeed, no desire to stop smoking, the tapering off method will not work, since the person can easily outwit a machine and have another source. Motivation to quit is a primary essential, and if it is strong, nothing else is needed. Heart patients in a hospital do not smoke after leaving if their doctors have told them (and they have believed) that the next smoke might kill them.

Cold turkey. The sudden cessation of some habits does not lead to any disaster if the habit does not actually serve some purpose. The person may feel great distress and discomfort—some suffer surprisingly little, according to their reports, and may even enjoy some boost in morale at finding themselves such stalwarts. There is nothing to say about this, since it is not a technique. It is simply a decision that is lived up to by some who are willing to undergo a period of stress and discomfort that is not all that serious with most habits below the level of heroin addiction. In the latter case, supervisory treatment appears to be desirable and recommended.

HALO EFFECTS   *(See PERSONALITY TESTS, STATISTICS)*

The *halo effect* refers to the fact that when people are asked to describe someone or recommend him or her for some position, they are likely to respond in terms of a rather general approval or disapproval or general impression. If they are asked to rate the person on a number of scales, they might rate him or her either high, or low, or average on all or nearly all of the items listed. Sometimes, because they are somewhat sophisticated about such matters, they might give a somewhat different rating on one or two items that they consider unimportant. The term *halo* suggests high ratings, but if one has a poor opinion of some candidate, he or she will give him or her rather uniformly low ratings, so that a "horn effect" might also be considered. Because it is considered unlikely that anyone is uniformly good, bad, or average on all possible measures, any finding of uniform ratings should be regarded with suspicion. All scale positions should be carefully defined with examples instead of consisting of terms such as high, low, average, and so on, since these terms are too vague and open to interpretation by the rater, who may have somewhat different opinions of what the terms mean. We can be reasonably certain that no one is average on all measures, and a consistent rating of average suggests that the rater does not really know the person being rated or is hesitant about expressing an opinion.

HANDEDNESS

This is a right-handed world, and most parents try to train their children, subtly or forcibly, to become right-handed. They know that the left-hander will have some difficulty in such matters as writing, various sports, and handling musical instruments, as well as with seating at the table. Actually, none of the problems is insuperable, and there are no really serious consequences to being left-handed. Most left-handers get to do many things with their right hands and may become quite ambidextrous. Left-handed violinists are rare, but they do exist, and left-handed baseball pitchers are prized.

Being right- or left-handed appears to be a matter of cerebral dominance, although it is not yet known why the right hemisphere should dominate in some people and promote left-handedness. The dominance extends to vision as well as to handedness, and the left-handed person may favor his left eye in aiming a rifle, for example. We are right-eyed as well as right-handed, and the same is the case with the left-handed person who is left-eyed. *Handedness* may be a matter of heredity, but that is not clearly appreciated or established. It does manifest itself early in life, and most parents introduce their own training influences as soon as a baby begins to reach for things. If the preference for left-handed operations is strong, there may be considerable stress, disturbance, and conflict for the child if strong efforts are made to change his or her apparently natural preference. Sometimes, this may lead to some speech difficulties, but such problems may be due to the stress and have no real relationship to the handedness. When the dominance or preference is strong, there appears to be no good reason to attempt to change the preference. Our society appears to have matured to the point where left-handers are no longer subjected to various insults. Even nicknames are no longer common.

HAWTHORNE EFFECT

The *Hawthorne effect* refers to the findings of a Western Electric Company investigation into worker morale and productivity in the 1930s. Female employees were selected to participate in an experimental series of changes in working conditions. They were assured about their job, given access to counseling, and were asked to work in a variety of changed conditions—for example, lights would be increased or decreased. It appeared to make no difference, regardless of environmental changes, since the productivity started to increase from the beginning of the experiment right on through to the end. The girls were led to believe that the changes were all likely to prove beneficial, and the production matched the expectations that were set up. As long as the employees were convinced that they were being treated as individuals, as real people, as participants in shaping their futures, productivity kept increasing. Later, after the experimental changes were terminated, productivity went back to what might be considered normal. The changes were attributed to the personal interest shown in the workers and to the novelty of the changes. Whenever any new condition is introduced, one may look for some such novelty effect. New drugs are frequently found to be very effective in curing diseases as are organizational changes, as long as the innovators maintain an enthusiastic and energetic level of operation. With time, the novelty wears off, and conditions tend to regress. The Hawthorne effect, then, is a label for a change brought about by boosts in morale, enthusiasm, additional activity, or energy consumption that may not be maintained for long but that might be well expected.

HEADACHE

Headaches can be caused by organic illnesses, such as infections, injuries, and tumors, and any persistent headache should be treated by a physician. But most headaches, those that many of us have suffered at one time or another, are clearly related to psychological stress. They are physiological reactions to psychological stress, or *psychophysiological* reactions. They range from mild to severe pain and from a brief few moments to prolonged periods, even days.

In the past few years, research on headaches has increased on the types, causes, and effective treatments of headaches, and some facts seem clear. First, there appear to be two major kinds of psychophysiological headaches: *migraine headaches,* which are somewhat rare, affecting perhaps 8% of the population, and the far more common *tension headaches,* probably experienced by most, and which are at least an occasional problem for about 30% of the population.

Physiologically, the two appear to be different. The common tension headache is caused by prolonged tension or contraction of muscles in the head and neck. The headache is a constant, nonthrobbing pain, often described as a tight band around the head. Although it can be severe, it does not ordinarily last too long. Tension headaches can be relieved for many people with aspirin and/or by resting for a few moments, closing the eyes, and relaxing the head and neck muscles.

The migraine headache is not due to tight muscles. Rather, it is caused by stretching of blood vessels in the brain, resulting in severe throbbing pain. For many migraine sufferers, the pain is often preceded by an *aura,* a vague feeling that warns the person that a headache is about to begin. The aura may include other discomforts, such as dizziness, nausea and vomiting. The migraine can last a few hours to several days and can totally incapacitate the person.

Psychological research consistently shows that chronic headaches are usually related to psychological stress. Both migraine and tension headaches are physiological responses to psychological stress caused by personal, social, or vocational demands and problems. People who experience prolonged or repeated headaches should consult a physician and be examined for possible organic illnesses. Once organic causes have been ruled out, then psychological treatment can be attempted. Both psychodynamic and behavior therapy approaches appear effective in treating psychophysiological reactions, including headaches. Research continues in the treatment of headaches, and it appears that more effective methods will probably be developed. At present, the chances of improvement, even for severe headache sufferers, are good, when treatment is provided.

HEALTH-RELATED AND ILLNESS-RELATED BEHAVIOR

The idea that our own behavior may lead to illness or improve our health is not new, but in the field of human health it is receiving a great deal of current interest. Traditionally medical doctors viewed illness and disease as organic events that happened by bad fortune, providence, accidental infection by microorganisms, or failures of body systems. Illness was seen as something that happened *to* a person who was passive in the matter, a victim of unfortunate circumstances.

Gradually, the realization grew that many human illnesses are brought on not by misfortune or providence but by our own human behavior. Epidemics caused by human beings' own unsanitary behavior in large cities provide early examples. Today, we are quite sure that much of that cluster of diseases we call cancer is caused by our own collective behavior in polluting our environment in general, our work places, and even our children's schools. Heart disease may be caused largely by inappropriate eating behavior and by our level and type of physical activity, as is obesity and a host of related disorders. Smoking behavior causes a whole array of serious illnesses; poor dental hygiene results in tooth decay and gum diseases; and so on. Common to all of those illnesses is *human behavior*. Behavior, the main subject matter of modern psychology, is, to a great extent, causally involved in major organic disorders.

The current professional interest in the individual and collective behaviors that are causally related to organic illnesses recognizes that perhaps the most effective approaches to combatting those disorders are to identify, measure, and change those behaviors. The major psychological questions then become the following: (1) What are the factors that maintain illness-related behaviors? and (2) what are the most effective ways to help people modify them?

All of us would benefit if we became more aware of our own personal illness-related behaviors that threaten ourselves and our families. Illness can still strike, no matter what precautions we take. We cannot avoid exposure in all our encounters with people, different environments, different foods, and so on. Yet it will pay to consider the risks involved before we take them and to make the necessary investment in personal and family hygiene.

A meaningful personal action is to avoid spreading our own illnesses by going to work, schools, or social functions when we are ill, simply because of some sense of obligation or misguided pride.

HEREDITY   *(See DOWN'S SYNDROME, INTELLIGENCE TESTS, SEX DIFFERENCES)*

You were born because an egg cell furnished by your mother was fertilized by a sperm cell provided by your father. Both egg and sperm at the time of fertilization contained 23 chromosomes. These chromosomes are so called because they can be stained or colored (chrome) and observed as colored bodies (somes) under a microscope. The fertilized egg contains 46 chromosomes or 23 pairs. The members of each pair contain genes, which are concerned with the development of all parts of your body. Each gene has a different function, so that one gene might determine that you will have blue eyes, another that your hair will be curly, a third that you will be likely to get some disease, and so on.

The genes for any particular hereditary trait are located in each of the two chromosomes involved in that trait. In general, then, you get half your physical characteristics from your mother and half from your father. But your father got his 46 from his father and mother, 23 from each, so that you actually got your chromosomes from your grandparents, 11 or 12 from each. They, in turn, got theirs from their parents, which in effect means that your present 46 chromosomes came from your great-grandparents, and so on back through the generations. The point is that chromosomes come down to you from all of your previous ancestry, although with each generation, there is a smaller proportional contribution. The reason for this is that the sex cells, the egg and the sperm, are passed on from parents to child without any change except for the fact that the sex cells consist of 23 pairs of chromosomes (a total of 46), but you only get 23 from each parent—that is, one of each pair. Thus, if your parent had a blue-eyed mother and a brown-eyed father, you would get from him or her either the blue-eye or the brown-eye chromosome, but not both. If the parent had similar parents—that is, one blue- and the other brown-eyed, you could get either one of the chromosomes, so that you, as a fertilized egg, would have two chromosomes carrying genes for brown eyes, two carrying genes for blue eyes, or one blue-eyed gene and one brown-eyed gene. If you did, by chance, and chance is all that is involved when the pairs of chromosomes separate (just before fertilization), get the two blue-eyed genes, you will have blue eyes. One brown-eyed gene will guarantee brown eyes, because some genes are dominant over other genes, which are called recessive; brown-eyed genes are dominant over blue-eyed genes, and so if either parent contributes a brown-eyed gene, you will have brown eyes. You may have deduced that two brown-eyed parents can have a blue-eyed child if at least one of each pair of grandparents had blue eyes. Two blue-eyed parents cannot have a brown-eyed child. For this to happen, the child would have to have a brown-eyed gene from one of his parents, and if both parents were blue-eyed, they could not have had a brown-eyed gene without themselves having brown eyes.

The physical characteristics a person will display, then, come from his parents, grandparents, and all of his earlier ancestry. If someone in your ancestry passes on a dominant gene, it is possible that you will also have it; if two recessive genes happen to be passed on, you will also possess that physical trait.

Skin color.   A special point should be made about skin color. Here, dominance does not operate to bring about one skin color or another. Instead, two color genes appear to mix and bring about a blend. Thus, a black and white mating will produce a brown offspring. This offspring, however, will have genes for both black and white skin, and if two brown-skinned individuals mate, they can have either black-, brown-, or white-skinned children. Note also that the child of two mulattoes may have a variety of other traits based on dominant genes in their parents.

What do genes control?   Genes determine a whole variety of physical characteristics. They do not control behavior except through such physical characteristics. Thus, a tall, rangy boy may become a good distance runner or basketball player, but he did not inherit running or basketball skills or talents. He inherited a good running or basketball body. Similarly with other skills or lacks thereof. Handsome people may be popular or admired, and such social reactions to them may affect their behavior. Less attractive people may be shunned or ignored and develop other behaviors. No one inherits intelligence, for example. He or she inherits a brain that may be healthy, fully developed, and without any defects; and with a suitable environment, he or she may become intelligent. In a very poor environment, without proper nourishment and medical attention for childhood diseases, he or she may become dull or even retarded.

Arguments and problems arise because people like to attribute the desirable characteristics of their children to themselves but do not like to attribute the undesirable characteristics or behaviors to their genes. Thus, a delinquent or criminal child will have parents wondering, "Where did we do wrong?"—meaning, of course, their training efforts and not their genes. A musically talented youngster will be described as taking after his or her parents if the parents are musicians. The fact that the child in such a case grows up in a musical environment may be ignored. Only rarely do we find musical children without a musical background, and even then, the influence of others can be detected. Arturo Toscanini's daughter had no musical talent. She was, however, it is claimed, possessed of criticial ability. With Toscanini for a father and Horowitz for a husband, there should be small wonder about her critical ability, which we can be quite certain was not inherited.

There is one area of interest where heredity must be seriously evaluated—the area of sex differences. Obviously, males and females differ in some physical characteristics, and in some cases some female characteristics may be prominent in a male, and vice versa, leading to difficulties in sexual identification. The simple fact of whether a child will be a girl or a boy is determined by which of each pair of sex-determining chromosomes happen to be contributed by each parent. The mother has two X chromosomes, whereas the father has an X chromosome and and a Y chromosome. At the time of fertilization, if both father and mother contribute an X chromosome, the child will be a girl. If the father's Y chromosome is contributed, the child will be a boy. Thus, only the father is responsible for a girl child, in that he contributed an X chromosome instead of a Y. Fathers should never blame mothers for the sex of a child, since the mother can only contribute an X chromosome. If there were any virgin births, the child would have to be a girl. Sometimes, the father contributes two Y chromosomes, and the child then has three sex chromosomes, an X from the mother and two Ys from the father. Some current research suggests, but does not establish or prove, that children with two Y chromosomes may grow up to be tall, rangy, aggressive, and somehow predisposed to crime. Since crime is a legal term and not a biological one, there are many difficulties with this hypothesis. In any case, this, too, would be the father's contribution and not the mother's.

We can conclude that heredity may well control various sensory functions through a mixture of genes, as well as such factors as height and weight (given a normal environment); body shape and bone structure; and, possibly, some features of reflex action, including glandular discharges; and, in general, some kinds of susceptibility to diseases, weaknesses, or strengths. One form of retardation, Down's syndrome, or Mongolism, is a direct genetic operation, and some other forms of nervous system disorder, with corresponding behavioral manifestations, are also hereditary. In general, however, we conclude that, given a so-called normal birth and appropriate physical surroundings, including nutrition, exercise, and health care, the behavior displayed by any person is more likely to be a function of his or her training and experience—that is, it is learned. In order to make our point, we can simply indicate that a mother who is constantly chewing candy and who quiets her children with candy and other sweets is going to have poor teeth herself and contribute to the poor teeth of her children. The children did not inherit dental weakness as much as they inherited a thoughtless mother.

HIGH SCHOOL DROP-OUTS

About a million adolescents a year drop out of school without earning a high school diploma, although in recent years the trend has been toward a slight decrease in school drop-outs, reaching about 800,000 a year. Young people drop out for many reasons—intellectual, social, and personal. It is very rare that financial need is the real reason for dropping out. In almost all cases, failure to complete school leaves the adolescent at a marked disadvantage upon entering the job market. Starting off one's work career at such a disadvantage leaves the young person with reduced chances for future occupational success. Those most seriously harmed by the lack of schooling are the young people who have the intellectual ability to succeed academically but who, for personal reasons, choose to drop out.

It is difficult to persuade a pregnant teenager or academic failure to remain in school, but the alternative in today's technological society is to work at low-level jobs— if one can be employed at all. A high school diploma is a kind of minimal credential for employment of any kind, and one kind or program or another can be completed by anyone who completed grade school. A high school diploma does not guarantee even so much as minimal literacy, as is shown by those who sue their schools for failure to educate them, but failure to obtain that diploma will lead to continual embarrassment for the rest of one's life, since the item, "Education completed—," appears on all kinds of application blanks.

In individual cases, there may be good reasons why some person might want to drop out of secondary school, but that person should not expect anyone else to take the time and trouble to understand the reasons. It will regularly be taken as a sign of incapacity or of some personality disorder. The high school drop-out will be welcome only in the society of high school drop-outs.

HOMOSEXUALITY

Our modern acceptance of what is normal sexual behavior is much broader than it was one or two generations ago. We recognize now that some sexual behavior is not necessarily associated with psychological disturbances. For example, very recently, the American Psychiatric Association changed its diagnostic system so that *homosexuality* is no longer considered a disorder in need of treatment. Rather, it is now considered an alternative sexual behavior, a preference expressed by some people, but not necessarily normal for all people. It is now recognized that homosexuals are no more psychologically disturbed than are heterosexuals; that, just like heterosexuals, they can live to any degree of good to poor psychological adjustment. The condition of homosexuality itself is no longer considered to be a disorder.

For the most part, the problems that are specific to homosexuality do not arise from the homosexual condition itself but occur in relation to the degree or acceptance and rejection by society—problems in obtaining a job or promotions, being socially accepted by so-called straight people, and so on. The rest of society still has difficulty accepting the presence of homosexuals, and most states still have restrictive laws against homosexuality. In time, however, there may be increased tolerance for the rights of homosexuals.

Homosexuality—or sexual preference for members of one's own sex—includes male homosexuality, lesbianism (female homosexuality), and bisexuality, where the person has continued experience with both male and female sex partners. There are stereotypes of the male homosexual as a prissy, prancing, and smirking effete and of the lesbian as a mannishly tough woman with wide shoulders and a deep voice. Of course, these are only stereotypes and do not describe most homosexuals, who are usually indistinguishable from heterosexuals in most ordinary social situations.

The origin of homosexuality is not clear. Whether it is a matter of physiological disposition or early life experiences has not been established. Homosexual practices were common before ancient Greek civilization gave it recognition and status. Freud thought of it as a regular stage in sexual development that normally gave way to heterosexuality. For Freud, homosexuality was a matter of failure to develop and was not a matter for treatment. The current view is that treatment should be a matter of personal choice for those who might want it. According to Masters and Johnson, 60% of those who do seek treatment can become heterosexual within about six months of sex therapy.

The majority of homosexuals are content with their homosexuality. They function in responsible social roles and experience no more psychological disorders than do heterosexuals. Long-term affectionate relationships are more common among lesbians than between male homosexuals. The latter seem to emphasize the sexual aspects more than the relationship aspects. Recently, public homosexual marriages have been performed, with some ceremonies conducted by priests or ministers, some of whom are open homosexuals.

In most cities, gay communities have developed where homosexuals, not easily tolerated as fully integrated members of general society, seek out each other's company in homosexual bars and other public meeting places. The recent emergence of homosexuals out of the closet will probably create some social changes as the struggle for gay rights develops.

HONESTY   (See TRAITS, TEST-TRAIT FALLACY)

Honesty as a character trait is probably never fully realized. To be completely honest one would never steal, cheat, lie, leave a wrong impression, not tell the whole truth, and so on. Some people try to be honest. They say, "Honesty is the best policy," but this is, itself, a dishonest statement. It merely means that one might get caught if he or she is not careful. It is essentially a selfish position, a concern that one will be thought of poorly or otherwise harmed. Honesty as a virtue is supposed to be pure and unmotivated. As such, it probably does not exist. We all tell lies, for example, to children about Santa Claus and tooth fairies; little white lies turn out to be convenient and sometimes beneficial to all concerned. Doctors may not tell some patients that they are about to die.

Dishonesty is more or less rampant. H. Hartshorne and M. May, in a famous study of children's honesty, found that most, if not all, children will lie, steal, and cheat on examinations if the motivation is strong. A bright child who is sure to get top grades does not need to cheat. He or she might steal, however, if he or she needs something and has no money with which to purchase the desired article. A child that does not steal may have no need to, but he or she might lie and cheat. People who return found wallets with the money intact may get their names in the papers, and might even be honest in that respect, but we can be reasonably certain that they did not need the money desperately. Most wallets are returned, minus the money—indicating some honesty. One should not pride him- or herself on honesty if the temptations faced are not great. Some people, like spies, are paid to be dishonest. Husbands and wives who cheat on each other may consider it unwise to be honest about their affairs. To be honest is sometimes to be brutally frank or merely brutal. What to teach children becomes a problem. They see others cheat on tests and gain some kind of distinction. The cheaters manage to create and maintain a kind of underworld morality where it becomes improper to report the violations. The educational system refuses to create cheat-proof tests and maintains a competitive atmosphere that supports dishonesty. The best parents can do is to teach their children about the real world and about how to work for a better one and to set examples of virtuous behavior themselves.

HUMAN FACTORS   (See ERRORS, FATIGUE, REACTION TIME, SENSORY THRESHOLDS)

During and after World War II, psychologists became involved in what used to be the work of efficiency experts back in the early years of the century. During the war, large numbers of people had to be put to work in the military or in industry without the necessary prior training, and psychologists became interested in ways of speeding up the training or modifying the tools and instruments or machines that had to be run by people who were not selected for the jobs by prior experience or expertise. As had been the usual practice of time and motion engineers in previous years, jobs were analyzed, their components were measured, and every effort was made to fit the job to the person instead of what is the usual practice when there is a surplus of employees—fitting the person to the job. A job would be analyzed so that a machine could be built to do it; people were regarded as not quite as good as machines. If a machine could be built to do the work, as in modern weaponry with guided missiles that home in on targets, that would be the ideal. Automation is the outcome of many job analyses, since a machine can function more or less indefinitely and does not create the problems that employees do.

A basic principle of the *human factors* practitioners was that of stimulus-response compatability—that is, every part of every job should be so arranged that a worker or operator will naturally do the right thing. A simple example would be to place elevator switches or buttons so that the up button is always above the down button. Probably no one ever reversed such buttons, but in aircraft or other complex machines a misplaced button or handle might cause a disaster. Aircraft instruments became a special interest of human factors people because of the split-second necessity for doing the right thing at the right time. A pilot should be able to tell at a glance what his or her altitude is and whether he or she is climbing or dropping; similarly, he or she should do something natural when it comes to turning a plane, with both hands or feet involved, and the devices for steering should not require any thinking or decision time.

As a result of human factors operations, many changes were made in the design of planes, ships, submarines, tanks, automobiles, and many other kinds of machines, such as washers, driers, and even tableware. An illustration can be drawn from the interest in numbers and their readability and in colors and their recognizability or detectability. What kind of print is easiest to read on what kind of colored paper? Many similar problems were investigated, with some appropriate adjustments made.

Human factors personnel broadened their interests into such business and manufacturing concerns as management, employee selection and training, advertising, labor-management relationships, and the like. Today, psychologists are employed by the armed forces, banks, factories, and all kinds of institutions where some problem relating to human activity might be of concern. Even the motion picture world and television broadcasters are using psychologists to anticipate the effects of certain productions. In this text, we will include descriptions of some of the findings of human factors or human engineering psychologists under appropriate headings.

The slogan of human engineers from the days of F. W. Taylor, one of the first efficiency experts, has been, "There is a better way." There probably is a better way to do anything if we count efficiency in terms of seconds. Consider the telephone, for instance. In its early use, people first had to crank a phone and talk to an operator, who would make a connection; later, dial phones were introduced; today, we have phones where one presses a series of buttons, even for long-distance calls. It is much faster to make an automatically controlled connection. If one enjoyed talking to an operator, all this efficiency is, of course, of no value. The time saved cannot be accumulated to provide an extra day or even an hour of vacation time. It is faster, but not necessarily better. Sometimes, something of value is lost when one becomes too efficient. Money saved by one person sometimes means money lost by another. Automation does mean unemployment for at least a while, if not permanently, for some people. Computers can replace people, who may not be able to get jobs making computers. Human engineers are rarely concerned with values or aesthetics, but they have already discovered many ways to improve efficiency, accuracy, and safety in many aspects of life.

HUMOR

Nearly everyone thinks he has a good sense of humor; that is, he or she can recognize something as funny. The same person, however, may be accused of not having a sense of humor if he or she does not laugh at something that happens to him or her and that others find amusing. There is no sense organ for a sense of humor, and so nobody has one; but we all laugh at some things, and the classical question has been why we do. Comedians who make people laugh are very serious at their business and sometimes indulge in very nonfunny seminars about the nature of comedy and what is funny. They have not yet discovered the secret, if there is one. Some comedians are funny to some people and not to others, and someone telling their jokes may not get the same laughter response. The joker then says something such as, "It's not what you say but how you say it."

Most interpreters of humor, from Freud on, argue that we think something is funny when something in a situation allows us to feel superior, to aggress against someone by laughter. There may be something to this view, since people do not like being the objects of laughter if they are not professional comics. Even children resent being laughed at or imitated in some ways. The classical pompous fat man slipping on a banana peel is supposed to be funny because we do not like pompous or pretentious people; and if they suffer some indignity, we can feel, at least momentarily, superior to them. Such superiority reactions can be detected in most jokes where a victim is hurt, ridiculed, or appears to be more stupid than we are. Most racial or ethnic jokes are based on some assumed inadequacy in the subject of the joke, and we can feel superior at someone's expense with no danger to ourselves. Sex jokes typically demean women or otherwise ridicule someone over whom we can feel superior.

Another explanation emphasizes the unexpected. Here, we are led down some path to some expected conclusion, and another conclusion is imposed on us that makes sense in some way that is unusual. We laugh because it is safe to do so in most cases, and the pun or paradox is regarded as clever. Once we have heard such a joke, however, it is no longer funny, and we may resent hearing it again.

In the usual case, the listener is able to identify with the victim of some allegedly funny situation and either can take some pleasure in not having been the victim or otherwise rationalize in a misery-loves-company sense. Thus, in a case where the victim suffers some humiliation that we know could also happen to us, we can identify with the victim and feel that we are not alone, getting some comfort out of it. The point is that a joke makes us feel good in a safe way. Tickling also makes us feel good if it is not crude and rough, and we know that we can control the tickler any time we choose to. Tickling, by its nature, is a series of unexpected stimuli for which we are basically unprepared. Thus, there appear to be at least two bases for humor: (1) the unexpected but safe stimulus when we are prepared for or expecting something else; and (2) a safe way of expressing our own animosity, hostility, or aggression against an undesirable source of real or imagined offense. The subsequent pleasure, satisfaction, or good feeling is what makes something funny to us, if not to others who do not share our animosities.

HYPERACTIVITY IN CHILDREN

It is no surprise to note that children, in general, engage in far more nondirected physical activity than do adults. Although adults may enjoy physical activity, they tend to organize it, to create rules and limits, to standardize it, and to aim it toward some justifiable goals. But children, being children, engage in a great deal of motor activity for no apparent goal or purpose other than the motor activity itself. Children make noises, jump and hop, swing their arms, run up and down the stairs and all over the house as if they were on a playground, and so on. It is activity for activity's sake—aimless, by adult standards, and inherently enjoyable to children. There are probably important learning experiences that the children gain from such activity, but these are difficult to detect and specify.

It is also true and nonsurprising to say that children's high rate of aimless motor activity is frequently very noxious and disturbing to older people—that is, anyone over about 18—who seem constantly to be telling children to sit down and be quiet. In school particularly, we demand that children "Sit down, be quiet, and do your work!"

In school more than in any other place, the annoyance value to adults has been magnified. In fact, it is so annoying to adults, that children's overactive behavior has been classed as a disorder, a problem that the *child* has, called *hyperactivity*. Many thousands of children have been put on drug treatment (methylphenidate; trade-name: Ritalin) for their hyperactivity. Although many teachers, physicians, school administrators, and psychologists use the term "hyperactivity," it is not at all clear if the problem is the disorder of the child or the intolerance of the adult. In one school system, the teachers, administrators, psychologist, and physician began seeing hyperactivity wherever they looked. They diagnosed an epidemic of hyperactivity and instituted a program òf drug treatments for a very large number of children.

Treatment by Ritalin does slow down some children and thus makes them more easily manageable by teachers. But it has its limitations: (1) It does not slow down all of the children dosed with the drug; (2) even for those who do slow down, it does not help them to develop better more attentive or more cooperative behavior; (3) it does not improve their academic achievement; and, probably most important, (4) it has possible negative side effects, such as high blood pressure, delayed physical growth, and increased probability of seizures. All it does is drug some children to a point where they can be more easily controlled by adults.

The wide-scale diagnosis of hyperactivity is probably wrong, and the large-scale use of drug treatment for hyperactive children is probably a serious mistake. Parents are urged to be cautious and skeptical when school doctors or school personnel recommend drug treatment to control hyperactivity in otherwise normal children.

There are alternatives to the use of drugs. First, of course, the adults should look at and recognize the degree to which their own intolerance, or perhaps their incompetence in handling active children, might contribute to or even constitute the whole problem. Secondly, if hyper- or overactivity does seem to be a real problem of the child in school, then a carefully detailed program of behavior modification, *with the child's knowledge and compliance,* should be tried. Using token systems or other reward systems to *increase the child's attentive and cooperative behavior* rather than trying to *decrease* the child's hyperactivity behavior can have good results and is ethically less objectionable.

The major problem, of course, is that using the psychological approach to increase children's attentive behavior requires planning and considerable work and involves a delay before results begin to appear. Drug therapy is much easier—on the teachers, that is—just get the child to take his pills every day, and the child will probably be slowed down enough so that he or she is no longer a major classroom distractor.

Our advice to parents whose children have been diagnosed as hyperactive is to question that diagnosis. Demand to see the evidence, the bases on which the diagnosis is made, and the competency of the person who makes it. Press the schools to develop nondrug alternative approaches. Know that serious side effects, possibly irreversible, can occur. Do not allow your child to be drugged into submission except under the most severe behavior problems—and then only temporarily, as an emergency measure, after all other psychological approaches have failed . The use of drugs is the least-preferred treatment, the treatment of last choice when nothing else works.

HYPERTENSION: HIGH BLOOD PRESSURE   *(See BIOFEEDBACK)*

Hypertension is a euphemism for *high blood pressure.* In the past, it had even a more impressive name, Essential hypertension. What was essential about it was never explained, although it is essential to have some blood pressure. If your physician tells you that your blood pressure is too high or too low, he or she will advise you properly.

High blood pressure is a medical problem, not a psychological one. As far as psychology is concerned, it is known that blood pressure rises with excitement and activity and declines with rest and repose or tranquility, within some reasonable limits. Some psychologists have been trying to teach people or train them to control their blood pressures by biofeedback procedures. Although there have been some small successes in the laboratory, it is probably impossible to institute the appropriate techniques in times of stress when blood pressure is likely to rise. Blood pressure increases with age and with arterial changes due to aging, and little or nothing can be done about such increases at the present time. Regular physical checkups and following your physician's advice are obvious precautions. Blood pressure is now a routine feature of any physical examination and is best left in the hands of your physician.

HYPNOSIS

Usually, people think of *hypnosis* as some kind of special state involving a trance of some kind, during which they become capable of unusual feats of strength or memory and are, perhaps, incapable of feeling pain. Newspapers tend to glamorize the activities of hypnotists as if they were possessed of special talents, such as restoring their subjects to some earlier incarnation. Most of such newspaper presentations is pure drivel designed to titillate unknowledgeable readers. We can dismiss the reincarnation nonsense as just that—sheer nonsense, unworthy of disproof—since there is nothing to disprove. There has been no evidence presented beyond some idle claims that someone today is reliving incidents of some earlier life. When hypnosis is studied by laboratory psychologists, they find that without any hypnosis at all, they can duplicate any kind of behavior that is allegedly possible only under hypnosis.

What the hypnotist does, and anyone can be a hypnotist if he or she can obtain the respect and confidence of the subject, is to suggest to the subject that he or she relax and put him- or herself at the disposal of the hypnotist, do whatever the hypnotist asks, and pay no attention to anything else that might be going on unless the hypnotist directs him or her to do so. Over the centuries, since Anton Mesmer (1734-1815) first introduced the practice as a way of manipulating animal magnetism, it has been convenient to create the condition of complete trust and reliance on the hypnotist by suggesting to the subject that he or she is falling asleep. The condition of sleep has some parallels to hypnosis in that, while asleep, we are uncritical and tend to be moderately cooperative, as when someone tells us to move over or turn over, we might comply without actually wakening. Some people talk in their sleep, and if gently talked to, they can carry on some modest degree of conversation. During hypnosis, however, the subject is not asleep, regardless of what the hypnotist says, unless, indeed, the subject does fall asleep. In that case, the subject is asleep and not hypnotized. Brain waves recorded from hypnotized subjects do not resemble the brain waves of sleepers. Usually, unless otherwise instructed, the subject is in a state of relaxation modified by a willingness to cooperate should the hypnotist ask the subject to do something that can, in fact, be done.

Having, in effect, entered into a contract to cooperate, the subject will respond positively to the suggestions of the hypnotist if they are not distressing. It would be embarrassing all around not to do some simple thing that has been requested. Most people can be hypnotized—that is, they are suggestible, within reason—as when some-one on a bench asks you to move over a bit, you move over. To do otherwise would be to start an altercation or create a scene. It is argued that people of low intelligence cannot be hypnotized, but intellectual limits should not be established in this way, since many intelligent people either refuse to let themselves be put into a condition that they do not understand or have little confidence in the hypnotist. If the hypnotist is a responsible-looking person with titles after his or her name, we are more likely to pay him or her some regard. Even such a person, however, cannot just focus his or her eyes on you and put you under. He or she must establish a condition of confi-dence in the subject wherein the subject is willing to surrender for a while, for what-ever reasons of his or her own. If the subject is looking for some help that is promised by the hypnotist, this will be of help in establishing the confidence relationship. Some people are more suggestible than others—that is, they tend to follow instructions from others without much restraint, and when asked to think of falling when their eyes are shut, they will tend to tilt over more than less suggestible subjects.

When relaxed and confident in the care of the hypnotist, subjects can appear to undergo painful stimulation that they would normally shrink from. Much of what we call pain is really a fear of harm, damage, or the persistence of an unpleasant stimula-tion. If we are told that something will not really hurt us (and if it does not), we stand much more if it than otherwise. Once the fear is removed (by suggestions of security), we can be quite heroic. A skillful dentist, sensitive to his or her patient's personality, can do a lot of tooth drilling without anesthesia. If he or she can convince his or her subject to relax and to believe that it will not hurt, it will not hurt as much.

It is frequently asked whether people who are hypnotized can be made to do something against their moral codes or against their wills. If the person does perform the act, it is difficult to assume that it was against his or her moral code or will; generally, it can be said that a person will do whatever he or she believes is right for him or her to do, and the hypnotist may be able to convince him or her that some-thing is right; in that case, he or she will do whatever seems right. It is probably unwise to blame hypnosis for whatever we do. We could be talked into doing the same thing without hypnosis if the talker is skillful enough and we are suggestible enough.

When hypnosis is defined as a heightened state of suggestibility, it implies that we are in a special state. Actually, we can be no more suggestible than we are, once we have let down the safeguards that might normally prevent us from doing whatever anyone tells us to do. If we have agreed to let someone hypnotize us, we have agreed to cooperate and to follow instructions: We are not in any different state of suggestibility; we are merely less critical. Those who worry about all the harm that hypnotists might cause are misplacing their worrries. There are enough persuaders around to cause all the trouble we need. Popular leaders such as Hilter could get others to do all sorts of horrible things without relaxing them and telling them that they were falling asleep. All they had to do was to promise to satisfy strong yearnings of their willing followers. The followers wanted to believe, and so they believed. Similarly, the hypnotized subject wants to believe; he or she does not dispute or argue, and does what he or she is told to do. He or she cannot do, however, anything that he or she could not do without the help of hypnosis. If someone wants to quit smoking, for example, he or she can quit. If the subject does not really want to quit, a hypnotist might be able to make him or her believe what is essentially true and what no one can deny: that smoking is a filthy habit, disease promoting, a public nuisance, and so on. The additional support to the belief may help the subject quit.

Hypnosis may help people concentrate on some specific point or issue and thus help learning and memory to some degree. Research results here are scanty and unreliable. Anyone who cannot pay attention to his or her lessons won't pay much attention to a hypnotist, but to the extent that someone can be helped to restrict his or her attention, he or she might be helped to remember things. One cannot remember what he or she has not learned, however, and stories of people speaking foreign languages they never learned are just that—stories. Under careful use by professional people, hypnosis may occasionally be employed to advantage in situations where it might work. It should not be the toy of sophomores or used as a party entertainment. That only brings it into disrepute. There is probably nothing to be done about entertainers who amuse theatre aduiences.

HYPOCHONDRIACAL BEHAVIOR

Almost everyone, at times, complains of not feeling well, and most of us exaggerate our aches and pains and imagined ailments. Usually, we do this as we try to decide if the ache is severe enough or sufficiently suggestive of something serious to arrange for a medical examination. Sometimes, we find our complaints and minor exaggerations get us a little attention and sympathy, at least for a short while. Occasionally, we even create or exaggerate an illness, such as a cold or headache, in order to develop an acceptable excuse for some failure, such as missing work or school or not going to a meeting or party. Imagining or exaggerating ailments is a common maneuver, probably recognized as such by everyone. When we engage in it, we usually know full well that we are exaggerating for a purpose, and we may feel vaguely disquieted as we wonder if the other person will really "buy it."

Some people, however, go much further with their imagined and exaggerated ailments and become quite preoccupied with them. Their repeated medical examinations show no organic or real illness, and they will continue searching from one doctor to another, refusing to accept the repeated diagnosis that they are really in quite good physical condition. That preoccupation with imagined illnesses is called *hypochondriacal behavior.*

Hypochondriacal behavior is developed over time, as the person finds that he or she can receive a good deal of positive reinforcement from others: attention, sympathy, excuse from normal responsibilities around the home, or even for a poor work record, or failure to provide for the family. In very extreme cases, hypochondriacal behavior can escalate to the point where the person takes the imagined illnesses to bed and remains there for months or even years, heavily reinforced by the family's attention, sympathy, and virtually complete hand-and-foot service.

The person gradually learns how to be a hypochondriac, how to act the role of a sick person. The hypochondriac is not organically ill, but, in time, he or she can become convinced that the illness is real and act accordingly. The *sick role* becomes a more convincing enactment and, in severe cases, can dominate the patient's entire life and the functioning of the rest of the family. Once having developed the sick role, the hypochondriac then interprets everything so as to be consistent with the role and to support and give further evidence that he or she is sick. For example, repeated examinations by a variety of doctors and specialists in many hospitals and clinics may all be negative—all showing the person to be in good health. But this repeated information does not change the hypochondriac's sick role or the personal thought processes. Rather, the information is interpreted as continued, convincing evidence of how sick one really is. "See," one will say, "I am so sick, with such a rare and complicated disease, that even the best doctors in the best hospitals are baffled, and they can't find out what it is!"

Probably the best way to help a family that is saddled with a hypochondriac is to shift the family's reinforcement—that is, attention, sympathy, personal service, and so on—from the hypochondriac's sick-role behavior toward more normal functioning. The family should gradually reduce and stop treating the patient as if he or she were really sick. Let the hypochondriac know, over a period of time, that he or she is better and is now expected to contribute more to the family and that special arrangements, such as meals in bed and other attentions, are not going to be continued. It is *not* useful to ridicule or criticize the complaints directly, because that strategy would only make things worse.

HYSTERIA   *(See AMNESIA, MULTIPLE PERSONALITY)*

The terms *hysteria, hysterical personality* and *hysterical neurosis* are terms without precise psychiatric meaning and are used interchangeably by the general public. To further complicate their meanings, there seems to be a general view that being hysterical is a female characteristic, whereas males are supposedly more reasonable, rational, and self-controlled. The stereotype—for that is what it is—of the hysterical female has a long history, with the term *hysteria* derived from the ancient Greek word for uterus, which, of course, by definition made hysteria a woman's problem some 2,000 years ago. Although we now recognize that men, too, become hysterical, the popular sex-typed stereotype has been maintained. Interestingly, in college abnormal psychology texts and in psychiatric and medical training, it is still taught that the hysterical personality is usually a female.

But what does it mean to be hysterical? In common usage, it means being irrational, emotionally upset, agitated, and not fully in control of oneself, particularly under pressure. As we noted above, men as well as women behave hysterically in this sense.

A related meaning is that of the hysterical personality; essentially, people so labeled act in the above manner much of the time. Their hysterical behavior works for them, and they come to rely on it at the expense of other, alternative, more adaptive behavior.

In professional use, hysteria is included in two psychiatric categories: *conversion hysteria* (conversion reactions) and *dissociative hysteria* (dissociative reactions). In the *conversion reactions,* the person appears to be suffering from some physical disorder that does not appear to have actual physical causes or damage. The disorders include hysterical blindness; partial paralysis; and disturbances in hearing, touch, and so on. The *dissociative reactions* include alterations in consciousness, such as amnesia, fugue, sleepwalking, and multiple personalities.

Thus, when we call someone hysterical, we probably mean to convey something like the more common meaning—that the person is upset, emotional, or irrational over something. If we refer to the typical female hysterics, we are using an old stereotype in a pejorative way, as a put-down of that person. We should recognize that hysteria occurs in men and women and that it has several meanings, all of which are descriptive but not too precise.

I

ID, EGO, AND SUPEREGO　　*(See PSYCHOANALYSIS)*

Freud recognized three sources of control over behavior and gave them Latin names that somehow came to be reified in much of psychoanalytic writing. Basic, natural, instinctive functions involving biological needs and urges were called the *id*. The id was supposed to be an unconscious force directing natural strivings for bodily satisfactions; in Freud's view, such strivings were primarily sexual and aggressive. The id was the center for the *libido,* another name for sexual urges. The id might be best appreciated by considering an infant's behavior as largely a matter of having bodily needs satisfied without regard to anything else: The baby eats, excretes, and sleeps; cries when cold, hungry, or in pain; and demands instant satisfaction. Its behavior is governed by the so-called pleasure principle.

Because reality and environmental factors impose certain delays and frustrations upon the infant—or on the adult, for that matter—needs cannot always be gratified immediately. A *reality principle* imposes itself. The individual has to come to terms with the real world. Sometimes he or she must wait for a satisfaction or do without it. He or she learns to eat three times a day, go to work, sleep at night, and so on. The culture imposes certain restraints. Recognizing such restraints, Freud introduced the term *ego* to describe behavior that involved taking environmental restraints into account in adjusting to id demands. The ego represents the impact of civilization, reason, learning how to get along, and so on. The basic needs are still there, demanding satisfaction, but the ego recognizes the additional need to plan, organize, wait, prepare, and so on. It is essentially selfish.

Besides the simple environmental restraints that control the id impulses, every culture develops folkways, customs, religions, and moral and ethical views that are imposed on the growing child. Freud referred to such moral and customary cultural restraints that also guide behavior as the *superego* because they were above the ordinary physical considerations that sometimes deny us instant satisfactions. Thus, a hungry person might starve rather than steal food because he or she believes that stealing is a sin, even though there might be no environmental restrictions around that would make stealing unwise—as, for example, the presence of a policeman. The superego is one's conscience. An ordinary thief with a weak superego would steal as soon as the policeman turned his back; he or she would be under stronger ego control.

The Latin names tend to obscure the fact that Freud did make a contribution in recognizing important influences over behavior. By introducing his particular concept of the unconscious, the significance of Freud's contribution was reduced. The so-called id, ego, and superego forces, according to Freud, were largely unconscious, whereas they are quite obviously conscious, in the sense that we all know when we want to satisfy bodily urges, that we obviously take the environment into account, and that some of us are also strongly affected by religious teaching that imposes restraints on our excesses. The Freudian contribution came from his recognition and emphasis on basic physiological drives, which opened new research areas for the physiologically oriented psychologists. The emphasis on superego sparked a great interest in how attitudes might be related to behavior.

IDEAS *(See MEANING, IMAGERY)*

We all have *ideas* from time to time, although no one knows what an idea is. Sometimes we have good ideas, and sometimes we have bad ones or ideas that do not work. Thus, whatever else we can say, ideas are not always correct or beneficial. When we say, "I have an idea," we usually mean that some image has occurred to us relative to some question or problem and that we are ready to describe it. When we do start describing our idea, it may not make such great sense to our audience. Why? Because what we are trying to do is to communicate a meaning, and meanings are what we feel and imagine and perhaps want to do. Our meaning may not correspond to what others image, feel, and want to do. Ideas are not some mental stuff that springs into some kind of ephemeral existence some place in our heads. They might be ephemeral images of how something might look or of how it might behave under certain other conditions. Ideas, in general, are prior to actual practice or observation; we are imagining or imaging how something might be. If we then state something—that is, describe the imaging—we now have a statement, not an idea. The statement, like meaning, is open to different interpretations, meaning that different people might react differently while stating the same words. Thus a term such as *democracy* or *republic* might be used to describe quite different governmental setups in the People's Republic of China, in the United States, or in Plato's famous work.

Whenever we try to solve a problem of some complexity, we may have a succession of images about the possible solution to the problem. Some of these will be discarded immediately because some new image will suggest the inadequacy of the one we just had; we will accept others for a while and work on the new hypothesis, which would merely be a statement of the new image. If that does not succeed, we wait for the new image, and, if we are lucky, it will come along, assuming that our prior experience is adequate and that there is some possibility for the new image to occur.

ILLUSIONS, DELUSIONS, AND HALLUCINATIONS
(See IMAGERY, DELIRIUM TREMENS)

The three terms *illusion, delusion,* and *hallucination* are frequently confused in common parlance. We can make a preliminary distinction by noting that delusions have little or nothing to do with sensory phenomena, whereas illusions and hallucinations do.

Delusions.   A delusion is a false belief. Anyone who believes something that is not true is deluded. Because that applies to all of us in some ways, we normally restrict the term to beliefs that are not common. If someone believes that he is Napoleon, for example, we call him deluded. A delusion can be relatively restricted in scope or expanded into a whole system. A person might have a complicated, interwoven, systematic set of beliefs about life on other planets; that would be a rather grand delusion. On the other hand, he or she might simply believe that eating yogurt will surely deprive him or her of his manhood or her womanhood. In all other respects, he or she might be quite normal and share quite common delusions, such as a belief in astrology. Systematic delusions about personal importance (delusions of grandeur) and of persecution are characteristics of psychoses. People who believe (without evidence) that someone is out to get them are diagnosed as paranoids.

Illusions.   Illusions are misinterpretations of sensory stimulation; these are common to every normal person and are the results of our own make-ups or sensory structures, which do not always tell the whole truth about our sensory worlds. You cannot always believe the evidence of your own eyes, since appearances can be deceiving. It is not our eyes that deceive us; rather, it is our beliefs and expectancies. If you draw a square with a ruler and measure very carefully, the result will be that the square will look taller than it is wide. Vertical lines look longer than horizontal lines. Sometimes this illusion is used to suggest to fat people that they wear vertically striped garments instead of horizontal stripes. The illusion, however, is not strong enough to make obese people look slim. They should try other measures, such as dieting. The full moon always looks larger when it is rising above the horizon than when it is high in the sky. On a hot summer day, as you drive along a highway, the road ahead, at some distance, may appear to be covered with water. Such experiences are common and can be attributed to the way various stimuli affect our sense organs. They are normal reactions, and not to have illusions that other people share would be abnormal.

Hallucinations.   Sometimes, under the influence of drugs or fever, we may report the appearance of objects, people, voices, music, or other forms of sensory and perceptual experience when there are no stimuli present to arouse these percepts. An alcoholic in the state of delirium tremens may report seeing snakes, rats, or tigers climbing all over him or coming out of the walls. People in some psychotic states hear the voice of God or of some other director of their destinies telling them that something must be done. Such people, of course, are in no position to be questioned, and their reports necessarily lack any detail. We cannot ask the desperate and frightened patient about the size or color of the tiger—he or she is too busy fighting it or fleeing. Hallucinations occur to normal people when they dream. Here, too, we have perceptual experiences without any appropriate external stimulation. The accounts that people give of their dreams are no more or less believable than reports of hallucinations, and sometimes they make as little sense. The hallucinator cannot give adequate descriptions of his or her reported perceptions, and we more or less take his or her word for them, but we are not obliged to believe them in any serious sense. Presumably, hallucinations are, perhaps, more intense images or are images of something we do not especially want to see or hear. We all do have imagery throughout our waking lives but we recognize the images to be such; that is, we know that there is no direct external stimulus present, and we take the image for what it is. The hallucinator, like the dreamer, does not exercise this censorship and takes the image as a present reality—that is, as a direct external presence of some object or person. The basis for this censorship under normal conditions is not known; children are notorious hallucinators, with their imaginary bears and other companions. Many children appear to be enjoying the company of some absent friend. Eventually, they learn to distinguish between the real and the unreal. The hallucinator, for some unknown reason, loses this ability, at least while he or she is hallucinating.

IMAGERY   *(See IDEAS)*

When you look at an apple and examine it for color, smell it, taste it, feel it, and so on, you are reacting to sensory stimuli and experiencing sensations and perceptions. No one knows what experiencing amounts to: It is a private, subjective reaction. At the same time that you are looking at the apple, you can describe it to some degree. No description is likely to be complete or perfect. If you try to describe what some person looks like to a friend, it is not too likely that the person could be picked out of a group of the same sex, general size, and age. Just as you can see an apple that is present you can think of an apple if someone mentions it. You can also think of some other things that are commonly associated with apples, such as pies, sauces, or salads. Thinking of an apple that is not physically present is what is meant by having an *image* of an apple. It will be a kind of sensory or perceptual experience rather like looking at the real apple, but this time, you will not be able to describe it as well, in most cases. Furthermore, you know that the apple is not present: If you think it is and it is not, you are enjoying an hallucination.

Normally, when we think that we are having a succession of images, each one is initiating another. At the present time, the best we can say is that an image is a neural reaction that is similar to the neural reaction we get when we actually look at, hear, or otherwise sense something. Sometimes, we think we hear a noise and ask someone else, "Did you hear that?" and are told that we must have imagined it. That appears to be as good a statement as any, indicating that something like what goes on when we do hear a real noise has happened in our heads. In such a case, however, the stimulus that provoked the reaction cannot be identified. "It must have been the wind," we might say, by way of explanation. Normally, when we talk we are, in effect, describing our own images and arousing imagery in our listener. His or her imagery is not likely to be the same as ours because of his or her different experiences, and, to some extent, we must settle for a lack of communication. No one ever really understands anyone else if we mean by understanding that he or she experiences exactly the same imagery that we do.

IMAGINARY PLAYMATES

Creating an *imaginary playmate* is quite common among children, occurring in about 30% of children between the ages of 3 and 10. The playmates are talked to, given names, described, and talked about to other people. The playmates can assume animal forms—friendly bears, horses, even dogs—when there are no pet dogs in the home. Firstborn and only children, perhaps because they have no other age mates to play with in the family, seem most prone to creating imaginary playmates, as are children who are creative and bright.

Around 10 years of age, the child quietly loses the imaginary playmate. He will remember the playmate and will sometimes say "Remember when I used to make believe that . . . ?"

Imaginary playmates are probably good exercises in a child's developing imagination. For the adult who is fortunate enough to be introduced to them, the imaginal activity can be a charming and pleasant interaction with the child. Having imaginary playmates is not a sign of mental disturbance, and parents should not try to talk their children out of such innocent fantasies. Imaginary playmates of adolescents or adults are another matter and call for investigation and treatment.

IMITATION   (See MODELING AND IMITATION)

Imitation amounts to copying, aping, or repeating what someone else does. It is a kind of behavior and not some special agency within a person that somehow controls behavior by itself. Imitation is something we learn to do under certain circumstances. Sometimes we imitate, and sometimes we do the opposite or do nothing at all. When it serves our purposes, we may mimic the behavior of others because we have found that what certain others do may also be useful to us. Imitation is, then, a learned pattern of behavior that occurs under certain circumstances of need and according to whom the model might be. In some situations, we are more or less forced to behave like others: For example, when marching in a parade, we must all step out with the correct foot first and keep in unison with the rest of the marchers. We all learn by show and tell; probably, that is the way in which we learn most of what we know.

An important feature of imitation is the nature of the model. We must approve of the model and, in a sense, identify with the model, or we will not imitate, except under duress. If the identification is strong and/or the need is great, we may imitate despite warnings or admonitions against imitation, as when the frustrated parent finds it necessary to say to us, "Do as I say, not as I do."

The process of imitation has been analyzed by O. Hobart Mowrer, a research professor at Illinois, as amounting to the following: A person we like does something we happen to observe. The action is remembered, at least for a time. Later, when we are in position to take similar action, we remember the model's action, and the good feelings associated with the model prompt us to repeat the action. According to Mowrer, our feelings guide our behavior, and we do what feels better to us.

Imitative behavior is not always successful because we may not be in a position to observe exactly what some model is doing. We may not be able to imitate a card trick because we may not have observed the preliminary preparations, for example. If our observations are inadequate, so will be our behavior. Imitation may require considerable additional instruction if the actual performance depends upon behavior we do not or cannot witness.

IMPLOSIVE THERAPY   *(See EXTINCTION, LEARNED FEARS)*

Implosive therapy is a little-used behavior therapy technique designed for the reduction of severe fears and neuroses. Like other behavior therapy approaches, it assumes that fears and neuroses are learned and that separate fears can combine and constitute complex neurotic conditions. Unlike other behavior therapy approaches, implosive therapy assumes that the content of fears and neuroses develop early in life and that they are organized around the psychosexual stages postulated by Freud. When trying to understand the nature of the client's neuroses, the implosive therapist makes psychoanalytic interpretations about the meaning of behavioral symptoms and uses psychoanalytic theory to guide and organize the information presented by the client.

The therapy procedure involves a verbal description by the therapist of the critical fear stimuli—these are identified in psychoanalytic terms—causing clients to feel extremely anxious as they imagine themselves being subjected to those stimuli. The therapist works hard to create compelling fear stimuli in the client's imagination and to generate as much fear and anxiety as possible. The basic ideas here are that (1) the extreme anxiety felt by the client is much the same as anxiety that would be felt in the real situation rather than in imagination; and (2) because the stimuli are imaginal only, what the client fears does not really happen in the therapy situation. In essence, the client goes through repeated experiences of being extremely fearful but never experiences the real fearful event or the ultimate punishment. For example, a client who fears rats can be made to experience intense fear and anxiety just by imagining in vivid detail being attacked by a horde of rats. But no matter how vivid the scene and how intense the anxiety, the ultimate and real fearful event—the actual rats attacking—does not occur. Theoretically, the repetition of the high fear and anxiety in response to imagined rats, but without the ultimate real punishment, constitutes extinction or gradual weakening of the fear response.

Implosive therapy is a dramatic technique. Some case studies suggest that it can be an effective and rapid method of fear reduction. But, for the most part, controlled experimental evidence does not support it as an effective technique. There have been a few cases in which implosive techniques were used with children, but some psychologists believe that it is too extreme and punitive an approach and, with too little evidence for its effectiveness, that such procedures should not be used in treating children.

IMPRINTING   *(See INSTINCT)*

In the last two decades, ethologists—students of animal behavior under more or less natural or nonexperimental or laboratory conditions—have emphasized a specific effect of early experience on later behavior. They noted that certain kinds of fowl, ducks, geese, and turkeys, at some critical hour, such as 15-18 hours after emerging from the egg, would tend to follow any moving object that happened to be around. In nature, this is usually the mother. Ducklings, for example, would follow the mother around wherever she went. If the object around and in motion happened to be some human, the duckling would attach itself to the human in the same manner and follow the human around as if the human were a mother duck.

Ethologists called such a strong attachment at this crucial infantile stage *imprinting* and speculated that it implied that other early experiences similarly affected future behavior. Actually, the phenomenon appears to be restricted to fowl, although claims have been asserted about some mammals. Even in fowl, the young grow up, ignore their mothers, and lay their own eggs, and become the imprinters of their offspring.

There does not appear to be any reason to assume that humans become imprinted in any way at some crucial hour or day in their lives, either positively or negatively, although the possibility need not be dismissed if one expands the period to some stretch of time where certain things might be learned better than at other times. A foreign language might be learned better by children before the age of 12 or so, at least as far as pronunciation is concerned. This might not mean that they were more susceptible to imprinting but rather that as we mature our vocal habits become more fixed, and we are unable to adjust our facial musculature and vocal apparatus to producing the guttural or nasal sounds of some language other than our own. It is also possible that some traumatic incident in childhood could have an important impact on future adjustments, but the evidence that such incidents are irreversible is in short supply.

IMPULSIVITY—REFLECTIVITY IN CHILDREN   *(See TEMPERAMENT)*

Children differ in their tendency to be impulsive or reflective in various situations. The *impulsive* child is one who wants immediate results, who gives the first answer that occurs to him or her, and who tends to jump right into action without much thought of alternatives or of consequences. The *reflective* child, on the other hand, takes a longer time to answer questions or to solve problems, thinks about alternative approaches and consequences, and, as a result, tends to make fewer errors. In general, the more reflective children tend to do better in school and to be more creative, since creativity seems to entail an appreciation of many alternative solutions or ways of doing things. The impulsive children are generally more daring, willing to make mistakes, and seem to enjoy doing new and different things.

It is not clear to what degree a child's impulsivity or reflectivity is learned or inborn. Such tendencies are reflections of temperament. Research studies tell us that middle-class children are more reflective than lower socioeconomic class children and that highly impulsive children can be taught in special education projects to slow down and be more reflective. Both of these sets of findings suggest that at least a good portion of a child's reflectivity-impulsivity is learned. It is also not clear if children's impulsivity-reflectivity is a generalized characteristic; that is, is an impulsive child impulsive across all situations, or is this behavior situation-specific—for example, does it occur only in school?

Is one better than the other? Under some situations, such as learning to read or taking an examination in school, impulsivity may interfere with concentration and thus reduce achievement. In others, such as new or different social situations, being more impulsive might be an asset, allowing the child to act quickly or more assertively.

The extremes are, of course, problematic; the extremely impulsive child may have reached near-thoughtlessness and probably gets into repeated difficulties; the extremely reflective one may have achieved nearly complete indecisiveness in action.

Because of the lack of facts to guide us, parents can be advised only to recognize the dimension of impulsivity-reflectivity and encourage each kind of behavior in its proper sphere. Children will grow up to be either impulsive or reflective adults, although experience will temper extreme manifestations.

INDIVIDUAL DIFFERENCES　　*(See PERSONALITY)*

One safe statement that psychologists can make is that there are no two people who are alike in all respects. The moment we begin to measure any characteristic or sample of behavior with a sufficiently fine scale, we find that people differ in size, shape, intelligence, behavior, vocabulary, and anything else we care to measure, including their ability to tell one color from another. The notion that all men are alike, as allegedly claimed by many women, is, of course, utter nonsense, as is the opposite— that all women are alike. Not even identical twins are alike when suitable measures are taken. We do have a tendency to assume that everyone else somehow belongs to some more or less general category or class, but we need not search too deeply to find differences among members of any groups.

In the military services, an effort is made to reduce individual differences to a minimum so that everyone walks and talks the same, dresses the same, and behaves the same in the same situation. This is desirable if one has the notion that a soldier is a unit, presumably a replaceable unit. When one soldier is killed, another is supposed to step into his place and do the job in exactly the same way as the previous unit had done it. The army has no time for personalities or individual differences.

Parents quickly note the differences in reactions of successive children, despite their efforts to treat them equally. There is, of course, no opportunity to treat children equally, since the parents will always be a little older and more experienced, and the older children will usually be better able to understand what is going on. In the time period between one child and the next, the financial status of parents frequently changes so that they are able to do more for the younger children as they are born. Toys differ from year to year, just like television programs, and there is no hope of providing uniform environments for successive children.

It is important to recognize that every person is different and to make allowances for such differences. To treat everybody alike may be democratic, but it can also be extremely unwise.

INFANTS' EMOTIONS　　*(See EMOTIONS)*

Parents know that their infants show a range of emotions, beginning at a very early age, and the alert parent is able to understand much of what the infant is expressing. From psychological studies over many years, it appears that newborns display a generalized emotional state of distress that we see when the child feels cold or hungry, is in pain, or is in some way physically uncomfortable. As the child grows older, emotional expressions become more specific than the general distress of the newborn. Emotional states associated with comfort, as opposed to discomfort, become increasingly differentiated in the child and responded to by the parent. Infants are soon able to smile, to coo, to reach out for people, to cry when upset, and so on. Recordings of babies' cries show different patterns of sounds and breathing that seem to be associated with anger, pain, and frustration.

Babies smile spontaneously by the time they are a week old, and the smiles seem clearly associated with comfort and soft sounds. In about a month, babies smile when their hands are playfully clapped together; by about three to four months, they will smile more at a familiar face than at a stranger. The baby's smile is an extremely important part of the nonverbal communication between baby and parent, and it will almost always stimulate a responding smile in the adult: Few adults can easily resist a baby's smile.

By about the fourth month, babies can laugh out loud, and they do so at all sorts of things, such as gentle playing, kissing, different sounds, and the funny antics of their delighted parents. The baby's smiles and laughter are powerful reinforcers for parents.

What do we know of infants' emotions, then? By four or five months, the infant can already differentially express pain, anger, frustration, and delight. Through smiling and laughing, they express comfort and satisfaction; through a variety of cries, they can express different discomforts. As the infant grows, these emotional expressions of delight and distress become increasingly refined and appropriate. By four or five months of age, infants are already able to express a considerable range of emotion that can be deciphered by a parent.

INSANITY   *(See PSYCHOSIS, COMMITMENT)*

Insanity is a legal term, not a psychological or medical term, and its meaning depends on the definition that a legislature chooses to arrange. It usually contains two elements: (1) A person does not know the nature of his or her acts—that is, whether they are right or wrong; and (2) the person cannot refrain from the acts that brought him or her before the law. A third element is also common: The person cannot participate in his or her defense. Such legal definitions lead to problems in courts where psychiatrists are asked to testify. As medical doctors, the psychiatrists are concerned with illness, not with the law. They may find the person charged with a crime to be psychotic even though he or she knows what he or she has done, knows it was wrong, and might appear to have been able to refrain from the act. The latter point may be disputed by a defense psychiatrist, who might also agree that the charged person is psychotic and in need of treatment, not punishment.

The general public uses terms, such as *crazy, mad, lunatic, maniac,* and many others to describe people whose behavior they do not like or find disturbing. The behavior might well be bizarre and extraordinary. If it is behavior that is dangerous or threatening to the person or to others, the police are often involved, and a judge may decide that a person is insane, usually following the recommendations of two physicians.

The term *demented* is often misused in this context. Demented refers to a decrease in mental skills or deterioration of mental faculties, often accompanied by behavioral and emotional disorders. *Aments* are retarded people who have never attained normal mental capacities.

INSOMNIA

Sometimes, one cannot fall asleep easily and may toss and turn. If you get concerned about the inability to sleep, the concern will add to the inability. One consideration to note is that it does not matter if you can't sleep some night: Usually, you do not worry about sleep if you are at a good party long after your normal bedtime, and you manage to survive the next day in spite of some loss of sleep hours. If the inability to sleep becomes chronic, so that night after night you cannot fall asleep, the problem may still be a result of lack of information or poor preparations. Nobody knows how much sleep anyone requires, and you may not need as much as you think you do. You may be able to get along on far less sleep than you try to schedule for yourself. Some people never sleep at all; they rest with their eyes closed, for some hours, and claim that they get along reasonably well. Obviously, if you feel tired, you should rest; whether sleep accompanies the rest may not be important. Shutting the eyes will rest them, too.

If you do not sleep, you might put the saved hours to some use—reading or some other activity of a not too strenuous nature. If it is desirable to be in bed at some hour, a change in a waking hour might be important. Get up early and have a long day.

Some people wake themselves up in the process of preparing for bed. They go through a detailed routine of clothes-changing, hairdressing, perhaps showers, and so on that wakens them from a previous drowsy state that originally suggested going to bed. Such people should go through their bedtime preparations an hour or two before actually going to bed. The extra hour should be spent in quiet and relaxing activity, watching TV or light reading. If you discover the kind of book or activity that makes you sleep, keep that kind of operation as part of the sleep schedule. Reading Chinese history used to put one Russian psychologist to sleep. After some time, the very thought of Chinese history would do the trick.

Do not take problems to bed with you. Trying to solve puzzles or work out logical conclusions will arouse you, as might any creative activity. Counting blessings instead of sheep is probably good advice, but any kind of routine reflection is just as effective. Some people can fall asleep by indulging in simply counting backwards from 100—imaging 99 as two numbers, then 98, and so on. Such a task has no intrinsic merit, but it prevents one from fretting over other problems. By the time they get to 37 or so, they are asleep. The sheep-counting routine may work for the same reason.

INSTINCT

The term *instinct* is in common usage and apparently refers to whatever the user thinks is somehow natural, inborn, innate, or biologically given. Sportswriters are the most frequent abusers, as they describe boxers with killer instincts or survival instincts, or other athletes instinctively doing the right thing. The trouble with such usage is that, for biologists, an instinct refers to a behavior pattern that is universal for a species—that is, every member of the species or race does it, without any opportunity to learn. Thus a turtle that is hatched in the sand at some distance from the sea will, upon hatching, start moving toward the sea instead of inland. If newly hatched turtles do this, we could properly refer to an instinct. When Baltimore orioles build a peculiar swinging nest, we are a little less certain, because the young are brought up in such a nest and may only be doing what seems to be right when they get around to building nests.

Most psychologists do not argue about the facts that homing pigeons come home and that salmon swim upstream to the place where they were born to lay their eggs. There may very well be some instinctive aspects to such behavior, although homing pigeons do get some training in finding their homes. What matters is the question of whether people have any instincts worth talking about. The most common alleged human instincts are those of survival and mother love, but when we consider the number of suicides that occur; the cases of abortion, child abandonment, and sheer murder of newborn infants by some new mothers; or the severe abuse of older children by their mothers; the notion of universality certainly comes into question.

On the human level, it is virtually impossible to find any behavior that is not affected by learning and training in the home. The child is completely unable to shift for him- or herself at birth, and for the first year, he or she is a gross incompetent at survival matters. There is no point to describing any human behavior as instinctive, since in all probability it is not so; and, in any case, all we are doing is pushing back a mystery by putting a label on some behavior that we cannot otherwise explain. Putting labels on events may bring some comfort, but no enlightenment. Sometimes a patient in a hospital may show all the signs of approaching death but fail to die on someone else's schedule. On such occasions, there will be talk of a will to live. The trouble with such talk is that the patient in the next bed, who has no desire or intention of dying, proceeds to do so despite the prognosis of recovery. He did not have the will to live. Such explanations are just too easy and fall into the general class of mythological agencies, such as susceptibilities, weaknesses, and so on. Again, we must be careful not to be too cavalier about what someone may be born with: He or she may have hereditary features that make him or her a more likely candidate for some diseases that other people, even those in his or her own family, do not have. Such hereditary factors, when established beyond doubt, are real enough, but they are not instincts. Instincts are supposed to refer to behavior patterns, not diseases.

INSTRUMENTAL BEHAVIOR   (See CONDITIONING, LEARNING)

Instrumental behavior refers to any response that is not a direct reflex reaction to some specific identifiable stimulus. Thus, a sneeze is a reflex. (Even if we do not know exactly what the stimulus is, if we have just seen someone take snuff, and if this is followed by a sneeze, we suspect the snuff to be the stimulus.) If a person presses a finger against his or her upper lip to prevent a sneeze, the pressing is an instrumental response. If the individual reaches for a handkerchief, that, too, is instrumental rather than reflex, even if he or she does so very quickly, and even if the act is automatic.

Speed is not the distinguishing feature in all cases. Instrumental behaviors are said to be *emitted* as opposed to *evoked* or *elicited;* the latter two terms are related to automatic reflexes. Thus, a knee jerk is elicited, but a football is kicked instrumentally. Another distinction might be that one does not have to perform an instrumental response, he or she can just refuse: A reflex response cannot normally be denied. Instrumental responses are not supposed to be voluntary, although they are frequently so regarded. They are considered to be responses that we will normally perform if our past history has been such that similar responses have been rewarded or followed by satisfaction. Thus, if we teach a dog to lie down and roll over, and if it now does so at our command, it is not assumed that the dog responded voluntarily; it had to do what it did because it had been trained to do so. Habits in which we engage without much thought can be instrumental acts.

The term *instrumental* was attached to such nonreflex behavior because usually the response referred to leads to some change in us or in our environment. It is instrumental in accomplishing something.

In the psychology of learning, a distinction has been drawn by some theorists between how instrumental responses are learned, as opposed to how reflexes become *conditioned*. The important factor in instrumental learning is supposed to be the immediate presentation of some reward following the response. Actually, the differences between instrumental learning and conditioning of reflexes are trivial, and the distinction is probably unwarranted, with both kinds of learning reducible to laws of association.

INTELLIGENCE AND THE I.Q.   *(See TEST-TRAIT FALLACY)*

Nobody and everybody knows what *intelligence* is. There is no generally accepted formal definition. In common language, we use terms such as *smart, wise, sharp, astute,* and a host of others in contrast to *dumb, stupid, retarded,* and so on. Psychologists have tried to measure the assumed foundation for such terms and have come up with tests that consist of problems or questions to be solved or answered. Whether someone can answer a question depends on a lot of things, especially experience. Some critics argue that heredity is the chief factor in the background. The argument runs like this: If you have the appropriate heredity, you will manage to acquire the appropriate experience. No parent likes to accept the heredity argument if his or her child is dull; on the other hand, the heredity argument sounds good if his or her child is bright. The brightness or stupidity is often described in terms of *I.Q.* or *intelligence quotient*. The quotient is based on a division of actual age into mental age. *Mental age* amounts to the number of questions you can answer out of a standard list arranged so that children can ordinarily answer more questions as they get older. Obviously, you cannot inherit I.Q.s. These are numbers, the results of some elementary arithmetic. You can inherit physical structures, including a good or healthy brain, although no one knows what a good brain amounts to. A good brain can become less good through accident, disease, poor nutrition, and, perhaps, through lack of appropriate experiences in the child's life. If the child never sees or hears many of the usual stimuli that operate in the general culture, he or she may turn out to be unable to cope with certain situations that others will find easy. In our culture, the I.Q. generally bears some, but by no means a strong, relation to progress in school. Children with low I.Q.s will not generally earn high grades in properly run schools. High I.Q.s will not guarantee high grades, since grades may depend on a lot of other factors. When a high I.Q. child receives poor grades, we find the label *underachiever* thrown about. There may be good reasons for underachievement, including boredom, dislike of the teacher, other interests, and so on. In general, there is not much that can be done to change I.Q.s, since the tests are designed to fit the average student in the average school; such students will maintain their average I.Q.s throughout the school years. If somewhat heroic measures are applied to a tractable child early in life, there can and have been some rather astonishing changes in I.Q. In general, again, the I.Q. does not matter. What does matter is how a child behaves, what the child can accomplish, and what skills he or she masters—not what his I.Q. might be. A high I.Q. by itself is of little or no value if the possessor sits in the sun twiddling his thumbs all day.

INTEREST TESTS   *(See PERSONALITY TESTS, VOCATIONAL COUNSELING)*

Interest tests are sometimes used to discover possible lines of study or employment when individuals appear to have no specifiable interests beyond some vague notions, such as "I'd like to work with people" or "I want to work outdoors." Even when some professional label, such as doctor, lawyer, or engineer, is mentioned, the label may not accurately reflect what some person would really find a rewarding occupation. There are many kinds of lawyers, engineers, and doctors, and thousands of occupations can be described as dealing with people. An interest test is usually developed by asking people who are successful at some occupation and who enjoy their work, identify with it, and stay at it a long time about their attitudes and opinions on all sorts of things, such as the kinds of books they read; their favorite sports, recreations, and hobbies; their views on art, politics, people, machines, and so on. A person might be asked, for example, if he or she would rather meet Charles Darwin or Florence Nightingale. The choice is then scored for a great many occupations in order to develop norms or profiles of the interests of those who are used as the standardization group. When someone takes an interest test, then, his or her responses are compared with the responses of those who comprise the comparison groups.

As with personality tests, there are no right or wrong answers, although a person is, of course, free to lie. He or she may want to come out looking like an engineer, but if he or she is not really familiar with what successful engineers are like, his or her efforts to outguess the test may prove futile.

The test results can be used by a vocational counselor to point out to a client that there are over 30,000 different occupations at which someone or other earns a living and that the choice is certainly not restricted to a handful of common professions or trades. Once a profile of interest is developed and matched against norms, the counselor may be able to suggest lines of work that never occurred to the client. The interest tests have nothing to do with capacity for any given field and only tell one what people already in a field are like and what one might more properly be like in order to fit in with those in the field. Most people who serve as vocational counselors argue that satisfaction with one's job is of considerable importance and that other considerations, such as money, might well be secondary for the long run.

INTROVERT-EXTROVERT   (See PERSONALITY TESTS)

The Swiss psychoanalyst Carl Jung formulated the now widely held notion that people can be categorized as *introverts* or *extroverts,* in perhaps the best known effort to typify or classify people into categories. According to Jung, extroverts were interested in the world of things, the external happenings, in so-called practical affairs. An extrovert, for example, would prefer to read the morning newspaper with his or her breakfast or to have breakfast with family or friends rather than to sit alone and think about him- or herself and his or her reasons for existence. The introvert would prefer no company and would be concerned with his or her own thoughts, with thoughts of personal worth, destiny, and so on.

The attempt to classify people appears to be a common human effort to handle social problems by some easy operation of labeling people as types and reacting to them as if the type had some reality. Studies of personality using a wide variety of scales, tests, and inventories do not support the notion of types to any degree of useful certainty, and the Jungian extroverts and introverts do not appear to exist in sufficient numbers to be worthy of classification. Most people are both introverted and extroverted at various times and situations. A 2-year old child will appear introverted to a stranger but will appear very extroverted when only mama is around.

Jung did recognize that pure introverts and extroverts probably did not exist and that one might be introverted at one time and not at another or that one might be introverted in social situations but quite extroverted in dealing with mechanical problems. Someone who likes to tinker with cars but wants to do it by him- or herself represents a contradiction in the introvert-extrovert continuum. Others might like to solve problems together in a brainstorming situation where the introvert's alleged preoccupation with thinking and imaginative speculations is socially rewarded and where one must push his or her proposals forward in a decidedly extroverted manner if he or she is to be heard at all.

INTUITION AND INSIGHT   (See GESTALT PSYCHOLOGY)

Intuition is alleged to be a kind of immediate knowledge that is not based on some logical process. In the past, it was used by men as a derogatory description of womens' thinking operations, on the men's assumption that women were less inclined to reason problems through and operate on facts. Today, this myth is no longer endorsed, and it is appreciated that men and women both will frequently assert, "I just know it," when they have no obvious and rational basis for a conclusion. The notion of intuitive knowledge is confused by the fact that the knowledge is frequently inadequate and incorrect. According to Piaget, the Swiss psychologist, children pass through an intuitive phase when they just know things to be true that are not actually so. They have not yet reached a phase of rational thought.

Intuition may be considered a form of insight, a kind of immediate awareness of the solution to a problem that was emphasized by Gestalt psychologists. According to these psychologists, a person could be trying to solve a problem by some trial and error method and be unsuccessful until he or she more or less suddenly *saw* the appropriate relationships between the elements of the problem situation; he or she would perceive the solution all at once as the parts of the problem fell into place. As with intuition, such insightful solutions are also frequently wrong, and we give them up and start hoping or looking for new insights.

There is little experimental research in the area of intuition, and the subject is ignored by most psychologists as amounting to lucky guesses when someone turns out to be correct in some prediction. When the hasty predictions turn out incorrectly, they are forgotten or regretted, depending on the action taken. It is true that many scientists arrive at new discoveries and inventions by taking a chance that something may be the case in the absence of a secure foundation of fact. If they are honest, they will admit that it was a lucky guess; otherwise, they can rationalize the outcome as a necessary consequence of what they now know to have happened.

J

JUDGMENT: DECISION MAKING

We are all frequently faced with conflicts and choices, with decisions that have to be made and, in some cases, lived with. If the choice is between two attractive alternatives (an *approach-approach conflict*), and when we can later enjoy the benefits of the other alternative, there is no great problem; we can choose whichever seems more attractive at the moment. If we cannot, however, make the alternative choice later, we do have a problem, one called a *double-approach-avoidance conflict*. Such choices are always hard to make, and only deadlines will force our hands. Later on, we can regret the choice and wonder what life would be like if we had taken the other course. When two unattractive alternatives are posed to us, we usually settle for the lesser of two evils if we cannot avoid the situation entirely.

Such conflicts or moments of indecision call for *judgments* about outcomes that cannot be made easily, since we cannot forsee the future. In such circumstances, we are told to use our heads, to think, as if we were not already using our heads as effectively as we can. We cannot think better than we already do think merely by trying to. If there is time, we can wait and hope that the problem will go away, and many problems do go away if we can afford to wait. We can, given time, muster up arguments for and against each position, but as we do this, we begin to recognize that our arguments are frequently only reinforcing a preference that has already been operating in the selection of arguments. In other words, we rarely make a choice that could not have been predicted by someone who knew us well.

We can more or less be counted upon to do what our past history would predict, and the choice or decision making is only a formal expression of a choice already made for us by our past. Sometimes, we forget some important past experience or misinterpret it, and our behavior then becomes unpredictable. In general, there is little freedom of choice in our most puzzling decision-making situations, since we have already made up our minds and merely seek for arguments that will support the decision already made. Using good judgment is not the application of some kind of intellectual force or procedure as much as it is a matter of the outcome. If the outcome is good, we obviously used good judgment, and vice versa.

K

KINESICS: BODY LANGUAGE

Some social psychologists and psycholinguists have studied the communication between people that takes place without the use of or in addition to words. Thus, various facial expressions and bodily postures inform the observant person that someone may be saying one thing but trying to communicate something else. The tone of voice and whether one ends a sentence on an upbeat or a downbeat may make all the difference between two different messages. There are many ways to say something, each of which means something else. A simple question, such as, Am I invited?, can mean at least three different things, depending upon which word is stressed. Whether one sits on the edge of the chair or crosses his or her legs at the knee or at the ankles may be highly meaningful. The white-knuckle airplane passenger or dental patient communicates a great deal without saying anything. The handclasp in a greeting can also tell a story without words.

Not only do gestures and bodily dispositions communicate, but the way we dress, wear our hair, have beards of various kinds and shapes, use decorations or jewelry, and so on all speak for the person. The shape, color, and care of the fingernails can also communicate to the observant.

The nature of nonverbal cues varies with times and cultures as well as with individuals. When two men embrace in France and other European countries, one must not jump to the conclusion that they are homosexuals. Both cultural and personal factors must be taken into account if one is to read another person's behavior or meanings.

One must also be aware that personal possessions can communicate a great deal about a person, regardless of the words he or she may be using in discussing them. The books on the shelf, the kind of car one drives, the very topics one discusses: All contribute to our appreciation and understanding of another's meanings if we but take them into account. They may, of course, be a facade, but if we know this, we again learn something about the person. We know what he or she might want us to think about him or her.

KINESTHESIS: THE PROPRIOCEPTIVE SENSE

When naming senses, most people do not mention perhaps the most important of all of our senses, the *kinesthetic* or *proprioceptive sense*. In our joints and ligaments, there are sense structures that are stimulated by any stretching or movement and that send impulses back to the central nervous system that we come to interpret as telling us where our various bodily parts are and to what extent they have moved. Without such a sense, we could not learn to walk or talk. The muscles in our larynx are specifically involved in the formation of speech sounds, and without the necessary stimulation of the kinesthetic receptors, we could not know how to create a particular sound. The interesting point is that we do not ever become aware of such laryngeal stimulation unless laboratory procedures are set up to demonstrate the stimulation to us. If we contract syphilis or some other disease that damages the sensory input from our legs, we are unable to walk without using our eyes to tell us where our feet are and which leg to move next. The staggering gait of people who have such diseases where the sensory nerves are damaged is called *tabes dorsalis* or *locomotor ataxia.* When a physician asks you to touch the tip of your nose from an outstretched hand position, he or she is testing your kinesthetic sense; knee jerk tests are also a measure of kinesthesis. We are normally unaware of this tremendously important sense, and yet it is the basis for the acquisition of any of our skillful movements, from that involved in feeding ourselves with fork and spoon to typing, playing the piano, playing golf, and so on.

The kinesthetic sense, sometimes called the proprioceptive or *muscle-tendon-joint sense,* is important in all motor control activity in terms of feedback. Whenever a muscle is contracted, the kinesthetic information is conveyed to the central nervous system as a consequence or result of that contraction. It is a movement-produced information source or stimulus, a feedback stimulus. Like any other stimulus, it can then serve as a conditioning stimulus in relation to any other stimulus and thus play a role in learning. When we throw a basketball at a hoop, all of the muscles and joints of the body have a particular disposition at the time of the toss. If the ball goes into the basket, those stimuli that have just been created will become conditioned to the pleasant emotion generated by the success. When we next have to throw the ball, we may try to assume the same position, as only that position will make us feel good and right. Professional players come to rely on arriving at a certain spot on the floor and let fly when they feel right. This is easily observed with foul shots, where each player develops his or her own style at arriving at the right feel. Good players can sink baskets by standing under the hoop and throwing backwards. They depend on bodily cues, as they cannot even see the basket from some positions. In golf, similarly, one gets to feel the proper stance from which a successful shot can be made. The pro tells us not to raise our heads, as this will interfere with the feedback from the swing.

Because the muscle-tendon-joint sense controls all of our adaptive movements, we should probably rate it above vision and hearing, however importantly we regard these other senses. If we are unable to do anything about what we hear and see, it might not be very meaningful. Even for seeing, we depend upon cues from eye muscles that control eye movements as well as the fixation point.

Because the kinesthetic sense is so intimately involved with the other senses, and because of its role in learning skills, we should certainly rate it as of major importance. Consider the example of a concert pianist practicing on a silent keyboard while flying to a concert. He or she sits in the plane seat, moving his or her fingers along with eyes shut—perhaps rehearsing a concerto. Without the kinesthetic sense, there would be no pianos, pianists, or concertos.

L

LATENT DREAM CONTENT: THE MEANING OF DREAMS
(See DREAMS)

The term *latent dream content* was devised by Sigmund Freud to describe what the real meaning of a dream was supposed to be. What a person actually recalls from a dream is called its *manifest content*. Manifest means obvious. The manifest content, however, rarely if ever meant anything serious to Freud. He chose to believe that dreams are controlled by some operation he referred to as a *censor*. The censor served to prevent unconscious repressed wishes or hostilities from entering consciousness, where they would be unacceptable. Through the censorship activity, a dreamer's thoughts, wishes, and hostilities would be changed into more socially acceptable forms. According to Freud, dreams might mean the exact opposite of the manifest content. If you dream of loving someone, this might really mean that you hate such a person; dreaming of taking a trip might really reflect a desire to stay home. Such an opposite twist is only one of the supposed operations of censorship. Another operation is translating wishes and the like into symbolic objects, so that objects, such as snakes, umbrellas, rulers, flagpoles, and so on, would really represent male sex organs. Boxes, houses, caves, and so on might represent female sex organs. Dreaming about flying might represent sexual intercourse. There has never been any evidence accumulated that such transformations take place. Healthy people have no trouble about dreaming about sexual intercourse directly, but since Freud dealt with neurotics, perhaps he was working with abnormal dream material.

Modern scientific assessment finds no reason to consider Freud's notions of latent dream content in any way a serious contribution. The average person should be careful about describing dreams to anyone who has a small grasp of Freudian thinking, since almost anything one reports can be made into its opposite or made to represent anything the listener cares to suggest. Despite the popularity of dream analysis, there is no reason to believe that dreams mean anything.

LATENT LEARNING   (See INSTRUMENTAL
LEARNING, CONDITIONING)

Edward C. Tolman, a great learning psychologist in the pre-World War II days, suggested that much learning takes place in the absence of any activity or practice and that we learn a great deal by merely seeing and hearing what goes on about us. We observe what leads to what, and observation is enough for some learning to occur. No one knows what we might have learned until we demonstrate our knowledge by some *performance*. Tolman insisted on a distinction between learning and performance because so many psychologists following the influence of Edward Thorndike and John Dewey felt that one only learns by doing, by acting. Later, B. F. Skinner, with his emphasis on *operant behavior,* was similarly concerned with action and reward. For Tolman, reward was not necessary in order for learning to take place. Learning occurred by Pavlovian conditioning as stimuli followed each other or occurred together. The hidden learning was called *latent* because no one had observed it occurring, including the learner.

In recent years, the subject of latent learning has dropped in interest and given way to so-called incidental learning, where experimental studies are arranged so that someone does perform some activity but is not asked to learn anything. Later on, one is tested and found to have learned something without trying to learn, without knowing that he or she had been learning, and without being rewarded for it. A great deal of our everyday learning is of the latent or incidental variety. Commonly, we do not know what we know until we try to state it or demonstrate it. We might come up with, "Oh, that reminds me, your mother called when you were out." If we are asked why we had not reported the fact until the subject of mother had been brought up, we mutter something about "I didn't think of it." If the subject is not brought up, it might never come to light and thus might still be latent knowledge.

Much of our incidental learning does call for some kind of activity, but it need not be identified or thought of as a deliberate learning operation. What we do in incidental learning is observe some items of interest and ignore others, as we do when we walk along the street window-shopping. We may note that a fire engine goes by without paying special attention to it or planning to remember it. Later in the day, we may report such information if the subject comes up. Tolman's point was that we know more than we show or care to admit sometimes and that we only perform when activity is required.

LEADERSHIP AND FOLLOWERSHIP

The term *leader* suggests that some people are more qualified than others to be labeled with such a title. Actually, for someone to lead, others must follow, and it is the needs and characteristics of the group that is to be led that determinine the characteristics of the person they might accept to follow. Basically, the members of a group will follow someone who brings them satisfaction or reinforcement. His or her other qualities will also be functions of the group. If it is a democratic group with a history of dependence upon parliamentary procedure, a person who tries to rule by edict or personal decisions will not last long, even if elected to lead. A leader appointed by higher authority may be followed with some reluctance unless he or she also happens to be likeable. Other features may vary considerably, and such factors as physical size, strength, good looks, and so on may be of no importance. People such as Mayor Daley of Chicago or Winston Churchill were not especially attractive physically, but as long as they gave their followers what they wanted, they were considered great leaders. In Churchill's case, his leadership qualities appeared to vanish shortly after World War II when his public needed other things that Churchill could not supply.

Historians sometimes argue about whether men make the times or times make the men. There appears to be no satisfactory answer to this question. When issues arise that call for group action, someone will be found or forced to take up the position of spokesperson for the group. If he or she articulates the needs of the group and is able to appear to solve some of their problems, he or she becomes a leader; on occasion, the leader can afford to suffer a setback or two; consistent failure to produce will lose followers.

The nature of the followers dictates the nature of the leader; a group of ignorant people will not follow an intellectual who cannot communicate with them, however much other intellectuals admire him or her. The search for character traits or personality features that distinguish leaders has not been highly successful, although within certain groups it is possible to predict that certain personality features are more likely to determine who will and who will not be a leader. In youth gangs, an outgoing, aggressive, physically adept individual is more likely to win over withdrawn, submissive youths for leadership posts. Reputations for prior success at solving the kinds of problems of importance to a group will also be important factors for a time, but success must follow success, or new leadership will be sought. Napoleon was a great leader all the way to Russia and not much of one on the way back. An ex-house painter named Hitler was able to mobilize the affection of many Germans, even though there was little about him that would make him stand out in a crowd. Much is written about the *charisma* of certain people, but the charisma is not a trait of the person alleged to have it but rather a projection onto some individual of fanciful and imagined virtues. We might not give a second glance to some person on the street until we are told that the person is a famous movie star, politician, or Supreme Court judge. Immediately, the person has charisma. The charisma vanishes with failure to produce or satisfy a following. Vice presidents, and even presidents who are deposed quickly, lose whatever charisma and leadership qualities were once perceived. In all cases of leadership, it pays to look behind the leader to see who is working hard and benefiting from the leadership. The power behind the throne is frequently the major leadership asset that the leader possesses.

LEAD POISONING

One of the many problems of our industrial age is that our environment is becoming increasingly polluted with toxic substances. Lead, one of the heavy metals, is encountered by people working in certain manufacturing plants where lead is used; it is found in lead-based paints and plaster; and it is breathed in by all of us because the lead that is in gasoline is spewn out into the air by the 60 million motor vehicles running in our country.

When a person's lead intake is heavy, there is an accumulation of fluid in the brain. In cases of severe *lead poisoning,* people hallucinate and become delirious; they can have convulsions and uncontrollable tremors. Children who are lead poisoned can become permanently mentally retarded. Of all children hospitalized for lead poisoning, one-fourth die and another one-fourth are permanently brain damaged. Children are particularly at risk of permanent damage from lead and other heavy metal poisoning because their brains and nervous systems are still developing.

How can children become lead poisoned? Young children tend to put things into their mouths or chew on many things, such as toys or furniture. When lead-based paint is used, children can chew the paint off those objects or can pick up and chew on the colorful paint chips that fall from walls or ceilings, particularly in old buildings.

Children breathe the same leaded air from automobiles as the rest of us. The colorful pictures in the Sunday comics are made with lead-based paint, and little children can chew them. Many glasses and dishes have designs or pictures produced with leaded paint. Some glasses, such as those given out by gasoline stations and fast-food chains, have the colorful pictures painted with leaded paint. As the child drinks from his or her favorite colorful glass with the friendly cartoon character on it, he or she may be slowly getting poisoned. The problem is greater for children living in or near cities, and nowadays that means more than 66% of all children.

Many states now have laws prohibiting the use of lead-based paints on children's toys or furniture or on the interior surfaces of buildings, and the Environmental Protection Agency has tried to reduce the lead content of our air by requiring lead-free gasoline in newer cars.

Children in high-lead areas should be tested. A simple blood test will determine lead levels. If toxic levels are found, the children should be detoxified. The procedure will not reverse any brain damage or mental retardation that has already occurred, but it can help to slow down and prevent continued brain deterioration.

Lead poisoning, as well as all heavy metal poisoning, such as that by mercury and arsenic, is a serious problem, particularly for children.

Parents should be alert to the variety of ways that young children can be subjected to heavy metal poisoning; they should use clear glass utensils and be careful of the paint on toys, furniture, and walls. City residents might find out about the lead content of the air. Information can be obtained from most city, county, or state health departments.

LEARNED FEARS AND PHOBIAS   (See ANGER, BEHAVIOR THERAPY, FEAR, FRUSTRATION, SYSTEMATIC DESENSITIZATION)

All of us experience fear: It is a common, normal reaction to stressful situations. Most of our fears are *learned reactions*. As we grow older, each of us learns to fear a variety of things. Among the most common adult fears are fears of animals, such as rats, snakes or insects; of dying; of losing one's livelihood; of supernatural events; of social situations; of enclosed places, such as elevators; of high places; of speaking before groups; of speaking up for one's own rights; and many others. Children are commonly afraid of the dark, of strangers, of ghosts and other supernatural events, and so on.

Some of these fears are realistic concerns, such as the fear of death, sickness, or losing one's job. However, we would be hard-pressed, for example, to find many city people who have ever been seriously injured by snakes or insects. These fears are examples of unrealistic fears, or *phobias*.

Regardless of the type of fear stimulus or the intensity of the reaction to it, the fear response is basically the same for everyone, consisting of at least three related reactions: (1) There is a physiological response or arousal, in which the body essentially prepares itself for emergency or defensive action. Such preparation includes increased adrenalin, heightened respiration and heart rates, a greater flow of blood to large muscle groups, and so on. (2) There is a cognitive or thinking component, in which people recognize that they are afraid, think of what to do, and so on. (3) There is a motor response component that includes what the person does—that is, runs, hides, avoids the fear stimulus, and the like. Although all three of these fear components have been noted and measured in some ways by psychologists, it is not clear that they occur in any particular order or even if they are all of the same order of intensity in any given fear reaction. In cases of severe fears, where the reactions are very intense and out of all proportion to the real threat—such as a person's near panic if a fly buzzes near or if it begins to thunder in a storm—the fear is labeled a *phobia.*

Severe fears and phobias are difficult to overcome by oneself, but the patient help of an understanding friend or family member can be effective. In extreme cases, where the fear or phobia does not decrease or disappear, professional help is recommended. Psychodynamic or psychoanalytic therapies have little documented success in the specific reduction of fears. The best available professional approach to fear reduction is provided by *behavior therapists* who use some variation of *systematic desensitization* for adults. For children, the most effective approaches so far documented by research are the behavioral approaches that use some form of *modeling* and *self-control.* In all of these behavioral approaches, the basic strategy is to reintroduce the person *gradually* to the feared object or situation, all the while *calmly* reassuring him or her of safety, and stopping the procedure as soon as fear or anxiety is felt. This gradual reintroduction requires much patience and reassurance and ordinarily requires many sessions or trials. Parents, concerned or sometimes fed up with their children's fears, often try to shame or ridicule a fearful child or even to force the child to encounter the feared stimulus or situation, such as forcing a child to pet a feared dog or to enter and stay in a dark room. Such approaches will probably only intensify the child's fears.

To help a fearful child, our best advice to parents is this: Be certain that you have correctly identified the fear stimulus—that is, precisely what the child does fear; do not ridicule the child or force the issue; have a calm talk, and try to get the child to agree to cooperate in getting over the fear. Throughout, be calm, patient, and highly reassuring; *gradually,* with the child's complete cooperation and knowledge of each step, bring the child closer to the feared object or event, always keeping the child calm and reassured. At the first signs of anxiety or upset, stop; try again the next day and go a little further each time; do not rush it; praise every small bit of success, and give some good rewards for good progress.

The most common adult phobia seen in mental health clinics is agoraphobia, a fear of leaving the safety of one's own home. The agoraphobic may have a cluster of fears, such as fears of open spaces; of crowds, such as those encountered in shopping centers or going to work; of loud noises; or of traveling. To avoid those fear-stimulating situations, the person learns to remain at home whenever possible. In less severe cases, the person chooses to remain at home on weekends and during vacations, leaving the house only when it is absolutely necessary to go to work or to shop. In more severe cases, the agoraphobia may develop to the degree that the person begins staying away from work as well as from social situations. Agoraphobia is obviously a fear that can interfere significantly with a person's life, and this probably accounts for the fact that so many eventually seek professional help. About 75% of agoraphobics are women, and most of them developed their fears as adolescents or as young adults.

Agoraphobics suffer in several ways: First, they experience the extreme anxiety and upset of the fears themselves; secondly, because they avoid going out, their family, social, occupational, or educational lives and development can be markedly disrupted and, in severe cases, destroyed; thirdly, the agoraphobics may become very depressed over their growing life failures. Agoraphobia, then, may be a severe problem.

Treatment of agoraphobia is more complicated than treating most other phobias. In general, very carefully planned and applied systematic desensitization by a skilled behavior therapist is the treatment currently available. But because agoraphobia may involve many complex fears as well as seriously disrupted social, personal, and occupational skills, desensitization alone may not be sufficient. The agoraphobic may have to be desensitized to more than one fear situation and then taught or retaught many social or other skills. Further, if the client is a family member, a mother or a father, and if the agoraphobia is eliminated so that he or she begins going out of the house normally, the family situation will have changed. Mother, for example, will no longer be dependably home all the time to take care of everyone's immediate needs. A whole variety of new problems might arise and have to be dealt with for the entire family system.

LEARNED HELPLESSNESS

People sometimes demonstrate ineptitude in some situations and appear to be unable or unwilling to learn. Someone might have tried to learn to drive a car at one time but gave up, never to try again. Students might avoid courses in certain areas as not their bag and demonstrate ineptitude when forced into some learning situation. When someone is unable to do something, he or she cannot be required to do it, and there may be some kinds of compensation for the inability. If one does not drive a car, someone else may be coerced into driving him or her around; if one does not want to face up to the challenges of an income tax form, someone else might be found who will do it and who will also provide company or other values. Of course, being helpless carries with it the onus of incompetence or stupidity. But, with sufficient ego-strength, one may be able to carry it off and act as if certain activities are unworthy of one's time or effort or even beneath one's dignity, as when a college professor cannot drive a nail into a wall to support a picture. He or she regards hammering as a tradesman's proper field and not something to be considered as an academician's skill. John Dollard, in *Class and Caste in a Southern Town*, reports that some blacks refused to learn to drive tractors or handle other complicated machinery, and such refusals would be interpreted as marks of native stupidity. Dollard called this negative behavior *pseudo-feeblemindness*. Dollard suggests that the blacks knew very well that if they did learn to handle the machines, those duties would be added to their burdens without any additional compensation, and they found it far wiser to appear stupid than to go through the trouble of acquiring certain skills under their unsatisfactory working conditions.

In the laboratory, if rats or other animals are given strong electrical shocks in confined spaces where they can do nothing about the shocks except cringe and squeal, they will not learn later on to avoid such shocks by operating some device or performing some particular avoidance routine. Such animals have, in effect, learned to be helpless; they no longer try to improve their situations because they have already learned that nothing works. Similarly, they will not learn to do anything on the positive side—to earn food, for example, by manipulating some device if food is presented sporadically and at random with no relationship between what the animal does and the reward. If no expectancies of consequences can be developed, the animal ceases to engage in problem-solving behavior and is again considered to have learned to be helpless.

From the animal evidence, it is assumed that when one presents the appearance of reluctance to try something that might appear to be new, there is a history of failure and frustration at that or related tasks. A child who has almost drowned at the seashore might not care for swimming lessons at school. A bad history at some athletic competition might sour one on future athletic activities. Some people who find that all they do when they try some do-it-yourself routine is to worsen a situation that then requires outside help may learn to be helpless in a variety of situations they could easily master if it were not for such negative histories.

As one cannot be a master of all trades any more, we all manage to acquire a bit of *learned helplessness:* We many not tinker with our modern automobiles, for example, since they have become rather tinker-proof in their complexity. Learned helplessness is not of great moment except in situations where nearly everyone has to qualify to some level, as in reading and arithmetic, and children should not be allowed to acquire techniques of avoiding lessons that they must eventually learn. Some children cannot learn to tie their shoelaces, and they wear slip-on shoes as long as possible. They might even avoid shoelaces all their lives, with a little effort. Where the physical facts do not preclude some activity, however, the parent who allows the child to get away with it because it is difficult for his or her child is only preparing the child to acquire a new technique of problem solving, one that calls for other people to solve the problem. Such luxurious training might be practical for rajahs, but the rest of us must learn routine skills.

LEARNING   (See IMITATION, LATENT LEARNING, MOTIVATION, CONDITIONING, GENERALIZATION)

Learning amounts to being changed in such a way that you respond differently from the way you did before. The amount of change will depend upon the time and kind of busy-ness in which you are engaged. Such busy-ness is sometimes called *attention,* and so learning might be described as a change brought about by paying attention to something for some time. Attention is usually an undefined term, only a shorthand or substitute term for describing behavior in which we react to some stimuli and not to others. We are always paying attention to something; what we learn is what we attend to, and if we do not learn what someone else wants us to learn, it is because we were paying attention to something else and learning that. If the time spent is too short for any biological changes to take place, the learning will be inadequate and poorly remembered in later tests.

Learning is only one source of change in behavior toward stimuli to which you formerly responded in some other way. If you are drugged or drunk, your behavior will also change, as it will with age and illness. Perhaps the most confusing factor is that of growth and development, a process called maturation where you grow into and out of various behavior patterns. Since maturation is always achieved in an environment with exposure to various stimuli and with corresponding experiences, it is sometimes difficult to know whether one has learned something or has just become able to do it. Striking examples are walking and talking. Parents usually try to get their children to walk: They hold them up and guide their steps. Eventually, the child walks, and one can wonder about how much learning was involved. We should note that if everything a child wanted was on the floor or on the ground, he or she might never get past a crawling stage. The crawling itself is a function of the environment, since the child would never crawl toward or away from objects if they were not there.

In general, there is no confusion about learning if we are dealing with the acquisition of knowledge, facts, or vocabulary. Here, it is clear that we learn correct answers by seeing or hearing, but we have to look and listen to the proper stimulus features and react appropriately for some future test. The reactions that we make sometimes confuse the issue. Sometimes, the reactions are gross bodily or vocal reactions, as in learning a maze. We cannot learn a maze without walking through it, and such performance has sometimes been emphasized as necessary for learning without recognizing that only some kinds of learning require a performance. We can learn a fact without saying anything out loud, and no one will know that we know unless he or she asks us, and we respond in the test. In such a case, the performance is only meaningful as a test and is not a necessary factor in the original learning. Most of what we learn is by observation and being told, where our performance is minimal and frequently unobservable. We might still argue that some kind of performance is necessary, in that in order to learn, we do have to look and listen or otherwise examine, judge, evaluate, compare, or check details in one way or another, perhaps label things, try to image or picture items in some relationships, and so on. Such activities are called *processing,* and probably no learning goes on without some kind of processing.

There is another complicating factor. Usually, when we learn something, there will be some consequences, good or bad. Frequently, learning is to our advantage in some way, and it can be argued that we were in some way benefited or rewarded for our learning. Some psychologists have chosen to infer that we only learn what we are rewarded for doing. There does not seem to be good reason for such a view, since we frequently learn bad news. We might learn that someone will harm us and that if we can stay away, a benefit can be inferred, but this is stretching the concept of reward. We also learn a great deal when there is no one around to reward us, and often we do not even know that we have learned something. Such learning, called *incidental learning,* is routinely acquired as we go about our daily business, neither trying to learn nor trying not to learn. We can learn things we do not want to know such as television and radio advertising jingles.

It is not necessary to engage in overt effort in order to learn some kinds of things, and it is not necessary to be rewarded for learning. Frequently enough, we do benefit from learning, but the learning occurs before the benefit. What is necessary for learning is time and attention or processing. Frequent trials or practice only increase the time factor. They may also allow the learning to become more complete in that, from time to time, a situation changes and still calls for the same answer. A child might learn that 5 and 9 make 14 but not know that 9 and 5 also make 14. Presenting the combinations in different orders means two separate learnings and not one, as might be inferred by the unwary. Although some *generalization* does take place, one should not expect a child to learn a complex pattern of relationships by having the child learn one sample. In teaching a child politeness, it is not enough to teach the child to say, "Thank you," for example, only when a gift is received. One has to take pains to see to it that "Thank you" is spoken whenever any favor or consideration has been received, perhaps even when some one asks, "How are you?" But saying "Thank you" is only part of politeness, and probably hundreds of politeness lessons must be learned, each one quite separately, before someone should be described as polite.

Learning is frequently related to motivation, as if one had to want to learn in order to do so. Actually, motivation or desire to learn can only bring the prospective learner into a learning situation; it cannot help him or her learn—only time and processing can do that. However, if a child skips school, he or she will not learn that day's lessons, even though he or she may learn other things that the school skipping permitted. Motivation for learning is a separate problem and should be recognized as such. Wanting to learn may even intrude on or interfere with the learning if one is spending his or her processing time entertaining his or her wants or desires for learning. Learning is a major interest to psychologists, and there are many related discussions in this text that should be consulted for separate issues. Motivation is one such issue and should be reviewed.

LEARNING DISABILITY   *(See LEARNED HELPLESSNESS)*

Anybody who suffers from any bodily disease, weakness, or defect may also be hampered in learning. Since most of what we learn we learn in school or from tutors who use language, both written and spoken, any defect of the eyes or ears is obviously going to affect the efficiency with which we see and hear. Blindness and deafness are obvious kinds of factors that lead to learning problems. There are many degrees of blindness and deafness or visual and auditory defects that are not detected and corrected early and result in a poor start in one's learning history. A host of other specific kinds of brain malfunction or disorder can also affect learning and retention. If one is seriously handicapped by some physical abnormality, he or she may not be able to learn enough to escape being classified as retarded.

Such physical handicaps are detectable, and special provisions can be made for education. Some children, however, do not show any physical abnormalities and still have trouble learning. There are many children with I.Q.s above the retarded level who do well enough on parts of I.Q. tests to score in the normal range and who stilll have great difficulty in learning basic skills, such as reading, computation, and writing. Such children, classified as *learning disability cases,* require special environments, special equipment, and special teachers who can help them surmount their problems to some degree. The nature of learning disabilities has only been recognized relatively recently as a consequence of the analysis of intelligence tests, which are commonly made up of a number of parts. Taking the whole score into account may hide the fact that someone may have done very well on parts of the test and poorly on others. Depending upon the weighting of the parts, a person could be classified as low in intelligence when he or she might actually be superior in some aspects of the test.

A learning disability must not be inferred from a low test score without further analysis. Some children may appear to be unable to learn to read, for example, and may make little or no progress, for many reasons other than a sheer inability to read. It might be necessary to eliminate such factors as anxiety, frustration, fear of competition—even learned helplessness. It must be established that the child has adequate vision, vocabulary, or opportunity to learn before the child is classified as learning-disabled. Special teachers are now being trained to work with children who are diagnosed as having a learning disability. It is still too early to tell if any great success can be anticipated.

LEARNING HOW TO LEARN: THE TRANSFER OF TRAINING
(See STUDY AND HOW TO STUDY)

Parents send children to school in order to prepare them for their futures. It is assumed that what they learn in school will somehow transfer to real life. Commonly enough, the college graduate on his or her first job finds out that he or she now has to learn the job more or less from scratch, since what was learned in school does not apply directly to what is now expected. Frequently, the world of work is well in advance of what is being taught in school. Such standard skills as typing may be applied immediately, but even with such skills, the typewriters may be different, and certain practices may differ. If a student spends his or her time studying Latin and mathematics, he or she may find little use for this kind of knowledge in the real world. He or she may have learned more than he or she believes, however. The study of Latin may have prepared him or her for a great many kinds of tasks where the language itself is not involved. He or she may have learned to stick to a task until it is done, to look beyond the words themselves for implications that are not apparent on the surface. He or she may have learned to enjoy a well-formed product and a host of other attitudinal and motivational patterns that might not be characteristic of someone who avoided Latin because it was hard, dead, and of no modern interest.

When habits or skills picked up in one activity are applicable to some other activity, psychologists talk about the *transfer of training*. It should be recognized that such factors as getting to work on time, sticking to the job instead of watching the clock, appreciating good work, cooperating with one's fellows, and so on can be common to many different kinds of jobs and might be expected to transfer from one job to another. If young people grow up without ever holding a job and are chronically unemployed, they will not adjust well to their first job because they have too many habits of not working, not taking responsibilities seriously, not following instructions, and so on.

As one gets exposed to one problem after another, he or she will acquire certain modes of attacking the problems so that he or she gets better and better at a given kind of problem. Monkeys in laboratory situations show tremendous gains from experience in solving certain kinds of problems—usually two-choice problems, where they are to pick out one of two objects that will be followed by a reward. Dr. Harry Harlow, who did many such studies, called this *learning how to learn*. In human situations, the problems that we deal with are not quite so simple, but humans are not monkeys and can handle much more complicated problems if they also have a satisfactory learning history. People acquire ways of approaching problems that they transfer from one situation to another. There is, of course, a danger if their experience is limited to one kind of problem and one kind of solution procedure. In such cases, people become set in their ways and can be ineffective in novel situations.

One of the areas where our educational world has not made much progress is in that of teaching people how to learn different skills and subject matters. Students are more or less expected, somehow naturally, to know how to study or how to go about picking up a skill. For every subject and skill area, there should be a preliminary period of training in how to go about learning X, whether X is Spanish, golf, or knitting. Only those teachers who have considered the problem are likely to take these preliminary steps. Others start right in with the lessons instead of analyzing what has to be learned and what are the best procedures for making effective progress. Many professional coaches recognize the importance of basics and drill students in what look like unnecessary activities to the students. If a student does not have a good instructor, the student must discover what there is to be learned and how the best learners have gone about the task. It can never be assumed that anyone can automatically hit upon the best way to do anything. Even pounding a nail involves a skill. The good carpenter knows how the hammer and nail will sound when a proper blow has been delivered. He or she may not know that he or she should teach the novice nail-pounder how the blow should sound.

Edward Lee Thorndike, the great educational psychologist, argued that only identical elements will transfer from task to task, but his elements included such things as motivation, approaches, orientations toward the tasks, and other general factors. The elements do not have to be identical for considerable transfer to take place; if there is sufficient similarity between one task and another, there will also be a gain. A problem arises if the similarity is not really great and only enough to lead to confusion, which will lead to negative transfer or interference. But if one learns to write with a pencil, the transfer to pen, to crayon, or even to toes in the sand is not beyond expectation.

LIBIDO

The psychoanalytic term *libido* refers to instinctual, basic energy that psychoanalysts believe drives human behavior and constantly presses, unconsciously, for satisfaction. Libido is not a term referring to an observed fact, such as the term *behavior*. Libido, like the concept of gravity, cannot be directly observed and measured. It is a theoretical concept that psychoanalysts use as a basic part of their theorizing. The term has no practical value, but it does carry some theoretical value within the psychoanalytic framework.

LOVE

Mountains of paper, including letters, have been used to write about *love*, but very little scientific information has been developed about this subject. Popular writers distinguish between true love and some other kinds, presumably not so true. We read about puppy love and first loves, mother love (fathers apparently do not rate a distinction), romantic love, and love-hate relationships. Dictionaries distinguish between love and like—we are not supposed to love ice cream or apple pie—we can only like material objects. Love is apparently reserved for people and, perhaps, animals. Pet cemeteries suggest that love of animals is strong with some people who lavish great sums of money on the care of their pets.

Scientifically, no one writes about love in the current psychological literature. Behavioristic psychologists, starting with John B. Watson, recognized that human infants would relax and smile when they were stroked in so-called erogenous zones. *Erogenous zones* usually refer to sex-organ regions, but if an infant relaxed when stroked any place else, that would also have to be an erogenous zone. In short, the definition of such zones is quite circular. Watson called the reaction to such stroking *love* and argued that it was an inborn emotional reaction, along with two other natural or inborn reactions—anger and fear. The trouble with Watson's description is that people proclaim their love for others when these others are not present to be stroking them or to be stroked. As a matter of fact, most expressions of love are for someone who is at the moment not present (as in love letters), and the strongest feelings of love are felt at such times. In fact, one might try to evaluate someone's love for someone else by the degree of discomfort he or she feels in the absence of his or her loved one. The folklore wisdom in this case is "Absence makes the heart grow fonder." Psychologists have measured sex drives in terms of how much shock a rat will undergo to reach a mate.

From what little is known, it can be assumed that love as a term refers to positive, pleasant, relaxed feelings that are aroused by some other individual: We ignore self-love as a misuse of the language. Such positive feelings are presumably aroused in the first instance by mothers who nurse and fondle their babies or by anyone else who performs these functions. Mothers typically become the first love objects, with gradual additions from among close associates. Commonly, by Pavlovian generalization, people such as the mother tend to arouse the same positive feelings. Freud was fond of saying that men marry women who somehow resemble their mothers. This is an unprovable assertion, since all women resemble each other to some extent, especially if ways of behaving are added to possible physical resemblance. It does appear to be true that people do develop positive feelings for certain types of other people—for example, short brunettes, tall blondes, or whatever. "He or she is not my type" is a common expression.

It has just been stated that one can love many other people of either sex and that the notion of one true love is probably a kind of romantic propaganda. What has been said so far has made no mention of sex, which is probably irrelevant to love. We can love others with whom there can be no sexual relationship, or we can avoid any great emotional commitment to those with whom there are such relationships. Sexual contact, of course, involves erogenous zone stimulation and might result in love attachments, but it is not necessary. To be faithful to one partner for life or for long periods is an ethical or moral matter and need have no relationship to love, since some people maintain a faithfulness relationship without any sexual contact or, for that matter, without love. It is important to discriminate between love and sex, since the latter involves many other variables besides a positive or relaxed, pleasant state. Some men, perhaps controlled by some machismo social influences, engage in sexual activity in order to demonstrate their manliness. Obviously, if they can get women to submit, they must be desirable, attractive, or important in some way.

In our culture, sexual activity is one way to demonstrate fondness or appreciation of a marital partner. After some marital conflict, a kiss and make up activity might symbolize a return to a peaceful coexistence. Husbands may even attempt rape of their wives, not so much for the possible pleasure involved but to demonstrate to themselves that their wives really love them; otherwise, they would not submit, and whatever objections or resistance are put up are regarded as the last stages of an argument.

It is clear that in any culture what is called love is a complex mixture of emotions, ethics, egoism, and experiences stemming from childhood. It is not some unique experience that descends on one from nowhere. Certainly, it is possible to fall in love at first sight. All that that means is that we have been prepared by our backgrounds to respond positively to a particular kind of person.

LYSERGIC ACID: LSD   (See DRUG ABUSE: TREATMENT)

A synthetic drug introduced to this country about 1950, *d-lysergic acid diethylamide* is used as a major hallucinogenic or psychedelic drug. Its users report experiencing fantastic internal trips with vivid auditory and visual hallucinations; intensely increased sensitivity to smells and sounds and to new sensory experiences, such as "smelling sounds"; and to a general, highly positive mind-expansion experience. During a trip, moods can swing widely from great elation to intense depression and, in a bad trip, to intense terror. Feelings of body growth and distortions are common, such as floating outside of one's body, feeling one's body grow larger or smaller, or feeling extremely powerful. The LSD trip usually lasts about eight hours, with the peak of hallucinatory experience occurring about the third to fourth hour. During the eight hours, the person's subjective experience of time might be quite different; he or she may feel as if he or she has been away for months. Coming off a good trip, the user can recall many of the sensations and in imagination savor the experience of having been in another world.

Users claim that LSD expands the mind and has great value in making them highly sensitive to new understanding and increasing their creativity. There simply is no evidence for such claims. No known great works of art or philosophical or sceintific achievements have been produced by LSD trippers in the past nearly thirty years of the drug's use in this country.

Sometimes, the user experiences bad trips in which intense hallucinations are horrific or frightening, causing grossly bizarre behavior and often leading to terror-induced suicide. A survivor of a bad trip has had an intense eight hours of terror that probably make the alcoholic's DTs appear mild.

One of the phenomena associated with LSD is the *flashback,* which sometimes occurs weeks or months after having taken LSD and without further use of the drug. Suddenly, without warning, the person will experience some of the earlier hallucinations. The flashback is a disturbing experience because the person has not deliberately induced it; the victim is out of control and is being forced into the unwanted trip.

Two other hallucinogenic drugs are *mescaline* and *psilocybin.* Mescaline is obtained from the peyote cactus and has been used for many hundreds of years by American Southwest Indians in religious rites. Psilocybin is obtained from a mushroom, *Psilocybe mexicana*. The most widely used of the hallucinogens is LSD.

M

MARIJUANA USE   *(See DRUG ABUSE)*

Cannabis sativa is a hemp plant that was extensively grown early in this country's history and used for making rope and cloth. In the 1800s, it was used as a medicine for a variety of disorders. But *cannabis* is a hemp plant with a difference; when its green leaves, known colloquially as *grass,* are dried and ground up, it becomes the drug, *marijuana.* Further, extracting and drying the plant's resin produces an even more powerful drug, *hashish.*

Today, marijuana is a common drug, easily available to anyone of virtually any age and at affordable prices. By 1974, 12% of adolescents were marijuana users; 5% of 17-year-olds were *daily* users; 53% of young adults (18-25 years) and 29% of adults (over 25) had tried it. Recent data continue to show its increasing use in these age groups. In some places, such as specific high schools, marijuana use involves more than 70-80% of the student population.

Ordinarily smoked in cigarettes and pipes, marijuana can be made into a tea, added to baked products, such as cookies, or even chewed.

Marijuana has an intoxicating effect, depending upon the amount used, its purity, and the user's previous experience with it. Users report a pleasant feeling of relaxation, a mild euphoria, an increase in amiability, and, some claim, a sharpness in perception. Activity levels and social participation decrease somewhat while under the influence of the drug. Physiologically, there is a slight increase in heart rate and an increased appetite, slowing reaction time. Short-time use of marijuana appears to have no serious ill effects physically or psychologically, provided that the person does not attempt anything particularly complicated, such as driving an automobile; the user is under the influence of a drug, just like a person who has been drinking alcohol. In short-term use, people do not become psychotic or brain damaged and do not tend to step up to hard drugs, nor do they particularly become aggressive or antisocial. Compared with *short-term* use of alcohol, for example, it is indeed a mild and innocuous drug. There is more violence and severe damage in a weekend of drinking than in months of smoking marijuana.

Some users believe that marijuana and other drugs, too, make them more creative and allow them to think more clearly. The evidence is clear that such benefits are simply not true. That the users think so is not hard to understand; when somewhat intoxicated, whether by beer or grass, people often think that they can understand and even solve many of the world's problems. It is a very common Saturday night experience.

Very recently, reports of studies of the long-term use of marijuana have begun to appear, and they seriously question the picture of marijuana as a harmless or innocuous drug. As we know, the long-term use of tobacco is an extremely dangerous behavior, causing cancers and a variety of other severe illnesses. Recent research indicates that a marijuana cigarette is far more potent in its toxic effects than tobacco. It is estimated that one or two marijuana cigarettes are the equivalent in damaging value to an entire pack of tobacco cigarettes. Thus, a teenager who smokes three or four reefers a day may be consuming the equivalent of many packs of cigarettes daily. Some researchers foresee a sharp increase in lung cancer when the current young marijuana users begin to reach late middle age.

Some parents and most adolescents still believe that marijuana is harmless. But the full impact of the use of this drug on health is not yet known. As we noted, recent research indicates that marijuana is far more toxic than tobacco, perhaps as much as twenty times more toxic. Current users must reconsider their earlier beliefs about its harmless nature.

One of the immediate dangers of marijuana use—or of any drug, for that matter—is what has been called the *amotivational syndrome*. Adolescents, for example, can become so completely dependent upon the use of marijuana for feeling good that they lose interest in virtually all other aspects of life. For them, in effect, they have given up all other options, all other possibilities for usual success. This is not a necessary condition of marijuana use, but it has happened often, and when it does, a life is wasted.

MARITAL PROBLEMS

Marriage is a social arrangement whereby two individuals, usually of the opposite sex, decide to live together as a pair with the approval of the state and, possibly, with the approval of some religious organization. The latter is not required by law. Licensing procedures were originally introduced in order to ensure some order in matters of property, inheritance, and later taxation. In some states, the licensing was a means by which marriages could be delayed for at least a few days in order to prevent a legal and formal union by people who might be drunk or otherwise incapacitated for rational decisions. It was also a means of requiring tests for venereal disease, thereby serving a public health function.

Marriage customs and patterns differ widely in different cultures, some of which permit a man to have several wives; others allow wives to have several husbands. In some cultures, marriages are arranged by parents, even for infants; whereas in others, more or less free choice is involved. The freedom to select marriage partners seems to be geographically limited, since studies show that people who marry frequently live within close proximity (about five city blocks) in a large proportion of cases.

Although some species of birds and animals mate for life with only one other individual, the existence of *polyandry* (many husbands) and *polygamy* (many wives) suggests that humans are not by nature committed to single pairings and that marriage of one pair "till death do us part" is a pattern developed in some cultures after long and complicated histories involving property and succession rights. The pattern has an equally long history of broken marriages, separations, divorces, and abandonments on both sides. The rising rate of divorce suggests that the pattern has no solid roots in biology or nature.

For most people, embarking on a first marriage amounts to starting a voyage on uncharted seas without a pilot of any experience. For two people who were strangers to each other for many developmental years, each living in a particular pattern and style, to work out a satisfactory and compatible arrangement of daily interactions is not an easy task. The partners in a marriage must work at it if it is to last for any period of time, each giving and taking in some appropriate measure. It is impossible to have a happy marriage if some kind of competition for dominance prevails. An arrangement where one partner is dominant and the other submissive is not the answer, since the submissive one might eventually revolt. The arrangement must involve appropriate sacrifices on each side; a recognition of each other's needs; and a cooperative life style, without exploitation of one by the other. Such arrangements are very difficult to work out if they are not planned, discussed, and tried out experimentally from time to time.

Although sexual incompatibility is frequently cited as the cause of marital disturbances or breakups, such difficulties may be the result of other sources of trouble and not the causes of a marital conflict. The major problems in marriage may often be traced to money—how it is obtained and distributed and in what quantity. Rich people have their marital problems, too, and they can also have difficulty over money, since wealth is a relative matter. How the individuals in a marital relationship will handle their incomes must be established to mutual satisfaction before the marriage takes place, and the arrangement should be mutually adjusted, since changes in economic status vary. Problems arising from money are ignored at the peril of the marriage. Another common source of difficulty is developed from in-law relationships, and these include not only the notorious mother-in-law but also the brothers and sisters of the marriage mates. The statement that "I did not marry your family" is not quite accurate, since what you did marry was the product of a family and its ways and customs as well as its relationships and influences. No one can deny his or her past, and people always marry someone with a past. The hope that someone can cure another from his or her past, whether this be alcoholism; religion; food preferences; or tastes in music, literature, or the movies is probably irresponsible and should never be assumed. In general, there are fewer marital breakups among people of the same religion and educational background than among those who choose to cross one kind of cultural line or another. The fact that some marriages among people of different backgrounds continue for years is not evidence of a happy situation. We do not have access to information about the intimate details of anyone's marital situation, and marital counselors frequently hear different stories when interviewing individuals separately. When a marriage gets to the level of requiring counseling, it is already a poor prospect for salvation. Marital counselors are not necessarily qualified to offer advice, regardless of their degrees or credentials. Each case is different and calls for a different solution, which is frequently impossible, because the original foundation for the marriage was improperly arranged.

Although all men and women are different, it appears unlikely that anyone who cannot get along with one person can get along with another. Men and women are not so different that a mistake can be corrected simply by switching partners. The rate of second divorces is higher than that of first divorces and is getting higher. If the members of a marital pair can appreciate that they probably could not do better, they might be able to adjust to the present partners more readily. The playwright, G. B. Shaw, remarked, "Whether you marry or not, you'll regret it." He should have modified his remark a bit by adding "sometimes." What he meant, of course, is that a marital arrangement was bound to become difficult at times and needed great care, consideration, and respect for individual differences if it was to succeed. The fact that there might be occasional regrets should not lead to rash and hasty decisions, since returning to a single or unmarried status will also lead to some regrets. Marriage is one way of remaining in a social community that depends on interrelationships in order to make the community function and survive. Until some other arrangements are worked out, marriages should be entered upon only after due consideration to such problems as money, in-laws, future job prospects for both man and wife, whether children will be involved, and so on. In general, a marriage between teenagers because of an unexpected pregnancy does not appear to be a good prospect. Some degree of experience, maturity, education, travel, and so on ought to be considered before a marriage is contemplated. Once errors are committed, there is little hope for success by way of repairs, patching up, advice, counseling, or psychotherapy.

MASCULINITY-FEMININITY   *(See SEX DIFFERENCES)*

We have been brought up to think of males and females as opposites, and most of us will say "male" when asked to give the opposite of "female" in a word test. The trouble is that, as with many other opposites, there are a great many similarities between men and women, and not all of the differences may be of great importance. Modern feminists emphasize that girl children are brought up differently from boy children, with different toys, household chore assignments, and different future plans. We can accept the fact that there are basic physiological differences (sex organs, mammary glands, pelvic proportions), but even these are sometimes difficult to establish. Olympic Games officials insist on chromosome tests. Men and women possess some of the same sex chemistry, and frequently, the characteristics assumed to be manly are found in women, and vice versa. The term *androgyny* has been introduced to emphasize the bisexuality of both males and females and is being used more commonly as feminists gain more ground in the struggle for equal rights.

It is incorrect to think of men and women as polar opposites, not only in strictly physical sex characteristics but also in any other respect. Although men are usually taller and heavier than women and are usually also stronger, there appear to be no important ways in which women differ from men that are not the results of culture or custom. Differences in behavior patterns are functions of the culture and may be of greater or lesser importance at any specific time. Tests are available, labeled Masculinity-Femininty Tests, which purport to measure to what extent a person behaves like or prefers what the majority of members of one sex or the other behave like or prefer. Such tests are of value if it is found that a man tends to respond like most women do instead of like most men, and vice versa. It may help in counseling such people to know that they are not like most members of the sex to which they nominally belong.

Where differences between the sexes do exist, they should not be ignored but taken advantage of in suitable ways. Girls do develop more quickly than boys; they show a more rapid grasp of language skills, and other differences may yet be found. To ignore such differences may prove costly or unwise in hasty efforts to achieve equality. Any real differences between men and women should not be eliminated by legislation but should be evaluated and incorporated into the culture.

MASTURBATION

Masturbation is genital stimulation for pleasure, either by oneself or with a partner. Traditionally, we have considered masturbatory activity in children and adolescents as morally wrong and even physically harmful. Many myths and outright lies have been told to children and adolescents about the disastrous physical damage caused by masturbation, as adults attempt to frighten children away from the activity. We now know that masturbation is engaged in by virtually every child and adolescent at some time and that there is no known physical harm that results from masturbation. The damage seems to be done by the effects of the misinformation given by adults—the guilt over doing something bad, the fear of being found out. For most adolescents, masturbation is a normal, personal, and private activity, engaged in for pleasure.

However, for some people, adults as well as adolescents, masturbation may be part of a larger set of sexual or other problems. In such instances, it is usually the other problems that are recognized first.

Masturbation ordinarily decreases with adulthood but does not necessarily disappear. Couples may engage in mutual masturbation, as may individuals when a partner is not available.

Masturbation remains a sensitive and controversial issue. For many adults, it appears somehow inadequate, abnormal, or improper. With current knowledge, it is no longer considered a deviation or a serious problem. Like *any* behavior, masturbation may be associated with other problems involving phobias about disease, fear of the opposite sex, and so on. Depending upon its frequency and the degree to which it inhibits other normal behavior, it may be a problem in itself.

MATERNAL DEPRIVATION   *(See EARLY EXPERIENCE)*

A distressing historical fact is that early in the century, many babies (from 30% to 90%) in orphanages died within their first year. Healthy, normal babies became listless, unresponsive, and soon succumbed to infections and died. In the 1940s, Dr. Rene Spitz observed and examined orphanage children and concluded that they were suffering and dying because of the lack of normal *maternal stimulation*. In the poorly staffed orphanages, where the caretakers might not have too much affection for their charges anyway, the babies were given little attention beyond meeting their physical needs for nourishment and cleaning. For the most part, they were left to lie in their covered cribs—alone, unstimulated, and unreinforced. They gradually grew silent, still, and sickly and died.

Dr. Spitz and, later, others found that when the babies were given more attention and stimulation by their caretakers, the children were healthier and survived. They had the caretakers play regularly with the children, allowed the babies to have physical contact with each other on mats on the floor, and so on, and the children did better.

It is clear that in normal parenting, with its playing, talking to, tickling, hugging, and so on, the continued contact, stimulation, and reinforcement is extremely important in the normal development of children. When the mother is missing, a substitute, such as a foster mother, a father, a nurse, an older sibling, and so on, can provide some of the all-important physical stimulation. Institutionalized children do not thrive where the staff is too small for the daily tasks, too busy, or too uncaring to provide sufficient maternal stimulation.

Research shows that when the institution provides adequate stimulation for the infants, the children do well. In some institutions, older, mentally retarded girls and women were instructed to play with their children; elderly patients became grandparents in another institution; and so on. In those projects, the special caretakers played with and obviously enjoyed the babies for many hours each day, and the children thrived. Early sensory and physical stimulation of infants, then, is extremely important and cannot be overemphasized here. New parents should know of this absolute necessity, for their child's well-being, of their gentle handling, playing with, and attending to their children.

MATURITY

Maturity is a term that has been, perhaps unwisely, applied to humans as something that is attained at some period in life. We may be able to tell when a tomato is ripe, mature, and ready for harvest; but when it comes to people, it is difficult to determine when they have arrived at some state that might be described as mature rather than as older. The analogy with vegetables might hold only to the extent that we do grow and change and, after some peak, begin to decline and become less capable or qualified. The difficulty arises in the fact that there are so many fields in which we might operate that we can be mature in one respect and not in another. Usually, the term suggests some state of wisdom and personal self-control that allows us to solve problems that others less experienced or younger people cannot handle. The trouble is that self-control and/or wisdom are not always attained by everybody, and some people will die at the age of 90 or older, never having reached a state of maturity.

We can become physically capable of doing various things at varying ages. A couple of teenagers are mature enough physically to produce children, but their emotional maturity might not be equal to the task, and their maturity as far as employers are concerned might be some years off. Physical maturity might be described as some stage where we cease to grow in height or cease to improve in some skill at which we practice. Emotional maturity is perhaps the key factor in most attempts at describing maturity. Some of us can learn to hide our feelings to some degree and explode inwardly. It is unlikely that one who does explode inwardly merits description as mature, but he or she is perhaps more mature than someone who explodes outwardly. Emotional control is perhaps the hardest kind of control to develop, and, even when attained, it might reflect some other kinds of mechanisms at work that might be described as maladjusted or immature, such as submissiveness, sublimation, repression, and the like. The term should not be used as a general description of anyone. It might be better to describe some behavior patterns as mature and others as still developing toward some proper criterion. A child might behave more maturely than an adult in some situations, and the use of the term as a trait description for the child might well be out of order, since the next thing the child might do is cry when he or she drops his or her lollypop. An adult with a dropped lollypop might not cry and still be thought of as immature by having a lollypop to begin with.

MEDITATION   *(See CONSCIOUSNESS)*

In the 1960s and 1970s, many people with time on their hands and some feelings of inadequacy were attracted to various Eastern philosophies and cultish practices. One, of these practices is an ancient one of simply sitting down, cross-legged, and trying to achieve what amounts to a blank state of mind. Various teachers of meditational practices surrounded the operation with philosophical verbiage and promises of great self-improvement in various ways, but the only people really known to profit from the practice are the teachers. In the form of meditation known as *Transcendental Meditation,* or TM, the meditator is told to pronounce, repeat, or listen to the sound of some word, the *Mantra,* provided by the teacher. Each person is supposedly given a different mantra, but since this is supposed to be a personal and secret word, and since meditators will not reveal it, we cannot be sure that the teachers do not provide everyone with the same word. In any case, after attempting to concentrate on the mantra for about 20 minutes at a time for two daily periods, a person will normally manage to become quite relaxed. He or she will not fall asleep, since the mantra-reciting task will keep him or her from falling asleep, but he or she can arrive at a state where nothing seems to be happening in the outside world, and, if he or she is in a quiet room by him- or herself, nothing much is happening. The same effect can be achieved in part by repeating any word—for example, "bubble", saying it over and over again. At first, one might think of a bubble, but in a short period, that sound of the word loses its meaning and becomes just that—a meaningless sound. When the meditator arrives at such a state, he or she will, in fact, be quite relaxed, breathing more slowly and less deeply, and feeling little or no stress. When he or she stops his or her meditation, he or she will frequently claim that he or she feels better, smarter, more creative, and less afraid of the world and its problems. The claims of some meditators make it appear that the procedure is little short of miraculous. The difficulty is that there is no known genuine result from all of the world's meditators thus far. They have not created any new ideas or solved any of the world's problems nor, as far as is known, made anyone else feel better except by talking him or her into meditating too. Like new converts to a religion, meditators are very enthusiastic about their success in becoming new people. Many meditators are former drug abusers who now feel no need for drugs. They have found a new way to take a trip. Busy people, such as factory workers, do not have the opportunity for such self-indulgence. Those whose work schedules allow it may enjoy a short nap or two during the day and feel refreshed and recharged. Thomas Edison was supposed to nap frequently. Edison's personality, however, as described by his biographers, does not appear to have improved from his napping practices. The question is whether meditators actually show any improvement in personality. Thus far, attempts to test meditator groups against other groups are not convincing.

Meditators have developed the notion that meditation is a way of arriving at an altered state of consciousness, as if that were somehow a desirable goal. Usually, we are in one of three states of consciousness—awake, sleeping, or dreaming. How dreaming is considered a state of consciousness is not made clear by describers of consciousness states, but meditators attempt to achieve a fourth state that is not liley any of the others, although it resembles all three. The meditator, for example, can demonstrate an increase in alpha waves, usually associated with the eyes being closed and not thinking of any problems. By taking fewer and shorter breaths, the meditator does not supply the brain with its normal oxygen and may thereby hamper its normal function. In any case, with the attempt to focus only on his or her mantra, he or she can arrive at the stage where nothing appears to be happening. Such a state is the desired altered fourth stage of consciousness. What value it actually may have is not known to anyone, including the swamis and yogas of the East.

Certainly, meditation appears less harmful than drugs, and if anyone with nothing better to do choose to meditate, we might tolerate such an inactivity. For the time of meditation, at least, the meditator is not bothering anyone and may even feel better for it. The point is to recognize that any claims to greater creativity or personality improvement have no foundation in any scientific studies. The practice may fill a gap in people who have failed to find solace in various religious practices, many of which also included some meditational operations, quiet periods, retreats, and other ways of withdrawal from the worries of the day. Some people get the same results from vacations, and scuba divers get rapturous about the marvelous feelings of communing with the eternal deeps.

MEMORY *(See MNEMONICS)*

Most of us think of *memory* as something of a possession, an agency, or power that resides somewhere within us and either works or does not work on demand. Psychologists like to think of remembering as an activity or a behavior that becomes active or apparent when something about the past comes up and we respond appropriately because of our past experience and presumed learning. Thus, we only speak of memory or remembering if there is some reason to believe that someone has been exposed to some stimulus previously and that it had some kind of impact on him or her. After we learn something, our nervous systems are changed in some way that allows us to respond to some stimulus in the way we came to respond in the past.Thus, if we do not know a stranger's name, we cannot remember it; after we are told the name and, perhaps, practice it a bit, we can now call the person by name when it appears desirable to do so.

How effectively we will be able to respond later on depends on a lot of factors that we frequently ignore, and we proceed to blame our failure to recall on a faulty memory. We have already mentioned one factor: In order to remember something, you have to learn it in the first place. Poor original learning will result in poor remembering. Another factor that is usually ignored is that if we only learn a few things, we may be able to remember them well. If we learn a lot, especially of a similar nature, we may suffer interference from other learnings when we are trying to remember some specific item. In a sense, the more you know or the more you learn, the more you will forget.

If we think of remembering as consisting of some connection between a stimulus and a response an $S_1 \rightarrow R_1$ (the 1 referring to some original learning) —and we now learn $S_2 \rightarrow R_2$, we may have trouble keeping the two associations from interfering with each other. When S_1 comes up, we may tend to respond with R_2, and vice versa for S_2. We rarely have a blank mind when someone asks us a question. We will think of something, but the answer need not be correct. Frequently, we will recognize the answer as incorrect and refuse to respond, claiming that we can't remember or that "nothing comes to me" when our trouble consists not of not rememebering, but of remembering the wrong thing. This is the *interference theory of forgetting,* and it is widely held by psychologists. Experimental evidence indicates that we will have more trouble remembering things as the similarity between S_1 and S_2 and R_1 and R_2 increases. If you try to learn the names of a lot of different roses or any other things that come in varieties, you will suffer a lot of interference. If you learn the names of one rose, one lily, and one daisy at about the same time, you will have less trouble remembering those names than the names of three roses.

Measures of remembering.   We usually refer to remembering when we try to *recall* something and fail to do so. When we fail to recall, it may be that the right question is not being asked—that is, the right cue or stimulus that might excite the correct answer is not being presented, or we misinterpret the question and remember some other answer that is not being asked for at the moment. Sometimes, we need a stronger hint than the question presents. If we can think of something only when some additional cues are presented, we are still recalling, but this is now an aided recall and is not so highly valued by us. Sometimes, we cannot recall, regardless of the cues. The actual stimulus itself must be present before we can recognize it. This kind of memory is called *recognition.* If we are shown a photograph of a person but cannot recall his or her name, we might be able to pick the correct name out of a list of five names that includes the correct one. We might be able to dismiss a hundred other names as not correct. Such recognition memory is not as useful as recall, since it calls for extra measures. Sometimes, we cannot even recognize something we could be expected to know, and we must *relearn* the association. Here, however, there is a strong probability that we will relearn much more rapidly than the time that the original learning took. In 1885, Ebbinghaus, the German psychologist, discovered what he called the *Savings Score.* He found that he could relearn any previously learned but now forgotten material with a substantial savings in practice time. This seems to hold true for anything you ever learned but now appear to have forgotten. If you once knew a foreign language or acquired some mathematical skill that now appears lost, you can relearn it in a fraction of the time you originally spent on it. It is like money in the bank. It takes a little effort to get it out of the bank. If you learn something, you still own it, in a sense, but you may have to do a little work in order to get it back. This, in a way, is the point of going to school. You will forget most of what you learn, but it is there for relearning as a savings whenever it becomes useful to do so.

MENTAL DISORDERS: TREATMENT   *(See BEHAVIOR MODIFICATION, CLIENT-CENTERED THERAPY, PSYCHOANALYSIS)*

There are many forms of treatment of the *mental disorders* or psychological problems, and they can generally be grouped into two major categories: *psychological treatment* and *somatic* (physical or organic) *treatment.* Psychological treatment includes all of the various psychotherapies, such as behavior therapy, client-centered therapy, psychoanalysis, and psychodynamic therapy, rational-emotive therapy, and so on. Psychological treatments can be applied to individuals or in groups, in residential settings, or in out-patient programs, and so on.

Somatic treatment includes drug therapy, psychosurgery, and electroconvulsive treatment (ECT). Somatic treatments are used by medical professionals, such as psychiatrists, neurosuregons, and psychiatric nurses. In general, somatic treatments, particularly psychosurgeries and ECT, tend to be used with the more severe cases of psychoses and depressions, although some psychiatrists use ECT more routinely. Drug therapy is very commonly used by psychiatrists with adults who are overanxious.

MENTAL HEALTH PROFESSIONS

Several major professional disciplines are included in the mental health field. The different professions are concerned with the same general goals: to provide diagnostic and treatment services for persons who have emotional problems. However, they differ in the education required for each profession and, although they overlap considerably in their actual functions, they also differ in the ways they work to achieve the common diagnostic and treatment goals.

Psychiatry.   People often confuse clinical psychologists and psychiatrists with each other. Psychiatry, the older of the two professions, is a *medical* speciality and has a modern history dating back to the early 1800s. The psychiatrist typically earns a four-year undergraduate degree (a Bachelor of Arts or of Science) and then completes four years of graduate studies in medical school, followed by a one-year clinical internship in hospitals or clinics. This is followed by two or more years of further clinical training as a psychiatric resident. The M. D. degree is the major degree in psychiatry.

Clinical psychology.   Clinical psychology is a much younger profession, having developed since the late 1930s, and is a *psychological* speciality. The clinical psychologist typically earns a four-year undergraduate degree (a Bachelor of Arts or of Science) and then completes four years of graduate studies in psychology, followed by a one-year clinical internship in hospitals or clinics. This may be followed by one or more years of further clinical training. The Ph.D. degree is the major degree in clinical psychology.

The number of years of graduate education is about the same for the two professions, and in each, one becomes a specialist: One profession is a specialized area of medicine, the other is a specialized area of psychology.

All states today have procedures for certifying or licensing medical doctors and clinical psychologists. Without such certification, no one can represent himself as a psychiatrist or as a clinical psychologist and offer therapeutic services.

Social work and psychiatric nursing. The social worker typically follows four years of undergraduate study with two years of graduate work in sociology and social work, followed by a year's internship. The Master's Degree in Social Work (MSW) is the major degree in social work. The psychiatric nurse is a nursing specialist who studies at least three years of nursing, with additional postgraduate training in psychiatric nursing.

Each profession has its own training and education programs and its own specified requirements for admission to and graduation from its professional schools. After graduation, these professionals, with their differing backgrounds, typically work together in the same hospitals, clinics, or schools.

Information on each can be obtained from state universitites; from county medical societies; and from state and county medical, psychology, nursing, and social work organizations.

MENTAL RETARDATION   (See INTELLIGENCE, HEREDITY)

Mental retardation is a term that refers to a condition of people who, from childhood, have a very low general intelligence (below an I.Q. of 70) and difficulties in learning adequate social functioning. Special programs are required for training, for education, and, in some cases, for total institutional care. There are approximately 6.6 million mentally retarded persons in the United States, or about 3% of the total population. This is a sizeable minority of Americans, and we can see that their special service needs present large demands on the rest of society.

Our society has tried to meet this responsibility. There are many state-operated total-care institutions for the retarded and many local governmental and private agency programs and sheltered workshops. Public schools and special classes are now provided by school boards, and the education and training of retarded children is now mandated by federal as well as by many state laws. Although many physical facilities now exist, the quality of their programming still needs much improvement.

Many mentally retarded persons, because of their extremely low functioning, require complete institutional care. The large majority, however, about 75% of all retarded people, function on a level of only mild retardation. With early diagnosis, good parental care, and proper education and training provided by the public schools, this majority of the mentally retarded can learn to read; develop good social adjustment; and, potentially, become self-supporting citizens, living outside of institutions.

A mentally retarded child means extra responsibility for a family, and too often this leads to considerable difficulties and hardships, since the family is taxed psychologically, in order to provide for that child's special needs. Perhaps the saddest thing is that we too often fail to see that a mentally retarded child is, after all, a child. We have to remind ourselves that this child, particularly one among the majority who function on the mild level of retardation, experiences feelings, concerns, emotions, fears, wonder, discovery, love, and so on, as do all children. A mildly retarded child can and does learn when given good support and training. A retarded child, when well cared for in a responsible and loving home, where parents are willing to and capable of the extra responsibility for meeting special needs, can learn to live a reasonably independent and self-supportive life as an adult. Institutionalization is not necessary for most retarded children.

Early diagnosis is extremely important so that special programs of education and training may begin as early as possible and thus give the child the best available opportunity to learn as much as possible. Some severe retardation, such as the condition *phenylketonuria,* or *PKU,* is caused by metabolic disorders. With early detection through a simple chemical test of the infant's urine, the metabolic imbalance can be detected soon after birth, the proper diet can be prescribed, and the retardation can then be prevented. In such cases, early detection is crucial.

When faced by the difficult problems and sadness of having a retarded child, the family must make some important decisions as to whether to institutionalize the child or to raise the child at home. When the retardation is severe and the daily care demands are great, institutionalization might be the best answer for both the child and the family. But the majority of retarded children need not be institutionalized; they do need particularly responsible parenting and family care and help. The family should consult with professionals who have made mental retardation their specialties—some physicians, psychologists, teachers, and the like. Most general practitioners do not know very much about retardation, and it is important to seek out those who do. Every state and most urban areas now have special governmental departments concerned with retardation, where advice and consultation are available. There are many private agencies, too, such as the Association for Retarded Children. These agencies are often limited and bureaucratic, but they are at least places where the parents can begin to seek help.

MNEMONICS: MEMORY TRICKS

Basically, an efficient memory is a matter of efficient learning. There is no way to improve your memory in general, since there is no such thing as a memory to improve. But you can remember better if you learn better, and there are some procedures that can help you to remember some things better than other people do who do not use these procedures. There are no exercises that will improve your ability to remember, but if you are concerned about forgetting things, that is a good first step. You can assume that you can forget anything you think you know. Certainly, professional singers forget the words to the Star Spangled Banner, and you could, too. Under some stressful conditions, you could even forget your own name. Having recognized this first point, you should, in general, consider everything you are learning as potentially forgettable and decide beforehand whether you really want to remember it for long and in what detail. Making a decision to remember leads to the second step: Ask yourself, "Why would I forget this? Does it appear to be similar to anything else I know that might interfere? Have I really studied it enough to claim to have learned it?" One recitation of a poem might not result in much retention. One recitation of a limerick might be enough for long-term retention. In short, make sure that you learn something before you complain about a poor memory.

Memory tricks. Some entertainers and popular memory experts who memorize telephone books and such material can astonish us with their capacities. These people are not specially gifted with splendid memories, and they work hard at their performances. In order to help themselves, they rely basically on the fact that if you spend a little time thinking about some simple pair of items (such as a name and a telephone number) and consider everything you know about that number and name, you might be able to remember it better than if you simply look at it, recite it a few times, and rely on some kind of memory to take over. When we say "think about it," we mean allow images of the two items to be associated to occur in some kind of meaningful interaction. Suppose that you want to remember that a number like 831-1619 is the phone number of someone named Jackson. If 1619 reminds you of the importation of slaves to this country and if Jackson reminds you of Stonewall Jackson, a Confederate general, you almost have it made. All you need is some association with 831.

Memory experts have prepared short words to stand for various numbers from 1 to 100. They memorize such words and numbers for which they can substitute to begin with, and they would have, in the case of 831, two words—one for the 83 and another for the 1. They would then combine these two words in sequence with slavery and have an almost unforgettable association with Jackson. Obviously, this takes time, effort, and some trouble; with 100 words previously mastered to represent numbers, one can image all sorts of combinations of other words and numbers and can then remember 100 items or numbers in sequence and baffle friends who do not know the original list. A simple list to help you remember 10 items in sequence is to associate 1-bun, 2-shoe, 3-tree, 4-door, 5-hive, 6-sticks, 7-heaven, 8-gate, 9-wine, and 10-hen. Now, in order to remember 10 things in sequence, all you have to do is picture the first thing with a bun, the second with a shoe, and so on. The success of such recalls depends on the person's ability to select suitable, active images. If the first thing in a list is a horse, the horse must be pictured as making buns, tossing them in the air with its nose, making a sandwich, or some other action. Then, when one wants to recall the first item, one thinks of a bun, and the horse image occurs more or less rapidly and automatically. The use of images for remembering is very potent and can be applied in many other situations than merely memorizing things in sequence. One should always think—that is, form images—of everything he or she is learning or is trying to learn. If you are studying the Battle of Waterloo, it will help to try imagining the opposing forces arrayed in certain locations; drawing maps (externalizing an image of a symbolic sort), picturing the uniforms, colors, artillery positions; even planning the battle for a different outcome and so on. Merely reading a description of the battle without making such additional efforts will not result in efficient retention. Reading is not learning or studying. Imaging the material is.

The basic point is that remembering anything calls for work. Prior preparation or familiarization with some kinds of cues may help in some kinds of material. No one has a photographic mind or some mysterious powers. In order to remember, you must learn and spend the time. For some kinds of retention, you must have spent the time prior to the present problem in learning a great many kinds of cues that can be readily associated with what you are facing. Thus, learning a list of dates, such as 1066, 1492, 1609, 1776, and so on, will help provide suitable images. Some people have a person or event associated with 1,000 or more names, places, or events; they learn the inaugural dates of all the presidents, the kings and queens of England, and so on. They are in a position to remember many new items by associating them with the already learned dates, numbers, or persons. It took time to learn all of that material, and that time can now be subtracted from any learning time related to the new material.

Other devices, such as rhymes and jingles, can help us to memorize some rules of spelling, the names of nerves, or which months have 30 days, but such devices are trivial, generally known, and not too helpful. If one forms a new poem for some new material, it will also help, but the trouble involved is probably prohibitive. We return to our first point: If you want to remember something, learn it.

In general, the retarded child needs special education and training and a good and loving home life where even more than normal patience is required of the parents. The demands on many families are too heavy, but for many more, they are met extremely well. As a society, we have not yet learned how to live with handicapped children, such as the mentally retarded, keep them in the family; and still maintain normal, healthy family relationships and activities.

MIDDLE AGE   (See DEVELOPMENTAL STAGES, HEALTH-RELATED AND ILLNESS-RELATED BEHAVIOR, OLD AGE)

Psychologists have typically thought of human development as occurring primarily in the early part of life, with little developmental change occurring through most of our adulthood. Developmental stages have been identified as infancy (birth to 1 year), childhood (1 year to 12 years), adolescence (13 years to about 19 years), and adulthood (20 years through the remainder of life). Most psychological studies of human development have focused upon those earlier years, up to about middle adolescence. Over the past two decades, however, other periods of life have become important areas of study, and psychologists have taken seriously the notion that people do indeed face new tasks and demands, learn new skills, and make new adjustments to changing conditions throughout their entire lives. The upper end of maturity, for example, from about age 60 through the remainder of life, is now actively studied as an important period of life with its own demands and adjustment problems, its own new experiences and personal satisfactions. Social, medical, educational, and recreational programs geared specifically for this age group have developed across the country, and senior citizens are recognizing that they can maintain an active and satisfying life and even wield some political power in our society.

Recently, too, *middle age,* that period from about 40 to 60 years, has been recognized as an important phase of life, different in many respects from earlier and later parts of adulthood.

Many physical, psychological, and vocational changes occur during this period, and, along with those changes, the persons' perceptions of themselves, their lives, and their futures also change.

The major general issue seems to be a vaguely felt and somewhat depressive belief that the bloom of life is over and that those over 40 are entering a period of personal decline. People recognize that they are physically changing, slowing down. They note that they have gradually gained weight over the years and now begin to feel it. They feel more aches and pains and more fatigue, and they begin to experience more serious illnesses that seem related to age, often after a lifetime of having felt quite good. Conditions such as serious gum diseases, heart problems, prostate difficulties, cancer, and so on begin to develop. It is a time of life, according to many medical researchers, when 40 years of neglected nutrition, too little exercise, and generally unintelligent health self-care begin to catch up with us. It is clear now that many of the degenerative processes associated with aging and formerly thought of as natural or inevitable, such as heart conditions, overweight, and degenerative gum diseases that result in the loss of teeth, could have been prevented by more sensible health-related behavior.

Women experience menopause, the ending of menstruation, during this time, and many women react with depression to these changes. Researchers believe that although physiological changes contribute to mood changes, the most important issues in menopausal depressions are psychological variables. People see their children grown up and leaving home, and they realize that one of their major functions for more than 20 years—family care—has virtually ended. Middle-aged people recognize that their levels of occupation are probably at their peaks and that they wll not advance much further, if at all. Add to those changes the recognition of physical slowing and increased ill health, and it seems understandable why some middle-aged people begin to feel somewhat depressed and vaguely disappointed about their lives.

But, as with older people, middle-aged adults are beginning to change their views of themselves and their period of life and to take advantage of their middle years to gain new experiences and satisfactions. Many middle-agers, rather than feeling saddened over the reduction of their families as children grow up and leave home, are beginning to recognize and to enjoy the advantages of lessened family responsibilities and to use their newfound free time to gain new experiences and satisfactions, indulging themselves for a change. Growing numbers of people are changing careers—not necessarily because of dissatisfaction with old careers but often because of the satisfaction of gaining new knowledge and skills. Many women, having been dutiful homemakers for 20 or so years, are returning to school and to the workplace, developing new careers for themselves. There has been a noted increase, for example, of women in their forties who attend graduate schools and become lawyers, teachers, psychologists, business executives, and so on, and who have an expected 20 or more productive years in their new careers.

Undoubtedly, society's views of middle age are changing from a concept that it is a mature period of little further growth or advances, a beginning of physiological and psychological decline and decreased activity and enjoyment. Our new concepts view middle age as a period of many opportunities for personal growth, for change, and for new experiences and satisfactions. If middle age begins at about age 40, then people can look forward to an expected 25 to 30 more years. How actively we enjoy those years, how much we grow personally, and, to a large extent, how physically healthy we are, depend upon our own personal, individual behavior.

For those readers who find themselves approaching or already in middle age, our best advice is to look around; to begin to note all of the advantages of your age, knowledge, skills, position, and so on; and to expect another 25-30 years of life and determine to use those years actively and enjoyably.

MIND: THE MIND-BODY PROBLEM   *(See THE BRAIN, CONSCIOUSNESS, UNCONSCIOUSNESS)*

Philosophers like to ponder over the *mind-body problem*. There would be no problem if there were no mind, only a body. Some have taken the over view: There is no body, only mind. The latter view, known as *idealism,* was the creation of Bishop Berkeley (1685-1753), the Irish philosopher. Since the time of Descartes (1596-1650), the great French mathematician and philosopher, people have thought that they possess a body, to be sure, and that some place within it, usually the head, they have another kind of something called a mind that thinks, wills, decides, chooses, and otherwise governs our sensing, knowing, and feeling activities. This view is known as *dualism.*

Psychologists generally try to get along without talking about a mind, since they feel uncomfortable with such a "something." If you consider the many ways in which the mind has been described, you begin to wonder if there could possibly be such a thing. Consider: Someone loses his mind, changes it, or makes it up. Someone has an evil mind, a dirty one, or a one-track one (presumably others have two- or multiple-track minds); some minds are healthy, others are destroyed; minds are also supposed to be divided, as in "I'm of two minds about this," or divided into conscious, semi-conscious, or unconscious kinds, stages, or levels. Apparently, some minds have backroads or recesses that may be deep; minds can be probed or read (without instruments—only procedures); some minds are venturesome; others are strong, weak, or simple; people can join minds together, as in with one mind; minds can be destroyed, boggled, warped, or blown; they can also be corrupt. Clearly, a mind that can do all or be all these things would be a marvelous thing. But if you examine the various phrases and adjectives involved, you see that when people use the term *mind,* they are really referring to somebody's behavior.

The mind is inferred from behavior as a guiding, governing, or regulating machine, but if the guidance or control can be traced to other recognizable and predictable factors, there would be no need for a so-called mind. This is the point of view of psychologists, who, although they are usually regarded as people who are interested in minds or mental events, actually study behavior and relate this behavior to the measureable aspects of the environment or to the person doing the behaving. Mental events cannot be observed or studied. At best, they can only be inferred. Because different kinds of behaviors in different animals have been related to differences in brain structure, most psychologists tend to identify mind with brain and prefer to study the brain rather than the mind. Actually, most psychologists do not study the brain as such but only the behavior that is controlled by the brain. Biopsychologists who do study the brain find no mental activities in the living brain. All that can be observed are chemical and electrical changes.

MINIMAL BRAIN DYSFUNCTION

When people behave in a peculiar fashion and we have no history of any specific cause, it is easy to attribute the behavior to something wrong with their brains. If there is no history of seizures, tumors, or other trauma, and if routine inspection does not reveal any serious damage to the brain from disease, lack of oxygen, and so on, the diagnosis of *minimal brain dysfunction* may be presented. The word *minimal* means the smallest, and so the term is really being misused, since no one knows what the smallest possible brain dysfunction could be. The diagnosis is usually made from abnormal electroencephalogram records and other neurological tests of reflexes, coordination, sensory defects, and slow development. Sometimes, the diagnosis is made on the basis of cognitive factors—that is, on such things as memory and attention span, as well as other perceptual and intellectual weaknesses.

The diagnosis of minimal brain damage or dysfunction is something that should be left to qualified neurologists and not to teachers in public schools. It is not a specific diagnosis that pinpoints a source of difficulty. It can be a catch-all kind of term to tack on to any weakness or lack, to uncoordination, or to language development problems, since it is true that all of our functions must be related to brain activity in one way or another. A child with faulty vision or hearing can be helped, although without glasses or hearing aids, his or her brain may be unable to perform its proper functions. If there are some kinds of general damage to a brain from a difficult birth, poor nutrition, diseases involving high fevers, and the like, there is a likelihood that there will also be difficulties in maturation, perception, and coordination, about which very little can be done.

MODELING   (See ADVERTISING, IMITATION, TELEVISION EFFECTS ON CHILDREN)

We have all seen the little child—or remember when we were the little child—who dresses up in parents' clothing and pretends to be so very grown up. That imitation of adult behavior is a charming bit of childish play; but the important point here is that the children are not merely playing; rather, they are very actively *imitating* and *learning*. Children try out what they have seen thousands of times—adult mannerisms, movements, speech, work, and emotion—and, in the process, they are definitely learning to behave in much the same way. Adults, including parents and teachers, television and movie stars, rock groups, comic book heroes and cartoon characters, athletes and people in advertisements, as well as other children and adolescents, are all powerful *models*. Children and adolescents learn a geat deal of their own behavior through the thousands—perhaps millions—of their observations of the way other people behave and then by imitating and practicing that behavior.

All of us know that children imitate their elders, but we tend to dismiss it as cute, childish play, and we adults generally fail to realize how powerful our own *modeling* is in shaping the behavior of children and adolescents. Parents and teachers who smoke cigarettes; who take drugs (prescriptions, of course); who are irritable, cross, aggressive, constant criticizers; and so on do not deliberately set out to teach the children in their care to behave that way. But, by consistently modeling such behavior for years, they are effectively teaching children just that. An irate parent or teacher might punish a child or angrily lecture about talking back, being late, making a mess, and the like. The adult might believe that the verbal message on how to behave properly is getting through to the child—and perhaps some of it is. But the angry parent or teacher might also, unintentionally, through modeling, be teaching the child how to browbeat children, how to shout, and how to be irrationally angry over only a little incident. A teacher might give a verbal lecture on the health hazards of cigarettes because it is part of the required curriculum. But when the students know that the teachers' lounge is filled with cigarette smoke, which lesson are they learning—what the teachers *say* or what they *do?*

Because adults do not believe in the power of their modeling, children are constantly faced with very mixed messages: Adults who *say* one thing but *do* another. One of the few groups who do understand the power of modeling are the advertisers. On television, on billboards, in magazines and movie theaters, wherever visual messages are possible, their basic advertising technique is to present an attractive person who models the behaviors that the advertisers want you to imitate (smoking, drinking, using drugs to help us sleep, buying a particular brand of soap, etc.).

Psychologists, too, use modeling procedures in working with both adults and children. One example is seen in helping a child to overcome some fear. The psychologist might model appropriate fearless behavior or arrange to have other children model it. The fearful child observes the models, and then, with the help of the psychologist, who tries to keep the child calm and reassured, the child gradually, in small steps, imitates parts of the desired behavior. Eventually, the child may imitate the entire behavior (for example, approaching a dog).

Adults should keep in mind that what we do may be far more powerful a learning influence over our children than what we *say*. If you want your child to learn some way of behaving, such as speaking clearly or politely, reading well, remaining calm under tension, and so on, then you must show the child how to do so by behaving that way yourself. If there is something that you do *not* want your child to develop, such as slovenly manners or aggression towards other people, then make sure that you do *not* model that behavior yourself.

MOTIVATION   *(See DRIVES)*

Motivation is perhaps the most mysterious problem in psychology. In common parlance, it covers the question, "What makes him or her tick?" That question is a good one, since it suggests that man is a machine that works in a certain way—sometimes in some undesirable or unexpected way—and that if we only knew what made him tick, we might be able to control his behavior in desirable (to us) ways.

The answer that psychologists have adopted to the motivation question is that man acts the way he does because of the way he is made (his heredity) and because of the way he was brought up (training, learning experiences), with an underlying assumption that the behavior involved is always related to some natural, biologically ordained, survival patterns. In general, survival means avoiding harm or pain, and, if not positively seeking pleasure, at least maintaining a proper balance of all the life support systems—that is, a suitable intake of oxygen and food and a proper amount of rest and bodily comfort, such as freedom from excessive heat or cold. The starting position for accounting for motivation, then, is a biological one that takes account of bodily conditions, including the internal organs, glands, and their secretions.

Over the millenia that man has evolved and survived, he has also learned to anticipate future needs, not only for the next hour or day but for years ahead. One only has to see an old man in some unsatisfactory state to consider one's own condition at that age and to give some thought to avoiding the same dissastisfaction. Once the development of man proceeded to the point where he could take account of future survival needs, a whole variety of behaviors became possible as different people, through accident or otherwise, discovered the kinds of activities or objects that could allay present needs and future fears. Different diets in different cultures or even different tastes in the same culture could be traced to specific experiences that had been recognized, not necessarily correctly, as benefiting survival. Thus, some people eat snakes and insects or each other, while others find such diets repelling. When any action is indulged in that does not appear to have an immediate survival—that is biological value—we ascribe it to a social motive. Social motives vary tremendously with various cultures, ages, and times. They include such things as desires for wealth and material objects, for appreciation of the arts, for preferences in clothing and recreation, for knowledge or academic degrees, for social recognition in politics, for community activities, for prestige, and, in general, for any values that anyone might endorse.

It is generally held that one learns his or her social behavior and values on a simple principle that the particular behavior and/or values were first a function of some chance responses to some situation and that there then followed some kind of consequences that can be described as a reward. Much of what we do that is a result of learning is also a result of having been rewarded for doing whatever it was. Subjectively, this translates into a principle of hedonism, or a pleasure-pain principle. We can stay on the objective level of rewards if we choose, since it is not necessary to bring up the notion of pleasure if talking about rewards will do.

The question of motivation, of why we do what we do, is then answered by most psychologists in the following way: We do what we do because we were rewarded for doing that and because we were not rewarded or perhaps punished for doing something else. Such an approach denies that anyone has any mysterious, subjective, internal mechanisms, such as greed, kindness, altruism, aggression, power-hunger, curiosity, or need to dominate or to be dominated. The greedy man only behaves in a way that some of us might call greedy: There is no independent greed motivating the person; he is merely doing what he has learned to do in the given circumstances—in his past he was rewarded for behaving in such a fashion.

In general, we do what makes us feel better and avoid doing what makes us feel worse. Such feelings become learned (associated, conditioned) to various stimuli, and we then report that we like this or that and dislike or hate something else. If there are no stimuli around, we do not have any feelings or motives either. It should be clear that we do not have any unconscious motives of the type that could be made conscious by any kind of analysis. We could have an unconscious need for starch, for protein, or for something else missing from our diets and not know precisely what we were needing. If a meal of spaghetti tastes unusually good, we may have been undergoing some starch deprivation without having recognized it. Such unconscious conditions are, however, a far cry from any alleged unconscious motive to kill somebody. Such motives, when they exist, are all too painfully obvious. Psychologists generally believe that if we want to change anyone's motives, we must first change his or her behavior. We must reward him or her for doing something that pleases us instead of doing what seems to please him or her. With careful control over the rewards—that is, making sure that what is done does not result in a reward—and simultaneously making sure that we reward him or her for what we want him or her to do, we can change his or her behavior without worrying about his or her motives.

MULTIPLE PERSONALITIES   *(See PERSONALITY)*

A dramatic form of psychological disorder, *multiple personality,* is very rare, with only about 100 reported cases in all clinical literature. One of the best-publicized cases was reported by psychotherapists C. H. Thigpen and H. M. Cleckley, in 1957, and became known as the "Three Faces of Eve."

In a multiple personality case, a person exhibits two or more distinctly different personalities, one of which takes precedence over the others at different times. While engaged in one personality, the person usually does not recall the other variations that he or she shows at other times.

Psychologists believe that in cases of multiple personality, the person shifts from one role or personality to another. The distinctly different roles are thought to be developed around personal conflicts, so that one personality might be quiet, industrious, serious, and somewhat sad, contrasting with another role that is mischievous, seductive, heedless, and adventurous, as in the case of Eve.

In essence, the multiple personality may be an exaggeration or escalation of the normal conflicts and role variations that all of us experience. Many of us have wanted simply to take off and have a good time instead of dutifully going to work as we do every day. Most people develop personal compromises and are able to contain these conflicting tendencies within the boundaries of their usual functioning. In the multiple personality, it is as if the person gradually separates the two or more kinds of conflicting desires, develops complex roles around each one, and then engages in them separately, one at a time, so that they do not directly conflict.

This *dissociation* allows the person to engage in behavior that would ordinarily conflict with other roles or personality. In psychiatric terms, this is considered an *hysterical dissociative reaction.*

How much credence one can place on reported cases of multiple personality is always a question. The patient may be engaged in a put-on. In any event, the individual does act or behave differently at different times—sometimes markedly so. Friends and relatives cannot understand the behavior because it is so uncharacteristic. We all behave differently at different times and places as we play various social roles. In multiple-personality cases, the behavior is extremely different from what might be expected. The best way to view such cases is from a behavioral aspect rather than from that of personality change. The behavior change is what must be explained, not some hypothetical personality.

N

NERVOUS BREAKDOWN   (See BRAIN AND NERVOUS SYSTEM, REACTION TIME)

The popular expression, *nervous breakdown,* is generally interpreted as some kind of personal collapse, usually attributed to emotional strain. Actually, nerves do not break down, and nothing snaps in the brain or nervous system as a result of any emotional activity. A physical injury to the body might sever some nerves, but you cannot worry yourself into any state wherein the nervous system is affected. There can be illnesses that involve the nervous system that can result in some damage, and some so-called psychosis may be the result of some kind of damage to the brain of a physical or chemical nature. A person in the third stage of syphilis, for example, may suffer from *general paresis,* which does involve a brain deterioration. Many popular expressions about neural structures are simple metaphors for other states. Thus, nerves do not tingle, jangle, or become frayed. Nerves cannot stand on edge, get jittery, or get lost, as in "I lost my nerve." Here, the obvious reference is to some failure to carry out some mission. The failure is not due to any nerve loss but to some other factor, such as fear. Similarly, other expressions about nerves refer to other states or conditions.

Nerves are actually long or short strands of specialized tissue, somewhat like strings: Some are covered with a sheet of cells called *myelin;* others are unmyelinated fibers. Each nerve that you can see is made up of hundreds of nerve fibers joining together to form the nerve itself. Although we react to all kinds of stimuli (electrical, mechanical, light, sound, touch, taste, smell, etc.), the nerves only react when the stimuli, through one means or another, set off what is called a *nervous impulse,* which amounts to a chemical-electrical discharge that proceeds along a nerve like the burning of a gunpowder fuse; it take time for a neural impulse to get from one point along a nerve to another or to a muscle. Once a nerve reacts, it cannot react again for something like .0001 of a second, or a millisecond. In a sense, the nerve has broken down, but actually, during that period, it is in its *refractory phase,* a kind of rest or restoration period. Immediately thereafter, it can react again. Nerves do not break down, even after thousands of repeated stimulations.

NEURASTHENIA

People respond to stress and anxiety in different ways. One of those variations is to give in to the fatigue that is often generated by long-term high anxiety and thus to feel constantly tired and weak, with aches and pains. When this becomes a person's major way of coping with psychological stress, the response is called *neurasthenia.* Psychologists believe that the neurasthenic has few other well-developed adaptive skills for responding to stress, even to the normal stresses that we all face in everyday life.

Interestingly, the neurasthenic's fatigue is highly selective, often overpowering during the day, when most of the stresses are operating, but disappearing at night, particularly if the person is going out for some recreation.

In its traditional meaning, neurasthenia means *nerve weakness,* and, in the early 1900s, psychiatrists believed that it was due to extreme overwork. But today, it is recognized that neurasthenics, as compared with other people, are far from over-worked, although they may succeed in giving the impression that they are. In truth, the demands made on them are no more than those imposed on all of us, particularly those who have accepted heavy responsibility, such as caring for a family. Neuras-thenia describes a condition of frustration, discouragement, lack of motivation— almost hopelessness—with feelings of fatigue. Neurasthenia has been called the *house-wife's syndrome* because so many cases are found among young housewives. They find themselves trapped at home while their husbands are out creating their own careers. They feel cheated, frustrated at giving up their own possible careers and other aspirations. They are frustrated and discouraged, and the major results are extreme listlessness, lack of motivation, and fatigue.

Neurasthenia is not easy to treat in therapy, since it seems to be so thoroughly ntertwined, created, and maintained by the person's life style. The most effective treatment would probably entail not only understanding the nature of the frustration but also actively changing the person's life, such as developing a career, getting a job, or continuing an education. In the case of a housewife, however, the changes might create other problems in a marriage, such as the wife's guilt feelings over not properly caring for her children or a husband's resistance and resentment over his wife's more active role outside of the home. It may be that as women achieve more complete occupa-tional and professional equality with men, neurasthenia will no longer be largely the housewife's syndrome.

In essence, the estimated two million neurasthenics in this country must learn to develop more active, personally satisfying lives—a difficult assignment for anyone to pursue after years of frustration and lack of direction.

NEUROSIS *(See CLASSIFICATION OF MENTAL DISORDERS, NERVOUS BREAKDOWN)*

Neurosis has been a commonly used term during this century, both professionally and by the general public. It refers to psychological problems or conditions in which the person experiences high anxiety and, as a result, has difficulties functioning. Ineffi-ciency, unhappiness, and anxiety were considered the basic symptoms of a neurosis. Because the neurotic could still function, although not up to his or her potential, the disorder was considered less severe than a psychosis. The neurotic has almost become a Western-culture stereotype—that is, he or she is the constantly worrying, fearful, and highly nervous person who always seems to be in some sort of crisis. Interestingly, although the neurotic was nervous and might have nervous breakdowns, there was not supposed to be anything wrong with the neurotic's nervous system. His or her prob-lems were supposedly psychological, not physical.

Traditionally, neurosis has been viewed as a broad category in which anxiety problems take on various directions or characteristics, resulting in several different types of neuroses. These include the following: general or free-floating anxiety felt almost all the time and not necessarily related to specific stimuli *(anxiety neurosis), phobic neuroses* (highly specific irrational fears), *obsessive-compulsive neuroses, hysterical neuroses, hypochondriacal neuroses, depression,* and so on.

Traditionally, the treatment of neuroses has been psychodynamic in nature. Since the 1960s, the effectiveness of such treatment has been questioned, and newer behavior therapy approaches, such as systematic desensitization, particularly with phobic problems, appear to be the most effective.

The category, neuroses, is too broad to have been very useful, and the people categorized within it were often far more different from each other than like one another. These and other problems led the American Psychiatric Association, in its most recent revision of its diagnostic manual, to abandon the general term *neurosis* entirely and, instead, to focus more descriptively and specifically on the characteristics of each case. Treatment, then, would focus on these specific problems rather than on the characteristics of the general category, neurosis.

Although the term has been dropped from the professional diagnostic manual, neurosis will undoubtedly continue as a common term in general and professional usage for many more years.

NEUROTIC VICIOUS CIRCLE   (See SYSTEMATIC DESENSITIZATION)

The term *vicious circle* describes some of the personal binds that people can develop around their own anxieties. For example, some people may typically feel very anxious and inadequate in social situations, feeling uneasy and unable to carry on simple conversations as other people seem able to do. The anxiety that they feel is uncomfortable, and, when invited to a party, for example, they might make excuses in order to avoid going. Avoiding the party removes that particular threat to themselves, but it also does other things: Having turned down the invitation, they typically begin to doubt and criticize themselves. "I've done it again!" they say. "Why can't I just go and have a good time?", and so on. Thus, turning down the invitations makes them feel even more inadequate and anxious, all of which can further disrupt their social functioning. Also, by refusing many invitations another thing happens: They do not allow themselves the opportunities to engage in such social situations and to gain practice in the needed social skills. The less practice they allow themselves, the less skill they actually develop; the less skilled they are, the more social failure and anxiety they experience; the more failure and anxiety they experience, the more they are apt to avoid future social situations. They have gone right around the circle, getting deeper and deeper into the progressively greater anxiety, poorer social skills, more failure, and growing avoidance of social situations. What makes the circle vicious is that it all progressively worsens as the victims trap themselves.

This kind of anxiety-mediated behavioral problem has been successfully treated by behavior therapists using combinations of *assertive training* and *in vivo desensitization.* People who realize that they have developed this circular behavior problem, whether it involves a social situation, work, personal relationships, or other settings, can help themselves break out of the vicious circle. One strategy is to try to attend limited, carefully chosen social engagements that might be very brief and not highly demanding. As experience and skill grows in such limited settings, a person can gradually begin attending longer, more involved social situations. The main idea is to gain skills and experience gradually in a sequence of situations that begin with limited demands, moving on to the more complex situations only as skills are gained. It helps if a sympathetic person, such as a spouse or a friend, goes along to give moral support when it is needed. With some thought and planning, this basic idea of gaining skills gradually can be used in other vicious circle situations, too.

NON-HOSPITAL TREATMENT OF MENTAL PATIENTS
(See COMMUNITY MENTAL HEALTH)

As the community mental health movement has grown, professionals have relied less upon traditional hospitalization for their clients. A variety of alternative services and programs is being developed and made available throughout much of the country, particularly in the larger cities. Among the alternatives to hospitalization are the following:

Special Classes.   Traditionally, both mentally retarded and psychotic (schizophrenic or autistic) children were sent to full-time residential institutions, frequently for their entire lives. Gradually, first for mentally retarded children and only recently for autistic and schizophrenic children, efforts have been made to provide useful services while keeping the child at home. Special classes in public schools have been developed to educate and to provide good social learning experiences for the children. The special education, combined with parent training, can maintain the children in their more natural environment—in their homes and with their families—rather than consigning them to residential institutions.

Parent Training.   Since the early 1960s, many psychologists have focused on the direct training of parents in how to work with or help their mentally, behaviorally, or physically handicapped children at home. The training focuses on how to teach appropriate behavior; on the development of language skills; on reducing inappropriate or troublesome behavior, such as tantrums; and so on. The parent becomes a knowledgeable and important part of the child's habilitation.

Group Home.   A group home is a residential unit in which about ten clients share a residence, supervised by the group home staff. The intent is to provide a more intimate, more homelike atmosphere than that found in the impersonal, dormitory living settings usually provided by hospitals and other large-group settings. Group homes have been established for clients of all ages, and they include both the retarded and the emotionally or behaviorally disturbed.

Sheltered Workshop.   In the process of rehabilitating mental patients, the mentally retarded, and physically handicapped people, a special, protective, work-training setting can be helpful. Called a sheltered workshop, the setting is supervised by professionals and their assistants and provides the clients with vocational training, work, and social experience. Many sheltered workshops operate as commercial subcontractors. They carry out commercially valuable tasks and provide paid employment to clients who would otherwise have no work experience or income. The intention is to help to train clients for later fuller employment in less protected settings. For many clients whose handicaps are severe, the sheltered workshop may provide their only work experience. As such, it can be of great psychological benefit for those people.

Halfway House.   A halfway house is a residential unit for mental health patients who were once hospitalized but who no longer require the complete care of a hospital setting. The halfway house is ordinarily a small residence unit, a group home, but it serves a specific function as a temporary living unit that bridges the transition from full hospitalization to more independent living in the community. The patient might live in the halfway house for a period of time and then perhaps move into another group home.

Walk-In Clinic.   Another alternative to hospitalization is the walk-in clinic. Located in the centers of cities where people can easily get to them, the walk-in clinics offer immediate services at low fees.

NORMAL VS. ABNORMAL

Some people are fond of saying we are all a little neurotic or abnormal. They get away with such expressions because there is no precise meaning to the term *normal*. This term commonly refers to the usual, the expected, the average, or the routine. When someone deviates from the routine, we might refer to him or her as *abnormal* or as a *deviant*. It is the degree of deviation that matters, since no two of us are alike in all respects. Normal, then, applies to what most of us are like—most of the time and within some limits. What determines the limits is the important question. There are three common considerations or views of normality or abnormality. We can think of these as the medical view, the cultural view, and the statistical view. From the medical approach, any infection or illness is abnormal. A broken leg is abnormal, as is a bloody nose. But even illnesses can be mild or severe, and many of us do not go to bed with a slight cold. An illness can run a normal course, to be sure, but it is an abnormal condition in itself. There are also variations of normal bodily functions—for example, heart rate and blood pressure. In such cases, physicians consider *normal limits*. Abnormality becomes a matter of exceeding limits that are set by physicians' experience.

From the cultural approach, the term *abnormal* is used to describe behavior that is normally regarded as undesirable. Some kinds of behavior are so undesirable that laws are passed against such behavior. The abnormal behavior then becomes illegal. Where there are no laws that grant rights, and where people are free to exercise their liberties, the behavior can still be regarded as abnormal if it goes beyond some poorly defined cultural limits. A boy can dress as a girl if he is playing a part on the stage. Wearing his costume outside the theatre might be viewed as a sign of deviance.

Statistically, normality is defined in terms of being somewhere in the middle area of what is called the *normal distribution curve*. If we measure 100 men for height and weight, for example, and graph the results, we shall find that most men will measure about 5 feet, 9 inches and weigh about 150 pounds. When we say most men, we mean that the middle 68% or about two-thirds will be between 5 feet, 6 inches and 6 feet tall. Such men would be considered normal. As we get below 5 feet, 3 inches and above 6 feet, 3 inches, we begin to run into rarer and rarer cases, and such people would be considered abnormal in height. But where do you draw any real line? Obviously, there is no particular height that is the normal height. Something like the average height might be taken for practical purposes as representing the ordinary or acceptable height that will not draw comment. In behavior patterns, we have a different story, as it is difficult to assess the extent and frequency of, to say nothing of the reasons for, some behavior. In general, it is best not to use the terms at all but to describe the behavior itself, taking reasons into account before considering it unusual.

O

OBESITY   *(See ANOREXIA NERVOSA)*

Obesity is a common problem that plagues 50 million Americans, with some 15% of adolescents being obese. It is usually defined as being 20% overweight for one's height, age, and body structure, and it is also measured in other ways, such as by flesh-fold tests, to determine the proportion of fat tissue at different places in the body. Being obese poses both physical dangers, such as the increased risk of heart attacks, and psychological problems, particularly for adolescents and young adults, who feel deeply different, rejected, and so on because of their weight and appearance.

Professionals know a great deal about obesity, its causes and problems, but are not very successful in treating it. The general population is equally unable to treat obesity, but, unlike the professionals, the public is extraordinarily ignorant about obesity. That combination of (1) millions of people suffering a disorder that (2) makes them uncomfortable and highly motivated to cure or change themselves with (3) extraordinary ignorance about nutrition, bodily functions, and human behavior makes us easy prey for all manner of professional and commercial hucksters, diet books, pills, quick weight-loss programs, and so on—none of which work.

What do we know about obesity? It is not a person's glands, heredity, or metabolism that causes him or her to gain weight no matter how little he or she eats. It *is* caused by *overeating* and *underexercising*. That is the behavioral combination that leads to obesity. If people ate less and regularly exercised more, we would not have so many obese people.

But what makes us eat too much and exercise too little? It is *not* because of deeply hidden, unconscious needs for love or some sort of unconscious self-hate, as the analysts might tell us. It is because we have developed extraordinarily bad eating habits and are controlled by external cues, such as the time of day; the amount, sight, and smell of available food; social pressures to eat; and so on. Normal weight people eat when they feel hungry; fat people eat when the environment tells them to, and it does so in a great multiplicity of ways.

What about obese children? They tend to become obese adults. Recent research suggests that children, by being overfed, develop a greater than normal number of fat cells. Once developed, those fat cells are never reduced in number, only in size, when the child later diets. The abnormally high number of fat cells remain, ready to swell up again when the person begins to overeat and underexercise.

Obesity is a physical and psychological problem that is caused by a lifetime of faulty learning. Some of us learn very bad eating and exercise habits. The successful treatment of obesity, then, if ever it is to be developed, is not going to be medical— through pills, special substances, diet wafers, and so on—nor is it going to be through psychotherapy, such as analysis. Rather, what is needed is a relearning process (1) to carefully alter those very destructive, habitual, eating behaviors; (2) to learn more about good nutrition and bodily functioning; and (3) to increase regular exercising.

Changing one's eating habits requires a great deal of planning and hard work and a long time. Fat people who think they might quickly lose weight in a few weeks through the latest fad diet, wonder pills, or wafers are cruelly fooling themselves and helping to make some sharp operators rich.

The best treatment approaches now available—and these may improve in their effectiveness as more research is carried out—involve extensive behavior modification programs. In these programs, people meet in groups that provide good social support; they learn about good nutrition and about how to exercise. Mostly, they learn how to alter their environment and their behavior to reduce eating and to increase physical exercise.

Probably the most difficult thing for very fat people to accept is that losing weight is not easy: It means work. It requires a major relearning of eating and exercising habits and nutritional information. It requires *time*—a good year for significant results—and it requires hard work and constant effort. There is no other way to lose weight successfully and keep from regaining it. But Americans will probably continue to spend millions for the promised quick weight loss of the magazine advertisers.

OBSESSIVE-COMPULSIVE BEHAVIOR

The terms *obsessive* and *compulsive* refer to repetitive, fixed, or stereotyped functioning in which the person repeats the same thoughts (obsession) and/or actions (compulsion) with little or no apparent success in controlling or stopping the activity. The person feels that he or she cannot control the obsessive thoughts and that the compulsive acts *must* be carried out. The person recognizes that all of this activity occurs against his or her will, and they almost always recognize that their behavior is irrational and even, at times, bizarre; but they cannot control it, no matter how much they recognize its disturbing nature.

Obsessive thoughts and compulsive acts can range from minor annoyances to major, highly distressful disorders. Most of us, for example, have experienced the annoyance of a tune or a thought that we cannot get rid of for a while. Many adults must knock on wood, avoid stepping on cracks in the sidewalk, and check a number of times to see that the door is securely locked before leaving the house—and even then be plagued with the persistent thought, "Did I lock the door?" These small bits of compulsive behavior, then, are quite common.

Compulsive behavior can become part of a person's character, or, more properly, the behavior can become a consistent or reliable part of that person's behavioral repertoire. Many people are extremely orderly and must keep their desks, closets, and the like all carefully arranged in some familiar, special way. The person with reliably compulsive behavior will usually become quite upset when the familiar oderliness is disturbed. But their compulsivity can also often be a considerable asset in their work.

On more serious levels, the obsessive thoughts may be very distressing, such as being unable to control thoughts about someone in the family getting sick or suddenly dying. Many psychoanalysts would interpret such thoughts as really being unconscious wishes for the illness or death of the other person, but there is little good evidence to support that interpretation.

Compulsive behavior may, in time, develop into full-scale, daily compulsive rituals in which the person spends many hours a day organizing, straightening, or checking each room in the house. In these cases, the person becomes distressed over the inability to control thoughts and behavior, and normal functioning is interfered with, largely taken over by time- and energy-consuming obsessive and/or compulsive ritualistic behavior.

The successful treatment of obsessive and compulsive behavior is difficult to achieve. Psychotherapy and several behavior therapy strategies are probably somewhat effective, but no reliably effective treatment approaches have yet been developed. It may be of help to obsessive-compulsive persons to know that there are many others like them and that their distress may be somewhat relieved in therapy or, perhaps, in time. Unfortunately, there is no evidence that the obsessive-compulsive can be helped by just talking to an understanding therapist.

OEDIPUS AND ELECTRA COMPLEXES

Freud considered his concept of the Oedipal situation to be of great importance in understanding neuroses. The *Oedipus complex* was named for the Greek tragedy in which King Oedipus was consumed by guilt and shame after learning that the man he killed was his father and that the woman he had married and loved was actually his mother. Because of Freud's emphasis on the son-mother relationship as basic to neurosis, the Oedipal complex has become widely known.

According to the psychoanalysts, every little boy must compete with his father for his mother's favors and attention, and his sexual desires for his mother are controlled by fear that his father will punish him. The feared punishment, according to Freud, is castration, that is, unconsciously, the boy fears that his father will cut off the little boy's penis. The Oedipal situation thus involves conflicts, sex and aggression, anxiety, fear and guilt, as well as direct competition with the father. The many complex problems of the Oedipal situation, then, according to the psychoanalysts, must be resolved, or else the child's continued psychological development will be in jeopardy.

Freud postulated a similar *Electra complex* for girls, who supposedly have strong sexual desires for their fathers and thus compete sexually with the mother. According to psychoanalysts, the conflicts and anxieties for girls are equally disturbing, and resolution of the Electra complex for girls is as important for their later development as is resolution of a boy's Oedipal complex.

Many neurotic problems are traced back by the psychoanalysts to this supposedly universal Oedipal or Electra complex. These assumed child complexes are offered as explanations for the adult neurotic problems. As with most of psycho-analysis, the theory is compelling and certainly interesting. But there is virtually no evidence that the analyst's interpretation of the Oedipal or Electra complex to a neurotic client is in any way a helpful or effective treatment for the adult neurotic. One of the most obvious limitations of Freudian psychoanalysis is that although Freud actually studied only a very markedly limited number and type of wealthy European adults—and never directly treated a single child—the ideas he gathered on his limited sample were assumed to apply to all peoples at all times in all places—that is, to be universal truth and basic human nature.

There is not much good evidence that little boys want to have sexual inter-course with their mothers or that girls also wish to do so with their fathers. Of course, if we believe the theory, we can interpret all sorts of normal behaviors in children—aggression, affection, anxiety, night-time fears, and so on—as indicating the operation of the Oedipal situation, but this kind of after-the-fact interpretation, the stock in trade of the psychoanalyst, does not constitute evidence that the theoretical notions are correct.

OLD AGE: SENILITY

Some people live into their eighties and nineties, and, in general, with advancing years, they begin to show signs of mental and physical decline. Despite sentimental proclama-tions about senior citizens and golden ages, older people begin to lose their sensitivities to sound and to visual as well as other stimuli. After age 45 or so, most people need glasses in order to see print and detail and show similar declines in audiometer tests that indicate they no longer hear high pitches. Other sensory losses are not well docu-mented because of the difficulties in measuring such senses as smell, taste, and touch. Old people also begin to lose weight and stature, in that they tend to bow over. With advancing years, arteries begin to harden, and people begin to suffer from arterial sclerosis, with an increasing probability of strokes; strokes can be mild or severe, and the subsequent damage to function depends upon the severity and location. Some people suffer numerous small strokes and show periods of inadequacy from which they sometimes make modest recoveries. As the years and cerebral damage go on, the aging person may begin to show peculiarities in behavior. He or she becomes more and more forgetful, especially about recent events; he or she misplaces things and is unable to find things, sometimes because he or she hides them in different places. The tendency to hide money, food, and other possessions suggests some feeling of suspi-cion about friends, neighbors, family, and surroundings, perhaps, some insecurity about status.

As people age, their friends die off, and they become increasingly alone. With a decline in intellectual acuity, they appear to be unable to appreciate the fact that there are fewer people around to pay attention to them. In advanced stages of debility, they are unable to recognize their own children, whom they might regard as intruders. If not supervised, they can wander off and get lost within short distances from their homes. What to do about such people is a complex moral question for which there are no easy answers. As medical science progresses, and as diseases that formerly killed off both young and old are conquered, people live longer. The American Social Security System was based on the hypothesis that most people would not survive long after 65. At present, this assumption has been shown to be wrong, and the financial base of the system is threatened. Old age does not represent golden years for many octogenerians any more than childhood represents the happiest years of anyone's life.

ONE-PARENT FAMILIES

Approximately one out of every ten children live in *one-parent families*. The reasons include death; divorce; desertion; separation; long-term illness and hospitalization of one parent; imprisonment of a parent; and, in a small but perhaps growing situation, having an unmarried parent. There are about six million American homes in which the only parent is the mother and about one million with a father only, making an estimated total of seven million families, or about twenty-one million people, living in one-parent families.

What are the effects on children of growing up in a one-parent family? A great deal of clinical research involving nearly 500 studies and cases has been done, but the only conclusion one can draw is a very general one: The two-parent family offers more support and help to children than the one-parent family; but the one-parent family is not necessarily any more pathological or disturbed than the two-parent family. What all of this psychological research boils down to is something that most reasonable parents already know: It is a far more difficult job for one parent alone to raise children than it is for two cooperating adults. It is not impossible, however, and, despite all the difficulties, extremely good, high quality, loving, and supportive one-parent families do exist, in which children do grow in perfectly normal, healthy ways.

It is true that many children in one-parent families have severe problems; it is also true that many children in two-parent, supposedly intact families also have severe problems. What appears to be important is the quality of the parenting provided, not the number of parents at home.

Our advice to those parents who must raise their children alone is this: Your task will be much more difficult because you will be alone and must assume all day-to-day parenting responsibility; but being alone does not mean that you necessarily must be a worse parent. If you have good parenting skills; if you work hard at it; and if you maintain affection, patience, guidance, concern, and interest in your children and your family life, your children can grow up just as healthy, normal, happy, and successful as children from "intact" homes. No one can ask more of any parent.

In those situations where divorce or separation has created the one-parent family, there is almost always a great deal of conflict and sharp disturbance in the family. Following the divorce, the children will be negatively affected and will need time, probably about two years, to adjust to the new situation. But once the turmoil and adjustment is completed, even the divorced family can then function in very healthy, normal ways. It all depends upon the remaining parent.

ONE-TRIAL LEARNING

Many associations and responses to new stimuli are learned in one trial. You need hear only once that your grandfather just died, for example. Commonly, what you can learn in *one trial* is some single association or response, but you are not likely to remember it for long if you do not practice or repeat the new learning. In the 1960s, psychologists devoted a lot of research to what they called *short-term memory* (STM). In such research, one would be shown some small amount of material—for example, three unrelated words for a time of three seconds. He or she would then be asked to subtract backwards by threes from some number, such as 948. After about 18 seconds of such subtraction, he or she might not remember the three words, especially after going through the exercises four or five times. The situation is parallel to looking up a new phone number, getting your party, and carrying on a conversation for a few minutes. You then find that you no longer remember the number. You remembered it only long enough to dial it. Any material that is briefly experienced is not likely to stick with you and requires rehearsal. What you remember depends on how it is tested. You might, for example, *recognize* the phone number or some parts of it even after a week. You would certainly know that it did not consist of seven zeros.

Some psychologists—for example, Edwin R. Guthrie—argued that you always learn everything in one trial. The trouble is that most learning assignments consist of a number of steps or items and that you only learn one at a time in one situation. If the situation changes, you may not be able to respond correctly. Thus, in playing golf or billiards or in any other task involving some motoric skill, you may learn a very particular and specific kind of stimulus-response association, but that stimulus may never be repeated precisely. It takes a long time to learn all the possible stimulus-response arrangements, and that calls for a great deal of practice and experience with different situations. The more you practice in what can be called a single skill (such as playing bridge or baseball), the better you will get, even though everything you learn, you learn the first time you do it.

Many psychologists agree that vivid, exciting outstanding, and isolated experiences can be remembered after only a single exposure. One fall off a roller coaster is probably enough for permanent retention—if you survive.

OPERANT BEHAVIOR

The term *operant* is Professor B. F. Skinner's word for *instrumental responses*. Skinner saw the really important kinds of behavior as consisting of operating on the environment and resulting in some kind of change—an effect bringing about either a positive or a negative reinforcer. The word *operant* is so closely identified with Skinner that anyone using it to the exclusion of the term *instrumental* is readily identifiable as a Skinnerian.

P

PAIN

Pain is not a well-understood sense, if it is a sense at all. The reason for questioning its sense nature is that, unlike other senses, it is not restricted to some specific type of stimulus energies but can be aroused by extreme stimulation of any sense. Very loud noises and very bright lights can be painful, for example. Although pain is usually discussed in terms of fine nerve endings under the skin, various kinds of internal pains, the intractable pains of cancer, the intense headaches, toothaches, and other organ ailments are difficult to trace to superficial nerve endings underlying the skin surface.

There are no good physiological indicators of pain. Ernest Hilgard, the Stanford psychologist, points out that a physiological indicator should show some increase with increases in reported pain and some decrease with reports of decreasing pain. No such indicators exist. Blood pressure does appear to be a promising candidate, but research has not yet established a strong correlation. Physiologists currently are making new discoveries about chemical secretions that are aroused in various ways and act as pain suppressants in ways similar to the effects of morphine. Sometimes, placebos excite such secretions, and patients actually feel less pain, even though the medicine they took has no direct action.

Pain is extremely variable in terms of individual differences, and even whole cultures appear to vary in the response to presumably painful stimulation. Members of some racial and national groups may be stoical or almost hysterical in their reactions. Women in childbirth vary from some who act as if there were no pain to speak of to those who appear to be unable to withstand the pain even with the aid of morphine, which, incidentally, does not appear to reduce pain in about a third of the people who receive medication for relief of pain.

Some people feel no pain at all because of some peculiarity or defect of the nervous system and are comparable to the blind and deaf in this respect. They are in constant danger of injury, since pain is normally a warning sign. Newborn infants apparently feel no pain, and children growing up probably learn to react with reports of pain as mothers rush to bandage small cuts and bruises. A small child falling down and picking himself up may not cry unless he or she notices a parent close by. Experiments with animals (dogs) at McGill University in the 1960s indicated that the dogs that were reared in individual boxes with no access to the sight of people or other dogs showed no signs of pain when they were tested after about a year of isolation from the time of birth. They would sniff at lighted matches and not retreat from hot radiators when placed against them. Learning presumably plays a major role in how individuals respond to painful stimuli.

When we expect pain, something might hurt. If we are otherwise preoccupied, we may feel no pain, as many athletes have discovered after a football game in which they have suffered various bruises. Soldiers in the heat of battle may not notice minor wounds. Under hypnosis, good subjects will report no pain from stimuli that they cannot stand if not hypnotized. Incidentally, their blood pressure may not rise under such stimulation, and the credibility of their reports of no pain is therefore rather high, since subjects who are not quite so good or who have not been given suggestions about anesthesia (absence of pain) will show the blood pressure increase.

After the opening of China, Americans became aware of the popularity of *acupuncture* as an anesthetic procedure, and some Americans have undergone surgery under acupuncture with no reported pain. It may be that acupuncture has some kind of blocking effect if the long needles that are twirled around by the manipulator actually stimulate some nerves, which stimulate other parts of the nervous system to engage in what has been called a *gating action*—that is, an action permitting or preventing the passage of nervous impulses to the brain. On the other hand, it may be that acupuncture, when successful, is analogous to hypnosis and, basically, to suggestion. The hynotized subject is generally relaxed, and the condition of relaxation, along with a freedom from fear, may reduce the stimulation we identify with pain to some minimum. Fear, as dentists have always known, is a major component of pain. Professor O. H. Mowrer of Illinois points out the common decrease in toothaches as we near the dentist's office and the relief we feel when we know the doctor is coming, even though no medicine has yet been taken or even prescribed.

Pain, then, is a complex, largely unknown reaction to unusual stimuli—unusual in that they are extreme. A needle is extreme in that the pressure involved over the tiny area it might penetrate is great as compared to some broad area of stimulation— for example, a bed of nails. We also report pain when the stimuli are unknown or are difficult to trace or remove. Internal bodily difficulties might be described as painful because we do not know what is occurring. *Referred pains,* for example, originate in some area where we may feel nothing and appear to occur in places where we are not suffering from any known source of pain. Once the pain source is established and a cure is promised, the pain also decreases, and one comes to live with it. The pain may remain as mysterious as is the efficacy of aspirin that relieves it, but knowledge of the specific origin and the probable duration always appears to be helpful. There is a great difference between a stubbed toe that we know will soon stop throbbing and a leg cramp that we cannot be sure will ever stop.

PALMISTRY

Palmistry, an ancient art of forecasting the future by looking at lines on the palm, has absolutely no basis in fact. Sometimes, people argue that there must be something to it because different palm readers told them the same thing. This argument has no virtue when it is recognized that people who claim to read palms have only read the same book. There are manuals on palmistry that state what various lines mean. Anyone who follows the book will then give the same interpretation. There are some things to be learned from hands. Hands that are soft, with polished fingernails, suggest that the owner is not a coal miner or farmer, although some coal miners keep their hands remarkably clean (using gloves). Chewed fingernails reveal that the owner is a nail biter, which might mean something more. A hardened hand might suggest karate or hard labor practice, and nicotine stains might suggest smoking. Probably nothing can be stated about a person after a thorough, even microscopic, examination of the hands on some one occasion, and certainly, nothing can be said about one's future unless the hands suggest something about one's past.

PANIC   *(See CROWD BEHAVIOR)*

Panic is irrational behavior in a threatening situation, and there is little that can be done if one allows him- or herself to get into a threatening situation in the first place. A crowded restaurant or circus tent or any enclosure without sufficient exits can be the setting for panic behavior should something go wrong. One can hardly avoid some crowded enclosures, but checking for exits and trying to be seated near one is about all an individual can do. Innocent observers are sometimes injured or arrested when trouble breaks out in crowd situations. The obvious remedy is to make such innocent observations by television rather than by personal attendance. Military personnel sometimes panic in situations of perceived danger and behave irrationally. Little can be done without the use of force, just as when a single individual panics and engages in hysterical behavior. A sharp slap on the face is the traditional prescription, but that may only work on the movie screen. Physical restraint will result in an eventual cooling off. One problem is that the appliers of the restraint may be close to panic themselves and may sometimes use more force than is necessary, with disastrous results.

The individual in a panic state sometimes appears to be stronger than one might expect. Such apparent strength is real enough, because there is none of the usual restraint that inhibits extreme exertion when one is unusually disturbed. A little old man can put up considerable resistance to restraint, as can a child in a strong temper tantrum, and the restraint of the person trying to control the person in panic makes the contrast vivid. When the restrainer is trying not to hurt the one in panic, the difficulty mounts. It can take four or five strong men to subdue a person in panic without injuring him or her. Just as in hypnosis, strong fears and terrors allow one to perform feats of strength that he or she would never consider under ordinary conditions. No one actually knows his or her own strength, and there may be dangers—for example, ruptures of various kinds—in excessive exertions. Because one cannot reason with someone in panic, there is little or nothing to do about such situations.

PARANOIA   (See SCHIZOPHRENIA, MENTAL DISORDERS: TREATMENT)

The term *paranoia* is used to label a type of thinking disorder. It is characterized by false beliefs (delusions) that are organized in a systematic and apparently logical fashion. The person may have delusions of persecution (that certain people or organizations are "out to get me") or of grandeur (that he or she is an extremely important person). The delusions have little basis in fact, but the person believes strongly in them and defends them.

An interesting characteristic of paranoia is that, despite the pronounced systemitized delusions, the person may appear very normal and rational in all other respects and continue to carry out his or her occupational and personal activities quite well. When the delusions become serious obstacles to the person and/or to his or her family, hospitalization is required, where the current practices of tranquilizing the patients will be followed.

There is a type of schizophrenia, *paranoid schizophrenia,* in which the person also has delusions of persecution and/or grandeur, like those of paranoia. The paranoid schizophrenic, however, suffers more severe thought and affective disorder and does *not* appear normal in most other respects. Paranoia and paranoid schizophrenia are two different conditions that have some similarities in the types of delusions they develop. Treatment of either is difficult and involves hospitalization.

PARAPSYCHOLOGY   (See EXTRASENSORY PERCEPTION)

Parapsychology is the general name for the study of alleged phenomena that are *outside* of psychology. *Para* means outside, beyond, alongside, or next to. Whatever it is, it is not psychology, and fewer than 5% of American psychologists are willing to admit that any of the claims of parapsychologists have any legitimacy at all. Those 5% take the position that anything is possible or that one ought to be open-minded about something until it is disproved. It is a curious situation, in that parapsychologists have managed to put the burden of disproof on the scientific world instead of presenting some proof in favor of their claims.

Parapsychologists have been very prolific in creating terminology at the expense of developing facts. Terms such as *psi, clairvoyance, telekinesis, paranormal, precognition,* and so on have gained wide usage with no factual backup. *Psi* refers to any paranormal phenomenon and is one of those sweeping terms that sounds scientific but is meaningless. *Clairvoyance* refers to some alleged ability to gain knowledge without the use of the known senses. *Telepathy* refers to some alleged ability to read minds or transfer thoughts (with senders and receivers); *psychokinesis* or *telekinesis* refers to the alleged ability of some (who claim to possess it) to affect movement in material objects without touching them (e.g., bending spoons by a power of the mind) or influencing the course of physical events, such as the number of spots that will turn up in a throw of dice (*Time* magazine referred to this as "Crapology"). *Precognition* refers to foreknowledge of coming events. Obviously, precognition would be a marvelous asset to anyone who had it and who also had a bent for betting or stock market investment.

The situation with regard to parapsychology is a sad one. Many people would like to believe that they had some special powers to help them along in an unfriendly world. The trouble is that there is no evidence worthy of scrutiny to support the claims of the honest believers, while at the same time there is a great deal of evidence that there are frauds and charlatans in this world who are taking advantage of the naive. Many stage magicians can duplicate any alleged psychic event, including conversations with your long-dead relatives. Such demonstrations will not persuade the believers, and nothing much can be done but to permit magazines and newspapers to continue printing hokum, just as they do with their daily astrological and bio-rhythm charts. The number of suckers in this world is, as Barnum said, increasing every minute. One difficulty is that even the alleged scientists who look into or do research in psychic matters are not always smart enough to detect fraud or error. Exposure of a fraud simply means this: "Well, yes, that one was a crook, but what about. . . ?" Disclosure of some source of error does not discourage the researcher: He makes the corrections in the procedure and continues gathering what he calls data. Uneducated people are in no position to evaluate the claims that come out of universities or from authoritative figures. Outstanding physicists have been taken in by charlatans because their area of expertise is physics and not fraud. There appears to be no hope that the parapsychologists will go away, and it will take a long time to educate their gullible publics to dismiss them as frauds or innocent dreamers.

PARENT-CHILD GUILT   (See GUILT AND SHAME)

Animal parents appear to have no capacity for guilt. Experimental attempts to create guilt in animals, notably dogs, have proved unsuccessful thus far. It is appreciated, of course, that for a dog to show guilt may be difficult, despite the folklore of the hang-dog look. What is known about birds and animals is that after a suitable period of nurturing, the young offspring are pushed out of the nest or otherwise abandoned to shift for themselves and that they do the same to their offspring, should they survive. Human parents, in general, do not, in our culture, eject the young. If anything, they hang on to them until the young, in rebellion, elect to remove themselves. There is no set age or period of maturity when children should, must, or do leave their parents. Some stay with their parents until the parents are dead. During the long period of years when human children stay with their parents, complex and numerous emotional ties develop on both sides, so that situational changes bring about the opportunity for both sides to feel *guilt*.

On the parents' side, the problem arises in connection with how much time, attention, and money should be spent on the children. Do they buy enough toys? Do they spend enough money on vacations, for college, for the wedding? Should they get the kids off to a good start by buying them a home, and so on? When the children get into trouble of one kind or another, the parent asks himself: Did I do enough? Was I too selfish with my time and money? Did I make the proper efforts to get help? These are good questions, but they are ethical-moral questions, about which no help can come from psychologists. The psychologist can only mutter platitudes about the fact that the behavior was a result of heredity and environment and make the point that the environment is something the parent cannot control effectively, any more than he or she could have done with the heredity. No one is responsible, and everyone does what he or she had to do. If there is no responsibility, there can be no guilt in any legal sense, but the parents can still feel inadequate, incompetent, worthless, and so on because of the cultural pressures that have made the parents believe that, some-how, the behavior of a child was their doing. They made the mistakes (of whatever nature) that resulted in the undesirable behavior. Their mistake might have consisted in or resulted from having more than one child which naturally enough prevents expenditures of time, money, and so on to the same extent that could have been afforded if only one child had been born. When single children get into trouble, the argument can be presented that he or she lacked siblings. It is a no-win situation.

Children's guilt. On the child's side, assuming minimal positive care from the parents, the child develops positive emotional ties toward the nurturing adults and may come to recognize certain sacrifices made by the parents. They give up a new car so that the child can go to college, or the father wears old clothes so that the child can have new ones, and the like. Such events can normally be taken in stride, and rationalizations such as "I didn't ask to be born" are probably pronounced by every child in times of stress. As the children and parents grow older, new problems develop. The youngsters feel the pressures to leave home and start out on their own, but by this time the parents begin to need attention, help of various kinds—perhaps even financial help because of decreased income from illness, unemployment, or other circumstances. Freud made much of the unmarried daughter keeping house for her invalid mother or father: It is the classical illustration. The sacrificing child develops neurotic anxieties and symptoms to go along with them. "When am I going to start living my own life?" becomes the slogan. Again, the psychologists are of no great help. To encourage independence for the child at the cost of depriving an aging parent of love, attention, and care violates the social pressures that have developed in most cultures. To honor your parents and other ancestors is a proposition that has found its way into many religions and cultures, and the child who has been raised in such a context is sorely tried. For the very wealthy, the problems do not exist in the same degree. There are always others who can be hired to look after the old folks, and, indeed, it is to the benefit of the young to keep wealthy old folks positively inclined toward them. For those at lower income levels, the problems can become almost unbearable, with any failure to cater to the old becoming a cause for misery and guilt.

There is no resolution for such guilts and conflicts in our culture that can be advanced as positive advice. The solution lies in a cultural change based on a principle of parents owing their children some to-be-established degrees of care but with children owing their parents nothing at all on the grounds that the children cite—that they did not ask to be born. Such a principle could operate only if other agencies were made responsible for such matters as care of health; nutrition; clothing; and, most importantly, education.

PERMISSIVENESS   *(See DISCIPLINE, PRAISE AND BLAME, REWARDS AND PUNISHMENT)*

Permissiveness is usually interpreted to mean that parents allow their children to do anything they feel like doing, including eating at any time they choose (a demand schedule), on the unsupported assumption that everything will turn out all right if everybody lives through the growing-up period. The promoters of permissiveness actually had no such license in mind: their position was more negative than positive, in that they really opposed punishment of children or overrigidity in scheduling such things as eating, bedtime, play activities, and so on. Such a position has some merit, especially if a more positive pattern of introducing rewards for desirable behavior is instituted at the same time.

The prevailing view among psychologists is that one should reinforce any signs of activity of a desirable nature and not reinforce any undesirable activity. This means that, although a child is not to be punished for something that a parent disapproves, he or she should not benefit by his or her misbehavior either. It is sometimes difficult to discover how the child benefits from some of his or her actions, but certainly a child should not be allowed to spill orange juice on a rug, for example. Until the child is old enough not to spill liquids, he or she should do his or her drinking in the kitchen or under otherwise controlled conditions. Although staying up late will probably not harm the child, it does interfere with parental plans for going out or having some peace and quiet, and some intelligent bedtime should be selected when the child is put to bed, whether he or she stays in it or not. A suitable schedule can be worked out by reinforcing successful occasions.

As part of the permissiveness operation, parents should never blame children for their accidents or even for deliberate nastiness. The *behavior* can be described as bad, not the child. The child is probably neither good nor bad, although behavior can be described as undesirable, antisocial, and so on. Permissiveness is therefore an attitude in which the child is accepted for what he or she is and is encouraged to behave along certain lines, while other lines are not encouraged. All of the available evidence suggests that beating children or otherwise threatening them is not effective and may have undesirable side-effects.

PERSONALITY

In casual conversation, people like to talk about the personalities of other people as if they possessed something unusual or peculiar, something that others did not have *Personality* is not something that you either have or have not. That might be charm, charisma, attractiveness, effectiveness, or something else. As far as psychologists have been able to come to grips with the issue, everyone has a personality, since personality amounts to how you differ from everyone else: It is your individual difference. If you are pretty much the same as a great many other people, then you might be referred to as having little that makes you stand out. Soldiers in the army are dressed alike, trained alike, and made to behave alike so that they, in effect, have no individual differences and, most importantly, can be replaced, like nuts and bolts in a factory. Soldiers are frequently referred to as replacements and are assumed to be able to perform just like the soldier they may replace.

To say that someone has a likeable or attractive personality is the same as saying that the person is likeable and attractive, or mean and ugly. What someone else's personality is does not depend upon that person as much as it does on who is talking about him or her. President Franklin Delano Roosevelt was a beloved figure to many millions of Americans, especially those from the lower economic levels. To the bankers and industrialists, who saw him as a threat to their activities, he was a monster, a radical, a real danger to the country. What Roosevelt was, in fact, was an individual with a certain physical appearance, certain speech patterns, certain manners, and a particular learning history. He did not have any more personality than the four Republican candidates he defeated in the polls. He was, of course, different from each of them, each of whom had his own social impact on the body politic. Social impact or effectiveness is not the same as personality; they depend upon those who undergo the impact or reject it. Great war leaders, such as U. S. Grant and Winston Churchill, could have been described as just full of personality, but once they had won their wars, they appeared to have lost their personalities and were no longer able to lead.

When we say of someone that he or she is not very good looking but has a swell personality, we are really saying that other individual difference characteristics of the person are pleasing to us, even if the person is not physically attractive. Incidentally, you cannot improve your personality. You might change in some ways, but then others might not like you.

PERSONALITY TESTS   *(See TEST-TRAIT FALLACY, INTEREST TESTS)*

Personality tests are based on a theory of traits—that is, that a person can be characterized as belonging to some type or as having certain specifiable features, such as aggressiveness, introversion, authoritarianism, liberalism, or whatever. There is sometimes some advantage to having some such information about a person you are about to meet, but behavior varies so much from time to time and from situation to situation that it is extremely difficult to predict how someone will behave in a novel situation. Personality tests, in effect, are designed to do just this. As with interest tests, the test makers select some samples of people who are said to possess some trait(s) and ask them a lot of questions to be answered by "yes," "no," or "sometimes" and try to develop a score for such features as hypochondria, neurasthenia, extroversion, authoritarianism, and so on. There is, of course, considerable difficulty with establishing such normative groups, since there are no tests for them other than rating scales or expressions of opinion, medical diagnoses, arrests, or whatever else is chosen as a criterion. Once some kinds of norms are developed, the test can be given to new candidates for evaluation.

Personality tests have no right answers, but people taking such tests can lie and attempt to develop a score that will present them in some desired light. Some more sophisticated tests have items built into them to determine if a client is telling the truth, and a *lie score* can be developed by seeing if the person is consistent in his or her responses and does not contradict him or herself. To attain some reasonable assurance that the score will be meaningful, personality tests are usually rather long. It should be noted that some of the questions may not appear to have any special signifiance to the test taker, but the answers may form a pattern that matches some kind of criterion norm. A sophisticated test taker may know what a queston is designed to reflect and may elect to answer it to suit his or her own purposes, but some tests may reveal patterns of interest, behavior, and symptoms that the taker is not aware of. It may turn out that someone who regards him- or herself as very masculine shares a number of feminine traits, and vice versa; a surface docility and modesty may mask a strong ego and some tendencies toward aggression, and so on. The great difficulty with personality tests is the accurate assessment of the criterion groups, along with the problems involved with trait theory.

PERSONALIZED SYSTEM OF INSTRUCTION (PSI): THE KELLER METHOD   *(See TEACHING MACHINES)*

It has probably always been recognized that students are individuals and that they would profit more from teaching programs that were tailored to their individual strengths and weaknesses, that they should proceed at their own paces, and that they should not be grouped into classes where the pace is assumed to fit some average student. Such personalized arrangements are expensive and available only to those whose parents can afford tutors.

Following upon the attempts of B. F. Skinner with his teaching machines and programmed learning proposals, F. S. Keller has tried to provide a solution to the expense problem by what has come to be known as *Personalized System of Instruction (PSI)*. In this system, college professors lecture only occasionally, presumably in order to help motivate students, if not to instruct them. The students themselves work alone (although they can consult faculty and other students), following course outlines and study guides that contain questions, assignments, and some instructional material. The student, in short, has a detailed syllabus of a course and learns the material by himself.

Keller has emphasized the concept of mastery, by which he means that each part of a course should be learned well before the student goes on to the next part. For meeting this need, Keller arranges his courses and proposes that others do the same in small units or sections to be learned in a serial and systematic order. A course is broken down into units—perhaps ten, or as many as twenty. Each unit is studied to the point where students can pass a test on that unit. The tests are administered and scored by student assistants, who then arrange for the next unit's materials to be provided. Tests can be taken as often as required to get a passing grade. No onus is attached to failure, and failure records are not kept unless someone is interested in statistical counts. The notion that failures do not matter, that only success counts, is commendable. The problem of time and assistance is solved by Keller through using student aides. For teachers in routine classes, scheduling tests for individuals would be a nightmare.

Studies evaluating the Keller method have rather generally demonstrated that students learn more and remember longer under the Keller system than students in courses that are taught in the traditional manner.

The results of evaluation studies also support the PSI concepts of mastery, especially in courses that are systematically organized so that what comes later depends upon what came before, as in mathematics and some science courses.

The Keller system calls on teachers to organize their courses in sections that can be mastered and tested and to provide students with considerable study guide material. The need for frequent tests and scoring calls for additional aides and supervision. Such an effort does not appeal to all those who have chosen the profession of teaching, and we cannot expect widespread adoption of PSI until Keller's own students multiply and encourage their students to multiply as well. Student satisfaction is commonly reported to be high, and we can expect the movement to continue. What Keller has emphasized should be the goal and guide of all teachers; namely, that the student must learn by him- and herself and at his or her own pace. The mastery of fundamentals is vital, and students should not go on if they have not learned the basic material. Teachers must expect to do more than talk at groups in lectures that may or not be systematically organized toward a goal. Syllabuses belong in the hands of the students as well as the teachers. All students are entitled to know what they are expected to know. Education should not be a mystique where the teacher springs tests as punishment for failure to learn or for what the teacher considers uncooperative behavior.

PHANTOM LIMBS AND PHANTOM PERCEPTS   *(See IMAGERY)*

People who suffer an amputation of a leg may sometimes report pains, itches, and other sensations, apparently coming from their toes, Similarly, finger tingles may be felt by people who no longer possess the arm of which the fingers were appendages. Such sensory experiences are called *phantom limb sensations* and appear puzzling to those unfamiliar with the fact that all sensory experiences are functions of activity in the brain. In certain parts of the brain, there are centers or connections for nerve cells that must be activated if one is to have certain sensory experiences. Normally, these are activated by nervous impulses coming from the source of the stimulation. Thus, if neural impulses are activated in the optic nerve, one will normally report some visual experience, but only after other centers in the back of the brain, the occipital lobe, are activated in turn. If the neurons in the occipital lobe are activated in any other abnormal way, as by a blow to the head, one may also have some sensory experience of light flashes. Popularly, we refer to such an experience as seeing stars. Electrical stimulation of these same neurons would also produce such an experience. During brain operations (under local anesthesia), the surface of the brain can be stimulated with tiny currents of electricity, and the patients sometimes report seeing and hearing things they experienced in the past. The Canadian surgeon, Wilder Penfield, reported on many such cases and concluded that many experiences we have appear to be like tape recordings in the brain. If the centers involved in such experiences are activated, we relive the experience.

When amputees describe sensations that appear impossible, it is because, in one way or another, the appropriate brain cells for the experience have been activated. An irritation at the stump of the nerve that had been severed at the knee, for example, might activate the neurons involved in what we experience as an itch.

People who suffer blindness or deafness after childhood may well imagine what things previously seen or heard look or sound like. Beethoven was able to compose great music after he became deaf, and blind students can visualize lists of numbers in rows and columns and appear to read them off. Such numbers are also *phantoms.* Actually, they are images that John B. Watson called the *ghosts* of *sensation,* perhaps more properly than he intended, since Watson had no use for a concept of images. The phantom sensations of amputees are truly ghosts of sensation.

PHYSIOGNOMY: READING FACES   *(See PALMISTRY)*

What can one tell about people by looking at faces and their features? We are familiar with the folklore about high and low brows, sensitive noses, sensuous lips, and granite chins—cleft or otherwise. Some con-artists make their livings giving *face readings* in department stores or at carnivals and similar places. Some even measure the sizes of various features and construct charts. No more can be told about your character from your face than palmists can tell from your hands. A face can be attractive to some, old or young looking, dirty, made up in various ways, and so on. These items tell you nothing certain about a person's character. Even typical happiness or sadness cannot be told from a face. Some people's faces are not especially expressive, and they might be called poker faces, but poker faces are not necessarily flat and expressionless. The good poker player might try to look pleased when holding a poor hand and depressed when holding a good one.

There are no established correlations between facial features and personality. A large, protruding jaw indicates only the bone formation of that face, not the personality behind it. Much has been written about people's eyes as the windows of the soul, their deceitful looks, and the like. Actually, the eyes are quite unimportant as far as the expression of emotion or anything else is concerned; they tell you little more than their color. Whether they are close set or far apart is of interest only to someone who is measuring you for eyeglasses. The mouth is much more revealing of some temporary mood or emotion. If you have a picture of someone who is angry or frightened, covering up the mouth will probably obscure any recognition of the emotion, whereas covering up the eyes might be irrelevant to an interpretation. But we know nothing more about a mouth than that it is large or small—possibly something can be learned from the teeth if they are missing, deformed, taken care of, or otherwise indicative of health and nutrition habits. Some judgments might be made about women from examining the make-up and hair-do, but these are poor bases for hard conclusions, especially from one examination. It is always better to observe behavior than appearance if you want to know what someone is like.

PLACEBOS   (See FAITH HEALING)

Many patients who are ill, or who think they are, demand and expect some kind of curative measures—some kind of medicine. Some people believe that they cannot fall asleep unless they take a pill. In many such conditions, only time will cure the patient, if anything will, and the physician or therapist finds that he or she can quiet the patient down for a while by offering a harmless pill that looks real enough but that contains nothing but sugar or dry milk. Such pills, known as *sugar pills,* are technically called *placebos.* Any treatment that looks to the patient like some possible therapy may also be a placebo if the treatment is not known to have any special effects or is presumed not to. Thus, the physician's bedside manner may be reassuring and relaxing to a patient, and the reassurance may help ease some anxieties, make the patient feel better, and allow him or her to have a brighter outlook. Whether such brighter outlooks or cheerfulness have any effect is not established. Some people begin to feel better if they are put on a waiting list, as compared to how they might feel if not on the list. If the placement on a waiting list is of some effect, it is also known as a placebo effect.

The use of placebos in research is common practice. In order to evaluate the possible effects of a drug, some patients are given the drug in appropriate dosages, whereas a control group of patients is given placebos. After an appropriate time, the recoveries in both groups are evaluated, and if the placebo group is the same or nearly the same as the treatment group, the treatment is recognized as meaningless. In all such research, matched groups of subjects are necessary—matched on age, previous history, duration and degrees of illness, and so on. The same procedures are followed in determining if some drug is harmful. Groups of animals are injected with some substance, whereas control groups are injected with saline solution. Any differential effects are then attributable to the drug.

An enormous amount of money is spent by people who take daily doses of tonics, vitamins, cold tablets, and so on that may do them no physiological good but may make them feel better. If a pill has a desirable effect on a patient, it becomes difficult to deny it just because its physiological action is known to be ineffective.

POPULARITY: HOW TO WIN FRIENDS AND INFLUENCE PEOPLE
(See PERSONALITY)

There is no question that most people like to be liked, to be popular, and to have a great many friends. There is also, however, no question that most people are not widely liked or popular and have very few, if any, friends. When people produce books designed to help somebody win friends and influence people, they are appealing to the great numbers of losers in our society. The probability is that there are no techniques available by which you can win friends and influence people if you have not already become the kind of person who does so, and such people do not use any special tricks. Books that pretend to help you will provide lists of operations or procedures you might try to follow, but the only one who benefits from such books is the author. There may be some advice of a modest merit that might make you more efficient or less dislikeable, but the probability is that if you need a book to help you to a more successful life, it will not help.

The famous Dale Carnegie made a fortune with his appeal to losers. He suggested a number of social tricks that might help. His first rule was to remember people's names. There is a certain superficial point here, because we all tend to forget the names of people who don't matter to us: If we want to meet someone, the likelihood is that we know his or her name perfectly well; if we do not want to meet him or her, there is little point to knowing his or her name. Some politicians practice the rule because they know that if they appear to know someone's name that person can feel that he or she must have had some kind of effect or importance. When politicians expect to attend a gathering of strangers, they will arrange to get a list of names and descriptions before the meeting for some study and rehearsal. It is important to most people to be recognized, and anyone that recognizes others will earn some brownie points. This, of course, is of minor value, because you can hate intensely someone whose name you know and who knows yours. The fact that you do call someone by name does not mean that he or she will automatically be your friend; at best, he or she might become an acquaintance who lets you do something for him or her. Friends are people who do things for you without expecting compensation.

Another Dale Carnegie trick is to let people do you favors. This kind of advice borders on the absurd. People will only do favors for you if they already like you, and you can only use the advice in reverse—that is, find out how much people will do for you and thus find out how popular you are. Many other popularity tricks are suggested in the numerous self-help books that flood the market. Some contain what appears to be good advice, but it is usually rather difficult to implement. It is not easy to be popular if everyone else wants the same thing. The only advice that can be suggested is this: Be nice to others—whether they appreciate it or not. You might like yourself better for it.

PRACTICE   *(See LEARNING, ONE-TRIAL LEARNING)*

Practice is normally identified with repetition and is equally normally assumed to result in learning. Some things can be learned in one trial, without any practice to speak of—for example, it only takes one hearing to learn that some dear one is dead. But even in such cases, we hear about it more than once and, in a way, practice this knowledge.

Usually more than one trial is required in order to learn more complex information or complicated skills. Most skills—for example, tennis or golf—are quite involved. In tennis, one must learn to serve, lob, and drive, anticipate where the return shot will come, handle the shot with a forehand or backhand, and so on. One might become good at one or some of these features and still lose games because all of the features are involved. Perhaps each separate feature of a skill is learned in one trial, with only one practice, but if there are thousands of features, thousands of trials are required. In tennis, for example, a ball may land almost anywhere and bounce in different ways. Thousands of response patterns may have to be learned.

Practice at the piano or at touch typing similarly involves numerous features, and no one learns to play the piano or type by touch all at once. Teachers prepare exercises or practice lessons that work out reasonably well, but no one has yet worked out any program or schedule that would fit all comers. No one knows how long a piano practice session needs to be. It could be that some people need shorter periods than others, but since the criterion of a satisfactory performance is a matter of opinion and not of numbers, there is no way to determine practice-period duration. If there is a willingness to work, then one could practice indefinitely and still not be perfect in somebody's opinion.

On the practical level, if one decides to set aside so many minutes per week to practice, it is better to practice more frequently for short periods than less often for long ones. Thus, for piano playing, two half-hour sessions are better than a one-hour session. There are other considerations, however, such as preparation time, warm-up, how long the material is, and so on.

All we can advise is that to become competent at anything worth doing—for example, playing the piano or any other instrument, typing, or various athletic skills—one must devote somewhere in the range of 5,000 to 10,000 hours to the procedures. Olympic champions nowadays are people who started their specialties at the age of 4 or younger. Great violinists start at age 2 or 3 and practice eight hours a day for years. We are describing top performers. Anyone who does not aspire to greatness need not practice as much, but he or she should not expect to win gold medals.

Practice does not make perfect, but it helps. If the practice is done in the absence of a teacher, the performer may practice errors. This will lead to perfection, of a sort, in performing errors. All practice should be supervised or at least include some objective criterion of success. Practicing foul shots on a basketball court gives immediate information about right or wrong moves, and one can improve by him- or herself. A coach could make suggestions about what is being done badly. Playing the piano is not so successfully done without a trained ear listening alongside. In order to get the greatest benefit, one should practice only with a teacher present.

In short, practice should be scheduled or arranged in keeping with goals. If you wish to remember some facts, they must be reviewed from time to time. A skill must be analyzed into components, and each component must be practiced to some satisfactory level of success. To become good at anything calls for many hours of work. Do not expect any real success without putting in the time. If you can afford it, get a teacher. Some things you can learn on your own, but a teacher can save you time.

PRAISE AND BLAME   (See PUNISHMENT, REWARD)

We all like to be praised and no one likes to be blamed. Psychologists generally agree that no one merits or deserves either. This is not to say that we should stop *blaming* or *praising.* Such acts are very effective in controlling behavior and represent forms of reward and punishment, but we should know what we are doing and what effects our own actions might have when we praise or blame others. The reasoning of psychologists is based on the general assumption of *determinism,* according to which, everyone always does what he or she has to do and could not help doing whatever it was, good or bad; and there is no more point to praising a person than praising a baseball for dropping when we release it. If a 7-foot basketball player slam-dunks a basketball, whereas a 5-foot, 8-inch basketball player cannot, there is little point to praising one and not the other. Telling your hostess that she served a beautiful dinner may get you another invitation, and it is the polite thing to do. Politeness will get you some praise in return, but such social niceties only represent the operations of our histories of training.

When an arsonist rapes your wife and burns down your house, you should certainly be angry, but there is no point in blaming the criminal. Certainly, action should be taken to prevent his doing it again, but that is another matter. The courts do not operate on a praise or blame basis; they operate on a guilty or innocent basis where the objective facts are examined, and where the question at issue is; Did he or didn't he? A soldier who saves his buddies by risking his life may receive a medal, and we may be glad that he did, but again, there are no grounds for praise unless we want him or others to do it again. Praise and blame are methods of controlling behavior. If used intelligently, they serve like other forms of reward and punishment. What we should appreciate is that there is no meaning to the concept that anyone *deserves* either; that notion is based on some belief that the person could have acted otherwise and chose to do what he or she did. Most people are extremely reluctant to accept a deterministic view because they would like to feel that they earned, merited, and deserved such praise as they occasionally receive. Our defenses against our own weaknesses and flaws make us only too ready to blame others. No one likes to be injured, and the emotional reaction to some hurt is frequently one of anger, with a felt need to aggress. Blaming someone helps to justify the aggressive attack.

PREJUDICE   (See ATTITUDES AND OPINIONS)

Prejudice is pre-judging. When you read in the papers that the police apprehended someone in a liquor store at night, you might assume that the person involved was a burglar. That would be prejudging the case. The person could have been in the store for some other reason. Even the smoking gun in the hand is not proof of guilt. In this country, we are supposed to believe that everyone is innocent until proven guilty. Hardly anyone actually sticks to such a position except those accused of some crime. In other countries—for example, France—it is assumed that one is guilty unless he or she can establish his or her innocence in the event that one is accused of some crime. This Napoleonic Code view is much closer to what people believe routinely, and when we do believe that someone is innocent, we do not do so because of any high moral principles but rather because we are prejudiced in the person's favor.

Prejudice is usually regarded in a negative way, as assuming or believing something bad about someone or some group without concern for the facts. Actually, we are all prejudiced in various ways about most of our life features, about people we work with, about other countries, about racial groups, and so on. The person who is prejudiced against blacks, for example, is prejudiced in favor of whites, and vice versa. One should not forget that black people are prejudiced, too. Prejudice is not a simple matter of preference, as, for example, for white meat instead of dark or for orange juice instead of tomato. It is a belief or a conviction that has been acquired without a consideration of the facts. An examination of the facts might support the prejudgment, but without such examination, a positive or negative conclusion is a prejudice.

Prejudice is obviously a learned affair. Black mammies used to nurse white babies, who loved them. In areas where both whites and blacks live, white children play with black children until their parents decide that they are too old to play with black children. Children are instructed by their parents about what is good or bad, right or wrong, without any thorough and realistic education, because that is impossible with children at the age when parents believe they should be taught such things, and they respond later on in terms of such emotional training. It is easier to believe something instead of constantly looking into a situation in order to establish the factual realities. The same holds true for adults who find it easier to believe than to check. Other people become prejudiced about foods, political parties, economic systems, movies, music, television shows, and the like.

We do not carry prejudices around with us as independent agencies that determine our behavior. Prejudices are emotional responses that are aroused by stimuli. We may not do anything when one prejudice is aroused because we may at the same time have some counter-prejudice aroused or because we may mask our views if it seems more useful to do so.

It is sometimes believed that one can be educated out of a prejudice by some kind of informational presentation. It appears, however, that prejudice, as an emotional reaction, must be eradicated in some other way. The emotion involved must be reconditioned through exposure to the object of prejudice with different consequences from those that might have been experienced or imagined before. Thus, it does no good to talk about the foolishness of some prejudice and its lack of substance. Emotions are not controlled by factual information. In the case of racial prejudice, for example, only actual physical association between members of the races involved will have any effect. If the results of the association are pleasant, a prejudice can be eliminated. If the results are unpleasant, the results will be negative, and the prejudice will be more securely established. Attempts at integration must be carefully controlled to ensure positive outcomes. Simply forcing people to be together will not do the trick.

On the other hand, if people are not forced together, they will probably not come together, and a legal forcing action may be necessary as a first step. The forcing of interassociation, however, should be planned to have positive results. Integration could certainly be more successful if begun with small children who are integrated to begin with, in the sense of there being no prejudice among infants and small children. Efforts to integrate at the child's level, however, do not appeal to those who want to solve the problem at once, without waiting another twenty years.

PROJECTIVE TESTS   (See PERSONALITY TESTS)

Projective tests are those in which the answers a person gives to questions or stimuli are supposed to reveal something about his or her personality, problems and conflicts, aspirations, and so on. The person being tested is supposed to project his or her inner conflicts and motives onto the test material. The two best known tests are the *Rorschach Ink Blot Test* and the *Murray Thematic Apperception Test* (TAT). In the Rorschach test, a person looks at 10 different ink blots—some colored; some black and white—and, in general, answers the question: What do you see here? No other instructions are given, and a person might respond to the blot as a whole or to any of its numerous parts. He or she might mention things that can be scored, such as color, movement, animal figures, and so on. The tester then interprets the answers according to his or her training in the use of various manuals. The manuals are based on other people's attempts to tabulate and interpret various responses from standardizing sample populations. After years of investigation, psychologists have not found any convincing evidence that the replies people make in the Rorschach situation are of any great help in interpreting a person's problems, and the use of the test is dropping. The test might be useful as a sort of groundbreaker and may allow a clinician to get some notions of a person's vocabulary and background, but such things can also be learned through routine questioning. There appears to be no good reason to take such tests, and if asked, one might well inquire as to why it should be taken, with the implication that one does not care to waste time.

The TAT is a test of 20 picture cards showing various people in situations that might be put to use as the basis for a story. The client is asked to tell a story about each picture (one card is blank) and to tell how the people got into the situation and what will probably happen. Again, the clinician tries to interpret the stories that are made up as reflections of the teller's needs, aspirations, prejudices, and so on. As with the Rorschach test, the validation of the TAT leaves must to be asked for and does not inspire confidence in continued use of the test. Again, one might well elect not to waste his or her time on such subjectively interpreted tests where the tester has such wide latitude to conclude almost anything he or she wishes. If the tests are to be used for experimental purposes, one might be inclined to cooperate, but any interpretation of personality based on such tests should certainly be suspect.

PROPAGANDA   (See ADVERTISING)

In European countries *propaganda* is regarded as a matter of spreading the word or educating the public; in the United States, the word has come to be associated with one-sided presentations or deliberate lying. It is usually distinguished from telling the truth, the whole truth, and nothing but the truth. Actually, we rarely hear all sides of any story in school, in the press, or from any other source, since frequently the other side is unknown, considered unimportant, or considered unsuitable for publication for any of many reasons.

Propaganda amounts to presenting a single point of view, although some opposing view may be presented inadequately or incorrectly in an apparent effort to appear honest or thorough. Advertising of commercial products is the obvious example, where a particular product is presented as the best. It should be noted that not only are commercial products sold by one-sided presentations but that personalities in the entertainment or political worlds are also packaged and sold to an innocent public in the same way. Any organization that wishes to alter people's views or habits may engage in propagandistic techniques, where an effort is made to enlist support by emotional appeals and promises that may be made in good faith but that are not necessarily supported by facts and reasoned argument.

The techniques of propagandists are similar to those of advertisers. What should be recognized is that we are all propagandists for our own views and that, frequently, we are not even interested in or concerned about the other sides of a story. We propagandize our children about moral, ethical, religious, political, and economic views as a matter of routine, long before they are even able to ask about other possible views or opinions. Professional propagandists are distinguished from the rest of us only in that they make their livings in the dissemination of one-sided presentations in favor of their clients. Losing one job merely leads to taking another where the opposing product, view, or personality will be sold with equal enthusiasm.

PSYCHOANALYSIS   *(See COLLECTIVE UNCONSCIOUS; UNCONSCIOUS)*

From about 1890 to 1939 Sigmund Freud elaborated and popularized *psychoanalysis,* a personality theory and treatment approach to mental problems. Psychoanalysis was the first comprehensive theory of personality development and functioning as well as the first systematic psychological approach to mental treatment. Freud's influence on the Western world has been enormous, and psychoanalysis has had impact not only on psychology and psychiatry, but also on literature, theater, philosophy, history and even politics. Psychoanalysis was further elaborated and modified by a long line of analysts, and its many current offshoots now form a major theoretical and treatment approach to psychological problems. In terms of the amount of research and writing in the mental health field, psychoanalysis is now second only to the more recently-developed behavior modification concepts and approaches.

At the time that Freud began to influence the field, the science of psychology was focused on the study of human *consciousness* and was just beginning to scientifically study human behavior. At the same time the practice of psychiatry was a medical speciality carried out in large mental hospitals, and was based mainly on biological theories. Against this background of biology, behavior and, mostly, the study of consciousness, Freud almost single-handedly turned attention to what he believed to be the most important but least-studied part of human personality, *unconscious* processes. The most basic ideas of psychoanalysis were not original with Freud, but had been developed almost a hundred years earlier by a small number of psychiatrists who had been influenced by the philosophy of the "Romantic Protest" movement in the late seventeen hundreds. Those Romantic Psychiatry ideas included a conception of a three-part personality consisting of an inherent "basic needs" level, out of which develops an *ego* and a *conscience*. These three systems were thought to be in dynamic interaction, and conflicts often arose between them. Ideas of unconscious, internal psychic conflicts, dynamically related portions of the personality, and psychological problems, were all part of the early Romantic Psychiatry that long predated Freud. In his writings, however, Freud did not refer to them.

Psychoanalysts today believe that current psychological problems are the results of long-buried unconscious conflicts that first arose early in life. The thwarting of a child's basic human drives of sex and aggression in the process of socialization, are considered to be the center of the adult's problems. The psychoanalyst listens to the patient's free associations, to descriptions of dreams, and to general talking about himself, and tries to interpret to the patient what the dream content and free associations mean in terms of the patient's basic drives and unconscious conflicts. In this process the patient will presumably come to gain insight or understanding of the problems. As these unconscious problems are solved, the associated overt symptoms should also disappear.

Psychoanalytic treatment is very lengthy compared with other treatments and is the most expensive psychotherapy now available. However, its high costs and lengthy involvement do not make it any better therapy than the many other psychotherapies available.

On evaluation, psychoanalysis offers a comprehensive theory of personality, but it remains a theory that is largely untestable. Laboratory research has been largely unsuccessful in supporting psychoanalytic hypotheses. While it is still influential in the mental health field, and many of its ideas and procedures have been adopted in other therapy systems, psychoanalysis itself is no longer the major psychological model in mental health. Its influence has weakened, particularly over the past twenty-five years. Although it will eventually become only of historical interest as more modern concepts and therapy techniques continue to develop, psychoanalysis will undoubtedly continue for many more years.

PSYCHOHISTORY

Psychohistory is the effort to write a biography of some person, usually dead, in terms of his or her personality, commonly interpreted in more or less Freudian terms or principles on the basis of whatever available evidence there might be in the form of documents, diaries, letters, or other records of activities. Since the person involved may be dead, anyone can say anything at all without fear of libel or direct challenge. Thus, Freud wrote psychological biographies of Moses and Leonardo Da Vinci, the latter work being developed from a part of a dream that Lenoardo recorded. Ernest Jones, the biographer of Freud, even attempted a biography of Hamlet, translating Hamlet into Shakespeare, since Hamlet was presumably a creature of fiction. Other psychobiographers have worked on people such as Martin Luther.

Historians with professional training are in general agreement that any effort to describe any period of history involves a selective process and that the historian cannot help being choosy about what he describes and what he omits. The history is part of the historian, and no two histories will be alike. To attempt to analyze the personality and motivations of some long-dead person is a challenge unlikely to be met and results in a work that is mostly fiction disguised as a factual demonstration of the truth of some analyst's principles. Only those already in agreement with the author's views are likely to accept the psychohistorian's effort. It is difficult enough to get the truth about a living person, even with his help; to attempt to do so about the dead appears to be folly.

PSYCHOLOGISTS

Although we are all psychologists in our own little ways, in most states, it is illegal to present one's self as a psychologist unless so certified or licensed by the state. In order to be certified as a *psychologist,* one must usually have earned a Ph.D. degree in psychology at an accredited university and have had two years of experience at work that is evaluated as psychological activity by the certification board. He or she must then pass a test prepared by a certification board. The fact that one has studied psychology or is interested in psychology is of no concern to the state. In order to be employed as a psychologist outside a college or university, one must be licensed. Psychologists who earn their livings teaching and doing research do not have to be licensed, but they cannot work as psychologists beyond the campus.

Most psychologists belong to the American Psychological Association, which has similar requirements to those of most states. The Ph.D. degree and endorsements of two members are required. In the United States, there are over 50,000 accredited psychologists, and the number is increasing every year. Most of the psychologists engage in clinical practice, either in private practice or in hospitals, clinics, community centers, and the like. In order to be properly accredited as a clinical psychologist, one should take board examinations administered by the American Psychological Association and be granted a diploma. Before consulting a psychologist on clinical matters, then, it is proper to inquire about certification and about the diploma in clinical psychology. Diplomas are also granted (following tests) for industrial psychology and for the practice of hypnosis. Although the various degrees and diplomas do not guarantee anything other than what they do represent, one should not accept anyone's claim to being a psychologist without such credentials. Quackery is rampant in the field of mental troubles.

PSYCHOLOGY   (See PSYCHOLOGISTS, PSYCHOSES, MENTAL HEALTH PROFESSIONS)

Psychology is a science and a profession. On the scientific side, psychology developed as an offshoot of physiology and philosophy and was introduced in universities as a separate discipline around 1880. The date of the first experimental psychology laboratory is in some dispute, but it is generally agreed that the first laboratory was that established in Leipzig, Germany in 1879 by Wilhelm Wundt. The early work in psychology was devoted to the study of sensation and perception; later, interest developed in learning, emotion, motivation, problem solving, and thinking. Psychology came to be defined as the study of behavior and experience, with the latter term, *experience,* referring to what one might ordinarily describe as mental life. The common factor identifying psychologists was the interest in discovering the principles or laws that describe human behavior. This interest was frequently described as one of being able to predict human behavior on the basis of discoverable cause and effect relationships. The causes might be hereditary background or environmental experience: The psychologist was concerned with assessing the role of each. With the passing years, psychology expanded into a great many different fields, so that the American Psychological Association now lists some 35 different branches or specialties, such as developmental, clinical, industrial, military, humanistic, historical, religious, and educational psychology, as well as over twenty others. Psychology is quite specialized, and members of one division or area are not too well prepared to communicate with members of other divisions. Psychologists are not simply people who run rats in mazes. In fact, very few psychologists work with rats, and mazes went out of style in the 1940s. Nor are psychologists people who can read minds or psychoanalyze you. Psychoanalysis is a specialized procedure in psychiatry and is practiced only by M.D.s, except for a few rare lay psychoanalysts.

As a profession, psychology is represented in a variety of areas. There are clinical psychologists who offer psychotherapy for people who are not medical cases (psychologists do not usually treat psychotics); other professional psychologists work in industry and business in the areas of machine design, advertising, and personnel work. Still others work in schools in areas of behavior disorders, testing, and teacher and student counseling. Still others practice hypnosis for therapy and other purposes. Some psychologists train animals for advertising and show business. Many psychologists are employed by the government in the military, in social work, in education, and in a variety of programs ranging from outer space to local ecology.

Psychology is distinguished from physiology because it studies the whole, intact, integrated organism. Physiologists are more concerned with separate and specific organs or organ systems. A physiologist might study the heart, for example, but a psychologist might be interested in the heartbeat only as one of a pattern of reactions of the whole person.

Sociologists study groups of people, entire communities, or populations without regard to individuals as such. Psychologists are more concerned with the individual, how he or she affects a group, or how the group affects the individual's behavior. Note that psychologists are not really interested in any single individual unless they are engaged in clinical, professional work. As scientists, they are interested in people in general or in the abstract human being, the man in the street, or the average human being.

PSYCHOPHYSIOLOGICAL REACTIONS: PSYCHOSOMATICS
(See THE BRAIN, BEHAVIOR MODIFICATION: THERAPY)

Investigators have long believed that emotional factors and physical health are often related, but it was not until 1935 that H. F. Dunbar put together the existing information that showed such relationships and helped to establish the resulting field of *psychosomatic medicine.* Since then, a great deal of research has been carried out to study relationships between psychological and physiological functioning. It is now recognized that many physical disorders involve psychological causes. Such disorders include obesity and anorexia nervosa; gastrointestinal disorders, such as peptic ulcers; cardiovascular disorders, including coronary heart disease; respiratory disorders, such as hyperventilation; endocrine disorders, including hyperthyroidism and diabetes mellitis; allergic skin disorders; and some forms of headaches. This is not to say that skin allergies, headaches, and the other disorders mentioned are completely caused by psychological factors but, rather, that psychological factors may contribute to the total causal condition. Some researchers argue that all physical illness involves contributing psychological variables and that therefore a special category, *psychophysiological disorders*, is not necessary. Most researchers in the field, however, agree that disorders such as those listed above involve some particularly important contribution of psychological causal factors.

The older term, *psychosomatic*, has been replaced by the terms *psychophysiological disorders* and, more recently, by *somatoform disorders*. All three refer essentially to the same set of issues—that is, physical disorders without clear physical causes or in which psychological variables play some causal role.

It has been estimated that about 30% of general medical patients show psychophysiological patterns in their illnesses. It is thus a major category of illness, involving a large number of people.

It should be emphasized that people suffering from psychophysiological reactions are not imagining or faking their illnesses. They suffer from actual tissue damage or change, such as with peptic ulcers, and their distress is real. It is important to treat those physical conditions directly with medical procedures and then, after the medical aspects are under control, to begin working on the emotional or psychological aspects of the disorders.

Physiological disorders involve primarily the autonomic nervous system, that portion of the nervous system that controls functions such as heart rate and breathing. This system operates automatically: We do not have to think about breathing or keeping our hearts beating. When suddenly startled or frightened, such as by a sudden loud sound, the autonomic nervous system immediately reacts to prepare the body for emergency defense: We breathe more rapidly; our hearts beat faster and circulate blood more rapidly, bringing more oxygen and nutrients to large muscles; adrenalin is discharged; and, in general, we get set to deal with some emergency. All of us have experienced this reaction when suddenly startled, and we likewise know that when the emergency is over, our defensive reactions gradually decrease, and we can feel ourselves gradually settle down and relax.

In the psychophysiological disorders, it is believed that the effective stimulus that brings about the emergency reaction might be a generalized stimulus situation, such as continued job pressure, or that it might be a brief but often repeated event. The emergency reaction becomes conditioned to the particular stimulus and will occur whenever that stimulus is present. In effect, the person with a psychophysiological reaction responds repeatedly as if he or she were reacting to an emergency situation that requires some maximum bodily defenses. With repetition or long continuation of those defensive physiological reactions, body organs begin to fatigue and even break down.

Because the tissue damage is real, medical treatment of the condition is important. In most cases, it is only after medical control has been achieved that attempts are made to deal with the psychological issues. Current research has used traditional psychotherapy, behavior modification approaches, and biofeedback procedures in therapeutic efforts. Some success has been reported with the first two, but biofeedback is probably too recent a development as yet to show any significant accumulation of data on its effectiveness in psychophysiological disorders.

PSYCHOSES   (See NEUROSES, MENTAL DISORDERS: TREATMENT, ILLUSIONS, SCHIZOPHRENIA, NON-HOSPITAL TREATMENT)

The term *psychoses* refers to a large variety of serious mental disorders. The psychoses are characterized by extreme distortions in thinking, in the way people perceive the world, and in their actual behavior. There are several types of psychoses, some much more severe than others, but all of them serious. Psychoses are typically diagnosed when patients show disorientation in time, place, and/or identity. They may quite literally not know what time (year or century) it is, where they are, and who they are, claiming to be someone else. In addition to the disorientation, they may entertain various delusions, often of grandeur or persecution.

Some psychoses are clearly the result of brain damage from injury, infections, and illness, and even from some progressive, severe deterioration in old age. For other types, such as the schizophrenias, the causes are as yet unknown and may include genetic, organic, and psychological factors. When no organic cause can be discovered, the psychoses may be labeled *functional,* as opposed to *organic,* where a physical disease or disorder can be diagnosed. The corresponding treatments then divide themselves into psychotherapy, which includes the interview, conversation, and behavioral approaches, and the physiological approach, through drugs, surgery, electroconvulsive shock, diet, and rest.

Whatever the causes may be, the psychoses are difficult to treat. Traditionally, psychotic people have been put away in state hospitals, where they do not interfere with families and the rest of society. For the patient, that is not necessarily the best solution. More recently, with the community mental health approaches, patients have been treated in group living settings, such as halfway houses, and in communities. Drug treatment and psychotherapy, in the relative freedom and normality of a group home, has been useful in many instances.

PSYCHOSURGERY

In 1949, the Portuguese psychiatrist, Antonio Moniz, received the Nobel prize for his development of *psychosurgery*—that is, brain surgery as treatment for mental patients. The early work in the late 1930s and the 1940s focused primarily on severely psychotic and/or aggressive patients. It was believed that the front part of the human brain is responsible for magnifying emotional responses that are produced in other parts of the brain, thus making some people dangerously violent or severely psychotic. Moniz and his colleagues developed surgical techniques to sever the neural connections between the frontal lobes and the rest of the brain. The operation, called a *lobotomy*, was performed on several thousand patients in the United States in the 1950s. Mental hospitals, it seemed, were engaging in wholesale lobotomies.

As with electroconvulsive treatment and other new procedures, many doctors became impressed and enthusiastic over the apparent good results, and, as noted above, Moniz was actually awarded the Nobel prize. But, because the surgeons and psychiatrists were practitioners and not trained scientists, they did not test and evaluate the effectiveness of their procedures objectively. Later, when researchers did begin to carry out careful evaluation studies, they found that lobotomized patients did not improve any more than those who were not lobotomized. In addition, the scientists found, the operation caused severe negative side-effects, such as seizures, deep stupor, general unresponsiveness, and even death.

By the 1960s, the use of lobotomies had decreased markedly, primarily because of the introduction of tranquilizers in the 1950s. The surgeons' and psychiatrists' enthusiastic large-scale use of lobotomies on thousands of mental patients had been a tragic professional mistake, causing irreversible brain damage to many people. Today, psychosurgical procedures are much more refined and are used only selectively.

Another psychosurgical technique has continued to be developed in which electrodes are implanted in the brain and an electric current is passed through in order to destroy certain areas of brain tissue. This approach has been presented by its developers as a way of reducing extreme violence in people by destroying the part of the brain that supposedly controls violent and aggressive behavior. It has been suggested that criminals and even urban rioters might be suffering from some brain dysfunction, and thus they are prime candidates for the tissue-destruction surgery. Most alarming is the suggestion made that we develop ways to test people—presumably children, too—in order to identify those who have brain dysfunction and who would thus be likely surgical candidates.

As with earlier psychosurgery, the scientific evidence does not support the claims, and these drastic procedures have little or no value in helping to reduce disturbed or violent behavior. The destructive techniques themselves seem to constitute a kind of professional violence that threatens people who fall under their control. It is to be hoped that society will be alert in protecting those people most likely to be threatened by such procedures.

PUNISHMENT   *(See PUNISHMENT IN CHILD REARING)*

When we punish someone our underlying motivation is to prevent someone from doing whatever we punished him or her for from doing it again. If our activity is not successful—that is, if the person does it again, and perhaps often—then our *punishment* has not succeeded, and some psychologists would argue that we did not really punish the person but that we merely abused him or her or aggressed against him or her in some way. B. F. Skinner, for example, argues that punishment has to be defined in terms of its effects, and that if there are no effects, there was no punishment. In his experimental studies, Skinner found no really permanent effects of punishment, merely temporary suppression of the activity that was punished. He concluded that punishment was largely a waste of time and might have serious side-effects, such as coming to hate the punisher. According to Skinner, punishment should be dropped as a method of behavior control in favor of a´more positive operation of rewarding desirable alternative behavior. Thus, to get prostitutes to stop their activities, there is no point in fining or jailing them. It is better to find them more rewarding activities, if this can be done.

In the history of mankind, the punishment concept goes back to our cave dweller days. It is prominent in the Bible, and many religions approve of either temporal or after-death kinds of punishment for our crimes and sins. Philosophers looking into the problem have distinguished a number of reasons why punishment has been and is practiced. (1) First is the revenge motive, based on some sort of notion that there must be some kind of balance in the world—an eye for an eye—the famous *law of retaliation* or *lex talionis*. Such a law seems to have a tremendous appeal for millions of people who appear to enjoy or justify feuding, capital punishment, and/or other punishments on a kind of get-even basis. Beyond the simple notion of a mystical need for balance, there appears to be no solid foundation for such a principle, and the trend in some parts of Western civilization has been to rise above such primitive notions of aggression merely to get even with someone. It should be noted that even though revenge is an emotional state or motive, it could have the effect of preventing the action being retaken, especially if the victim is now dead. (2) The second alleged motive for punishment is that of rehabilitation, or reform of the one punished. Somehow, he or she is supposed to learn a lesson, improve, or change his or her ways because he or she had been punished. This point of view is essentially illogical, since it is based on the expectation that someone who preferred some other course of action should now prefer one the punisher indicates as more acceptable, without rewarding him or her for behaving in the now sought way. We can assume that a criminal, for example, has been rewarded for criminal behavior in the past and may have been rewarded many times before he or she was caught. To expect him or her to change because of some negative treatment is a hope without any foundation in theory or evidence. (3) The third alleged reason for punishing those who get caught is to provide examples for those who have not yet been caught—in short, as a deterrent. Actually, we are all deterred from some crimes if the punishment is meaningful. If we must pay a $10 fine for illegal parking, and if the $10 is meaningful to us, we may not park in the same place illegally again. If the fine is trivial, we may not be deterred. If someone else pays a fine for his or her crime, we may also be deterred by knowing that it could happen to us. Many people slow down when they are told that a certain section of highway is a speed trap, and, in general, most people avoid crime or law breaking if the penalties are serious. Even a professional criminal waits until the police car goes by, although in his or her case, it is only a temporary deterrence. Sometimes, it is argued that capital punishment does not deter murderers, because the number of murders is not affected in states that do not have such laws. Most murders are crimes of passion or are committed without any plans beforehand to exterminate someone, and they are not even considered murders as much as manslaughter or, at least, as not premeditated. We have no good data on the number of premeditated murders in any state before and after capital punishment laws are passed or repealed, and the argument is empty. The actual degree of deterrence has never been assessed appropriately enough to suggest that it does not pay to punish malefactors. Before we draw conclusions, we should assess the kind of punishment involved and evaluate whether or not it was indeed a punishment. (4) A fourth reason for punishment is that of the prevention of crime or serious misbehavior by simply removing the culprit from the scene by locking him or her up. This is obviously effective but is also costly and negative. It solves no general problems but gets rid of a specific problem for a while.

In laboratory studies on animals and on children, certain interesting and parallel facts have been observed. One cannot punish children in laboratories in any serious way, of course, and the usual punishment amounts to delaying children from playing with certain desirable toys, letting them play with less desirable toys, segregating them for short time-out periods, mild reproofs, and the like. Rats, on the other hand, are commonly given electric shocks, blasts of air, cold water, slaps, or other forms of abuse. In the rat studies (as well as in the children studies), certain principles have emerged that might be applied usefully.

1. In general, punishment will suppress ongoing activity if administered at the time of the activity. One cannot wait any serious length of time, such as till daddy gets home, and expect that the punishment will affect the behavior in question. The only consequence will be that daddy will come to be regarded as an ogre.
2. If the punishment is relatively weak, the period of suppression will be short, and the behavior will be reinstated at some later opportunity. The longer and stronger the punishment, the longer the period of suppression to the point of permanence. Punishment does work if the punishment is drastic.

Our problem, of course, is that we do not want to be drastic with children; despite the felt need to punish, we still want their love, respect, and admiration. Such contradictory goals are self-defeating. If children are to be punished at all, the punishment has to be divorced from any indications of revenge, arbitrariness, or personal pique. A parent certainly has to show anger when displeased and more anger when greatly displeased, or a child may never learn to discriminate between minor and major issues. When children are old enough to carry on conversations and can be told what punishment fits what crime, the personal features of a punishment situation may be reduced. The kinds of punishment (temporary isolation, deprivation of some toys or desserts, frowns, inattention, etc.) can be spelled out and related to misbehaviors. The notion that children can be brought up with never a harsh word or any other expression of reproof represents some tender sentiment. Although some psychologists believe that a mild spanking is sometimes appropriate, many others disapprove of any kind of personal physical affront, such as a slap. What can a child think or feel about a parent who indulges in personal abuse? Children must be prepared for a world that does not especially care for them or make room for all their desires and fancies. A code of behavior must be instituted, and a careful manipulation of rewards and withholding of rewards has been the only positive means so far developed by mankind.

Parents should anticipate the occurrence of accidents and misbehavior and arrange a program of rewards for more desirable behavior wherever possible. Certainly, there is no basis for any violence, abuse, tying up children, or otherwise assaulting them in serious ways. Such behavior is more criminal than anything a child can do. Children should be taught to handle matches, for example, at the fireplace or at a campsite, under supervision. They should simultaneously be taught the dangers of uncontrolled conflagrations. The same advice holds for any potentially dangerous act.

PUNISHMENT IN CHILD REARING
(See CHILD ABUSE, PUNISHMENT)

Virtually all American parents use a great deal of *punishment* in raising their children. In fact, some psychologists estimate that punishment in various forms, ranging from scoldings or taking away privileges to the actual beating of a child, may be the most commonly used child-control methods in the United States. Punishment is an attempt to weaken and eliminate undesirable behavior by inflicting some painful or otherwise highly aversive stimulus following the undesirable behavior. A misbehaving child may be loudly scolded by a teacher; a child's hand may be slapped after touching forbidden objects, and so on. It is consistent across all levels of society in our country that punishment for undesired behavior is allowed to proceed in only one direction—that is, the adult assumes the right to punish the child, but the reverse would be considered an extreme breach of conduct and would probably bring down even more severe punishment of the child. Although children are not allowed to punish adults, adults are allowed to punish other adults who are in subordinate postions: A sergeant can punish a buck private; a jailer punishes an inmate; and husbands can still punish their wives with relatively little concern or retaliation by the rest of society.

The common use of punishment is probably far more destructive than it is helpful in child rearing. Punishment of any type is, by definition, aversive. It is unpleasant, and it creates pain and often a great deal of emotionality in both punished child and punishing parent. The emotionality; the crying and upset of the child; the anger and, perhaps, guilt feelings of the parent, often escalate, creating a whole new situation, a new battleground that often goes far beyond the original undesired behavior of the child in its disruptive effects. It appears characteristic that the original point or lesson is either never made or is lost in the ensuing emotionality, anger, pain, and—too often—hatred that the punishment can create between parent and child.

Another problem is the usually poorly timed use of punishment. "Wait until your father comes home!" is heard too often. Hours later, long after the behavior is over, the family disciplinarian must inflict his punishment on the child, but, again, the point or lesson has been lost. All that has come across to the child is that the parents have again acted in a cruel and mean manner.

In general, punishment, as used by most parents, particularly physical punishment, does not work very well. The fact is that many children are punished often but they still do not learn the lesson, a clear indication of the ineffectiveness of parental punishment. If it is so ineffective, then what keeps it going as a common child-rearing practice? Psychologists believe that one reason is that the parent who inflicts punishment is reinforced immediately in two ways: (1) The punishment usually interferes with the undesirable behavior, stopping it momentarily; and (2) the angered parent seems to feel better after the blow-up. In psychological terms, punishment continues to be used against the child because it is reinforcing to the parent.

But in the long run, punishment—particularly physical punishment—may create many more, and more severe, problems than it can solve. Children who are punished may grow up into parents who punish their children. Sometimes, if punishment is applied immediately, is commensurate with the behavior to be corrected, and is mild enough not to create undue emotion, it may have its good effects of teaching the child a lesson.

Punishment is a decremental approach—that is, it is an attempt to *reduce* undesired behavior. A better alternative, of course, is to use positive reinforcement or rewards to *increase* alternative positive or desirable behavior. Some people think that there may be a risk of spoiling a child with too much positive reinforcement; but even if spoiling were to happen, psychologists generally believe that it is still preferable to creating permanent anger or hostility with too much punishment.

R

RACISM

Racism is a negative emotional and prejudicial reaction toward some group identified by race. It is generally considered to be a feature of the majority group, but the victims or targets of one group's racism may also react negatively toward the other and are equally guilty of racism. Any kind of racism involves a failure to recognize that groups consist of individuals who vary as much if not more within the group than the groups differ or vary from each other. On every known measurement, there is considerable overlap between groups, regardless of average differences, if there are any; and responding to someone on the basis of race alone, as if that necessarily included some behavioral feature, is irrational.

Racism is, of course, official policy in some governments or cultures. The American experience with slavery was an obvious case of official racism at one time in our history, and we might wonder, too, about our official Indian policy. Even if not official, racism can be the cause of conflicts and wars or other violence. Added to ethnic, national, and religious conflicts, conflicts between races can be just as deadly, with each side trying to wipe out the other with various final solutions. There appears to be no easing of the problem of group conflict, and as populations grow and the earth's bounty dwindles, the conflicts may well increase in scale and scope.

RANDOM SAMPLES AND STRATIFIED SAMPLES

You may have never been interviewed by Gallup, Roper, or any of the other pollsters who keep telling us that 86% of the people believe such and such or that so and so will win an election by a 10% majority. You may not believe such reports, but the well-known pollsters know almost exactly (within 2 or 3%) what they are talking about. It actually only takes about 1,200 or 1,500 people to represent the viewpoints of all of the rest of the citizens of the United States. We are not talking about just any 1,200 people—that would be a *random sample.* A random sample simply means that you might stop anyone, anywhere, and anytime and ask for his or her opinion about something. You would need a great many such individuals to come up with any reliable findings. You might, for example, ask all of the adult white males in a small Southern town for their opinions and get some fairly uniform answers. The responses, however, might not correspond at all with the opinions of women, blacks, Northerners, or big-city residents. In order to get reliable opinions, you must *stratify* the sample—that is, try to match the sample with the population statistics of the whole country. You select the same percentage of males and females; young and old; black and white; rich and poor; various religious denominations; people from the North, South, East, and West; and so on as you would find if you polled every citizen. Such a sample is a miniature United States, and it turns out that the opinions found in such a sample will correspond very closely with what the country's citizens think as a whole.

Random samples should not be used for polling, and one only uses random samples from a known group. For example, if we want to know what 18-year-old white girls think, we need not ask all of those who are alive at the moment; we need only to get a relatively small number—for example, about 30—if we have not selected the girls on some special basis, such as all of the girls in one high school or in one neighborhood. A telephone directory would be used to call every tenth name, for example, in order to locate 18-year-old white girls, and every tenth such person could be interviewed in order to provide a random sample. What we would lose in such a search are all of the girls who might be unable to afford a phone in the home, and so the sample would not be purely random. Random means that no special selection has been exercised, as when a lottery is held, and a number is drawn by a blindfolded child from a fishbowl full of numbers. If the sample is not stratified, we must be very wary about results based on so-called random samples.

RATIONAL-EMOTIVE THERAPY

Rational-emotive therapy has been developed over the past twenty-five years by psychologist Albert Ellis who believes that disturbed behavior is largely caused by the things that people habitually tell themselves. We all develop some ideas about how we should, must, or ought to be, says Ellis, and in different situations we repeat them, silently and often without even realizing it, to ourselves. These internal statements then affect how we behave.

The statements habitually recited may be irrational and may cause a variety of difficulties. For example, many of us believe, "I must be perfect in everything I do." This belief about what one must do or be is irrational because no one can approach such a state of perfection. Such persons will fail in many things in life, big and small, just like the rest of us fail in many ways. But to them, failure can be psychologically devastating because they have, for years, been telling themselves that they *must* be perfect—or always successful. That idea of what they must be is self-defeating.

Another common irrational belief, according to Ellis, is the idea that "I must be liked by everyone." Such persons will periodically encounter the many rejections and hostilities we all experience and will also be devastated when they are not liked.

The rational-emotive therapist focuses, on the client's irrational, self-defeating statements. By bringing these ideas to the client's attention, examining them, and changing them, the therapist tries to substitute produtive rather than self-defeating self-statements.

Rational-emotive therapy is not a widely used approach, but it is growing in popularity. Like the other verbal psychotherapies, such as psychoanalysis, there is as yet limited scientific evidence for its effectiveness.

RATIONALIZATION AND DISSONANCE

Rationalization is offering an acceptable explanation to ourselves or to others for something we are about to do or, more usually, have done for some other reason than the one we offer. We all do this occasionally. Freudian analysts like to think of rationalization as an unconscious process, a *defense mechanism,* but there is no evidence that people go about lying unconsciously. It is often just too uncomfortable to tell the truth, even to ourselves, and so we invent some presumably plausible and socially acceptable reason for our actions. If we should have an automobile accident, it is easy enough to blame another driver, a defect in the road, or the like. After a while, we might even come to believe it ourselves. At that point, something approaching the Freudian notion appears more acceptable.

The rationalization concept was introduced into laboratory psychology, via the notion of *cognitive dissonance,* by Leon Festinger. According to this conception, people might find themselves in an uncomfortable situation and, in some sense, be forced to do something unpleasant. This might happen frequently and appear inappropriate to others. In order to justify the action, the person involved might then invent some plausible excuse, plausible even to him- or herself. If he or she can accept the new reason, he or she may come to forget or at least ignore the former reason and make a new adjustment. Parents, for example, might be forced by law into sending their children to a school that they do not like, for whatever reason. Friends may ask them why they do so, and, instead of admitting that they are unable to afford another school or that they are knuckling under to the law, they begin to look for and perhaps find good reasons for having their children in that school. The rough conditions will make a man out of his or her boy; he has a better chance of getting good grades; it is the honorable thing to do; and so on. When they find an acceptable reason, they resolve their dissonance or conflict and can now ignore the issue. We are constantly resolving our dissonances in one way or another, since we are frequently called upon to unpleasant things. We buy expensive cars or clothes because it is necessary to look smart or prosperous to our clients. A doctor who drives a cheap car cannot be making any money, and therefore he or she cannot have many patients because he or she is probably not a good doctor, and so on.

Whenever we conform to pressures we do not really like and come to accept them for really improper reasons, we are resolving our dissonances. It might be helpful at least to recognize what we are doing before we accept what should be rejected.

REACTION TIME   *(See HUMAN FACTORS)*

How quickly can one react to a signal or stimulus? That all depends on the nature of the stimulus, whether one is ready for it or not, and what the reaction may be. The auto driver in a long line at a traffic signal may be puzzled about why the line does not move when the signal changes to green. Some people in the line may not be ready; they are paying attention to something else; the cars themselves have a reaction time, in that it takes some time to overcome the inertia of the standing car; the reaction is rather complex, calling for arm and foot movements, such as releasing clutches, accelerating, and the like. Each driver reacts to the motion of the car ahead. By the time all the reaction times involved are added, the last person in the line will arrive in time for the signal to change back to red.

In the laboratory, *reaction time* is measured by presenting a signal that simultaneously starts a clock and having the subject press or release a key to stop the clock. The interval between is called the *latency* or *reaction time*. The average person can respond to a touch or a sound signal in about 0.15 of a second; the response to light takes a little longer, about 0.18 or 0.20 of a second. It takes about a half-second to taste something and about 0.60 second to react to pain. Such rapid reactions, however, are obtained from subjects who are prepared to respond and who are given a ready signal prior to occurrence of the stimulus. If the stimulus occurs in a background of noise, it will take longer. If people are in normal good health, they do not vary much from the times cited. Sometimes, we are told that some athletes are faster than usual in their reaction times, but this does not appear to be so. They are better prepared to respond, or they anticipate signals better than we. Even the best baseball hitters strike out often enough when they fail to react quickly enough to fast pitches; a foul ball to the right of the plate for a right-handed batter indicates a slower than needed reaction time. It takes time to see and hear; even such reactions are not instantaneous. For most purposes, our reaction times are adequate; it is our attention that might need some preparation. If we are slow and sluggish in our behaviors, it is not because our nervous systems cannot carry the messages fast enough; other factors are operating.

READINESS   *(See DEVELOPMENTAL STAGES)*

There are two uses of the term *readiness,* one describes a kind of attention or immediate preparation for a response, in the sense of "ready, set, go"; the other indicates a more or less chronological or developmental readiness, in the sense of "She's not ready for marriage" or "He's not ready for long division."

The first kind of readiness refers to being set or prepared to receive certain stimuli and to react to them efficiently or rapidly. A rat that has just been fed is not ready for his or her daily run in a maze. One is not ready to take a test if he or she is nervous, unprepared, or has no pencil in hand. Such readinesses are not of great importance, in that they can be remedied. A pencil can be supplied, and perhaps something can be done about the nervousness and lack of preparation. Instructions to get ready usually suffice for most situations where a person is capable of responding.

The second kind of readiness is a matter of maturation. An 8-month old child is not ready to walk, talk, and read, although there might be exceptions. Children in the fifth grade might not be ready to learn how to type, even if they do make some progress during the year. Had they waited another year, they might have made much more rapid progress. The trouble with this second kind of readiness is that one never knows if a person (child) is ready for anything until it is tried. We do not allow children to drive automobiles until they are 16 or some other age controlled by a state licensing bureau. Yet 8- and 9-year-old children can, and some do, drive tractors and trucks on farms with reasonable skill. Other children with wealthy and indulgent parents fly airplanes, after a fashion—some very well. Public school teachers sometimes advise parents against teaching children to read at home on the grounds that they are not ready and will pick up bad reading habits. They endorse some concept of *reading readiness*, which is somehow supposed to come into being in the first grade (age 6). Actually, many children do some reading at age 3 and, in some exceptional cases, learn to read Greek or other foreign languages by the age of 4 or 5. In all probability, no harm is done in testing a child or trying him or her out in one form of activity or another; if the progress is satisfactory, there is no harm in continuing. Some authorities, Jerome Bruner, for example, argue that every child is ready for some stage of learning in any area of instruction. Mixing soap and water is a kind of elementary chemical operation that infants can begin to appreciate. The learning operations must be adjusted to the sensory capacities and motor development of the children, and the child can be encouraged to move ahead at a rate that is compatible with his or her capacities. We might not have had a Mozart if his parents had waited till he had reached some kind of hypothetical age for taking piano lessons.

In general, children should be taught what they can learn without concern over the calendar. Although in some cases, the learning may be inefficient, wasteful, and expensive, there is also a danger that interest may die while the child is waiting to become old enough to try something. Difficulties do arise if most children are not ready to learn, say, algebra, and not enough teachers are available to push each child to his or her limits. In such cases, the average child benefits if he or she waits until he or she is ready—meaning that most children of his or her age can handle the skill or content of some course.

READING AND READING PEDAGOGY　　*(See DYSLEXIA)*

Reading consists of making sense out of writing. The writing can be a footprint in the snow; a feather on the ground; or, in what we normally regard as writing, letters in one kind of script; print; or symbolic pictures. Only people properly trained can make sense of Chinese ideographs. Similarly, only people properly trained can make sense out of messages presented in the Roman, Greek, or Arabic alphabets. If we keep in mind that reading involves making sense out of writing, then we know that someone who merely recites words as he or she looks at them is not necessarily reading.

Most English-speaking people can read an Italian newspaper, in the sense of phrasing the words in sequence. They could perform such a feat for hours and make virtually no sense out of what their eyes and mouths had done if they were not familiar with the Italian language. We note next that the verbalization is unnecessary: you don't have to pronounce the words correctly or at all to get the sense or meanings involved. In fact, silent reading is normally the desired technique. You do not have to read all of the words in a message in order to get the basic sense. Of course, teachers will downgrade beginning readers if they do not pronounce every word correctly. The beginner must go through the mechanics of reading before he or she can more or less ignore individual words. Even whole sentences can be ignored when one is reading for a specific purpose. In reading a book, it may not be necessary to read every paragraph or even every page in order to get something out of the material, and what is learned may be satisfactory.

The real problem of reading is to get as much sense as you need to out of whatever you have to deal with in terms of words. This, in turn, means that you have to have a vocabulary that meets your needs. To read material beyond your vocabulary is a meaningless exercise and cannot qualify as reading. Children's primers start with words that are familiar to the children, but improvements in reading skills call for a continuing vocabulary growth. If parents do not supply this vocabulary through their own speech and efforts at explaining words, including instruction in dictionary use, the children will not become good readers. The most important factor in reading is the example of parents reading. If everyone in the family is watching TV, reading suffers.

Teaching methods.   There are two traditional teaching methods, the *phonetic method* and the *look and say method*. Both are effective and inseparable. Children learn certain words from television advertising, box tops, street signs, and the like. The parents explain that a certain sign says "Stop," and the child will learn this word by seeing and saying it. Slowly, a child learns that certain letters and combinations of letters are alike in sound. Most children get off to a bad start by learning to sing-song the alphabet and learning to say A, B, D, and so on by sounding the letter names instead of the letter sounds. Eventually, they learn that "B" is *beh* and not *bee* and that "C" is a hiss instead of *see*. Once they learn the letter sounds, they can sound out words, and if they sound like something familiar, they have read the word.

A problem arises in that English spelling is not consistently phonetic, and no one could read a word such as "weigh" correctly the first time by relying on letter sounds. It is not necessary, however, to pronounce words at all as far as reading is concerned. There are, for example, picture-language books in which a Russian word in the Cyrillic alphabet is shown alongside of a picture of a book, a window, or some other recognizable object. With a little care, work, and attention, one can learn that when he or she sees "Kniga" in Russian spelling, he or she is supposed to think of "book." He or she can learn to *read* Russian without ever hearing it spoken. Normally, the process involves spoken sounds along with visual stimuli.

The ability to read appears to be well within the grasp of everyone, even of people who have various visual problems to the extreme of blindness. All that it takes is the patient presence of someone who already knows how to read along with the learner. Children can and do teach each other. Others learn from comic books and funny papers, quite on their own. Only time and effort and a speaking vocabulary are required if one is concerned about oral reading. The translators of Egyptian hieroglyphics did not know how the ancients pronounced their words, but they were able to make sense out of them.

REASONING AND THINKING   *(See RATIONALIZATION, IMAGERY)*

We all like to think that we are reasonable and wish that other people were too. When we ask someone else to be reasonable, what we usually mean is that we want that person to agree with us. The difficulty is that most if not all of our decisions and conclusions about anything are made for us by our history, by emotional conditioning, and from necessity; little, if any, logic played any role. Even something as important as a job that may last a lifetime may be accepted without any logical analysis or from some immediate necessity. We often find reasons for our choices or decisions after they have been made.

The concept of *reason* plays a role in legal matters, where children are not considered to have reached the age of reason or responsibility until some arbitrary number of years selected by a legislature. Thus, the age for permission to purchase alcoholic drinks may vary from state to state and within states from time to time as legislators reason their way to decisions aided and abetted by the liquor industry. Similarly, the age for operating a motor vehicle varies with states, as do the ages for marriage. Females are usually permitted to marry at earlier ages than are men. Do they reach the age of reason sooner? Although some religious groups or legislators may announce some formal age of reason, there is actually no age when something called reason enters into the developmental picture. College professors of logic find the reasoning processes of sophomores rather wanting and in need of instruction.

Behavior is not always guided by reason. What does happen is that everyone learns to approach and deal with certain kinds of problems that enter into his or her experience, either at home or in the schools, by following certain rules or instructions. Habits are acquired and control behavior. In social, religious, family, and personal affairs, other rules or instructions are followed, highly affected by emotional states. Certain religious tenets are to be taken on faith or from authority. Precepts from the Bible or other religious books may be followed without question. Superficial explanations and superstitions may guide much of our behavior, and as long as we avoid disaster or difficulty, there is little role for reason. When we are very young, our reason for doing anything is expressed simply as "because." As we grow older, we find that word insufficient, although the reason for the insufficiency is that our interrogrator has some other explanation as his or her "because" and doesn't like ours. Decisions by nations to declare war on each other or to exterminate other populations represent the thinking of the leaders of nations but hardly represent anything like reason operating in the decisions.

Usually, we refer to reason or thinking when we can detect some hesitation or lapse of time prior to some action. John Dewey argued that we would not have to think if we had enough habits. What goes on during a thinking period might be the basis for some reference to a reasoning process. The nature of the *thinking process,* however, is poorly understood by anyone, including psychologists. Prior to any scientific efforts to determine what thinking is, some philosophers entertained the notion that people were endowed with a faculty of intellect that did their thinking for them. When the intellect was finished with its task, a faculty of will took over and decided the action.

Psychologists could not find any evidence or support for the existence of separate faculties and attacked the problem of thinking from other orientations. John B. Watson, the first behaviorist, suggested that thinking was only a matter of talking to one's self. Ivan Pavlov suggested that talking itself was only a matter of responding to new kinds (verbal, vocal) of stimuli (a second signal system). At present, many psychologists are ready to recognize that when we think, we both talk to ourselves, if we are language-using creatures, and also respond in terms of a series of images wherein a variety of actions might be visualized or where the results of such actions might be represented in imagery. Along with such imagery and verbal activity, there would be an underlying emotional activity at various levels. A chess player might look calm and somehow purely mentally engaged, but he or she is also talking to him- or herself, imaging, and undergoing emotional stress. Only computers can play tick-tack-toe without speech, imagery, or emotion, but they are built to follow rules on purely mechanical principles. They do not reason or think.

REFLEXES   *(See CONDITIONING)*

A *reflex* is usually thought of as a simple, unlearned, automatic reaction of some part of the body to some specific stimulus. Thus, if the knee of a relaxed person is tapped, the leg will swing outward in a so-called knee jerk. Similarly, if a puff of air is blown at someone's eye, the lid will close. A drop of lemon juice on the tongue will result in a discharge of the salivary glands. A sharp prick on the hand will result in withdrawal of the arm. There are literally hundreds of such automatic reactions that we do not have to learn. Our nervous system is prepared by heredity to deal with certain stimuli without our taking time to think or learn what to do.

Reflexes are, however, by no means simple. The entire body and nervous system is involved in an integrated way whenever any action is performed. Consider the knee jerk again. To get a good knee jerk, the person must be sitting upright and yet be rather limp or relaxed. If the subject clenches a fist at just the right moment, he or she can exaggerate the jerk. Clenching at the wrong moment will inhibit the reflex. All muscular reflexes involve antagonistic muscles, so that when one muscle of a pair of antagonists contracts, the other relaxes. If you pull a dog's front leg, some muscles in the hind legs will contract (a crossed-extensor reflex). Walking is largely reflexive in nature. You carry your weight on one leg as the other extends; simultaneously, your arms swing out in a crossed-extensor pattern.

Most of our internal activity (heart pumping, breathing, swallowing/digestion, excretion, various glandular secretions) is performed reflexively. We not only do not have to think about it, we do not even know how to think about it.

Reflexes are normally identified with specific organs or muscle groups, even though they do not operate alone or in a vacuum. When we are engaged in some activity that involves the whole body in some coordinated effort, we do not usually think of this as reflex activity, although reflexes may be involved. In such cases, we usually look for other explanations and typically invoke the notion of learning. Learning however, may be, as Ivan Pavlov proposed, a matter of *conditioning* reflexes. This was also the view of John B. Watson, the American behaviorist. The Russian physiologist, Sechenov, thought that thinking was a matter of the reflexes of the brain.

Sometimes, reflexes are distinguished from instincts, which do involve the whole body. A spider spinning a web of a particular design (depending on the variety of spider) is using all of its parts in the architectural operation. A turtle, newborn, crawling toward the sea that it cannot see is also reacting with the whole body. The behavior in both cases is unlearned and automatic, but since it is a complex pattern of activity, it perhaps requires a different label and is not called reflexive.

Simple reflexes habituate, that is, they cease to occur if the stimulus for the activity is repetitive and prolonged. Thus, if someone is pounding on a roof in a shingling operation and you find your eyes blinking with each hammer blow, you will adapt to this stimulus and stop blinking if the hammering is regular and consistent. With a short recovery, the adaptation will, in turn, cease, and you will be back to blinking again.

Reflexes are, of course, of enormous survival value. They take our hands out of a fire quickly; they wash away the cinders in our eyes; they allow us to regurgitate improper foods; and, in general, they leave us free for more complex adjustments. In some circles, reflexes are treated almost contemptuously, as if they were mere muscle contractions. We should recognize that we are bundles of reflexes, and perhaps that is all we are, if we include all of our conditioned responses.

RELAXATION AND PROGRESSIVE RELAXATION

The muscles of the body are arranged in antagonistic pairs—that is, when one muscle of a pair contracts (shortens), the opposing muscle relaxes (lengthens). If you make a muscle by flexing your biceps, the muscle along the back of the arm lengthens. Normally, if the body is at rest, some muscles are in some state of contraction, whereas others are in a state of corresponding relaxation. The normal uncontracted state of a muscle is said to be in a state of *tonus*. When you try to do something and not do it at the same time—for example, close a fist and keep the fingers stretched out—you will be contracting or trying to contract antagonistic muscles and will feel tense: The stronger you try, the greater the tension, rigor, tremor, and so on that will be observable. You can also reduce the tonus or tension in any muscle system by making an effort to do nothing. You can let your arm fall limply at your side and just hang there; there will still be some muscle fiber contraction and tonus, but such a state of limpness is what we usually identify with *relaxation*. When you sprawl or slump in an easy chair or collapse on a bed, you think of this as relaxation; actually, some muscles have to be in some state of contraction for you to maintain any position at all, including that of lying down.

In training people to relax, special techniques are sometimes used, such as those introduced by E. Jacobson in 1938. A person is told to think of some muscle group—for example, those involved in tensing the forearm. He or she is then instructed to tense these muscles strongly so that the forearm tightens and is under strong tension. Then the learner is asked to relax these muscles slowly and pay attention to the feelings that accompany the relaxation. He or she then tenses the arm strongly and relaxes again. After some practice, he or she becomes more closely aware of how his or her arm feels when tensing and relaxing. Another muscle set is then selected—for example, the muscles involved in frowning or in tightening the scalp, neck, buttocks, calves, or ankles. Each set of muscles is tensed and relaxed many times. Facial muscles used in smiling or grimacing are exercised in a similar way until a person begins to show appreciation of when a muscle is tensed or relaxed and to what degree. With such training, a person can be asked to lie down, tense the toes, ankles, calves, thighs, buttocks, back, neck, scalp, and so on in succession, and then relax the muscles in the same or reverse order. Such *progressive relaxation*, after sufficient practice, can be accomplished quickly, and the whole body may be tensed or relaxed in a matter of seconds. A person with the appropriate training can then relax, slump, or sag into a kind of loose state as far as bodily tension is concerned whenever he or she wants to or is asked to. Long ago, William James, the first great American psychologist, pointed out that our bodily tensions are the basic operating factors in emotional life. If we are relaxed, we cannot feel fear or anger, since these are emotions that call for flight or fight and require considerable bodily contractions of the arms, legs, chest, and so on. Without the support of such tensions, we will feel calm and, if not completely fearless, at least not panicky.

In desensitization therapy, people with phobias are asked to think about something that would frighten them under normal conditions, and as soon as they are starting to think about the situation, the therapist asks the client to relax. If the client can manage to relax while entertaining a thought of some normally fear-inciting circumstance, he or she can eventually learn not to be afraid through the simple process of relaxing when something that used to scare him or her enters the picture. The treatment is not so simple, of course, and much more goes on in therapy than simply thinking and relaxing. The therapist talks a lot, sets an example, uses other models who are fearless in a particular situation—for example, holding spiders in their hands. With the assurance and security as well as the examples, the patient may get over a phobia after a few treatments. He or she may feel uneasy but may not panic in situations that formerly prevented him or her from normal reactions.

RELIABILITY AND VALIDITY

Reliability means dependability. The notion of dependability, however, has an implication of worthiness, of positive value—something you can count on to do you good. In its psychological usage, the term has no value rating. All that it means is that if the conditions do not change, you can expect to get the same behavior, the same test score, or the same measurement the next time you look for it. Even the notion of same is a bit strong, and we should accept similar as more likely. Thus, a bathroom scale that shows you the same weight every time you step on it (let us say you try it 10 times in one hour and do not eat in between tests) is a reliable scale, even if it is broken and always shows the same weight no matter who steps on it. You can depend on it to show the same reading. You cannot depend upon it to show a true reading of your weight unless you happen to be just heavy enough to match its broken features. The true reading would be called a *valid* one, and although valid readings should also be reliable, being reliable, by itself, may mean nothing.

If the child is sick and you take his or her temperature, the temperature may be up or down from reading to reading. In such a case, the reading is not reliable, but it could be valid. The child may be having chills and fevers in some alternation. You would not expect the temperature to change every three minutes, however, and a repeated measure within three minutes should show about the same reading as the last one. Such correspondence would mean that your thermometer was reliable. How valid is it? Unless you had some other measure of temperature, you could not find out. If you test it against another thermometer, how do you know if the second one is valid? We expect that thermometers we buy from reliable pharmacists are both reliable and valid, and they probably are, since the manufacturers are charged with the responsibility of testing their instruments before sale. Bathroom scales are another matter.

The subject of reliability comes up mainly with tests and with the grades that students get on such tests. If tests are made professionally, they are tested for reliability by several methods, chiefly by repeating the test on the same people at some appropriate interval. When teachers make up tests to give to your children, they hardly ever test their tests to see if they are, in fact, reliable. Would the child score the same if he or she repeated the test? Teachers do not have time to test tests; they just give them. Unless they are extremely talented test makers, the chances are that the tests are not really reliable. Of course, if the teacher is experienced and has given similar tests in the past frequently, there may be sufficient reliability to assume that not much improvement could be achieved by an extensive program of test testing. As to validity, again, the teachers' questions may or may not have much to do with what the child was supposed to learn in a particular course. Grades that children are given in art, music, sports, or gymnastics are heavily loaded in subjective appraisals where the validity of the judgments is extremely difficult to assess. Such grades should probably not even be assigned. Similarly, prizes for paintings are often highly questionable, especially to those who did not win the prizes. We should be very wary about such ratings.

The greatest problem arises in tests of intelligence, where reliability need not be a great problem. With sufficient work, one can make a test very reliable: all you have to do is keep adding and dropping questions until you have a set that will always produce just about the same score or standing. Validity is another matter. There is no way to establish that any test actually measures intelligence because we have nothing available with which to compare the score. We would have to have an independent assessment of intelligence to compare with the test score, and there are no such independent assessments. Most commonly, school grades are used to establish the validity of I.Q.-like tests, and the school grades themselves have no established reliability or validity. It turns out that there is a modest relationship of a relatively low order between school grades and I.Q. scores, but the relationship rests on the assumption that school grades are a result or product of something called intelligence in the first place. If school grades are actually a function of something else (good looks, good manners, effort, helpful parents, etc.), then the relationship loses even more as far as supporting the validity of a test.

Never take a test without asking about its reliability and validity. The reliability of a test should be reported as a statistic called the *correlation coefficient* and should be above 0.90 to be considered seriously. The coefficient for validity will not be likely to be anywhere near that high, but you should ask for the criterion against which the test was assessed and how that was measured. If all prospective test takers asked these questions, the test makers would go out of business.

REMEMBERING NAMES AND FACES
(See MEMORY, MNEMONICS)

One commonly complains that one remembers faces but not names. An element of surprise is generally included, since one makes a simple equation of seeing someone once and hearing his or her name once. Actually, hearing something once is slightly better than seeing something once as far as remembering is concerned, but that is true only if we examine the meaning of *once*. If we meet someone, we usually look at him or her for at least a minute or two, perhaps even five or more. In a minute, one can *see* something or someone well over 60 times, since it does not take a second to see something at the level of taking it in. A flash card of an automobile exposed for a tenth of a second will be recognized as an automobile; if you are familiar with various automobiles, you might even recognize it in a tenth of a second, and you would certainly do so in a full second. Using a second as a standard, then, you may hear a name for less than one second and see the person for a minute (60 viewings). Should you now be surprised if later on you *recognize* the face but cannot recall the name? You might recognize the name, too, if it is spoken.

There is no question, then, that everyone remembers faces better than names. If we face the question directly, however, we should appreciate that we learn so many names without effort of any kind that we come to expect to be able to recall any other names of new people we meet equally easily. This is where we meet the problem. When we are actually meeting new people, whether one at a time or in a group, an effort does have to be made. No one can remember the names of five or so strangers mentioned one after another if he or she does not do some work before, during, or after the introduction. Politicians expecting to meet some new voters or supporters may undergo a briefing before they make their appearance. They are told whom they will meet. The names are examined, rehearsed, and tied to cues relating to physical features, wives, and so on. Businessmen make an effort to find out who will be there before attending some function. When they actually meet the parties (with whose names they are already familiar), they pronounce the name, repeat it several times, and try to tie it to some distinctive feature. After the session, they rehearse the names again, using notes, programs, and pictures. Some people who meet strangers constantly take pictures of them, a flattering gesture to begin with, and a considerable aid to memory. Others take occasion to write the name down, perhaps in a way of alluding to some future correspondence. Writing down the name is an extra rehearsal. Some take the trouble to write out the name in their hands, using a finger as a pencil, while asking something about the spelling of the name. Such learners do not have complaints about a faulty memory.

In short, if you do not remember as many names as other people might, it is quite probably the case that you do not go to the same trouble as others do. There are no poor rememberers, there are only poor learners.

There is no point, of course, to remembering the names of all the people you meet; you will never see some again. At a reception, you might meet 200 people very briefly. If you had no previous preparation and no time to stop and chat, write down names, practice, and so on, the probability is that you will remember very few of the names without using special tricks and devices, such as taking a little time to picture the name, analyze its components, and tie these components into some association with physical features. That is what stage entertainers do. They remember 200 names of people they met only once because they went through 200 learning exercises in the process of meeting them. They concentrated on the names and faces and not on any other feature of the people that could not be associated with the names. Remembering names is hard work, and most people are too lazy to go to the necessary trouble.

REPRESSION

In psychoanalysis, *repression* was supposed to be a defense mechanism by which unpleasant thoughts, memories, and/or illicit desires could be somehow removed from consciousness and relegated to the unconscious, where they continued an independent existence and constantly struggled to emerge back into consciousness. With successful repression, a person could carry on in a more or less normal way on the surface but might have dreams that, in disguised form, could allow the illicit material some opportunity to operate. A slip of the tongue might reveal the real thought a person might have repressed; similarly, an accident might be the result of a repressed thought or wish coming through.

There has never been any substantial laboratory evidence for any mechanism such as repression, and most psychologists do not entertain the concept in their work. Everyone, however, has occasion to tell someone else to "forget it" or stop worrying over it, and we frequently do forget and stop worrying, not by some mysterious agency such as repression operating but by the simple expedient of thinking of something else. We cannot worry constantly: There are too many obligations and interruptions in our lives, and even if something to worry about does come up, we eventually have to turn to something else. After sufficient terminations of worries or thoughts, illicit or otherwise, we come to forget various insults, traumas, defeats, or injuries. We have not really forgotten them, in that we can more or less easily be reminded of them by one cue or another, but they have not been bothering us in the meantime. To say that they were repressed is of no merit, since we can remember many unpleasant memories even with slight provocation. Some people, however, adopt formulas that help them over difficult times. In *Gone with the Wind,* Scarlett O'Hara would frequently say to herself, "I'll think about it tomorrow," and go about some other business. Such a technique could work fairly well in avoiding unpleasant situations. We could even school ourselves to have some specific counter-thought with which to busy ourselves when trouble of any kind comes up. A person who might lust in his heart every time he saw some particular kind of woman might learn to recite the Twenty-third Psalm or the Bill of Rights as soon as the lust arose, and by the time he was through with his ritual, the lust would be gone. It is possible to, in this way, put things out of your mind. Once they are gone, they no longer function, and the notion of an unconscious harboring all sorts of repressed desires trying to escape and make our lives miserable is quite unacceptable and certainly unnecessary. Most of us recognize quite clearly our various illicit wishes and desires and make the necessary adjustments to stay out of trouble, knowing full well that although we are not angels, we must, on occasion, try to act as we think angels should.

Freud considered repression to be the major principle underlying his entire system of psychoanalysis, which was designed to bring out the repressed memories, especially those of some childhood traumatic incident, and have the patient relive the experience in a now adult frame of reference. Most of us are quite clear about the kinds of desires and experiences we have had, and if the memories are painful, it would be highly desirable and gratifying if they could actually be forgotten. We would then have no need of psychoanalysis or any other therapy.

RETIREMENT   (See OLD AGE AND SENILITY)

Modern civilized society is based on the proposition that people should be employed at some kind of job and that they should work at this job for a long stretch of their lives. At various times, the principle applied to children, who labored in mines or mills for 12 or more hours daily, except for a Biblical day of rest. Currently, women are urged or are urging that women also be employed in some kind of regular job, meaning something outside the home where daily attendance for some fixed number of hours is required and where a wage, or preferably, a salary, could be earned. Such a program is sometimes called the *work ethic*. There is no scientific evidence that supports the proposition that anyone really wants to get up at a fixed hour and go to some place of work and stay there for a fixed time. All evidence, such as there is, suggests that people would prefer to sleep until they awakened naturally, eat when they are hungry, and do nothing except what interested them for as long as it did interest them. There does appear to be some kind of drive or physiological need to move around to some degree, but the nature of the activity called for seems merely one of stretching muscles from time to time.

When people attain some age where their productivity appears to be lowering, employers would prefer to see them leave and be replaced by younger, more productive wrkers. Governments get into the act with pension or social security plans to provide some basic income for those who are unemployed for reasons of age. Because governments must take budgets into some consideration, they make the age of retirement as late as possible, with the expectation that the retirer will not live too long. The age of 65 was selected by the German chancellor Bismarck as a good time to retire, since in Bismarck's day, few people reached that age. With modern medicine, more people live longer, and governments now try to keep workers at their posts as long as possible, creating new problems by preventing young workers from securing jobs or promotions as the older worker remains on the job.

To add to the problem, some people prefer to work over whatever else they might do, perhaps because they enjoy power or the income, or, perhaps, they fear to admit that they are no longer useful, respected, admired, or feared. Politicians push for legislation that allows them to retain office as well as to get the votes of the elderly by maintaining that old people are wise, experienced, skillful, prompt, and reliable, along with a lot of other virtues. Some old people even believe this, although it is perfectly clear that everyone slows down with age. Although there are exceptions, nearly everyone past 40 needs glasses to read and could use a hearing aid to hear all that goes on around him or her. He or she also needs notes to remember what he or she has already said and to whom. The simple facts of the matter are that after age 25 or thereabouts, one begins a more or less steady decline in his or her capacities, whether they be mental or physical, and whatever he or she is doing, someone younger could probably be found who could do it better.

It is well established that in science, poetry, and other literature, as well as the arts, the greatest achievements have been the work of young people who lived on their reputations from then on. Einstein, for example, achieved his greatest feats by the time he was 25 and did not make any serious advances after that; Newton, whom Einstein displaced in physical glory, similarly did his finest work before 45 and contributed nothing of importance after that. In the arts, some people can remain great performers into their seventies and beyond, and they should be so credited: If anyone wants to observe their performances, they can pay to do so. No one needs to employ an old artist who is no longer productive. In the arts, it is difficult to set up standards of productivity. Picasso painted pictures at the age of 90, and if some people wanted to pay for these, it was their privilege. Other people never liked Picasso's work even when he was young. In a factory or office, however, an older person's work might be more effectively measured and evaluated, but again, it is difficult if the worker owns the corporation or is chairman of the board. In any case, there are no indispensable people. Death sees to that. If one is forced to retire by death, the question is why one should not retire before that, making room for others as well as doing what should have come naturally but which has been trained out of one by necessity and by long years of habit. For a while after a period of getting up at a fixed time, one will continue to do so, but if the alarm is not set, one will soon get to waken when he or she has had enough sleep. One can get used to retirement as easily, if not more so, as he or she got used to work.

The problem with some retirees is that they did not foresee the day when they might not be useful to an employer any more, and they made no plans for their new leisure time. What is needed is an educational program wherein retirement is considered at some early age when skills appropriate to leisure time can be developed and looked forward to. Such skills should not only be physical affairs such as sports; one can be too frail, weak, or otherwise disabled to engage in these. The skills should include intellectual operations, such as playing bridge, chess, poker, or other games; handicapping horses; or following some sport played by others—for example, professional baseball, football, and the like. The skills should also include aesthetics, the appreciation of art and music beyond some casual level, so that the retiree would find less than enough time to follow pursuits such as photography or plant propagation. Hobbies should certainly be part of one's education and training, since hobbies, however strenuous, are not work. The wealthy among us never had a problem of retirement as they retired at birth and did what nature probably intended for man in general: eat, sleep, and move about a bit.

RETROGRADE AMNESIA

If one suffers a blow to the skull or if the brain is shocked or damaged by a stroke, one may be unable to recall the events that occurred at some period prior to the trauma. When patients in mental institutions are given electroshock therapy, they do not remember the shocks or the events leading up to their coming to the place where the shocks were given. Laboratory rats also forget habits learned just prior to convulsive shocks. Failure to recall recent events is called *retrograde amnesia,* and it is characteristic of aging people, who appear to have excellent recall of events of their childhood but cannot remember what they had for breakfast. We should, of course, recognize that we were not around at the time of the childhood of some older person and that what passes for a good memory may be largely a confabulation or some frequently rehearsed and well-learned story. It may have little correspondence with the facts.

In *senile dementia,* it is common for people to fail to recall many simple activities, but we should note that they are frequently not interested in much that we might think they should appreciate. They might be able to remember better if they bothered to learn better, but the effort of learning does not appear to be sufficiently rewarding. Laboratory studies have shown that old people can learn the kinds of laboratory tasks young people are asked to learn, but that the older person will usually require much more time to learn. If he or she learns to the same level as the young person, he or she will remember it almost as well as the younger subject. The problem consists of getting the older person to learn what amounts to nonsense and unimportant, uninteresting material.

In homes for the elderly, the old people may be resigned, depressed, and rather hopeless, seeing themselves as useless burdens on their younger relatives, and they may be preoccupied with problems of illness and approaching death. They find it unimportant to note the time of day or the day of the week and might find nothing of interest around them. There is no point to remembering most of what occurs, and they prefer not to make the effort to exercise the sclerotic brain that brought them to such a state in the first place. Retrograde amnesia is more frustrating to the relatives than to the old person who is no longer in a position to affect his or her own life.

REWARD AND REINFORCEMENT   (See MOTIVATION, EXTINCTION, PERMISSIVENESS, PUNISHMENT)

In 1891, Edward Lee Thorndike captured the fancy of American psychologists by restating the ancient hedonistic doctrine that we learn by rewards and punishments, that is, by the consequences of our acts. Thorndike called it the *law of effect*. Ever since then, most educators and learning psychologists have behaved as if they accepted the assumption that one learns by being rewarded or punished for what he or she does. In the intervening years, no progress was made in discovering *how* rewards and punishments worked, but a lot of systematic information about how rewards and punishments had to be manipulated for efficient learning has been accumulated. For example, both rewards and punishments had to be administered immediately if they were to be of value. The amount of reward does not appear to be important in itself, but it must be appropriate for the learner involved: Babies will not learn if they are given dollar bills. Anything associated with a reward—for example, a cup in which food is given—can become rewarding in its own right as a *secondary reward*. In order to maintain a habit or learned behavior pattern, the reward need not be given on every occasion, and, in fact, spreading out the times of providing a reward *(periodic reinforcement)* can maintain a response pattern longer when rewards are no longer provided *(extinction)*.

The term *reward* had a subjective tone, one associated with pleasure, and the more objective sounding term *reinforcement* was introduced as a substitute to describe any kind of object or event that seemed to strengthen some behavior pattern.

By 1932, Thorndike had decided that experimental data could not be developed to support the notion that punishment weakened learning, and he discarded one-half of his law of effect. Again, he was followed widely by psychologists, who more or less abandoned studies of punishment in connection with learning as unproductive. An era of permissiveness in child training was the result of such statements by Thorndike and his latter-day followers, especially B. F. Skinner. Actually, Thorndike never demonstrated and neither did anyone else that learning depended upon some rewarding consequence to a behavior. Much learning occurs by imitation, where the learner is not rewarded directly but may see someone else benefit by some behavior. In *incidental learning,* a person learns without knowing that he or she is learning anything and without being asked to learn or to be rewarded for learning. What rewards actually do is motivate people to remain in a learning situation. They also provide stimuli for emotional reactions that become conditioned to other stimuli in a learning situation. A rat, for example, will learn to run down an alley to the end where it is fed. If the food reward is small on every even-numbered trial and large on every odd-numbered trial, the rat will run slowly on the even-numbered trials and quickly on the odd. The rat has learned that there is a reward and what kind of reward is there, but the learning was not accomplished because of the reward, except indirectly. The rat already knew how to run down that or any other alley. It only had to learn where the reward was. Had it run down and found no reward, it would also have learned that there was no reward and no point to running in that direction in the future. Rewards, then, function as motivators and not as learning agents, except in the sense that, in some situations, a person will not bother to apply him- or herself, look into a situation, examine the circumstances, and so on if there is no payoff at the end.

The old hedonistic philosophy did not apply to learning. It applied to what people would do regardless of what they knew or came to know. Thus, a person could lead a life of pleasure seeking or one of ascetic denial and still know the same things in various degrees. Most people learned to sacrifice immediate and minor satisfactions for later but greater pleasures of one kind of another. For some, the pleasure of dying in grace was compensation for a lifetime or personal denial. Today, the same kinds of behavior are observable all around us. Most people seek pleasure to the extent that circumstances allow and avoid painful consequences. Also, most people make immediate sacrifices, some of them painful, as in the case of a surgical operation, in order to attain some more satisfactory later objective. When rewards are used in teaching dogs to do tricks of one kind or another or in teaching children, what we are doing is manipulating the motivation of the child or the dog to continue to follow our operations. Obviously, rewards are more pleasant to deal with than are punishments, and they are also often easier to arrange without negative aftereffects, such as fear and hate. In general, it is much easier to train someone if you say, "That's a good boy" (or dog) than to swing a whip for any lack of activity or deviation. By careful selection of rewards, we can manipulate most people to do anything that we want them to do. At the same time, they may be learning something and will certainly learn who is doing the rewarding, when, and what the rewards amount to.

ROLE PLAYING   *(See MULTIPLE PERSONALITIES)*

Because we have only one legal name and one body, we grow up thinking that we are but one person or self and do not recognize that we all have to learn to behave differently with different people and in different circumstances. Sometimes we search, vainly, for a true self, the real or inner *me,* when there is no such thing. What we have are different behaviors, different ways of getting along in various circumstances. Such different behaviors are referred to as *role playing,* since we do play various roles—for example, the brave soldier, the indulgent father, the political activitist, the steady worker, and the loving husband. We have our *social self* and our more private selves. The social self will, itself, vary with the societies it encounters. As long as the various roles can be kept apart, we can get along. It is only when someone else finds us playing a role unfamiliar to him or her that the question, "What is he or she really like?", arises. He or she is really like the roles he or she plays is the only answer to the question. Novelists, dramatists, and newspaper feature writers like to play around with the notion that sometimes two or more different persons or personalities inhabit the same body, and we accept the sensational reports of multiple personalities as if these were some unique or strange creatures. Actually, we are all multiple personalities, inasmuch as we play different roles or parts as parents, workers, or party-goers. Very few of us behave in the same way with a priest, doctor, child, wife or husband, boss, or employee. Some of the roles we play cover up a host of undesirable feelings. A wife may be apparently loyal, loving, kind, self-sacrificing, and patient and have a profligate roué for a husband. Someday, she reaches the end of her rope and does something out of character, and the friends and relations report their surprise. There was nothing out of character about the matter. The kind and loving wife had been playing one role while living another (miserable) existence hidden from the observers, possibly even from her husband. Sometimes, extreme departures from one role confound us, but they should not lead us to assume that at last the true personality asserted itself. It was the same person all along, with a different repertoire of behavior on display in the hope, perhaps, that one role might lead to some greater satisfaction than another. In extreme cases, various roles might be so different as to create disorder in a person as he or she changes from one role to another. In such cases, a person might assume different identities and names to go along with different roles. He or she is no longer in touch with reality and is said to be dissociated. Such multiple personalities are virtually psychotic and need treatment. The question of which personality to treat may be a real puzzle, along with the puzzle of what treatment to attempt.

S

SCAPEGOATING   (See FRUSTRATION, RATIONALIZATION)

Scapegoating is a popular and common practice of *displacement*—that is, placing the blame for our troubles onto other people, animals, or even things, as when we kick a chair that somehow got into our way. The practice is an ancient one and stems from the Biblical reference to the custom of placing one's sins on the back of a goat and then sending the goat out into the desert to die, along with the sins.

It is easy to blame the Congress, the president, big business, the labor unions, other races, and so on, for any of our troubles. Hitler aroused the German people to attack and exterminate the Jews, whom he blamed for the sorry state of the German economy after World War I. The scapegoat selected is usually one that cannot defend itself and whom it is safe to attack. Usually, the effort is made to select some kind of evidence to justify the attack, without going into any vigorous analysis and looking at all sides of a question. Scapegoating is frequently a form of rationalization, in that there is a prior underlying animosity toward the subject of our attack that surfaces only when we are frustrated to the point of some felt need for action. Scapegoating becomes serious when groups of people join in blaming other groups for their troubles.

All manner of crime, violence, and brutality can emerge when large, powerful, or dominant groups find themselves a convenient scapegoat.

SCHIZOPHRENIA

Insanity, a general term for what we now consider to be a variety of severe mental disorders, has been recognized for more than 2,000 years. Actually, *insanity* is a legal term, and its meaning varies with changes in laws. It usually includes the notion that a person does not realize the nature of his or her acts or that they are wrong. Attempts to understand and treat insanity have ranged from believing it to be caused by demoniacal possession, overpowering id impulses, chemical imbalances, and brain damage or malfunction. Attempts to cure insanity have included exorcism, torture, confinement, psychotherapy, brain surgery, electroshock treatment, and tranquilizing medications. None of these approaches has cured insanity, and most of them have made the patients worse. Tranquilizers have been effective in reducing bizarre symptoms and in helping to keep patients calm, thus making it possible to release many patients from mental hospitals. But tranquilizers do not cure the condition, and, as is only now being realized, they do have serious negative side-effects.

In the 1800s, a particular type of insanity was recognized and described by the psychiatrist Emil Kraepelin. He observed that people became confused, bizarre, unable to think correctly, or keep their attention on anything for too long and that they could not readily take care of themselves. Kraepelin believed that the disorder was an incurable, progressive mental deterioration, or *dementia,* that begins in adolescence. The sex glands, he believed, malfunctioned and caused a severe chemical imbalance in the body that affected the nervous system. Because he believed that this dementia began early in life (i.e., adolescence), he termed it *dementia praecox.*

In 1911, the psychiatrist Eugene Bleuler described the same set of bizarre behaviors as a *splitting of the mind,* or *schizophrenia.* Like Kraepelin, he thought it due to organic factors. However, although Kraepelin thought it incurable, Bleuler believed it could be arrested at any stage in its development.

Today, the term *schizophrenia* continues in use, but we no longer believe in its literal meaning of split mind. The schizophrenic patient is recognized as a person whose mental functioning is extremely disturbed. The very thinking processes are disturbed; the ways in which the world is perceived are distorted; emotional responses are lacking, exaggerated, or inappropriate; delusions or false beliefs are common parts of the reaction; and hallucinations are experienced by many schizophrenics.

Because of the severity of the disturbances, it is very difficult for most families to live with a schizophrenic. Although most schizophrenics are not assaultive or dangerous to others, their bizarre beliefs and strange behaviors cause unease and impose a great deal of responsibility on others in the family. For those reasons, many schizophrenics are sent to institutions where they can receive some care.

But the isolated institutional life is not good or helpful for these people. In the past fifteen years, as part of the community mental health movement, schizophrenics have been released from hospitals to live in special small centers, such as group homes, within cities, and to become more a part of normal society. For the most part, they can remain outside of hospitals successfully for long periods of time, requiring occasional emergency rehospitalization mainly to calm down and to readjust their medication. In their new, more normal surroundings, they seem to do fairly well, seldom causing any problems for other people. Unfortunately, neighbors and businessmen are too often fearful and suspicious and do not like the looks of some of these admittedly different-appearing people, and they object to the attempts at community placement.

At present, after nearly a hundred years of recognition of this condition of *dementia praecox* or *schizophrenia,* we do not yet know its causes. It may be physiologically caused, or it may be more psychological in its beginnings. Nor can we cure it, even with all of our modern approaches. The best treatment available now includes emergency hospitalization for those who are in an acute schizophrenic condition, in order to calm them down; the use of tranquilizers to help them maintain a more even functioning; a highly structured, carefully supervised social training or retraining program. It is very important to be aware of the possible negative side-effects of the prolonged use of tranquilizers. Finally, probably the best advice for those who have to try to find suitable treatment for a schizophrenic relative or friend is to recognize the critical importance of keeping the person in *active contact with other people.* Probably one of the worst things that can be done is to keep the person in social isolation and physically inactive, either at home or in an institution. Active contact with other people and continued physical and social activity are critical. Such social interaction can best be achieved in well-run group homes and day-care centers. Unfortunately, these centers are not yet common enough to take care of all of the people who could benefit.

SCHOOL PHOBIA

Nearly all children complain at times about going to school, probably with good reason. Every year, about three out of every 1,000 school children will refuse to go to school and, in refusing, exhibit extreme upset and anxiety. These children are clearly afraid of something; their anxiety is real and is extreme. They resist, fight, and even tolerate harsh punishment, but they will not go to school. Fear and anxiety, refusal to go to school and sometimes to leave the house at all, crying, and pleading are all part of the picture. Often, this is accompanied by physical complaints, such as headaches, stomach aches, and nausea. The children can be seen trembling and breathing rapidly; they often experience diarrhea and sleep disturbances and, in older girls, dysmenorrhea. Faced with such severe behavior, obvious anxiety, and the physical problems of the child, many parents find themselves going through a highly emotional battle each morning but eventually giving in and allowing the child to stay home.

The school rejection has been termed *school phobia,* and it is important to note that the reaction includes that of the parents as well as that of the child.

Although the ultimate behavior—refusal to attend school—is the same in all cases, the important factors vary from one case to another. Some children may be highly afraid of school itself; some might fear the trip to school, either on the bus or walking; others may fear leaving the house; others may have an intense, highly dependent relationship with their mothers and fear a separation. For some children, the school phobia may begin suddenly, perhaps because of an incident at school or because of finding themselves assigned to a teacher they fear or dislike. For others, the pattern of refusal might slowly develop over months or even a year. Although some children who exhibit severe school rejection have many psychological problems, most of the school-phobic children have no other serious problems, and, once the school phobia is successfully removed, they functon in a normal manner.

It is generally agreed that treatment for school phobia should be started immediately and that attempts should be made to get the child back in school as quickly as possible. Delaying treatment makes the task more difficult, since the child settles in and strengthens his or her staying at home the longer he or she is allowed to do it.

In general, the best treatment is started immediately and consists of the following: (1) reducing the child's rewards for staying at home (for example, no TV, no playing, no special foods or staying in bed late; and, on the positive side, making the child do schoolwork, housework, etc.); (2) helping him or her get to school, taking him or her if necessary; (3) increasing his or her rewards for going to and staying in school. Details of treatment, such as whether school re-entry will be all at once or gradual, depend upon the nature of each case. In some instances, part of the difficulty is a parent's reluctance to let the child become more independent. In those instances, counseling for the parent is also needed.

The best advice for parents who see this highly anxious school-refusal pattern is to seek help from the school without delay. Get the child back into school immediately, do all you can to support and reward good school-attending behavior, and be aware of your own behavior that might be reinforcing the child's tendency to stay at home.

SELF-ACTUALIZATION   *(See CLIENT-CENTERED THERAPY)*

The concept of *self-actualization* is central to humanistic psychological models of personality and of psychological treatment. Psychologists Abraham Maslow and Carl Rogers assume that every individual develops a set of ideas, perceptions, and values, specific to one's own personal self. This self-evaluation includes physical, moral, and psychological characteristics, and according to these psychologists, critical in determining how we perceive the world, other people, and how we behave.

One of the key ideas of Maslow and Rogers involves the natural strivings of people. According to most psychological theories of personality and of learning, people naturally strive to maintain *homeostasis,* or balance, among physical and psychological systems. When something happens to upset that balance, the person presumably feels anxious and is motivated to correct the imbalance and return to a state of equilibrium. Maslow and Rogers believe that people naturally strive to achieve a level far beyond equilibrium or balanced survival; that we also strive to improve our physical, moral, and psychological well-being; to express ourselves; to grow as human beings, reaching to achieve the fullest possible human potentialities. In their terms, we strive toward self-actualization.

The human striving toward self-actualization is expressed differently by different people. Examples include striving toward creative self-expression in art, music, science, and writing; enriching life experiences, such as in traveling; increasing our relatedness with other people through developing warm relationships; answering basic humanistic questions, such as "Who am I?" and "What and who is this self?" By struggling with these questions, one gradually refines a concept of self.

The concept of self-actualization is consistent with humanistic philosophy and with much of what we believe to be our democratic ideals that emphasize individual self-determination. In humanistic therapies, such as Carl Rogers's client-centered therapy, the concepts are used to help guide the client toward greater personal self-actualization.

Although these concepts have theoretical value and a great deal of appeal for many people, they do not constitute any well-validated theory. Like psychoanalysis, they can be used in a general way to guide a therapist and a client working together, but they cannot be used to make specific predictions about human behavior. The theory of self-actualization is more a philosophical and moral position, such as that developed by humanistic philosophers in the 1800s, than a scientific psychological concept; and as such, it may have considerable value and appeal. But it should be recognized as philosophical and not as either scientific or practical.

SELF-CONTROL   (See WILL)

Self-control is not a new idea, but it is a topic of increasing interest for psychologists. Traditionally, we have thought of self-control much as some internal reservoir of strength that a person has, an inner strength that allows good restraint even in the face of powerful external forces. *Willpower* is the common term for this trait, and people are thought to have or not to have sufficient amounts of it. There is a heavy value-loading in the concept of willpower that implies virtue and personal strength in those who possess it and weakness in those who do not. The traditional willpower concept has little functional value. It does as little good, for example, to exhort someone to use some self-control or "pull yourself together" as it does for persons to lament, "I wish I had more willpower"; or "I really have tried to stay with a diet many times, but I just don't have your willpower"; and so on.

The belief that some kind of willpower exists within the person as some kind of force or capacity that people have in different amounts is no longer accepted as a useful concept by many psychologists. Instead, the willpower concept has been altered to one of self-control, and the change is more than a mere semantic shift. Self-control refers not to a given trait or characteristic generally possessed by the person but rather to sets of learned skills that are used by an individual to perceive, monitor, understand, organize, and direct his or her own behavior. These learned skills are not generalized skills that can be applied across the board; rather, they are thought of as skills specific to particular demands or stimulus situations. Thus, a person might very reliably display excellent self-control under certain circumstances—for example, when faced with a variety of highly attractive foods—but the same person might also characteristically fail in self-control when faced with an array of easily available alcoholic beverages, or he or she might be unable to moderate excesses of temper when angry. The learned skills required for self-control differ from one set of conditions to another, and a person's self-control successes under one set of circumstances do not necessarily generalize to others. Thus, all of us have self-control under some conditions but lack self-control skills in some other situations. None of us is without some self-control, but neither does anyone have complete self-control across all situations. The person who laments the lack of willpower and repeated failures at dieting to lose weight might nevertheless display considerable willpower (self-control) in many other situations. Self-control, then, is not an all or none, have or have not characteristic.

Self-control, thought of as learned skills, is an optimistic concept, for it assumes that people can learn them. Psychologists who study the development and use of self-control skills try to analyze each situation that requires self-control. They assume that a person's behavior is largely controlled by the stimulus conditions and by the rewarding and punishing consequences of one's behavior. Those stimulus conditions and consequences include a variety of verbal signals and verbal reinforcers and punishers used by the person. The major tasks, then, are for the person to identify what those controlling factors are and how they operate. In order to do this, the person first carefully self-monitors his or her behavior, keeping careful records of how often something is done (e.g., eating, smoking) and under exactly what conditions it is done. Having developed such a record of performance, the person can then try systematically to rearrange the controlling environmental conditions, including the deliberate use of rewards and punishments, and thus come to alter the behavior—that is, to develop self-control skills.

Our lamenting dieter, for example, who keeps falling off the diet, could keep records of all the food eaten, all the exercise taken, and the conditions under which he or she eats. The self-control behavior change program would then aim to alter those conditions so that they will bring about both less eating and more exercise. The person might discover, for example, that excessive eating occurs largely during food preparation rather than at the meals themselves; or primarily during certain times of day, such as after 7 o'clock at night; or perhaps through all-day snacking on a variety of high-calorie foods that are kept conveniently handy all around the house. The dieter can systematically change some of these important controlling conditions by altering food preparation practices; perhaps by eating some meals out; by having someone else in the family prepare some meals; by purchasing already prepared diet meals; by getting rid of all the unnecessary, excess foods available around the house; by altering his or her schedules so as to be busier at night; perhaps by arranging to be out after 7:00 P.M. on several nights; and so on. Each person's self-control program would be different, depending upon the particular controlling factors in each case. At present, personalized programs to help develop self-control skills are best supervised by a psychologist who has had experience in the field. Gradually, as the person's self-control develops, he or she depends less on the professional supervision. Recently, numerous "how to" books have appeared on developing control of eating and smoking behavior and, for students, of study behavior. Many of these books offer good suggestions but, of course, cannot provide personal supervision.

Self-control, then, in its modern psychological meaning, refers to a set of learned skills that allows the person to alter systematically the environmental conditions, including verbal behavior and thinking, that now control the troublesome behavior in question and thus to alter systematically his or her own functioning.

SELF-FULFILLING PROPHECIES   (See PLACEBOS)

In mythology, Pygmalion, sometimes referred to as a king and sometimes as a sculptor, fell in love with a statue of a beautiful woman and wished that it would come to life so that he could wed her. It did, and he did. The myth underlies the folk saying,

"Would that wishing made it so." In psychology, the myth has been interpreted to represent a principle that people see what they want to see and behave in such a way as to make their original vision come true. In the special application in psychology, a teacher, for example, might consider some pupil stupid. If this teacher then behaves toward this pupil as if the pupil was, in fact, stupid, the pupil will become stupid—or at least he or she will get poor grades from that teacher. Because teachers talk about their problem cases to other teachers, a child who gets the stupid treatment in the first grade may continue to get it all through school and, with the inattention and abuse, may actually turn out less well than he or she might have. The evidence for such a principle is not strong. It rests on studies where teachers have been misinformed about the I.Q.s of their students. Those that have been labeled bright might then be treated by the teacher in some fashion that differs from the treatment accorded those labeled retarded or dull. Subsequent grades are then evaluated for evidence of the treatment effect. The studies have been criticized for various weaknesses and cannot be considered to support the *Pygmalion principle* strongly.

There is, however, considerable evidence to support the notion of *experimenter bias*. In many studies, researchers expect to find certain kinds of results. Frequently, they have research assistants who know the expected outcomes and know what will be pleasing to the chief. They tend to find such results without any conscious awareness of faking data. It is somehow easier to make mistakes in one's own favor, make modest adjustments that tilt the scales, or otherwise fudge a little here and there and accumulate data that favor some desired hypothetical outcome. Fortunately, many researchers are fully aware of such biases and arrange their experiments so that assistants do not know what hypothesis is favored or which experimental subjects are getting what treatment. Such blind or double-blind experiments are especially important in assessing drug effects: The experiments are arranged so that the subjects do not know if they are getting a drug and so that the administrators do not know if they are giving a drug or a placebo.

SELF-INJURIOUS BEHAVIORS IN CHILDREN

Many retarded and psychotic children display *self-injurious behaviors (SIBs);* they bang their heads, punch, stab, gouge, and bit themselves, and so on. It is not known why this occurs, and its treatment is, as yet, uncertain. SIBs are obviously potentially dangerous behaviors. In some extreme cases, the SIBs are extremely disruptive, violent, and frequent. For example, head-banging children have been known to punch or bang their heads violently at a rate exceeding 1,000 times a day, if allowed the opportunity. In such cases, it is difficult to teach any alternative behavior because the children remain so completely involved and seemingly overpowered by their own SIBs. Language, toilet training, simple social skills, and so on are interfered with and must sometimes be given up because of the interference of the child's violent self-abuse.

In institutions, where SIBs are most likely to occur, the most frequent control methods are drugs and physical restraints, such as straitjackets and tying the child in bed. Neither is a good treatment because (1) it does not produce alternative, non-injurious behavior and because (2) when the restraints are removed, the SIBs recur.

Further, the negative side-effects of drugs and physical restraints may be enormous. Essentially, the child is largely immobilized and might be kept so for years. During such long-term immobilization, muscles may atrophy, and the child loses critical opportunities for learning—opportunities that might never again be possible.

In recent years, contingent electric shock has been used as a treatment for SIBs. The shock is painful, but it does not damage tissues. It is administered to the child as a punishment and must be carefully timed to occur immediately following the self-abusive behavior. Although contingent shock has been dramatically successful in some cases (and not successful in others), immediately eliminating the SIBs after all else has failed, there is considerable concern over the ethics of the procedure. Some psychologists believe that we should not use severe punishers, such as electric shock, no matter what the reasons or good intentions may be. Others argue that the shock is not physically dangerous (it is a high voltage shock, causing pain, but a low-amperage shock that does not damage tissues); only a few painful shocks are needed. The shock users ask, is it better to keep the child wrapped in a straightjacket or otherwise restrained, perhaps for years, or to inflict brief pain, possibly eliminate the SIBs, and then go on to teach more adaptive behaviors?

The best treatment now available for severe SIBs may be a combination of contingent electric shock to decrease the frequency of SIBs immediately and then to follow it up immediately by beginning a detailed program of social skills training, using high positive reinforcements.

SENSATION AND PERCEPTION   *(See BRAIN AND NERVOUS SYSTEM)*

Psychology as a science began in 1879 in Leipzig in what is now East Germany, in the laboratories of Wilhelm Wundt. The main preoccupation of Wundt and his students was the study of *sensation* and *perception,* neither of which was ever defined satisfactorily. *Sensation* was supposed to be some relatively simple personal and conscious reaction to some stimulus energy, divorced from its source. Thus, if one looked at a piece of blackboard chalk, he or she would experience sensations of whiteness, length, and breadth. The whiteness would be of a certain brightness or intensity, and the experiencer would possibly note other attributes of the sensory experience he or she was undergoing, such as clarity and duration. We already mentioned the attribute of extension (length and breadth). The job of psychologists was to analyze such sensory experiences as might occur when one smelled, tasted, felt, heard, or lifted something that might serve as a stimulus. If one reported that he or she saw a chalk, Wundt might be displeased and would identify such a response as a *stimulus error;* a stimulus error would be committed if one named the stimulus rather than the attributes of the sensory experience. Committing the stimulus error was the same as reporting a perception. A *perception* would be made up of a combination of sensations, along with imagery and feelings, a complex mental product that involved past experience. No one could name some white cylindrical object a piece of chalk without having had certain prior experiences with such an object.

For some psychologists, a sensation was a kind of primary mental reaction, whereas perception would be secondary elaboration involving past experience. For an adult to have a pure sensation is virtually impossible in real life. In the laboratory, it is possible to have one look through a tube, for example, at some colored surface so that only a circle of color is exposed, without any cues as to its origin. The viewer then sees a surface color, and if he or she tries to prevent speculations about its source, he or she might be able to talk about its hue, saturation, brightness, and perhaps some other pure sensory experience. When we hear a sound, we usually respond in terms of its source and not its pitch, loudness, and timbre, the attributes of a tone. To identify it as a piano note would be a perceptual response, a stimulus error. Again, in order to hear a pure tone, one would have to be in a specially prepared room in an acoustical laboratory where every effort has been made to prevent echoes, reflections, and differential absorptions. A pitch would be produced by an oscillator at some frequency and loudness, and we would be experiencing a pure sound sensation.

According to Wundt, all perceptions would be combinational experiences involving past experience. If anyone responded meaningfully on the first occasion of stimulation, he or she would be having a perception without past experience, and this would violate the Wundtian theory. Some psychologists have tried to demonstrate that depth perception, for example, is a native, inborn reaction in various species and, perhaps, in human babies. If this were true, then sensation would be indistinguishable from perception. Baby chicks, for example, peck at corn fairly accurately as soon as their eyes are suitably developed; human babies, at the crawling age, appear to perceive depth and avoid what looks like a dangerous lower level if they are placed on a visual cliff (a sheet of plate glass divided in the middle with a checkerboard pattern just under the glass at one side and several feet below the glass on the other). It can be argued that the babies have already *learned* to perceive depth at the crawling age.

The interesting thing about sensation and perception is that although a hundred years have passed since Wundt opened his laboratory, no psychologist has ever explained what such sensory reactions as seeing, hearing, smelling, and so on really comprise. What happens when we look at and see an apple? Psychologists and neurologists can explain what happens on the retina, on the optic nerve, and in certain parts of the brain in terms of electrochemical impulses and neural firing, but at no point in the course of the neural activity is anyone able to identify a seeing activity. Certain observations on people born blind, with cataracts, have proved very provocative. When the cataracts are removed, the people should be able to see like anyone else if they are provided with lenses to replace the clouded lenses that were removed in the operation. Even without the lenses, they should see something. The usual report is that they certainly do not see any objects. They do report that something seems to be out there, and they can follow a line with their fingers, but they cannot recognize squares, triangles, balls, or faces without several months of experience. They do react to colors as different from one another and can learn the color names very quickly, but they still have to learn to see objects in a very arduous and slow manner, with such slow progress that, according to the findings of M. Von Senden, some refuse the precious gift of sight and take up their dark glasses and white canes and go about as before— blind.

Such findings suggest that for any sensory input, our nervous systems react in terms of neural activity going on in our nerves and brain but that such activity does not mean anything to us when we are infants. As we grow older, we begin to respond to such internal activity with some kinds of motor responses (our eyes follow a moving light, for example, as soon as our eyes are open—an inborn reflex). We may not know what our eyes are doing, however, perhaps for years, until we see other babies' eyes following lights. Our own eye movements are not very strong generators of stimuli for ourselves although such movement-produced stimuli may become involved in many complex reactions which are of great meaning to us, as in reading, for example. Babies will often cry if they bump their heads. The cry may come along a little late, but the three year old baby will cry immediately and sometimes when the bump is hardly serious. As we learn to react with cries, and later with words or other adaptative movements other observers can tell that we see or hear or feel but still no one knows what these terms mean. Saying that we are having a conscious experience is of no help because no one knows what consciousness means. The best we can say is that we "see," for example, when our eyes are open and when we react to the occurrence of stimuli that reflect light into our eyes. If we react adaptively and can name the stimulus we are perhaps better off than if we react maladaptively and/or cannot name the stimulus. If we do not react at all we are not *seeing*. Babies that do not react to a light approaching their faces are not seeing even if something is going on in their nervous systems that is different from a lightless situation. In the words of William James, they are having a big, booming, buzzing confusion, not so much of consciousness but of stimulation and neural activity that is not being channeled into appropriate reactions. Apparently, as human beings we are able to respond to the presence of lights and sounds as different kinds of events which generate activity in different parts of our brains and, as adults, we have learned to label such internal activity with suitable terms; presumably the same kind of activity goes on in the brains of cats and dogs, but we hesitate to refer to them as conscious creatures. In recent years, some interesting studies have been done on human patients whose brains have been divided into two halves by surgically cutting through the corpus callosum, an area in the brain that joins the two hemispheres and through which nerve fibers pass from one side of the brain to the other. Such split-brain patients now have, in effect, a right and a left brain. The left brain contains structures that appear to be specialized for language, whereas the right brain lacks these. The right brain, however, can, by suitable manipulations of stimuli, be shown things that the left brain cannot see. Using their left hands, such patients can identify objects (by feel) and demonstrate that they, in fact, did see the objects shown; they are unable, however, to tell anyone what they saw or felt. In short, they do the right thing but have no awareness or consciousness of the events in which they have just engaged. Objects shown to the left brain are readily identified, and we might assume that the person saw the objects, but the only difference between the two experiences is that one is describable by words and the other is not. The implication from such split-brain studies is that both our sensation and perception experiences are neural activities that we have learned to identify over a long history of experiences, aided and abetted by our parents, who really tell us that it hurts when we suffer a bruise instead of waiting for us to cry; some children appear not to know enough to cry (perhaps they feel nothing special) except when the parents are around.

B. F. Skinner has pointed out that we are not very clever about describing our headaches, toothaches, and various internal miseries because no one else can see the activity that is occurring and help us find words that would make sense. No one can feel our headaches for us and we are told to take an aspirin. With such internal sources of sensation we are still in the stage of a buzzing confusion. We may know that "it hurts" but we do not know what the "it" is. We can be grateful for an evolutionary history that has endowed us handsomely with inborn reflex responses and a language capacity which we are able to apply to some varieties of stimuli.

SENSORY THRESHOLDS

For anything to be seen, heard, smelled, felt, or sensed in any way, some minimal amount of energy must affect the sense organs and their corresponding sensory nerves. The amount of energy required to sense something is remarkably small. Our ears are about as sensitive as they can be when we are young and healthy. If they were any more sensitive, we would hear the air moving about us in a quiet room. Similarly, our noses are so sensitive that very minute quantities measured in micrograms of some odoriferous substance can be detected. Our eyes can detect very minute amounts of light against a dark background. From the top of a tall building, at night, one can see a match flare miles away in the darkness. In short, our senses are normally about as keen as they ever needed to be for our survival under primitive conditions in our evolutionary history.

The amount of energy impinging upon our sense organs required to be just barely noticed is called the *absolute threshold,* or *limen.* The threshold varies slightly from time to time and has to be considered in statistical terms as an average amount. Usually, it is defined as the amount of energy that can be detected 50% of the time across a series of tests.

Once we have determined the threshold energy level, we can ask, How much change in stimulus strength does it take to detect a difference? That answer would be called the *difference threshold* or *DL* (difference limen). Here, we encounter some interesting variations among the senses. It takes a smaller percentage change to detect a change in the amount of light than in the loudness of a sound. In general, a 1% difference in light strength can be noticed, but it takes almost a 25% change in loud- ness to be noticed. To tell the difference between two weights, they must differ by approximately 3%. In practice, this means that one could not easily tell the difference in weights between two children weighing 30 and 31 pounds: They would appear to weigh about the same.

At the other extreme of intense stimulation, there is another threshold, the *terminal threshold.* At such a level, no light can look brighter, no sound louder, or no smell stronger than at the present level. At such points, the sense itself seems to change, so that something that was just called very hot now changes to pain, as does something noisy or bright. The pain protects us from exposure that might damage the sense if we are able to turn away or escape. Thus, looking at the bright sun will damage the retina; it is also too painful to continue. A problem does arise if the change is introduced gradually, as with hot water in a shower or the sun on the beach; we can become adapted and not notice when the intensity level changes to a dangerous point. Similarly, when the temperature drops, we cannot tell that it is getting any colder after reaching a point around 12°F. With numbness taking over, we can remain in the cold long beyond the point of safety; we can even lie down, relax, and die in the cold after a kind of adaptation—numbness—has occurred.

Much of the early work in psychology was dedicated to the study of thresholds, and the first law, and still one of the only laws of psychology, was described as *Weber's Law,* or the *Weber-Fechner Law.* This law dealt with the fact that just because a stimulus increased by some amount, there need not be an increase in sensation or awareness of change by some similar amount. In order for one to notice a change, there had to be some percentage change in the magnitude of the stimulus as compared with some standard. Actually, the percentage changes with the size of the standard, and so the law is not a particularly useful or elegant law, but it still has some bearing on practical affairs. If someone asks you to cut the volume on a radio, it might not do to turn the volume knob some small amount. The difference might not be recognized. Merely to get the difference noticed calls for quite a change in the knob setting. To get a change that the requester will consider pleasing might call for an heroic twist.

SEX AS RECREATION

It has been said that sex was once primarily a procreational activity, but it has now become a recreational activity. The pleasure of sex, as distinct from the duty of sex, is now openly accepted and sought after. There is now a great deal of room for varying opinions, values, and behaviors. We now openly discuss sexual pleasures, study sexual activity, and even have specialized professionals who deal with sexual problems, such as the inability of some couples to experience fully satisfying sexual activity. This elevation of sexual pleasure to such widespread acceptance is a significant change in our society's beliefs and behavior.

Not long ago, normal sex was that engaged in by married couples, both to carry out their procreational duties and to share intimacy and love only with each other. Their normal sex activities were limited to coitus—that is, genital contact with some, but not too much, foreplay. Husband and wife could enjoy sex with each other, but they could not enjoy it too much. All other sexual activity, such as masturbation, oral-genital contact, homosexuality, extramarital and premarital sex, and so on, were considered illicit and/or deviant.

Today, our definition of normal sex activity is much wider. It still includes husband-wife intercourse, but with two major changes: (1) The heterosexual couple is no longer necessarily a married couple, and (2) the pleasurable value of sex has been elevated over its duty for procreation. Couples are now expected to engage in sex as pleasure, to enjoy it to the greatest degree they can, to experiment with variations in sexual acts, and no longer to limit themselves to simple coitus. Women are now encouraged to take a more active part in the sexual activity, and illustrated manuals are available for couples, showing dozens of different positions for coitus and variations in techniques for mutual stimulation. In fact, the pleasure of sex is now so stressed that a lack of great pleasure for both partners is considered by many psychologists to be a problem of sexual inadequacy. Actually, a couple's degree of enjoyment of sex is their own affair. If not all of us can—or want to—match every contortion of the sex manuals or the implied high frequency and intensity of sexual activity, it is a mistake to think that we therefore have a problem. What is important to emphasize here is that a wide variety of heterosexual practices engaged in by consenting adults for the pleasure of sex are now considered by psychologists to be normal, acceptable behavior.

The degree to which people pursue sexual pleasure is a matter of their own choice, and the less sexually troubled or zealous among us are not necessarily inadequate.

SEX DIFFERENCES   *(See MASCULINITY—FEMININITY)*

The differences we are concerned with here are those that derive from the fact that women have two X chromosomes and men one X and one Y chromosome. These chromosomes and their genes control a variety of structural differences, some of which are responsible for some functional differences. The obvious differences between men and women are in their sex organs themselves and in their corresponding glands, which secrete different kinds of hormones. In the female, two kinds of endocrine glands secrete *estrogen* and *progesterone.* The latter is chiefly involved in reproduction (implantation of fertilized eggs and nutrition of the fetus); the former is responsible for secondary sex characteristics—for example, breast development. In men, the testes produce *testosterone,* which controls the development of secondary sexual characteristics. The *secondary characteristics,* called secondary because they develop slowly in adolescence, include such things as distribution of pubic hair (the patterns differ in men and women), subcutaneous body fat (women have more), breast development, and sexual arousal. The hormonal secretions interact with all other hormones and affect other body structures so that men in general grow taller and heavier than women and consequently are, in general, stronger. The pattern and distribution of bodily and facial hair differs in obvious ways. Women also tend to develop more rapidly; talk and walk sooner; and, in general, seem to stop growth about two or three years before similar declines in males.

Despite the average differences in height, weight, and strength, some women are taller, heavier, and stronger than some men. If women were encouraged to engage in athletics and strenuous sports, the present differences might well be reduced. One additional difference should be pointed out: Women after adolescence undergo a monthly period of menstruation until menopause. The menstrual period tends to be accompanied by some changes in emotion and behavior that vary in degree and quality from woman to woman. In some cases, the period is almost incapacitating, in others, there is hardly any change from normal feelings and behavior. One cannot generalize.

Although the sexual differences can be traced to the glandular secretions, it should be appreciated that both men and women secrete the same hormones; only the relative amounts differ, and so both men and women will share some of the traits of the opposite sex.

Over the centuries and in different cultures, men and women have been reared differently and have adopted various roles. Modern feminists claim that all of the important and serious differences in male-female roles are cultural in origin and that there are no reasons why women should be treated differently from men in modern times. This is an unproven assumption. In the United States, at present, some women regard themselves as unequally treated and exploited. Male antifeminists might well merit the accusations. The question of male-female differences may or may not be resolved by changes in the law. Men still cannot bear children, and if children are to be born, women will have to bear them.

Psychologists can only advise that female children tend to develop physically earlier than do male children and that they appear to have more language fluency than do male children. All of the testing that has been done that shows some kinds of male superiority in mathematics and design problems after age 14 or so cannot be evaluated until, and if, some suitable population of boys and girls is raised under absolutely equal conditions until the age of 12 or so. This is a most unlikely prospect. In the meantime, it should be pointed out that testers who make up tests have generally assumed that there are no sex differences, and when they find test items that are handled more easily by girls than by boys (or vice versa), those items are excluded. Tests, then, in general, will show no sex differences, because all of the items that might have demonstrated a difference are excluded by the deliberate choice of the testers.

The development of girls tends to stop earlier than the development of boys, so that girls, in general, show declines in developmental rate starting at about age 15, whereas boys continue to develop until about age 18 or so. Full height in boys is not attained until about age 20; in girls, it occurs about age 16.

Child-care problems regarding how a girl should be dressed; what toys she should play with; what household chores, tasks, or skills should be encouraged; what kinds of books to read; and so on are matters of some concern to parents. Because the future is uncertain, no one really knows what to do in these regards. The answers depend on parents' emotions and not on reason. There is no reason why a woman cannot be a coal miner if she wants to (there might be a good reason to question her wanting to). In some countries, women do mine coal, collect garbage, work in steel mills, and perform all kinds of tasks that some people in this country consider male occupations. The question is whether the women in such countries are not being exploited. If they have to mine coal, that is one situation. If it is a matter of choice, it is another matter entirely. The ideal situation would presumably be one where each individual, regardless of sex, is engaged in activities for which the person is suited, competent, and satisfied and where other people would not be disturbed because of the individual's activities. That is a Utopian situation that does not represent the present realities.

SEX DRIVES AND NEEDS

In modern Western culture, sexual activities are perhaps the most highly promoted, discussed, sold, and worried over aspects of existence. Problems related to sex are so highly and frequently publicized that the entire culture could be described as sex-ridden. Pornographers of various sorts (magazine publishers, movie producers), prostitutes of both sexes, newspapers, and even psychiatrists and psychologists find sex a source of profit in one way or another. In some allegedly more primitive cultures, sex is treated far more casually, and more time is devoted to other aspects of life. We cannot explore all the complications of sex over the centuries, but we can and should recognize it for what it basically amounts to and, perhaps, relegate it to its proper sphere.

Except for one-celled forms of life and some flower species that happen to have both sex organs (male and female structures in the same plant), all reproduction of life depends on sexual intercourse, so that the continuation of a species depends on such activity. The question of whether or not a species should continue is rarely raised, and since there are no good answers, the question will not be raised here. We start, then, with the biological function of sex—reproduction. In nonhuman animals, there appears to be no other function, and animals mate only at certain seasons when the female is likely to become pregnant. With humans, reproduction might cause problems for young people who cannot provide for offspring, and a great many other variables, such as property rights, make problems for adults if they should also reproduce, so that sexual activity is probably more commonly engaged in when reproduction is undesirable. Nature has apparently arranged for ensuring the reproduction of the species by eliminating the mating season for humans so that mating can be a year-round activity, with only certain periods of fertility in the female. Both males and females are equipped with sex glands that secrete substances that increase female and male inclinations toward indulging in sexual activity. Such secretions appear to underlie what is called the *sex drive*. Both males and females vary in the strength of their inclinations to engage in mating behavior, and the strengths vary from no inclination at all to some degree that might be called excessive.

In our culture, the reproductive aspect of sexual activity has been reduced in importance, whereas the activity itself has been inflated in importance. We can note immediately that any needs or drives can be met, relieved, or satisfied by simple masturbation, which is, in fact, indulged in by both sexes at one time or another, so that sexual intercourse itself is not necessary for any *biological* reasons other than reproduction. Sexual activity, in short, has become a social activity surrounded by social values. A female might be valued for the number of males she can attract, and a male might be valued for the number of females he can attract. The attraction is measured by some in terms of sexual acts, and, in fact, the term *score* is used to measure social-sexual success. The act of sexual intercourse has become a game surrounded by all sorts of rules, some of which are related to marriage, property, and various social rituals—for example, engagements, which are publicized in the press.

Sexual pleasure.   If a pair of people, whether of same or different sexes, gets involved in a positive relationship, finding each other acceptable, they usually find it pleasant to have physical contact with one another; and under appropriate conditions of security and relaxation, they may extend the contact to petting, touching, embracing, contact with so-called erogenous zones (breasts and sex organs) and find such stimulation pleasant. The mutuality of the contact, besides whatever cutaneous stimulatory pleasure may be involved, generates considerable psychological or emotional satisfaction from the obvious fact that one person accepts the other and finds this other person agreeable, worthy, satisfactory, or otherwise acceptable. Such acceptance is ego-enhancing and provides for feelings of security, status, trust, and any number of satisfactions. If the contact extends to actual intercourse, the feelings of worthiness are greatly increased because of the social taboos that have come to surround such behavior. Sexual intercourse is thus a sign of personal commitment, and both of the mutually consenting people can enjoy their feelings of worth. Rejection of contact at any level implies unworthiness or inadequacy in some regard.

In marital situations, after some difficulties or quarrels, a husband may try to get his wife to engage in intercourse without any great physiological needs motivating him but simply to obtain the assurance that he is still acceptable. He may go so far as to, in effect, rape his wife, believing that her resistance is not based on his inadequacy but on her anger and that the anger might disappear if he can restore the commitment implied by the act.

Psychiatists and the other practitioners of the healing arts like to believe that sex is at the root of all marital difficulties or personal problems. Counselors abound who are willing to teach sexual tricks in order to make sex more pleasant or rewarding. It is probably more correct to assume that any marital problems are based on money, in-law relationships, or behavior patterns that were not evaluated fully or correctly prior to marriage. If a woman marries a drunk with the conviction that her love will cure him, she has a surprise coming. By the time people get married, they are not good candidates for behavior changes that suit the whims of someone who was brought up in a different life style. The increasing divorce rate is not the result of sexual incompatibility, as it might have been in days when virgins married.

Most marital counselors place great stress on feminine orgasm. This stress, too, seems to be misplaced, since many women never have an orgasm during intercourse and do not care to. Statistics in this area are difficult to obtain, since people are particularly careful about their private lives, feelings, and capacities. Even so, some studies report over 50% of married women as not experiencing organisms at all and as not especially interested in sex. The "I've got a headache" excuse is a feminine, not a masculine, ploy. Besides the orgasm interest, there is much doubt about the frequency of intercourse that couples are willing to report. Some couples live happy lives without any sexual contact. Others indulge every day. Many couples have intercourse only 2 or 3 times a month, not the widely advertised twice a week of the nightclub comedians.

Only those couples who would like to get more out of sex than they are getting should seek counseling from sex experts; if they are satisfied with their present activities, they should not be taken in by fantasies exploited by salesmen. No one knows how much sexual activity anybody needs. Probably none is needed in any serious sense of that word, but nearly everyone enjoys being accepted and cared for. It is notorious that children cannot get enough loving. Perhaps we are all children in this regard, and what we may want is love. Sex has become a way of proving that someone loves us or of demonstrating how important we are.

SEX THERAPY   *(See SEXUAL INADEQUACY)*

Sexual issues and problems have traditionally been thought by mental health professionals to be of major importance in the development of adults' psychological disorders. Accordingly, for nearly three generations, psychotherapists have been particularly interested in the sexual activities, fantasies, and problems of their clients. Traditional psychoanalysis emphasized its hypothesis that much of complex human behavior—even behavior that appears to most of us to be remote from any sexual implications—is derived from sexual issues. The psychoanalyst's concerns are not so much with the client's actual sexual behavior but rather with the hidden or repressed sexual fears, fantasies, and drives that were supposed to have resulted in the person's problems. We can make quite accurate predictions that whatever the problems their

clients might present to them—anxieties, fears, specific phobias, interpersonal problems with the mother-in-law, compulsions, paranoia, enuresis, hostility, obessive
thoughts, marital problems, or vocational failures—the analysts would interpret and
relate them all to basic, unconscious, sexual issues.

Modern psychotherapists, of course, now realize that the psychoanalytic notions
are, after all, speculations and not established facts and that complex human behavior
is multiply determined by social, interpersonal, personal, and psychological factors;
and modern psychologists are increasingly skeptical about the speculative importance
of unconscious variables, such as repressed sexuality in emotional disturbances.

Although the hypothesized sexual origins of psychological problems are no
longer so strongly emphasized, the interest in human sexuality has not decreased;
rather, it has increased. A major difference, however, is that although the older
therapists focused on repressed sex as causative variables in psychological problems,
modern psychologists are now studying sexual behavior itself and developing therapies
to deal directly with overt sexual problems, such as the cluster of problems labeled
adult sexual inadequacy.

The pioneering work of Alfred Kinsey and, more recently, of Virginia Johnson
and William Masters, has shown us the range of problems, degree of disturbance, and
variety of behaviors that humans experience in their sexual activities. Modern American society expects and encourages adults to enjoy active sex lives and to overcome
any particular disturbances and sexual inadequacies that might interfere with their
normal, healthy enjoyment of sex. A fairly new therapeutic field, *sex therapy,* has
been developed to help adults overcome their sexual inadequacies and/or deviations.
Sex therapists work with consenting adults who voluntarily seek help. In many
instances, the clients are married couples, but single people also seek and receive sex
therapy. Some of the common issues treated are frigidity, impotence, premature
ejaculation, general sexual anxiety, vaginismus, and so on. A less common condition
is ejaculatory incompetence, in which the male is unable to ejaculate within the
vagina but is able to do so with masturbation. The condition is serious, particularly
for couples who want children, because it prevents conception. The therapist provides
corrective information; helps the couple to reduce anxieties regarding their sexual
abilities; and helps the couple, often through programs such as those developed by
Drs. Masters and Johnson and by Dr. Joseph LoPiccolo, to learn more effective,
satisfying skills.

Many people are still quite reluctant to seek help for sexual inadequacies and
dysfunctions, but there are now many qualified sex therapists in the country. Those
seeking help are encouraged to seek referral information from public mental health
agencies or from state and local professional organizations, such as the state's psychological association.

SEXUAL DEVIATIONS

Despite our society's growing tolerance of sexual variations, some practices remain
strongly disapproved. Some variations from normal heterosexual behavior are considered "kinky", and their practitioners are labeled *deviates,* or *perverts.* The perversions are generally condemned on moral grounds and are legally prohibited. A greater

proportion of the people who practice them are considered psychologically disturbed compared to those who practice alternative sex. One of the most important distinctions is that in deviate sex activity there is often a victim, an unwilling adult or a child, upon whom the sexual acts, often violent in nature, are forced. The people who practice these sexual acts, then, are not only deviant sexually but also pose a threat to other people, forcing or imposing themselves on unwilling victims. In these instances, people are being victimized to some degree by another person's sexual behavior. Society can not tolerate victimization, whether the behavior involved is sexual, commercial, or otherwise.

Exhibitionism—Indecent exposure: The Flasher.   The most common of these acts is *exhibitionism,* or *flashing,* carried out almost exclusively by men. It involves the sudden exposure of the genitals to unwary people, such as passersby. The flasher derives sexual excitement from this act and may follow it by masturbating. It is the most frequently reported deviant sex act in the United States, although it is extremely rare in many other countries. Although offensive, and involving an unwilling participant or victim, flashers rarely do any more than expose themselves. Many flashers are psychologically impaired, and, once caught, most of them do not repeat the activity.

Voyeurism—The Peeping Tom.   Some men obtain sexual excitement and orgasm by surreptitiously watching other people undressing or engaging in sexual activity. Although many adults would probably find some pleasure in such observations, most do not depend upon it for their major stimulation. The Peeper rarely does any more than "just look." Many voyeurs have psychological problems and, like the flasher, rarely repeat the activity, once caught. Some people believe that the increasing availability of X-rated movies might decrease the incidence of voyeurism, but we have no real data to support that.

Fetishism.   Achieving sexual excitement and orgasm primarily by handling certain objects—usually clothing, such as women's shoes, underwear, or scarves, or parts of the body, such as a foot or hair—is called fetishism. Almost all fetishists are men, and most have psychological problems associated with their sexual deviancy. Some fetishists may experience orgasm only by looking at certain objects or parts of women's bodies. Whatever the sexually exicting object, the fetishistic activity becomes a major preoccupation of the person's life, and he does not usually engage in other, more normal sex activity.

In many cases, the fetishist will steal the sexually exciting object, robbing stores, breaking into houses, and occasionally assulting and robbing women. The excitement of the illegal activity becomes part of the sexually arousing pattern, and some will have orgasms as they engage in the robbery. For some, setting and watching fires becomes their means of sexual excitement.

The fetishist is potentially more dangerous to others than the voyeur or the flasher and is usually more psychologically disturbed.

Sadism.   Sadists achieve sexual excitement by inflicting pain and injury on another person. Although most sadists are men, many women also achieve satisfaction in this way. It may be that with more male-like behavior in women, the incidence of female sadism might increase.

Sadists can be homosexual, heterosexual, or bisexual. The means of inflicting pain include verbal abuse; tying or chaining up the partner; hitting; pinching; whipping with straps or belts; and, in more extreme cases, slashing, cutting, stabbing, and choking the victim. In the most extreme cases, the sadist tortures and murders his or her victims and may repeat the acts for many years before being caught.

For the sadist, the activity of inflicting pain is highly sexually exciting, often the only way he or she can achieve orgasm. In some cases, the partners, often their wives, submit to mild pain as a prelude to more normal sexual intercourse. The wife may be masochistic in these cases (see the next section).

The sadist is clearly a psychologically disturbed person and is potentially dangerous to society. Although treatment has been attempted and has been reported successful in mild cases where the sadistic acts were carried out only in fantasy, there is probably no effective psychological treatment at present for the more extreme instances. In those extreme cases of victimization, torture, or murder, the sadist should be incarcerated or otherwise closely controlled for life or at least well into old age.

Masochism.   Masochism is deriving sexual pleasure from inflicting pain on oneself or having another person do it. The masochistic acts are generally less severe than those of the sadist, probably because the masochist can control the degree of pain or injury. Little is known about masochists, probably because they do not usually victimize other people and come to the attention of the police. They are psychologically disturbed people, and there is no known effective treatment for the condition. The masochist is not as much of a potential threat to society as the sadist, since he or she does not ordinarily victimize other people. Masochists commonly employ others (prostitutes) to administer the pain.

Incest.   Incest is the term applied to sexual relations among blood relatives. Psychologists have little data on incest. When it occurs, it is in private, within families, and seldom becomes public. Kinsey's estimate was that 5 people out of 1,000 have had incestuous experiences.

The most common pattern appears to be brother-sister incest, with father-daughter incest as the next most frequent. Sexual activity between mother and son is very rare, as is multiple incest within a family.

Incest, in particular father-daughter incest, where the child is more a raped victim than a willing partner, can be psychologically devastating for the child. Most incest goes unreported because of family shame or fears of legal punishment.

Rape.   Rape is sexual activity that is forced upon another unwilling person. Most rapes are committed by men against women. The rapist, most often a marginal person intellectually and socially, tends to frequent his own city or town, often not far from his home. He usually attacks single women at night and in places such as empty parking lots and dark streets, where there is little chance of discovery. Some rapists break into or gain entrance to a house or apartment by posing as a utilities meter reader or repairman. About a third of all rapes are committed by two or more men together, sometimes by a gang of youths.

Rape has traditionally been considered to be a sexual act, but it is primarily an act of *violence* committed against a weaker person. The raped woman is often severely beaten or otherwise physically injured and almost always suffers a lifelong psychological trauma. Many rape victims are killed by the rapist. A raped woman is a victim in many respects; not only is she victimized by the rapist but often also by the police, the courts, and the public, all of whom are often skeptical of the woman's innocence, assuming that she actually instigated or in some way encouraged the rape.

Rape is slowly coming to be recognized for what it is—an act of violence—a physical, aggressive attack upon a person. The traditional biases against the raped woman are disappearing.

There is no psychological treatment for rapists. When rape is proved in court, society protects itself against repetitions by long prison terms. In prison, the rapists may themselves become victims of homosexual rape. Such experiences may or may not have therapeutic value. We do not have data.

Pedophilia.   In pedophilia, the adult's sex object are children. Usually a man, the adult entices the child into sexual activity that includes genital stimulation; oral sex; and, with girls, partial or full intromission. The adult might be heterosexual, homosexual, or bisexual. In many cases, the child is known to the person.

It is clear that the child is a victim in every sense. In cases studied, it was rare to find instances where the children were willing or active participants in the sex acts. As with any sexual victimization, extreme psychological damage can be done to the child.

The child molester is a psychologically disturbed person. Although psychological treatment, such as some forms of behavior modification, may be effective for some cases, society must decide whether this offender, like the rapist, is too much of a social threat to be allowed social freedom. Imprisonment of molesters appears to be the only option society has for the protection of children.

SEXUAL INADEQUACY

Alfred Kinsey, in the 1950s and 1960s, carried out pioneering work on the prevalence and kinds of sexual behavior engaged in by Americans. Since the 1960s, William Masters and Virginia Johnson have created a large, important area of the study and specialized treatment of *human sexual inadequacy*—that is, of persons who are not achieving appropriate and/or adequate sexual satisfaction for themselves or their partners, and clearly are having personal problems.

Sexual inadequacy includes male impotence (the inability to attain or maintain an erection), female frigidity (having insufficient or no feelings of sexual arousal), painful coitus, and/or a variety of other problems. The treatment of sexual inadequacy must be individually geared and very flexible. In some cases, providing good information to clear up misconceptions about sex is sufficient. For some couples, reading a sex manual dealing with their particular problems may be helpful. For others, extended conversations with a sex therapist and pursuit of a carefully defined sex-training program is needed. When treated by competent, professional sex therapists, some 60% or more of the couples are significantly helped. However, there are now probably several thousand sex-training programs and clinics in the country and countless published manuals. The teachers and/or authors range from serious and competent professionals through outright charlatans, and any potential client must be wary. For any couples who might consult a sex therapist, it is wise to check first with local and state mental health organizations. This will not guarantee competence, but it should at least steer clients away from self-styled sex therapists who are not professionally recognized.

SICK ROLES   *(See HYPOCHONDRIACAL BEHAVIORS, SELF-FULFILLING PROPHECIES)*

Hypochondriacs are people who become preoccupied with imagined and exaggerated illnesses, gradually creating and enacting the role of a sick person, although they are not really organically ill at all. With much practice and reinforcement from others, the *sick role* can become quite convincing. Most importantly, it becomes convincing to the persons who enact the sick behavior. They soon come to believe their own enactment fully and to feel hurt when some others refuse to believe them.

There may be a great deal of similar sick-role behavior involved in many mental disorders. Schizophrenic patients in a state hospital, for example, gradually learn the pattern of treatment and the nature of the rewards and punishments given out by the staff. They also learn how to act the roles of cooperative mental patients, to act withdrawn, listless, unresponsive, vague, dependent, and so on. Thus, in addition to whatever biological or psychological problems might have sent them to the hospital in the first place, after a stay in the hospital, the patients come out having learned a new way of behaving—how to enact the *sick role*. Other people, of course, will respond to the sick role by treating the former patients accordingly and will thus help to perpetuate it.

We must be careful that when we treat people in hospitals and clinics, we do not inadvertently create and strengthen the sick role. Instead, we must actively teach the patient how to develop and strengthen normal role enactments.

SIGNIFICANCE AND STATISTICAL SIGNIFICANCE
(See STATISTICS)

What difference does it make? This is probably the most common question that is asked. We are always concerned with statements about the effects of this or that effort, drug, policy, and so on. Research is conducted to determine whether one condition is different from another. What will ordinarily happen is that in any research that is conducted, one group of subjects is put into some form of treatment or exposed to some condition, whereas a control group is not. Thus, in order to determine if smoking is a factor in lung cancer, the number of cancer patients is counted in a sample group of smokers and a sample group of nonsmokers. The chances that there will be exactly the same number or percentage of cancer victims in each group is very remote. No two groups ever measure exactly the same in any test. If you simply take two groups of men, say 100 coffee drinkers and 100 nondrinkers, and measure their heights, the average height will not be exactly the same—there will be some small variation: Perhaps one group will average 5'9.017", and the other will average 5'9.002". This difference is trivial, and we would regard it as insignificant. It might be *statistically significant,* however, meaning that by applying certain rules of computation, one could show that this difference would hold up if additional samples were taken from the groups that provided the original samples. By hold up, we mean only that if we kept taking many samples from each original population, we would find similar differences. If in 100 additional tests, we found that 95 times out of a 100, the coffee drinkers were taller (even by that trivial amount), we would have a statistically significant finding. That is what *statistical signficance* means—that 95 times or more out of 100, a difference is found in the direction (not necessarily the same amount) between two groups of measures.

The word *significance,* of course, suggests something important; in statistics, no such suggestion is involved. The statistician does not care if the difference is important or not; he or she is only concerned with its truth, its consistency, and its persistence. He or she is looking for a finding that he or she can rely on, and if something is true 95 times out of 100, it is a good bet. Note that some difference might work out to be true only 51% or 55% of the time. This is not regarded as statistically significant, because too many chance factors are operating to make prediction meaningful. You lose a lot of bets with odds of 51-49 and even 80-20. The closer you get to 95, the more confidence you have that there is something specific operating to create the difference. Of course, any odds are better than none in an even bet, but the statistician is not interested in bets. He or she is trying to establish that there is some specific factor involved in one group that is making it different from another, and he or she wants to find that factor. If the difference between two groups is large, as in the height differences between men and women, the difference is attributed to sex. Such an attribution directs the nature of future research to determine how sex hormones, for example, control growth in men and women. If there were no large difference, or if samples did not differ consistently, there would be no problem to worry about.

Whenever you are told that two groups differ in any way—for example, that some drug cures cancer or causes it—ask for the amount of difference in order to determine its importance and for the statistical significance—that is, the chances out of 100 that the difference is a real or true one. If it turns out that taking a spoonful of some tonic every morning will increase your life span by one hour, you might consider the cost of the tonic and the desirability of an extra hour before you adopt the program. If some other factor will cut your life by 20 years, and the chances are somewhat more than even, you could give that factor some appropriate consideration, taking the odds into account. Never simply accept a reported difference between two groups or two conditions. It may be insignificant in both senses of the word.

SLEEP AND LEARNING   *(See LEARNING)*

Some people are attracted by advertisements that offer for sale pillow speakers that can be arranged to present taped information to a sleeper while he or she is asleep. Hypothetically, if the process worked, the sleeper would wake up with some additional knowledge over what he or she had before going to sleep. There have been some reports in responsible journals that there were some positive results from such practice, but, at least in one case, the report was a fraudulent one, and there is no good evidence that you can learn anything when you are actually asleep. It should be recognized, however, that sleep itself is not a unitary process. Sleep appears to consist of some three or four stages, ranging from sleepiness to sound sleep, with another stage of relative wakefulness. The phases of sleep are measured by recording brain waves, which show different characteristics at different phases of what appears to be a 90-minute cycle. If a pillow speaker is presenting some kind of material that you could learn while awake, you might be able to learn some of this material if it is played during periods of light sleep. Such periods, however, are so close to waking brain activity that it does not appear wise to label them as sleep; possibly, the only difference from waking would be that you happen to be in bed. On the whole, it appears that more efficient learning occurs when you are as awake as possible, with the corresponding conclusion that when you are sleepy, you should go to bed to sleep, perchance to dream, which is also the kind of activity that occurs when you are in a period of light sleep. Considering the irrational nature of dreams, it might be best not to confuse learning operations with the dream activity, since the results might very well be quite confused. It should be pointed out that the experimental demonstrations referred to above were done with rote material (vocabulary items) and not with any logical or theoretical material. It might be possible to learn some more or less meaningless material while sleeping, but one might be best advised not to count on even that.

SLIPS OF THE TONGUE AND OTHER ERRORS

The popularity of Sigmund Freud's views can be measured by the rather widespread awareness among the general public of his interpretation of accidents and especially of his notions about common *slips of the tongue*. When someone says something he or she obviously did not mean to say, a listener might, if influenced by Freud, interpret the remark or work to be exactly what he or she really meant to say. The so-called *Freudian slips* are supposed to be the successful emergence of some unconscious wish or, more correctly, the failure to repress the unconscious desire. The notion that one has an accident because he or she somehow wanted to smash up his or her new car is a bit difficult to accept; breaking a mother-in-law's dish while washing it might be a little easier. In neither case, however, is there any evidence that Freud's views on such matters have any merit. We all have accidents of one kind or another, and our speech is frequently mangled and distorted. Anyone listening to a tape recording of a conversation in which he or she took part will become quite uncomfortable if he or she counts the errors of grammar, hesitations, mispronunciations, and other distortions that he or she commits. It is only when the error or accident can be interpreted to show some hostility or illicit feature that the Freudian view is invoked. Public speakers sometimes deliberately introduce a mispronunciation of an opponent's name with a hasty and apparently embarrassed correction, but we can assume that they are only playing.

In the nature of the case, it is impossible to do research on slips of the tongue or other accidents because we cannot arrange for them to happen and are forced to rely on interpretation after the event. When we are upset or preoccupied by some stressing factors, we may, of course, have accidents, and an explanation in terms of wishes can often appear appropriate. We can, in excitement or in hasty action, say one thing and mean another, but the notion that it is the working of an unconscious force is without any support. One's relationship to a mother-in-law is probably about as conscious as anything can be. Frequently, we are careless with other people's possessions, and if we are not fond of these people, we may be even more careless. The unhappy fact is that we know we are not fond of them and that we do not have to make Freudian slips for them to also be conscious of that fact. It is not easy to pretend that you like someone you actually do not feel positive about. Even devoted husbands and wives need frequent reassurance.

SPEED READING   *(See READING AND READING PEDAGOGY)*

We are constantly being informed that the schools are failing to teach children to read, and, at the same time, we see advertisements offering to make *speed readers* out of us. We hear that our president is a speed reader who can cover enormous amounts of material in a very short time and that reading speeds of up to 1,500 words per minute are not out of our reach. Actually, the physical and physiological facts about the eyes in reading make it most unlikely that anyone can read more than 800 words per minute, if we mean by reading, seeing or somehow taking account of every word read. When we read, we can only perceive words when the eyes are not in motion—that is, when they are employed in a *fixation;* the fixation lasts about one-quarter of a second, and, during that fixation, we can take note of about 7 letters. The time spent in reading, then, amounts to fixation time and eye movement time, and reading speed would depend upon the number of fixations per unit time. Obviously, if we make fewer fixations, we will speed up our reading time, but we will also see less. Any part of the material that is not seen cannot be read, nor can it have any impact, unless one guesses at what it might be.

Speed readers are trained first to preview the material and then to look at the middle of a page or column, presumably going down the page with a moving finger to guide them. Photographic records of the eye movements of speed readers do not show them doing this. Rather, they fixate like normal readers, try not to go back (regress), and make fewer fixations. Experimental studies comparing speed reading course graduates and those without such training show that the speed readers will, in fact, say that they have finished a given assignment faster than the controls, but their comprehension of the material will rather regularly be far poorer than that of the controls. Speed readers, in effect, do not read all of the material; they skim and select as well as they can, but if there is no basis for the selection, they are not going to benefit much. Much of the material we get involved in reading is not worth our time, and one might as well skim. If the material is difficult or important, one must read carefully and slowly. If the object is comprehension rather than speed, skipping about in the material is hardly of any value. What helps most is to be familiar with the subject matter, to have an adequate vocabulary, and to stick with the reading rather than attending to other stimuli. Running the finger down the page has not been shown to be of any value in experiments comparing moving fingers and nonmoving fingers, but in such studies it can be assumed that both groups or readers in both situations will be attentive. In a private setting, keeping the finger in motion may help the concentration on reading, as such, instead of permitting daydreaming.

In general, psychologists concerned with the problems of reading (see E. J. Gibson and H. Levin, *The Psychology of Reading*) see no point to taking courses in speed reading, since such a course will be of benefit only with easy material. Probably everyone can increase his or her speed of reading by making the effort or recognizing that perhaps he or she reads too slowly. But, as mentioned earlier, one cannot increase the speed to any serious extent and maintain comprehension, and the time spent on speed reading courses might well be better spent reading something of value.

STATISTICS

Statistics is a branch of mathematics that deals with probability. Some people do not trust statistics or resent them, but they are only resenting mathematical exercises. One sometimes hears the expression, "Figures don't lie, but liars can figure." That may be true, and one should resent liars, but not the figures, as they are essentially blameless. Basically, statistics deals with odds. The odds are that you might die of cancer or heart failure if you live a very long time. That is, the odds are greater that you will die from these causes rather than from ingrown toe nails, dandruff, or measles. If you do die of measles or for any other reason, the statistics do not matter. As far as any individual goes, statistics are not important. If a woman about to undergo a Caesarean section is told that the death rate is only one out of a thousand (or whatever figure), the statistics can only give her some minor comfort. She might be the one. There is no comfort at all for someone to be told that he or she has a rare disease or that only a few people get what he or she has. If he or she has it, there is no point to the statistics. In short, statistics is a branch of mathematics that deals with large numbers and may be of value to institutions, governments, corporations, businessmen, and door-to-door salesmen. Taking the last example, if the history of some business shows that 5 out of 100 housewives will buy some article, the door-to-door salesman should know this and not resent a rejection, even after 100 turndowns. He or she might make ten sales in the next hundred. All he or she has to do is keep knocking. In all probability, he or she will not sell more than 5 in 100 regardless of how hard he or she tries.

The average citizen should know a few things about statistics, because he or she is frequently confronted by them. The major statistic that one runs into almost daily is also one of the most deceptive. It is the statistic called *the average.* We read daily about the average person and his or her needs and achievements. We read about the average tax increment we will have to pay, the average cost of living, the average wage, and so on. What should be recognized is that the average is just a number obtained by dividing some total number by the number of measurements. Thus, if there are 100 wage earners in a shop, the average wage might be $100 per week. This means only that there was a total weekly payroll of $10,000. Now if 50 workers were paid only $50, and if the other 50 were paid $150, the average would be $100, yet nobody in the shop was actually paid the average wage of $100. If someone got $1,000 per week, that would also figure into the average, which could still be $100, although it would mean that some people were certainly getting paid less. The trouble comes from the general impression that the average is somehow typical: We read about the average man, for example, when there is no such person. Everybody is different, and one is only deluded if he or she thinks that there is some kind of representative person who exemplifies the rest of us in some way. If we mean something such as what most people are like, we should use another statistic called the *mode*. The *mode* means the greatest number; thus, if five people out of 100 have the same score, and if no other score is attained by as many as five people, 5 will be the mode. It is the same as a plurality, not necessarily a majority. If you are concerned about what the middle person in a group scores or earns, you must line up all the scores or numbers from lowest to highest and count off each score until you reach the halfway point; this is the *median,* and it usually is more representative of a population than the average, or *mean,* as it is called in statistics. In any case, you should never be content with some statement about the average. Always ask for the distribution, the spread of the scores, the highest and lowest, the top 10% and 20%, and the lowest 10% and 20%. This will give you some appreciation of what the average reflects.

STEREOTYPES AND INSTITUTIONAL THINKING   *(See PREJUDICE)*

When we react to some individual as a member of a group, a class, or a category instead of regarding him or her as an individual, we are reacting in terms of a *stereotype.* Some stereotypes are rather general—that is, shared by a large proportion of some population. Thus, a film director needing someone to play the part of a banker would never think of going to a bank to find someone interested in acting. He or she would probably not find anyone in the bank who looked like a banker. Instead, he or she consults some casting lists and calls for someone who has played a banker before, a person who may know very little about banks and their business but who looks the part. Actors commonly resist being typed because that may limit the number of jobs they can secure. But the director is happy if he or she can feel sure that the audience will accept his or her choice; it saves him or her a lot of trouble in establishing the authenticity of the role. In the movies, such deception is not of any serious importance. The audience knows that it is watching actors, while at the same time it is being reinforced in its own thinking about how bankers should look and act, and they may be a bit disappointed when they go to the bank on their next visit. Too bad that their banker does not look like one.

In the area of social relations, the matter becomes more serious. To think of all Chinese, Russians, Jews or Negroes as somehow all the same is to invite immediate difficulties. The moment that you respond to any person as a member of a group, you will lose the essence of that person and be operating on assumptions that may be largely erroneous. The fact that someone is Chinese may only mean that his or her skin is somewhat more yellow than that of a non-Chinese and that his or her eyes may be somehow a bit different. Unless you are specifically interested in skin and eyes, however, that information may be the least important data you might have. What matters is how the Chinese person thinks and behaves, and if you are not considering such factors, you lose out in understanding. There are some things you might infer about a person if you know him or her to be a member of a certain group, profession, class, race, or religion. But he or she may be only nominally a member of such categories and not share their beliefs or customs. To the extent that you assume that his or her membership in a group includes his or her sharing the beliefs and practices of the group, you are prejuding him or her and are therefore prejudiced. In this sense, we are all prejudiced in favor of or against a great many people who happen, always, to be classifiable in one way or another.

Origins of Stereotypes.   Probably most stereotypes and the accompanying prejudices are passed on to us from family and friends; some are acquired in schools, since teachers are rarely inclined to present a complete description of the other side. Newspaper cartoonists and writers of fiction contribute heavily to our stereotypes in their efforts at economizing on work and words. When parents make remarks about members of some groups, the children find it easy to acquire a satisfactory, to them, position on various issues. The clearest case is in the area of religion. Catholic parents have Catholic children, and so on throughout the various religious denominations. We can assume that the children are not given to a critical analysis of the religious views that they are brought up with. They then fight members of other religions, as in Northern Ireland, with, we assume, little thought about the reasons for conflict and how to avoid it.

Institutional Thinking.   One extension of stereotyping is to forget about individuals when dealing with persons or groups who are operating under some group label or title. Thus, we tend to forget that a president is a human being and that his or her election has not endowed him or her with any special gifts or talents he or she did not possess before the election. He or she selects some other individuals as his or her cabinet, and they become secretaries instead of individual people. Similarly, the *government* only consists of people. It has no policy, mind, or position that is different from the policies, minds, or positions of individuals. When judges are appointed to the Supreme Court, they are still individual people with their own biases, prejudices, strengths, and weaknesses, and the fact that they are now members of a relatively exclusive group does not make them any wiser than they were before. Yet we all submit to governments and office holders as if they were something other than people who are filling positions that they intend to protect. Instead of being servants of the public, they are regarded as masters, and the public puts up with bureaucratic nonsense because it does not deal with the realities. Similarly, we elect or appoint members to a committee, and then the committee does things for which no individual is blamed. A committee, for example, can fire someone, and each member of the committee can absolve her- or himself of the action. Similarly, corporations consist of people who take various actions in the name of the corporation and reject individual responsibility and liability. We hear that the company decided on some action when no company can decide anything—only individual people can make decisions. When the government does something, we should examine *who* actually did what. As long as we continue to act as if a company, a corporation, a committee, or an officeholder is not an individual or a body of individuals, we are bound to make errors in judgment or appraisal.

The only advice that can be given with regard to such *institutional thinking* is to keep asking the question, "Who is this person I am dealing with?" This one person, regardless of where he or she comes from, what he or she looks like, or what clothes he or she wears, what language he or she speaks, and so on. If the person turns out to be unsatisfactory to us, we should take the appropriate steps to either change him or her, avoid him or her, or, depending on the situation, make the best of him or her, but at no time should we mistake him or her for something he or she is not.

STIMULUS AND RESPONSE—S→R
(See CONDITIONING, DISCRIMINATED STIMULI)

By far, the most common words in psychology are *stimulus* and *response*. For convenience, they are usually abbreviated to *S* and *R* and are casually interpreted as amounting to causes and effects. The behavioristic school took a rather mechanical view of human behavior and attempted to portray all activity as a matter of responses of muscles and glands to some kind of physical energy change that could be labeled as a stimulus. For this reason, behaviorism came to be known as an S→R psychology. According to its founder, John B. Watson, the basic assumption of psychology was that eventually we would arrive at the position where, knowing the stimulus, we could predict the response or, knowing the response, we could *postdict* the stimulus—that is, know what preceded the response.

Difficulties arise with both terms. A stimulus is usually defined as some energy change (the onset of a light, the occurrence of a sound, etc.). If someone who is being observed does not react in some observable or measurable manner, the energy change would not be a stimulus. Thus, the stimulus is defined in a circular way: It is something that is followed by a response. A response, similarly, must have a stimulus; it cannot be spontaneous, but the stimulus frequently cannot be identified. Someone gets up and does something, and there has not been an identifiable energy change observed. In such cases, the stimulus is presumed to have occurred internally in some way. In some instances—for example, when a bladder is full—the stimulus can be identified with the internal pressure. If the responder, however, remarks, "I think I'll go to the movies," it might be rather difficult to pinpoint the stimulus. In such cases, a chain or train of internal stimuli and responses, none of which is observable from the outside, can be presumed to have run off, starting from some earlier external stimulus and terminating in the remark. Such internal stimuli and responses, assuming they occur, are called *mediating stimuli* and *mediating responses,* because they go between some externally observable stimuli and overt responses. When we go through any serial action or sequence of movements, one movement produces internal (kinesthetic) stimuli (movement-produced stimuli, or mps) that lead to the subsequent responses. If we spell or type a word, one letter follows the other because the production of the first letter generates the stimuli for the next.

Additional problems arise for stimulus-response psychologists, in that responses are studied as if they were behavior, but behavior itself is never studied, since behavior itself has not been defined in any precise way. An observable response is selected for study as a sample of behavior. A person may be seated in front of a light bulb with a finger on a button. He or she is told to remove his or her finger when the light comes on. A clock can be arranged to measure his or her *reaction time.* The psychologists involved in such a study would be studying reaction time, a part of behavior. The subject would be doing a lot of other things besides moving a finger, but these other things would not be observed. In all laboratory studies, some sample of behavor is chosen for observation, and conclusions are drawn somewhat more broadly about behavior, but all we really have are collections of observations on samples. If the samples are not wisely chosen, we may be grossly misled. In the familiar Pavlovian experiments in conditioning, Pavlov thought that he was observing the conditioning of a salivary response because that was the sample he selected. Professor O. H. Mowrer of Illinois argues that the dog was being conditioned to have an emotional reaction (feeling better) and that the salivation was only a sign of that positive good feeling. A completely different psychological interpretation was developed by Professor Mowrer when he considered different samples.

Another difficulty arises from the common observation that we do not always respond in the same way to what appears to be the same stimulus, and a great deal of speculative theorizing comes into play, involving all sorts of unobserved events such as changes in mood, previous activity, learning, sets to respond, instructions, and so on. The difficulty increases when we are not in a position to identify the stimulus at all, as mentioned earlier. Most human behavior appeared to B. F. Skinner to be of this variety, where we do something in a situation that might be very complex and difficult to describe in stimulus terms. When the stimulus is simple and known, and when the response is more or less direct and immediate, the S→R psychology appears adequate. When there are dealys between S and R, or when S is unobservable, we get into difficulty. Skinner solved the difficulty for himself by more or less disregarding the stimuli, except for certain classes (discriminated stimuli) and concentrated on the response itself, counting its frequency over some period of time. His psychology can be described as an R psychology instead of the S→R approach of Watson.

STRESS AND COPING   (See LEARNED HELPLESSNESS)

Stress is a general term used by psychologists to mean any demands on a person that strain one's capacity to cope with a situation. The specific nature of the stress varies not only between people but, within people, from one situation or one time to another. The usual stresses that make demands on adults are different from those on children, and so on.

When stress occurs, the person typically feels anxious and upset. Thus, under stress, we are usually faced by two related tasks: One is to deal effectively with the stressful events, to successfully get through them, and the other is to control our anxiety and upset sufficiently to be able to function.

To cope with stress means to deal actively with it and successfully master that particular event or situation. Children cope with stress on first entering school, on entering high school, on graduation, on seeking a job, or on beginning college. The serious illness of a child poses severe stress for parents as well as for the child. In coping successfully, the person keeps focusing on the stressful events and attempts to deal successfully with them despite the upset, fear, or anxiety that might be felt. Coping fails when the person tries to deny, ignore, or in other ways escape from the stress. For some people, using tranquilizers to reduce anxiety represents a failure to cope with the original stress, although such people may feel more calm and comfortable.

There is no great mystery about how to study. Anyone interested in finding out something can generally start and proceed without any special guidance. A problem arises when some child is not doing as well in his or her school work as his or her parents might expect him or her to, and even when they force the child to get busy with his or her books or lessons, the results are frequently less than satisfying. The problem really amounts to a conflict of interests; the child is interested in some things, and teachers and parents may be interested in something else. To blame lack of academic success on poor study habits is probably to indict the wrong operation. There are a few misconceptions about study that should be clarified for anxious parents. The first point to recognize is that study is work and that work takes time. If a child likes a particular activity, he or she will not consider it work. Work appears to be intrinsically unattractive, if by work we mean doing something at someone else's bidding when we would rather be doing something else, such as playing football, which is much harder work than reading and writing as far as physical energy is concerned.

Granting that study is work, however pleasant for some, there are some ways in which it can be done more efficiently, as is true of most activities. Sometimes, a child gets the wrong instruction or impression, as when he or she is told to read something as an assignment. Reading is not studying—it is reading. A child who faithfully follows the instruction to read may learn very little from that operation and his or her lack of results may sour him or her on the activity for the future. In order to learn, one does not read, one looks for answers—one must have questions. Some text writers are aware of the need for questions and even insert questions into paragraphs or paragraph headings. But the basic question that must be raised is this: What am I supposed to know? This question is rarely answered in most school classrooms, from kindergarten through college. Teachers are apparently afraid to let their charges know what they are expected to know on some vague grounds that they will only learn that much and will not learn some ill-defined additional area of knowledge.

If the questions that are to be answered are presented to the student, he or she can begin the basic study operation—that of finding or creating answers. Parents are usually not of great help because they do not know what questions the teachers have in mind, but they could at least ask the child, "What are you supposed to know?" The answer cannot possibly be, "Chapter III," since even the author of Chapter III could not recite it or even know what was in it in true and complete detail.

There are ways to contrive or discover the questions in a lesson by assuming that a textbook has some basic organization and that an introduction to a section may spell out the questions; that a summary might reiterate or confirm that these were, in fact, the questions; and that heavy print and italics might point to items of importance. Once the questions are deciphered in any assignment, the answers may also be available from that or other sources.

When a lesson has been mastered to some degree, a test of the mastery should be imposed. The best test of such mastery is to have the learner teach somebody else who has been primed with the appropriate questions but who may not know the answers. A parent can be a convenient foil for such purposes, since he or she is able to play the role of the naive learner and still ask the proper questions. But the responsibility for teaching others plays an important role in learning. Teachers usually learn their lessons because they face the duty of imparting their knowledge to the unprepared. The operation seems to work at all levels, so that children who are just learning to read can teach other children who are less competent than they are.

An additional problem with study is that learners sometimes think that once they have gone through some exercise, they now know it forever. They should learn quickly that forgetting is universal and general and that no one remembers everything. In order to remember anything, there is a need to review at intervals that are short enough to have some retention present to be reviewed. Systematically scheduled reviews are required for any learning, and for school materials where tests are given at semester ends, the reviews must be introduced at something like weekly or monthly intervals in order to keep the mastery alive.

Some academic advice-givers try to encourage parents to set aside rooms and equipment for the student. Many people have learned a great deal under the most trying conditions, and there is probably no great gain from any elaborate or expensive facilities, especially if these are not going to be used. For any effective study, there cannot be any competitive attractions, such as a TV show, in the same room. Radio music or records do not seem to have any great effect one way or the other. Some children cannot really study without some kind of noise around.

What is essential for learning is that the student works at the activity involved in terms of trying to construct or reinvent the answers to questions that have been posed for him or her, largely by others. The great inventors in history might have generated their own problems; the student has problems dumped into his or her lap. He or she must now take these problems for his or her own and try to construct the appropriate answers. There should be some way for him or her to discover when he or she is on the right path, close to an answer, or off on a dead-end trail. If the student is a beginner, he or she will need all kinds of cues in order to make progress. As the student matures, he or she will be able to recognize a good answer when one appears or will be able to check its value. Checks, of course, are part of the learning process, and many children never are taught the value and purpose of checks. They turn in their own incorrect answers and are disgruntled and discouraged by failures, when simple checking could have saved them. In short, some way must be provided for discovering the correct answers. The Skinner teaching machine had this favorable feature built into it so that a student always knew where he or she stood. A great deal of study time is wasted if the student does not have answers available under appropriate controls—that is, that he or she attempts answers first before looking them up.

To summarize, study is work; it takes time, and more time is needed for reviews. The study requires checks on progress, and this can be arranged through having the student teach or through some arrangement of a learning situation that permits a student to have a continuous appraisal of his or her progress, with appropriate criteria established by teachers, parents, or companions.

SUBLIMINAL PERCEPTION

The term *subliminal perception* is made up of a pair of self-contradictory words. The words refer to the alleged ability of people to respond to stimuli when these stimuli are not actually affecting the sense organs. As an illustration, we have the report that some advertisers managed to insert into a film some message, such as "Eat More Popcorn" or "Drink Coca-Cola." The message on the film would go by so rapidly that the viewers would not be able to see the words, but it is claimed that more popcorn and Coca-Cola were sold when such messages were flashed than on nights when no messages were presented. There are actually no scientifically acceptable reports of such experiments.

Ordinarily, when we do perceive something, it is because we are presented with some stimulus that does have an impact on the sense organs. It has sufficient strength. If the energy level of the stimulus is too low, it will not be perceived. As the energy level increases, we come to some point where the subject is able to report the presence of a stimulus. With repeated trials, we find that this point varies slightly from time to time, and the point where the stimulus is reported half the time is called the *stimulus threshold,* or the *limen.* A stimulus whose energy is below the threshold or limen is subliminal. If it is close to the limen, it may be seen, heard, or otherwise sensed some of the time. The meaning of a limen can be easily illustrated by lowering the amplification on a radio from some level where you can easily hear the radio to some point where the sound disappears. Some people might be able to hear it after you do not; their loudness limens are lower. As you raise the intensity, you will again reach your threshold and begin hearing the sound again. If you cannot hear a sound, it cannot affect you, although if the sound is repeated rapidly, there might be *summation,* and you could then hear it again. The point, however, is that if you do not hear it, you do not hear it and cannot be influenced by it. If it is above your threshold—that is, superliminal—you will hear it. The presentation of subthreshold stimuli will not affect you in any way. Even superthreshold advertisements do not move you into immediate action. Why should advertisements that you cannot hear or see?

SUICIDE   *(See DEPRESSION, PSYCHOSES)*

There are some 260,000 attempted *suicides* in the United States each year, and up to 60,000 people succeed in killing themselves. Suicide is increasing, and is now the eleventh most frequent cause of death in the U.S. It is sobering to realize that suicide is the second highest cause of death in young people 15 to 24 years old.

There is no single personality type that can be called suicidal. Rather, a person can start thinking about suicide for many different reasons. In most cases, the suicide is a result of some severe life stresses. Psychological depression is a major element in most, perhaps all, suicides. The most prevalent feelings of those who attempt suicide are feelings of hopelessness—that they have no control over life events, that nothing they can do will change or improve anything.

There are many popular misconceptions about suicide, including the following:

1. "If a person talks about killing her- or himself, he or she won't really do it." This is incorrect. The suicide usually gives warnings of his or her intent and talks about it with other people, often just joking.
2. "Suicide is a form of psychosis." The person who commits suicide may be severely depressed, but he or she is not necessarily psychotic or mentally ill.

3. "If the attempt is unsuccessful, the person really did not mean it and had no real intention of killing him- or herself." If a suicide attempt fails, the person will probably keep trying. They *do* mean it.

4. "Suicide is stimulated by changes in seasons or moon cycles." No. There is *no* evidence for that belief.

5. "When a depressed, apparently suicidal person's mood improves, the danger of suicide is over." This is not necessarily true. Many depressed people do not attempt suicide until after they seem to improve somewhat. A lifting of spirits or mood should *not* be automatically interpreted as a decrease in suicidal risk.

The treatment of those who attempt suicide includes increased supervision over their activity and treatment for depression. This would include a combination of drug therapy and behavior therapy. Recently, there has developed an active professional area of suicide prevention through crisis centers. This has been part of the development of the community mental health approach of the 1960s and 1970s. Crisis centers have developed in many cities in which troubled, perhaps suicidal, people can telephone and talk to a staff member and, later, go in to see the staff at the center. These crisis centers operate their hot lines 24 hours a day. The crisis center personnel hope that when a potential suicide calls in, they can delay the attempt until the person's crisis has passed. There are no data as to whether these crisis centers are actually effective. However, given the high rate of suicide, particularly among the young, maintaining the crisis centers, even without good data as yet, is certainly advisable and is, perhaps, a socially useful contribution.

SUPERSTITION   *(See DELUSIONS, STATISTICS)*

Many people throughout the world believe a lot of things that simply are not true. If the belief is in some involved series of ideas, we tend to call it a delusion, but if the false belief involves some rather isolated or random idea, such as knocking on wood to prevent bad luck, we call it *superstition*. We could not begin to catalogue all of the beliefs that are considered superstitious. We note that even the people who engage in some rituals to ward off bad or bring good luck do not always take them seriously, although we do not usually test them or make an issue of the matter. Thus, if someone drops a fork at the dinner table and announces that more company is likely to come, we do not argue the point. Such superstitions do not matter; most do not. Some people make light of their superstitions by saying that they don't really believe in them because to be superstitious is to bring bad luck.

The real point to observe about superstitions is that they are statements, some of which control behavior, that are believed without any evidence. As such, they do not differ much from many other statements we believe for which we have no greater amount of evidence. Thus, if we ask a superstitious person why he or she believes that throwing a hat on the bed will bring bad luck, we regard his or her answer as silly. We know that he or she has not made a systematic and serious study of the kinds of luck that befell people who threw their hats on beds and those who did not. But if a person tells us that Columbus discovered America in 1492, we do not regard that as silly for a very simple reason: We believe it, too, and we have not made a serious and systematic study of Columbus and his voyages, in all probability. In short, if we believe something that somebody else says, it is not superstitious to us; it is a fact. Thus, two children can walk along the sidewalk, carefully avoiding the cracks, because each believes that to do otherwise is unlucky; neither accuses the other of superstition. Similarly, the natives in some primitive culture might all believe that some crocodile is their tribal god and would regard anyone not sharing this view as a dangerous heretic. When we tell them about our religious beliefs, they might regard us as superstitious.

There does not appear to be any mystery about how we acquire our superstitions. Someone tells us that we will have seven years of bad luck if we break a mirror. If we are inquisitive, we might ask him or her how he or she knows this, but we usually hear such statements when we are very young and unlikely to quiz our betters too extensively. We have learned that most of what we are told seems to be more or less reasonably true, and if we trust the speaker to almost any small degree, we can accept such statements uncritically. Certainly, in the case of breaking a mirror, we have already had some bad luck. We might have to replace it or pay for a new one. Gamblers often display their superstitions quite openly. A poker player may not look at cards he or she is given without shuffling them around a few times; a dice player might blow on the dice or ask someone else to do so. Sometimes the action is followed by good results, and the gambler might try it again. After all, indulging in most superstitions costs nothing and may even be amusing. One false belief is likely to prove costly to gamblers. They sometimes believe in what is called the law of averages, which to them means that there are such things as runs of luck (good or bad) and that, sooner or later, a particular run will change to its opposite. Thus, if you have a run of bad luck, it is bound to change and be followed by a run of good luck. Now no one can deny the fact of runs of luck, in the sense that someone may keep losing for a long time. The law of averages, however, deals with extremely long runs, such as thousands of events in succession, where no known factors are biasing the events. Thus, if one tosses 100 pennies in the air, when they land, there should be almost 50 heads and 50 tails, but any different count of either may also happen. It is unlikely that all pennies will fall heads up even if we toss the 100 pennies a million times. When we get down to tossing one penny, we cannot predict that it will fall heads on any trial or sequence of trials. If it fell heads 20 times in a row, there is nothing in statistical theory that says that it is about time for it to fall tails. The gambler would have to have sufficient funds to keep increasing his or her bets on every new play if he or she is to count on the law of averages to do him or her any good. In practice, very few people are able to keep increasing their bets and thus take advantage of a law that only says that eventually all gamblers should die broke.

SYMPTOM SUBSTITUTION

Symptom substitution is a key concept in psychoanalytic theory and treatment. The psychoanalytic model asserts that disturbed behavior is produced by unconscious processes within the person. The behavior itself, according to the psychoanalysts, is but a symptom of the underlying unconscious processes. The symptom may be very serious, such as fire setting, stealing, or paranoid thought, and may cause further problems for the person. But according to the psychoanalysts, however serious the symptoms might be, they are not the important foci of treatment; the most important parts of the problems and the treatment are the unconscious causes of the observed symptoms. In treatment, psychoanlysts try to discover, understand, and resolve those all-important underlying unconscious causes. If that is done successfully, then, according to the psychoanalysts, the symptoms should disappear.

The symptom substitution hypothesis has been a serious point of difference between psychoanalysts and behavior therapists. It follows from the psychoanalytic position that removing symptoms alone, without resolving the unconscious causes, might provide some temporary relief to the person but that, soon, the unresolved conflicts would only produce a new symptom that would substitute for the old one. Thus, behavior therapy that approaches problem behaviors directly—that is, deals with the symptoms themselves—*must* result in symptom substitution, according to the psychoanalysts. The enuretic child whose bedwetting is eliminated through direct conditioning, the highly phobic person whose fear behavior is reduced, the schizophrenic whose bizzare mannerisms or paranoid talking are directly changed: All, according to the analysts, will produce new symptoms unless the underlying unconscious causes are also resolved.

The symptom substitution hypothesis, then, is this: If a psychopathological symptom is removed without resolving the unconscious causes, a new and perhaps even more severe symtom(s) will be produced.

Since the late 1950s, there have been many clinical cases treated and research projects on therapy carried out by behavior modifiers. What were the results in those thousands of people whose symptoms were eliminated through direct behavior modification. without paying attention to presumed underlying unconscious causes? The fact is that symptom substitution rarely, if ever, was observed. The psychoanalytic prediction, so basically important to the theory, has not been supported by the evidence of either research results or clinical cases of behavior therapy.

The failure to confirm the symptom substitution hypothesis casts serious doubt on probably the most basic idea in psychoanalytic therapy—that is, that unconscious conflicts are the major causes of disturbed behavior.

SYNESTHESIA

Synesthesia refers to responding in some sensory fashion that is inappropriate to the stimulation. Some people will report having a dark brown taste in their mouths on some occasions. They are speaking colorfully but not communicating precisely, since there are no such things as dark brown tastes or tastes of any other color. One can taste only sweet, salt, sour, and bitter. More often, people will report seeing colors when listening to music. They may very well be having some kinds of visual fantasies, and these may well be colored, but it is the scene they are fantasizing that is colored, not the music. Some music teachers try to teach students to identify notes on the piano by color so that when they hear a certain tone, they will "see" a color and, having associated the name of the note with the color, they will then be able to identify the note. Experimental research on trying to associate colors with notes has proven unsuccessful even after thousands of trials, and so-called *chromastesia* does not appear to be a genuine phenomenon, in spite of some people's claims. If someone chooses to claim that he or she sees colors when he or she hears tones, there does not appear to be any harm in such claims if the person also hears the tones. Certainly, any stimulus object or event can remind us of some other kind of stimulus that affects a different sensory modality. Such imagery harms no one and might as well be enjoyed. We should not take the claims of people seriously in this connection, and efforts to teach someone to react with a different sense from the one normally employed seem to be of dubious value.

SYSTEMATIC DESENSITIZATION   (See BEHAVIOR THERAPY, RELAXATION AND PROGRESSIVE RELAXATION)

Systematic desensitization is one of the most widely used of the many behavior therapy techniques. Applied mostly to adults, it is used to teach clients to reduce and control their severe anxiety or fear. All of us have experienced fear and anxiety as a normal part of life. For some people, however, the fear or anxiety has become an intense feeling of upset that occurs whenever certain stimuli or events occur and that anxiety disrupts the person's normal functioning. For example, a person might have powerful fears of failing at his or her job. Whenever challenged by a particularly demanding task—the boss might give him or her a special project to carry out or tell him or her to present a report at a big regional meeting of businessmen—one might react with high fear or anxiety and find that he or she cannot carry out the task. Ordinarily, such a person will have learned a variety of ways to avoid the task—getting sick is one common way. The result, though, is failure and then even more upset.

All of us feel some anxiety when challenged with such special tasks; but for some people, the anxiety is far beyond normal limits, and it interferes with their good functioning. If only they could learn to relax and control their anxiety, they would be able to function far better. Such relaxation is what the behavior therapist tries to bring about with systematic desensitization; the therapist tries to *desensitize* the client to the fear-provoking challenges.

First, the therapist trains the person in deep muscle relaxation. When the client is able to relax well in the therapist's office—where there are few anxiety-provoking stimuli—the therapist and client proceed to the next step, the desensitization itself. While deeply relaxed, the client is asked to imagine a scene or a situation in which he or she is faced by some minor challenge. As the scene is imagined, the client will feel some anxiety, but the deep relaxation should overcome the small amount of anxiety. Several repetitions of that imaginal scene will probably be necessary before the client is able to imagine it without anxiety, to remain completely calm. The client then proceeds to other scenes, each successive scene presenting a greater challenge. In this systematic fashion, step by step, the client learns to remain calm and relaxed even when imagining scenes that used to cause great anxiety.

Although the process of systematic desensitization is quite straightforward, it demands skill and experience for the therapist to judge which clients might benefit from the approach, to train good relaxation skills, to create and arrange effective imaginary scenes, and to lead the client through them gradually. The therapist must constantly evaluate progress and determine if any other form of therapy is also needed.

When there has been sufficient success in desensitization to the imaginary scenes, the therapist often helps the client to begin a series of anxiety-control experiences in real-life situations. The client gradually, under the therapist's supervision, gains increased control over his or her anxiety in an increasing variety of real-life situations.

T

TALENTS AND SKILLS   *(See HEREDITY)*

In any field of activity, some people are better than others. For some activities, certain physical conditions might be of supreme importance, and bodily strength, speed, dexterity, and so on might count heavily. For professional football linemen, sheer weight becomes important. Assuming the necessary physical capacity (or building that into being), the great performers are not necessarily endowed with some special inherited blessing or *talent*. In most cases, they have worked at their special fields for long periods. Mark Spitz, the gold medal winner of the 1976 Olympics, started swimming at the age of two. Jimmy Connors, the tennis champion, was in the courts at the age of 4. Jascha Heifitz, the violin virtuoso, started practicing the violin at the age of 2. If your child is not showing championship qualities in some field, you might reflect on how he or she spends his or her time. It is important to recognize that one cannot be first rate at everything, although one might be good at related activities if he or she practices one. Some authorities argue that it takes 5,000 hours of practice to become adequate at any activity—for example, dancing or playing the piano, bridge, golf, and the like. If you have not put in that much time, do not expect to win many prizes.

Merely putting in the time is not by itself sufficient. Competent teachers are required. Musicians frequently have musical children. They are in a position to oversee the practice, select teachers, and provide successful models for their children. The fact that musical ability runs in families does not then mean that any hereditary talent was passed on from parents to offspring. A musical environment is obviously of help. Despite the strongest efforts and pressures of parents, however, some children do not take to the regimens their parents might try to impose. Here, again, we encounter the problem of what is best for the children. Many professionals familiar with the difficulties in their own fields urge their children into other fields about which they may know little and may be unable to provide the environments, teachers, and so on that might make for success.

Some children, at some early age, manifest some unusual aptitude, such as an aptitude for mathematics, even if their parents are not especially skilled in the area. Such geniuses are not easy to understand, since they are too rare to be studied in any systematic fashion, and by the time they come to the attention of psychologists, the influencing factors have been obscured beyond recovery.

One big difficulty for parents is to decide on how they should attempt to influence their children toward careers. In a democracy without a royal line, no one's future can be spelled out in terms of a future job. The parents might want a child to be a doctor, but a medical school might not choose to accept the student. Success in any field cannot be guaranteed, and a great deal is controlled by chance factors. For a parent to decide that a 2-year old should become a champion swimmer is a serious step. Failure to make decisions, on the other hand, will probably promote only average abilities in a wide variety of activities that come to affect a child as he or she matures. It takes a very confident, if not arrogant, parent to decide a child's future, and, given the fact that there are other sources of influence, the strongest efforts of a parent may not prevail since the child may rebel against the parental pressures and go off on his or her own. The issues involved are ethical and philosophical, and psychology cannot provide answers to some of these questions.

TASTE AND SMELL

The senses of *taste* and *smell* are usually referred to as the *chemical* senses. The curious feature of the sense of taste is that apparently we can only taste stimulus objects that dissolve into solutions that can affect the taste buds, and, if our sense of smell is blocked off, all we can taste is whether the object is sweet, bitter, salty, or sour. It appears that different parts of the tongue are specialized for the different tastes, with the tip of the tongue most sentitive to sweet. Once the stimulus affects the back of the tongue, we can detect bitter tastes that might not have been detected by the tip. Most of the taste buds are on the tongue, with some scattered in other areas of the mouth. Besides the four tastes mentioned, we can also have taste experience that we usually describe as metallic, but that is about as far as taste sensitivity is refined. What we taste depends upon what other things we have just tasted, so that prior experience with something salty will make a sweet stimulus taste sweeter. Some people put salt on watermelon or pepper on strawberries to bring out the taste.

Most of what we call taste is actually a matter of olfaction or smell. Potatoes, onions, and apples taste the same if we cannot smell them. Taste tests for cigarettes or beer are largely smell tests. No great progress has been achieved in studies of the sense of smell, and even today, there is no physical or chemical scale by which we can arrange smells in any kind of order or sequence. We are forced to rely on words that refer to objects—for example, we say that something smells like burning rubber, goats, wet dogs, fruits, flowers, and the like. Our senses of smell are very acute, and a tiny amount of a substance may be detected if we really try to smell it; but the American culture is an antismell culture, and we usually try to avoid odors of many kinds, especially body odors. Sniffing in someone else's kitchen is regarded as impolite, although each kitchen and home does indeed have its own smells. As with taste, we quickly adapt to odors, and within a couple of minutes, we can no longer smell something that was almost overpowering when we first met it. If we visit a hospital, the prevailing odor may be quite potent, even with air conditioning, but we will soon become adapted. People who work with odoriferous substances appear to adapt to them on an almost permanent basis or at least to pay them no heed, even on first encounters at the beginning of a work day. In order to be able to smell effectively, we must be free of pollutants, colds, and prior exposure to other odors, since what we are trying to smell may be a combination that includes stimulation from some substances to which we may have become adapted. Professional wine and perfume testers, really smellers, must take precautions to keep their noses in good health. Such professionals have developed their own vocabularies to describe the somewhat complex combinations of elements they encounter. A wine might be described as robust, challenging, or whatever the taster chooses to say. He or she can only smell the fruitiness, taste the sweetness or bitterness, sense some of the astringency of a dry wine, and enjoy its color, a visual aspect. A fresh stalk of cold celery might provide a small excitement at the table, since it excites the senses of sight, sound, taste, smell, feel, and temperature. To say that something tastes like celery is to engage in a conversation without much communication, since the taste is probably the least recognizable feature.

TEACHING MACHINES AND PROGRAMMED LEARNING
(PERSONALIZED SYSTEM OF INSTRUCTION)

Any device that can be used to assist learning can be called a *teaching machine.* Flash cards, for example, are teaching machines, as are pencils, maps, calculators, and so on. S. L. Pressey, in the 1920s, introduced a novel approach to learning by developing a self-testing machine where students pressed buttons in answering multiple-choice questions. Students would press one button after another until the correct answer was found. The procedure was found to help with learning the material that could be adapted to it. The term *teaching machine,* however, properly refers to the creation of B. F. Skinner, the Harvard psychologist, who first developed the idea that any lesson must be properly created in a systematic and organized form so that one starts out from what he or she knows and progresses by simple controlled steps, building on what he or she knows, to achieve final mastery of whatever is to be taught. Such a procedure was described by Plato and is known as the Socratic method. It consists of asking questions and building new questions on the answers to earlier ones.

Most education prior to Skinner's emphasis simply started somewhere convenient to a teacher's interest and proceeded by steps the teacher thought were appropriate, ending when some convenient criterion was met. What Skinner emphasized was the concept of a *program.* Any lesson can be considered as having a beginning, a development, and an end. The trouble is that we rarely analyze something to be taught in such terms and do not recognize that the intermediate steps have to be manageable by the learner.

In Skinner's approach, a learner begins by answering a simple question. He or she must be able to answer this question, or he or she is not ready for that particular lesson. On the basis of his or her answer to the first question, a second question is asked, which the learner should also be able to answer. Similarly, the third, fourth, and final questions are all built on the foundation of prior questions; and if the program is constructed well, a student should be able to go through the program without an error. Skinner saw no virtues in errors or mistakes. They merely waste time. It should be evident that the heart of the matter, then, is in the analysis of the content of a lesson and its arrangement in a logical sequence of carefully prepared negotiable steps.

Programmed learning involves some other features. Because the program has been well prepared in the first place, one can ask the questions as fast as the student is ready to answer them—that is, the student controls the learning time and can go at his or her own rate, as slowly as necessary. Programmed learning is, then, individualized learning. No teacher is required, since the questions can be presented in a variety of ways, generally in printed form. Entire textbooks can be prepared so that the student faces a series of carefully scheduled questions as he or she goes through the text. With small children, various devices or machines can be arranged so that the question appears on a screen or in a window, and the student composes his or her answer on a strip of paper if he or she can write, or he or she can type the answers, press buttons, or indicate his or her answers in some other way. Skinner originally thought that the correct answer should be revealed as soon as the student formed his or her answer; providing the correct answer was regarded as a way of reinforcing or rewarding the learner. Skinner was committed to the belief that we only learn what we are rewarded for doing. Studies have shown that one does not have to produce any overt response or answers nor does one have to be shown the correct answer in order to make learning progress. Mechanical devices are not required for presenting questions. All that is really important is the program.

Many people have learned a great deal from the kinds of programs that have been prepared for aspects of mathematics, grammar, biology, logic, and similar subjects. The greatest success has been met where the subject matter has a logical progression. The successful programs are the result of hard and extensive work by programmers, subject-matter experts, and testers. To produce a good program is a very expensive venture, and there has not been enough enthusiasm shown by publishers, teachers, or others who might have gotten involved to keep the programming proposal alive. In more recent years, the teaching machine has been more or less forgotten. Teachers feared that machines would replace them, and they resisted efforts at development. It is obviously difficult to introduce new procedures and methods in education, since it calls for giving up old ways and sometimes calls for a lot more work than anyone cares to give to the effort. There is no question but that Skinner's approach was sensible, logical, and effective. The educational world was perhaps not ready for it, just as it was not ready for Pressey's teaching machine in the 1920s.

TELEVISION EFFECTS ON CHILDREN

In the very important years between ages 5 and 15, the average American child witnesses nearly 14,000 violent deaths on television. A little arithmetic tells us that that works out to 27 violent deaths per week, or nearly 4 every day. This figure includes only the depicted killing of people; a good deal more violence is shown that stops short of killing or that involves animals rather than people.

Does witnessing this great amount of violence on television affect children? According to psychologists, the answer is a clear "yes!" Children observing television violence tend to imitate it and to act violently themselves. Researchers have found that children, immediately after watching violent television programs, played more violently, were more willing to hurt other children, became more willing to accept violent solutions to problems and to be more tolerant of lawbreaking, as well as being more willing to break social rules themselves. A finding that appears to be of particular concern is that by watching so much violence, children became less sensitive to *aggression* in real life.

The general public seems to believe that there is still a great deal of debate among social scientists over this issue and that it is not at all certain that TV violence is bad for children. Psychologists, through their research, clearly agree that TV violence has negative effects on children, including normal children. The apparent controversy occurs not because of real differences among scientists but because the public hears a very powerful television industry and their powerful allies, the advertisers, assert that television violence does not hurt children. The research data is virtually all on one side of the issue; the special interests groups, wielding their own power and seeking their own profit, are on the other side.

Responsible parents will realize that any set of information that pours over their children so intensively for so many years will have effects. It is important for parents to monitor their children's viewing and to limit the type and number of shows that children watch.

The United States has now seen the growth and development of a new generation of children, now adults, who have spent a good portion of their lives watching television. Some children spend 35 hours or more per week watching television programming, much of it directed at preschool children. Although some mothers have found the television set a cheap baby-sitting service, others have become alarmed at the possible damaging effects of the programming and advertising that encourages children to demand foods of doubtful nutritional value, sugared foods, and toys that may or may not be selected by parents. Some advertisers testify before Congressional committees that the exposure to television is not harmful and is without any lasting evil influence. There is no question that television advertising is effective; if it were not, there would be no sponsors. Whether the programming has good or bad influences depends on the programs. Again, there is no question that children will imitate what they see on the tube. Because there is so much violence and aggression depicted on the programs, some researchers blame the violence in our society on such programs.

The studies by psychologists interested in aggression and imitative behavior appear conclusive. Children will imitate what they see on the tube, granted the opportunity and the motivation. Children would, of course, imitate what they read in juvenile fiction, comic books, or any other medium of communication. The fact that many children are now poor readers is also blamed on television, and it is certainly true that when watching television, children cannot and do not read.

TEMPERAMENT   (See IMPULSIVITY, CONSTITUTIONAL TYPES)

Temperament, or, better, temperaments, are those aspects of an individual that are determined primarily by a person's constitution or biological make-up. They are the inborn tendencies that underlie individual differences in personality. It is clear, then, that personality is the more inclusive term: It includes temperamental traits and more. Temperamental traits are part, but only part, of what we refer to as personality. The interesting question is this: How much of a part and how significant a part of personality can be seen as temperamental—that is, related to inborn tendencies in nature?

The ancient Greeks, in writing attributed to Hippocrates, answered this question by describing four temperamental traits, each associated with a corresponding body fluid, or humour. Thus, the person with an excess of black bile would tend to be melancholic and the one with yellow bile, choleric; an excess of blood would lead to sanguine personality traits, and too much phlegm would determine a phlegmatic character. Over time, this particular theory of biologically determined personality traits has been discredited, although the general notion that humours (or, as we refer to them today, hormones) can affect behavior patterns certainly remains as a viable idea.

There is little current research in support of a biological predisposition for such specific characteristics as stinginess, ambition, orderliness, politeness, or a host of other traits that are often alleged to characterize people. However, research does suggest that there are certain broad classes of behavior that can legitimately be seen as temperaments—that is, that reflect a biologically based predisposition. One of these is certainly the simple *level of activity* or energy output characteristic of a person. Another is the general level of *emotionality*—how much it takes to get a person emotionally aroused, whether that emotion is fear, anger, or distress. A third is *sociability,* or *affiliativeness,* the tendency to want to be with others, to avoid being alone. (This temperament factor is what makes some breeds of dogs better house pets than others.) A fourth is *impulsivity* and its opposite, *inhibitory control.* We refer here to the degree to which a person responds to stimulation—either in a very quick way or with deliberation. These four characteristics and little else in the way of person variables have been shown to be influenced by constitutional factors and are reflected in individual differences early in life, sometimes as early as the first few days. They can, then, be described as human temperaments.

TEMPER TANTRUMS

It is the rare child who has not had a *temper tantrum.* The tantrum can range from a small, angry sound, a pout, and a momentary stamp of the foot to a full-blown, screaming, rolling-on-the-floor, kicking tantrum carried out in public places, such as supermarkets, with the embarrassed parents and all the other people looking on. The extreme tantrum is rare, and it takes a child and the parents a fairly long time and considerable practice to build up the child's normal, mild objections to the full-blown tantrum level. It is not that parents deliberately intend to create that level of behavior, but, effectively, that is what happens.

Temper tantrums do not usually appear until after the children are walking, getting around the house and into things that may be breakable or dangerous. When denied something they want, children will feel badly and make a protest, usually by crying. If the crying is generally rewarded by allowing the child to have the originally denied object, a crying-protesting strategy will probably develop that, in time, works well to get much of what is desired. The temper tantrum, whatever its severity, is essentially a strategy developed by the child and parent in interaction. It serves to express the child's protest and becomes effective in forcing the parent to give in to the child.

The major elements of a childish tantrum, then, are clear: The child wants something; the parent says "no"; the frustrated child protests in whatever way has been learned—in this case, with some degree of tantrum behavior. We have then escalated to a whole new problem, the tantrum itself, and the parent now has to deal with that. Too frequently, parents respond to the obnoxiousness of the tantrum behavior, becoming angry and upset and punishing the child by shaking, yelling at, or even hitting the child. In doing this, the parent has further escalated the entire exchange to a whole new level of intense conflict far beyond the original, simple want of the child. A main point here is that the temper tantrum is not wholly the child's behavioral creation; it has been built up in close interaction by child and parent together.

In this situation, the first mistake the parent makes is in thoughtlessly saying "no" to the child's original request or, if the denial is truly justified, in the manner in which the "no" is spoken. A young child can be told "no" gently, with patience, and be immediately distracted with some other equally or even more interesting activity or object. Doing this smoothly, with patience and good humor, can avoid the gradual build-up of tantrum behavior.

But if that is not done, then the second mistake occurs after the tantrum has begun. The parent can still save the situation by gently distracting the child, as described above, in the early stages of the tantrum behavior. But if the parent fails to take this action, an escalated conflict erupts into a full-blown tantrum, and the whole situation has suddenly become far more serious and complicated. At this point, the parent has only a few choices left: Ignore the child's tantrum until it stops; give in to it and let the child have what is wanted; get angry and punish the child for crying and throwing a tantrum. None of these is a good solution, since they all create further problems, and whatever the parent does is a mistake. The most destructive mistake at this point is to get angry, lose control, and punish the child. This does not teach the child anything about moderating his or her demands or about how to behave nicely; all it does is to embroil the parent and child in an intense and painful conflict that has gone far beyond the original issues.

Once the tantrum starts, about the only thing the parent can do is to wait it out, being careful not to talk to or in any other way to reinforce the tantrum behavior. This will work only if there are no other people around who might inadvertently reinforce the tantrum while the parent is trying so hard to ignore it. In public settings or in situations where the child might be injured during a tantrum, the parent obviously cannot ignore it. Under such conditions, the parent has to use some restraint and remove the child from the situation where the demand was originally made. The two biggest mistakes here are to give in eventually because the child has worn you down or, worse yet, to lose control and create an angry, punitive, and even more serious conflict.

The best way to deal with the problem of tantrums, of course, is not to allow them to develop in the first place. Learn when and how to say "no." When a child does cry in frustration over being denied something, comfort the child and gently and reasonably reiterate the "no." Try to provide some alternative activity or thing for the child. If tantrum behavior has already developed, then you have to plan on reducing it. The main ideas are to maintain your own control, to make sure that you do not eventually give in and thus reinforce the child, never to become aggressive and punitive, to ignore the tantrum when possible, and to remove or restrain the child when necessary.

Most children go through a period of at least mild temper tantrums; they are trying out the strategy, and most seem to find it is not a particularly good way to get cooperation from their parents and friends. Many, however, never learn that and we all know adults who still have what are clearly temper tantrums whenever they do not get their own way. When an adult, such as a teacher, a school superintendent, a manager, or a boss, has tantrums and also has decision-making power over other people, the lives of other people can be made very difficult.

TERRITORIALITY-PECKING ORDERS   (See INSTINCT)

Some *ethologists* (students of animal behavior in natural settings) and other more casual observers, along with some sociobiologists, have popularized the old notion of a *pecking order* into a broad explanation of human behavior. In the barnyard, it might be observed that some hen or rooster appears to dominate the flock and that other members of the group appear to dominate others while submitting to the most dominant and aggressive leader. Similar observations made of deer, baboons, and various species of birds have led to the notion of *territoriality*, the idea that creatures in natural habitats stake out some area of the terrain (jungle, seashore, etc.) where they hunt, nest, breed, and keep out all intruders. Such territorial boundaries are not always well defined, but there appears to be support for the general notion that creatures try to dominate a personal space and ranking within a group.

How meaningfully such an idea as territoriality applies to people living in so-called civilization is debatable. Strap-hanging commuters packed into subways, trains, and buses have little choice about how close they may stand. When hordes of adolescents invade Southern beaches during spring holidays and pack football stadia for rock concerts, one might be inclined to postulate some sort of herding instinct. It is, of course, true that people like their own chairs or positions at the table and that youth gangs define their so-called turf. There are obvious social and learning explanations for such personal preferences and arrangements, and there is, of course, a variety of reasons why people might group together very closely or set up arrangements, where possible, for more private and exclusive living. Apartment dwellers might resemble ant colonies, but suburban estates might suggest other comparisons. All sorts of customs prevail around the world that dictate how closely we stand when talking to someone, whether men embrace other men on greeting each other, whether we gaze into others' eyes or avoid them, why peasants flock to cities and live in cardboard and tin huts, and the like. To invoke biological instincts to explain crowding, herding, pecking orders, and personal desires for some elbow room may be premature. It may be a question of whose elbows are pressing against you.

TEST-TRAIT FALLACY   (See PERSONALITY TESTS, INTELLIGENCE TESTS, ATTITUDES AND OPTIONS)

Any test, whether of intelligence or personality, is a sample of behavior. Responses are observed to questions or situations, and, if possible, some kind of score is attached to the responses. The score is then compared with some other behavior or sample that can be scored—for example, school grades, criminal records, hospitalization, or some other criterion—and a correlation, if present, is noted. If there is a correlation of some degree, the test is then identified by a label as a test of intelligence, honesty, neuroticism, primary mental abilities, or whatever. Note that at no time has anyone ever observed intelligence, neuroticism, or any real thing or process corresponding to the labels. The test makers or administrators simply *assume* that they have been measuring some aptitude, trait, or learning potential. It is then further assumed that the aptitude or trait now plays a causal role in controlling the responses made to the test items. Because the traits, aptitudes, potentials, tendencies, susceptibilities, or predispositions are not independently observed, such assumptions remain what they are—assumptions—and however appealing the assumptions may be, they are not supported or justified by the circular reasoning involved. What we have is a logical fallacy of begging the question, assuming that which is to be proved. The *test-trait fallacy* has been brought to the attention of psychologists on many occasions, but the test makers continue at their craft, producing more and more tests.

It is not to be concluded that tests are of no value. Their value depends upon the correlation with some criterion. Certainly, if a sample of questions can be asked in five minutes that will enable us to predict how well someone will do in school or at a job, it is much easier and cheaper than to enroll him or her in a long program or in a serious position. We are dealing strictly with numbers that do or do not correlate. We never measure intelligence, ability, or personality traits. These are and remain inferences—that is, assumptions—and when we base serious social actions on the assumptions that such things as intelligence are real, we may make very serious blunders. It is necessary to be extremely cautious about reifying any inferred property or characteristic of a person.

THUMBSUCKING

Young infants put anything they can into their mouths, and the thumb is the safest of all possible things: At least, it will not be swallowed. The usual advice is that they will grow out of it, and most of them do, although there have been reports (unverified) about adults who still enjoy a lick or two, especially in moments of stress. Some people interpret cigarette, cigar, and pipe smoking as a variation on the thumb, and some individuals manicure their fingernails with their teeth. Outside of the sanitary problem, there is no great harm in *thumbsucking,* and it may even have some value in infancy in the development of jaw muscles. It is still not determined whether infants need to suck for some unknown amount of time.

Interpretations about security are probably ill-founded, since a whole variety of substitutes enters the picture. Anyone really concerned about the problem can bandage the thumb with enough bandage to prevent entry. There is a constant danger that small infants will swallow small objects, and, of course, they must be watched. Oral exploration and examination must teach infants something about the taste, feel, and solidity of objects, and one should not expect to prevent such aspects of the child's education.

TICS   *(See HABIT BREAKING)*

A *tic* is a frequently occurring, involuntary muscle spasm or twitching. Tics may occur in any muscle group but are most noticeable to others when they involve the facial muscles. Tics may also be vocal, involving sudden, uncontrollable, loud sounds. Tics vary greatly among those who suffer from the disorder and may range from eyelid trembling and blinking to large movements of the head, limbs, or torso; lip smacking; and explosive sounds.

A person with a tic may become aware of it, but most often, the behavior has become so habitual that the person does not even know it is occurring until someone else calls attention to it. Often, when made aware of a tic, a person can become self-conscious about it, even more anxious, and, as a result, produce the tic even more than before. It is important, then, to be careful about when and how we point out a tic to someone. Although tics can occur at any age, they seem to occur mostly in childhood and adolescence, between about age 6 and age 14.

Psychologists do not know a great deal about tics. Questions of their causes, frequencies of occurrence, types, treatment, and so on must await future research. Three points of information seem clear: (1) The majority of tics are psychologically caused, with the person's tension or anxiety playing a very large part in the disorder; (2) tics seem to be usually, but not always, temporary, and they eventually decrease and disappear in time. However, the concern, embarrassment, and upset can be very great when a tic is known to occur; (3) treatment, particularly by behavioral methods that involve relaxation training and negative practice, appears promising but is still experimental.

If a child or adult is observed to have a tic, it probably means that there is some fairly great psychological tension. Any attempts to embarrass, ridicule, scold, or punish the person will probably increase anxiety and make things worse. The best advice at this point is to wait and see if the tic fades and disappears by itself and to put *no* pressure on the person. If it does not decrease, or if it begins to create other problems in the person's life, then professional help should be sought. The use of tranquilizers might generally calm down the person but will not necessarily teach him or her to decrease the tic. The best treatment at present is probably the following: (1) verbal counseling or therapy that tries to determine the anxiety-causing conditions that are pressing upon the person, followed by (2) active behavioral methods of *relaxation training, systematic desensitization,* and *negative,* or *massed, practice.* The latter are essentially experimental techniques in which the person is urged to practice or produce the tic at a very high rate, perhaps while watching him- or herself in a mirror. The basic idea here is that fatigue—a negative physical and psychological condition—will weaken the tic, whereas the unpleasant sight of oneself engaging in the behavior will constitute a negative feedback or punishment, also having the effect of providing cues to responses that can control tic behavior. Negative practice must be carried out only under carefully supervised professional conditions.

TOILET TRAINING   *(See ENURESIS)*

Most children are bowel trained by about a year and a half and by about age 3 have learned to be dry day and night. There are large individual variations in training times between children, and differences that seem great to parents probably do not mean much of anything important in terms of the child's development. Appropriate times to begin training are at about the age of 11 or 12 months for bowel training and around the age of 20 months for bladder training. Of course, the time to begin training will vary from one family to another and even between children within the same family. Some parents begin as early as the fifth month, whereas many do not begin until into the second year. Starting too early amounts to training the parents, not the child. There is no precise time that appears best for all parents and children; rather, the quality, patience, ease, and pleasant character of toilet training seem to be the most important aspects, according to child psychologists.

Several things seem fairly certain: (1) The process of learning to control bowel and bladder elimination is a set of complex tasks for and demands on the child, who must learn muscle control, recognition of physical cues, and the social appropriateness of when and where to eliminate; (2) the child's physical control will not be learned until the child has sufficiently matured, no matter what training approaches might be used; (3) putting great pressure on the child, scolding, and punishing will probably create considerable upset, anxiety, and discomfort for the child and make the entire process totally unpleasant. The problems created by a too demanding, too tense, and punitive parent in toilet training may or may not result in long-term or permanent psychological problems, but they will undoubtedly create immediate unhappiness for the duration of the training.

What this means for the parent is that one probably cannot speed up the toilet-training process by starting the child at a very early age; by zealously holding the child to a rigid, demanding schedule; or by getting tough about it; but one can easily make a demanding process even more difficult and, effectively, slow it down. The best advice is to begin at a reasonable age; to view the training as a learning experience for the child; to appreciate the demands that are being made on him or her; and to proceed with plenty of patience, support, rewards, and soft, quiet praises. Know, too, that children do not progress at the same rate and that even after training is completed, children will have occasional accidents: Such occasional relapses, even around the age of 12, are not at all unusual for normal children.

TRAITS   (See TEST-TRAIT FALLACY)

There are thousands of adjectives in the dictionary, such as kind, mean, honest, and so on, all of which really describe some behavior. But since the behavior is performed by some persons, the adjective is attached to the person; thus, one who does something that someone else might choose to describe as "kind" becomes a kind person (even if the next day he or she burns down an orphanage), and somehow the kind person is now presumed to possess something called kindness as a personal feature or mechanism—some kind of special part of him or her that then controls his or her behavior and, in effect, makes him or her do kind things. Such adjectives are called *traits,* and the basic psychology of the man in the street is to try to understand people's behavior by trying to find out what the controlling mechanisms are that other people possess in terms of these adjectives. Such adjectives are reified or embodied as traits. It should be clear that there are no traits that control behavior. Of course, some people can be described as predominantly of one kind or another, in the sense that their behavior is frequently, if not always, described by some term such as fair, stubborn, rude, brave, or the like. If someone seems to be strongly describable as honest, we might describe this as a dominant trait and perhaps take advantage of it in predicting behavior, but all we are doing in that case is basing a prediction on past performance, just as we might in betting on a horse. If someone appears to be driven by some single (or by a restricted few) goal(s), we might refer to him or her as having some *cardinal*—meaning outstanding—traits; for example, we can describe Caesar as ambitious or Napoleon as authoritarian; someone else might be grasping, malevolent, inhibited, egotistical, or whatever.

Psychologists have spent many years trying to measure personality traits by various inventories or check lists, usually of adjectives, but all they have accomplished in this regard is to obtain some data on how a person usually or commonly behaves, assuming that the tests had any validity. People are frequently surprised by the behavior they observe on the part of someone who, according to the observer, should not have behaved in that way, as when a politician is found to be taking bribes. All that means is that the earlier observations were not complete enough. In many cases, people are fairly consistent in their behavior, and if their circumstances do not change seriously, they can be counted on to behave as they did before. This consistency, however, does not point to anything more than the habits they have acquired; there is no great harm done in thinking of the person as having traits—that, in itself, is no more incorrect than thinking of him or her as having habits. In both cases, it is necessary to remember that consistency can be counted on only under consistent conditions and that when things change, one should not be surprised by so-called surprises. One will make better judgments about people by finding out how they have been reinforced in the past than by looking for nonexistent traits.

TRANQUILIZERS   (See DRUG THERAPY)

A number of tranquilizing medications have been used for years as somatic treatment for emotional or psychological problems. The tranquilizers have been used alone as the sole treatment or in conjunction with other, sometimes psychological, treatment. As their name suggests, *tranquilizers* are used to calm people down, to help reduce their anxiety.

A group of minor tranquilizers, carrying trade names such as Milltown, Equanil, Librium, and Valium, are being prescribed to millions of people by general practitioners as well as by psychiatrists and have become a familiar part of our society. These minor tranquilizers are prescribed for outpatients from all levels of society whose anxieties and tensions, although troublesome, are not overwhelming. Many people have been kept on the tranquilizing medication for many years.

Although these minor tranquilizers do help a large number of people to get through each day, many psychologists believe that such wholesale use is, in the long run, more damaging than helpful. They suggest that the person who comes to depend upon the tranquilizers may be preventing him- or herself from learning how to control anxiety without drugs. However, despite the misgivings, the wholesale use of tranquilizers appears to be here to stay.

The major tranquilizers, such as Thorazine, Stelazine, Mellaril, Haldol, and Taractan, are used primarily by psychiatrists in the somatic treatment of the more severe psychological disorders, such as schizophrenia. In fact, the major tranquilizers have become known as *antipsychotic drugs* because of their effect in reducing schizophrenic symptoms.

Research carried out with schizophrenic patients has been quite clear in showing that these major tranquilizers are effective in keeping the patient on a more even emotional level and in shortening hospital stay. Sometimes, the effect of the tranquilizers is quite dramatic, and the patient is able to function much better. It is largely because of these major tranquilizers that people are no longer kept in mental hospitals for as many years as they once were. The drugs do not cure schizophrenia, but they do reduce many of the bizarre and interfering symptoms, and they help the patient to function much better. There seems little doubt that proper use of tranquilizers has been of considerable help to many severely disturbed people.

Very recently, however, we have seen a growing concern over the possible negative side-effects of the major tranquilizers, with questions also raised about the minor tranquilizers. Long-term use of some of the major tranquilizers may result in a number of small-muscle control problems. For example, a small percentage of patients begin to show uncontrollable mouth and lip twitching, and lip smacking, chin wagging, and sucking motions and sounds. All these are uncontrollable and may become permanent, irreversible. Low blood pressure and jaundice are also negative side-effects sometimes seen in the long-term use of major tranquilizers. The negative effects on children are not yet clear, primarily because not too many researchers appear to be too concerned about the problem and have not carefully investigated the negative side-effects in children. Certainly, caution must be carefully maintained in the use of any drug, particularly with children.

Long-term use of any medications must be carefully monitored, not only for their intended positive effects but also for their unintended negative effects. Tranquilizers have their effective use and have been important in the treatment of severe psychological disorders such as schizophrenia, but, like any medication, tranquilizers may be overused and thus become another instance of drug abuse in our modern American drug culture.

U

UNCONDITIONED RESPONSE   *(See CONDITIONING)*

The term *unconditioned response* has a technical meaning in Pavlovian research, where it refers to any response that is made naturally to some stimulus. The stimulus is normally regarded as somehow related to and determining the response, as, for example, if a branch of some tree grazes one's face, the eye will close or blink, and we tend to assume that the response is singularly appropriate: The eye blinks because it was touched or threatened with contact. Pavlov worked with digestive juices and glandular secretions and regarded the secretion of saliva or gastric acid when food was in the mouth or stomach as natural reflexes that would occur despite anything else that might be going on. Actually, a frightened dog would not salivate to food in the mouth, and it might not salivate if not hungry. Thus, the term *unconditioned*, in the sense of not dependent upon other factors, is not quite appropriate. In general, however, there are many bodily reflexes that are quite dependable most of the time, and they can be elicited readily upon demand. Pepper or snuff drawn into the nose will tend to elicit a sneeze; a tap on the patellar tendon will evoke a knee jerk; a shock to the fingertips will evoke a hand withdrawal; running a pencil along a baby's sole will result in a spreading or upward extension of the toes (Babinski reflex). Generally, then, we regard any immediate reaction to some specific stimulus where no prior training has been involved as an unconditioned reflex. Actually the term unconditioned is more or less redundant, since all genuine reflexes are unconditioned, if the term *conditioned* is to refer to learned responses of an apparently reflex nature.

Any simple behavior that occurs reliably upon the presentation of a specific stimulus can be considered as the basic reflex or starting point for a conditioning exercise. Thus, we can tell a child to squeeze a rubber ball when we say, "Squeeze" or "Ta Ra." If the child proceeds to squeeze upon our command and waits for the command, the squeezing is playing the role of an unconditioned reflex, regardless of the fact that the child had to learn the meaning of the word or of the instruction and, to some extent, master control over his or her finger and hand muscles. We can accept the general meaning of unconditioned as referring to some original reaction to a stimulus in any given situation or stage of training.

UNCONSCIOUS   *(See CONSCIOUSNESS)*

There is no *unconscious* in the sense of some kind of mind or operating equipment in the human body. As an adjective, unconscious is acceptable, although confusing, in its meaning and usage. It is correctly used to refer to someone who is not responding to the normal range of stimuli as, for example, when someone faints, is anesthetized for some operation, suffers from a severe blow to the head, or is otherwise knocked out. When a person is asleep, he or she is also unconscious most of the time and will not respond to modest levels of stimulation. The term is also used as a synonym for lack of awareness. When we are aware of something, we can tell other people about it, point to it, if it is an object, or respond in some appropriate way. Awareness is similar to attention, and since we can attend in any serious way to only one thing at a time, we must be unaware of what is happening around us in many other regards, most of which we can dismiss. If a soldier on patrol is investigating what he thinks he heard under some bush, he may be unaware of an enemy about to attack him from the rear. To say that he was unconscious of the enemy is abusing the term.

Sigmund Freud, the popularizer of psychoanalysis, chose to divide what he called the mind into conscious, preconscious, and unconscious levels, and he chose to assume that there was some kind of activity at each level. In the *unconscious mind,* for example, one might be entertaining wishes, desires, or anxieties of various kinds. One might, for example, unconsciously wish that his or her father was dead or have some lustful desires for one's mother or any other person. The unconscious, for Freud, was some kind of locus for repressed desires, where they presumably continued to operate but could not break through to conscious awareness because of various protective or defense mechanisms and because of another hypothetical operator or figure Freud called the *censor.*

The problem with the Freudian model is that we rarely are unaware of our desires, whether these are noble or evil; our problem is not with the desires but with the difficulty of satisfying them and meeting other needs. If the desire is for sexual intercourse with someone, we might have to reckon with other factors, such as beliefs in sin, knowledge of disease, fear of discovery (if the affair would be illicit or illegal), and so on. We need not fear our unconscious desires; our conscious ones can be troublesome enough. Freud believed that one could get through to the unconscious and make it conscious by means of the process of having people relax and talk freely about anything that came into their minds, about their dreams, or even about made-up dreams. What he was allowing his patients to do was to pretend that they were really fine, upright people who could not be blamed for what their unconscious minds were doing to them. In modern, more liberated times, people are more willing to admit that they occasionally harbor desires that they do not really like to broadcast. Even a United States president is willing to admit that he has "lusted in my heart" for women other than his wife. Some people pretended to be shocked at the candidate's admission but probably few really were, since lusting for a variety of sex partners is probably the normal or standard condition in our culture.

The notion that one is unconsciously striving for some kind of goal—that is, working toward something without knowing what it is—is a bit of non-science fiction. Of course, some people attain some ends they did not anticipate. In that case, they may or may not be lucky. They may have been unaware of where they were going to arrive, but that does not mean that the unconscious drove them there.

UNDERSTANDING

Whenever we say something to anyone, it is our hope that the other person will *understand* us. It is a vain hope if we really expect that someone will now know or feel exactly what we know, think, or feel. Sometimes, we put the matter in the form, "Do you get my meaning?" Again, we are acting as if meanings were something that we somehow transferred from ourselves to some other by talking or showing something to someone. We say, "Here's how you do it. Get it?" An affirmative reply satisfies us that a meaning was communicated. We then find, frequently enough, that the other person is now telling someone else some garbled version of the communication or doing the wrong thing.

The confusion about understanding arises from the fact that understanding is not something that is communicated to someone else as a reproduction of our appreciation of some matter. When a person is giving an explanation of something, he or she starts talking, says as much as he or she thinks is necessary, and then says, "Do you understand?" He or she should ask, "Are there any questions?" If there are no questions, the explainer assumes that he or she has done a proper job. Actually, there may be no questions because some may be afraid to ask them and appear stupid or because the matter does seem to be clear, and thus no questions occur to the one receiving the explanation because he or she has not paid attention to the correct items in the explanation and has concentrated on others: He or she may have had his or her own ideas about something and heard or thought he or she heard these ideas confirmed; he or she may have been in a hurry to get it over with and assumed that he or she could look it up later or that he or she would get the points when he or she faced a situation. In any case, he or she misunderstood.

If a misunderstanding is based on the fact that the explanation seemed clear, the misunderstander could feel perfectly satisfied, fully knowledgeable, and ready to go on to the next matter just exactly as he or she would if he or she actually understood. In short, there is no difference in the reactions involved between understanding and misunderstanding. You feel exactly the same way. *Meanings* are not something that we communicate to anyone. They are reactions that we arouse in someone else when we try to say something or explain some matter. Everyone reacts with his or her own imagery and feelings to what we say, and we cannot arouse *our* feelings or imagery in anyone else. Sometimes we come close, and in simple matters, we can find some common ground and even common action. If we say, "I'll see you at noon," another person can arrange to meet us at precisely 12 o'clock. Clearly, he or she understood what "noon" meant in terms of a clock, but the word "noon" may have meant one thing to us and something else entirely to the other. It might have meant missing another appointment, making all sorts of other arrangements, losing out on an opportunity, or any of thousands of reactions. There was a successful communication, but only in a narrow and limited sense. We can rarely appreciate just what our words and messages mean to anyone else, and, in that sense, almost every communication is a failure. Even when people agree on the wording of some document, they might later fall out and argue that they did not understand the wording to mean *that*. In international affairs involving different languages, diplomats may appear to be quibbling for weeks or months over the wording of some apparently simple item. It is probably a good thing to take the time to quibble before the document is signed, because meanings are very personal things, and agreeing that now we understand each other is about as meaningless a statement as one can make.

V

VALUES

It would be extremely helpful if we could pigeonhole people into various but limited categories in terms of how they would be likely to react in various situations. In an attempt to do this, many psychologists have tried to, in effect, summarize many traits into some smaller number, perhaps as few as two groupings or classes. Thus, some people are categorized as *extroverts* and the rest as *introverts,* with a possible middle category that is neither too much of one or the other. People are commonly described as *optimists* and *pessimists.* Robert Benchley categorized people into two groups: those who categorize people and those who don't. That humorist's effort was probably closer to the truth than the categorizations attempted by psychologists.

One prominent psychological effort was to break down people into six categories in terms of the *values* that could be presumed to guide their reactions in a wide range of situations. The categories selected by G. W. Allport and P. E. Vernon were labeled as follows: *theoretical, political, social, aesthetic, religious,* and *economic.* These psychologists prepared an inventory consisting of statements that could indicate whether a person in some situation would presumably choose to respond along one of these orientations rather than along another. If you were a witness to an accident, and if your first reaction was in terms of how much money it would cost to repair the damages (to people and materials) as opposed to a reaction of how you might be able to help the victims, you would score positively on economic and negatively on social. If your reaction was in terms of statistics and accident causes as opposed to how dreadful and ugly the scene appeared to be, you would be scored positively on theoretical and negatively on aesthetic, and so on. To the extent that a person was more interested in science than in art, politics or power rather than moral principles, he or she would then be characterized in terms of his or her scores as high on one category, low on others, and so on. It might be of some help to know that a person was more aesthetically inclined than inclined toward business or politics if one had to engage in some relationship with him or her, but the Allport and Vernon scale was designed to appraise the relative values for an individual; and if the individual was more or less equally interested in all of the six categories, one would not be able to categorize him or her very effectively.

Actually, most people vary in the kinds of interests or values they might demonstrate in different situations. When in church on Sunday, they might be high on religious values but put these aside in the workaday world of Monday through Saturday. Social values might be very strong with respect to some groups and very low toward others, and one might be very wrong in judging the social values of someone at a jovial Ku Klux Klan meeting. It is highly improbable that any kind of typology will prove useful, since individuals vary too greatly in different situations and times of their lives. It is better to note how a person responds in a specific situation and use that as a guide for similar situations than to make judgments about more general circumstances. Doctors may well speed past the scene of an accident, not because they are inhumane or antisocial but because they know that good Samaritan doctors have been sued for malpractice because they were unable to work effectively at the scene of an accident and needed the equipment available only in a hospital to do any real good. Very polite people can stomp on old ladies while rushing for exits in a building that is on fire.

VESTIBULAR SENSE

The *vestibular sense* is the sense of equilibrium, or one through which we become aware of changes in the positions of our head, of gravitational pull, or of accelerations or decelerations of our bodies. If we are riding in a car, and if the driver suddenly applies the brakes, we lunge forward if we are not belted in. We feel such lurches and lunges in our legs, neck, and chest muscles, but sensory stimulation also occurs in tiny organs in what is called the *vestibule* of the *inner ear*. In our skulls, surrounded by cartilage, the inner ear consists of a complex arrangement of tubular bony structures. One of these, the *cochlea*, is concerned with hearing. In close proximity, other structures—the *semicircular canals* and two other rounded structures, the *saccule* and the *utricle*—are concerned with bodily balance and acceleration changes. Most of us do not even know we possess such organs, since they appear not to provide any sensory information directly. They do not even appear to be necessary to normal adjustment if both are destroyed; if one is damaged, however, we may suffer a variety of discomforts and disorientations with dizziness, nausea, lack of balance, and other difficulties, such as unappreciated tilts of the head.

The semicircular canals are three in number, roughly at right angles to each other, containing a fluid that responds to change in inertia. As long as we are in some constant state, not accelerating in any direction, nothing seems to happen; as we do accelerate, the liquids lag behind and then surge forward, stimulating hair cells that are the endings of the vestibular nerve. The action of the liquids can only be observed on experimental animals, and the best indicator of such activities is through the action of other organs, notably the eyes. Vestibular stimulation results in *nystagmus*—that is, a slow drift of the eyes in one direction with a fast return, followed by another drift, another return, and so on. *Otologists* test us for vestibular adequacy by syringing our external ear canals with hot or cold water and watching our eye movements.

The vestibular sense is apparently involved in such reactions as seasickness, air-sickness, sudden rises or drops in elevators that people report as "feeling my stomach drop," and the like. Presumably, such *motion sickness* effects are related to vestibular stimulation. Not all people suffer to the same degree, suggesting wide differences in sensitivity to vestibular activity.

VISUAL DIFFICULTIES

Although our eyes are remarkable instruments, they are subject to a variety of weaknesses or anomalies that are frequently undetected until children begin to have trouble in school and someone tells the parents that they should have the child's eyes examined. Some people grow to adulthood and never know that they are not enjoying all the possibilities their eyes could provide. If they are nearsighted, they may manage to focus on print and have no great trouble in reading, but they may be unable to see things at a distance and, not seeing them, may never know they are there. Thus, a scenic view from some mountain height may hold no interest for them. What they see may be a foggy vista of no charm whatever. Many visual deficiencies are correctable by properly prescribed glasses, and regular visual examinations by an optometrist should be undergone. Even if one can pass the casual examination for a driver's license, one should not assume that he or she sees like everyone else. You may not know what you are missing. Twenty-twenty vision is not anything more than that—seeing at 20 feet what most people can see at 20 feet. What about 400 feet or 14 inches?

Various specialists deal with visual problems. *Oculists* are physicians who deal with eye diseases. They usually prefer to be called *ophthalmologists*. Such physicians are qualified to perform operations on the eyes, remove cataracts, transplant corneas, and otherwise deal with the eye itself. *Optometrists* are not medical doctors, although they have doctoral degrees, and are specialized in testing the eyes and prescribing lenses. One should visit an optometrist first when some visual defect is suspected. He or she will refer appropriate cases to an opthamologist when necessary. An optician is someone who manufacturers lenses according to prescription.

Some of the typical difficulties people might suffer from are the following:

Amblyopia—a dimness of vision without any special disease or apparent defect.
Astigmatism—fuzziness of vision, lack of clear images in part of the visual field.

Myopia—nearsightedness; distant objects are focused in front of the retina so that they appear blurred.

Hyperopia—farsightedness; images of objects in the field are focused beyond the retina, making distant objects appear clearer than near objects.

Most people reaching the age of 40 or so will begin to have trouble with telephone book print and newspapers. They will complain about the poor quality of the ink or print. Simple magnifying lenses may demonstrate that the print is good but that the vision is no longer the same as it once was. Bifocal glasses are frequently prescribed for such people.

Many other defects or diseases of the eye can be detected and treated by opthamologists. Psychologists are concerned only with getting the maximum use out of the eyes.

VOCALIZATION AND LANGUAGE DEVELOPMENT

Anthropologists inform us that by the age of 2, children all over the world learn the language used in their homes. There appear to be no racial or other differences that make one language or another easier or more difficult to acquire. Such worldwide uniformity makes it appear that language development is a natural process, a native human feature, and one that will appear without any special instruction as long as some language is being spoken around the child. Noam Chomsky, the linguist, even urges that there is a native predisposition for acquiring grammar, so that by the age of 5 or so the average child will be speaking fluently and grammatically, even if he or she cannot begin to describe the rules of grammar he or she uses so well.

Speech and language begin with baby babbling and vocalizing, usually of vowels, less commonly of consonants, with various squeals, gurgles, and grunts. Most parents try to encourage the alteration of these spontaneous vocalizations into words, but the first word is not likely to appear before the child is a year old. Parents should not be trusted in obtaining information about when a child began to talk, since they will interpret any sound as corresponding to a word in their anxiety to have their child appear bright. It does appear that children who will later test out to be bright begin to talk sooner than others, but since intelligence tests are made up of verbal items and depend largely on vocabulary appreciation, it is difficult to decide if bright children have better language mastery or if better language mastery makes for brightness. Girls appear to be somewhat advanced over boys in language acquisition, according to most studies, but this is a matter of averages, with no special meaning for any particular child.

Parents need not attempt to teach or train children to talk, since it is a waste of time. All that is required is that a good language environment be supplied in which people talk to and around the child. Correcting mistakes and pronunciation is of little merit, since it may only create problems, in the vast majority of cases, and the children will eventually speak appropriately. It is probably unwise to yell and scream around a child in family quarrels, since the loud sounds may be frightening and may inhibit some speech tendencies. People who accept the responsibility of having children should carry out their fights in private, preferably in the woods.

Children commonly invent their own words for favorite playthings, blankets, and so on and may not be understood by strangers unfamiliar with their private vocabularies. There is no point to parents learning the child's language; the burden is on the child to communicate with the rest of the world, and a parent might better use the standard words for a blanket instead of reinforcing a child's "banky," or some similar noise. This should be done without reproof but in a noncommital way; as long as the parents speak correctly, the child will also come to do so. Parents should appreciate that children pick up four-letter words as easily as any others and that the vocabulary and grammar of the parents will become that of the child.

It should be recognized that the words a child uses may not mean anything to him or her. A child can learn to count to twenty without knowing what a number means, and he or she can sing and say words that mean nothing to him or her. The use of abstract words is probably not really meaningful before the age of 10 or 12.

Bilingualism.   Many children learn two languages: one at home and another in the streets and schools. Children apparently have no difficulty in mastering another language along with that used in the home. Once they reach their teens, a second language will not come as easily as far as pronunciation is concerned. Apparently, the habits involved in using the first language make it difficult to use the vocal apparatus for the different sound structure involved in some other language. If children are to learn a second language, there appears to be no reason why it should not be started before they reach high school. There are, of course, many problems of a social nature if the bilingualism is forced upon a child in what amounts to an alien culture. If all of the children in a school speak one language as a native tongue, however, introducing a new language in the primary or middle-school grades can be done effectively as far as a spoken use of the new language is concerned. It should also be expected that time spent on learning another language must be subtracted from time that could be spent in learning something else, and some poorer achievement levels can be expected in other areas. It should be appreciated that school children in European countries commonly learn a number of languages along with the rest of their courses; it is not the second language that is the cause of problems foreign language-speaking children experience when they enter American schools.

VOCATIONAL COUNSELING AND JOB SELECTION

Children are commonly asked, "What are you going to be when you grow up?" The equally common answers are fireman, doctor, or nurse. The actual number of firemen, doctors, and nurses is relatively small, and so we must assume that childish vocational choices are not realistic. But neither are those made by many other people who find themselves in the wrong jobs, in the sense that they are not pleased with the kind of work they are doing, with the compensation, with the prestige, or with other features of the work. The problem arises only in a society where the children are taught that they can be anything that they want, including the president, and are not brought up to expect to enter a specific position, as they might in a society where class membership might automatically exert certain restraints upon ambition. A crown prince can be fairly sure about what his job will be. No one else has any real control over his or her destiny.

By the time we become 18 years old, we must begin to consider the future, with its economic aspects. If one is not independently wealthy, the prospect of some kind of employment (a trade, a profession, or a business) has to be considered. Parental advice is usually overabundant and not necessarily apt. Certain careers call for certain skills and abilities, and, in some cases, they are precluded if one has waited for 18 years before starting to prepare. No one is likely to become a concert pianist who has not been praticing since the age of 5 or so. If mathematics was avoided in high school, the probability of becoming a nuclear physicist is low, if not impossible. Deciding to become a doctor or lawyer may be self-satisfying, but whether one can get into the appropriate schools often depends more on the school than on the applicant. Medical schools turn away thousands of aspirants, as do all other professional training institutions. One cannot merely decide that he or she will be anything at all—except unemployed.

Obviously, parental influence, home background, family occupations, geographical location, friends, and grammar school and high school teachers are all important in what notions a new adult entertains about what his or her prospective employment role may be. Sometimes, parents with their own experience of work will advise and take steps to prevent a child from entering their own occupations because they have not been happy with their experience. An orchestra clarinetist may say, "No kid of mine is going to blow a horn." He or she may, of course, be depriving the world of a great musician, but no one can really stop him or her.

The common advice the adolescent receives is to pick something that will be interesting to do, to get a job that he or she likes and would like to do even if he or she were not paid to do it. There is some merit to such advice, since one is likely to spend a large portion of his or her life at earning a living, but what one might like at age 18 and what the job might be like 20 or 30 years later are quite likely to be very different affairs. Most jobs have a way of changing. New techniques, machines, and organizations take over, and a job that was interesting becomes dull and unsatisfying. A doctor trained in certain skills at age 25 may find himself old hat and useless at age 40 because the disease he or she learned to cure has been eliminated or because he or she did not keep acquiring new skills, since he or she was too busy. Computer experts at age 25 may be unemployable at age 40. Training to become a teacher may not be meaningful if the population of students keeps declining and schools are closed. In short, one must project the prospects of the job lasting over the working lifetime of the candidate, and one must also recognize that the job will inevitably change into something that may not be recognizable. Learning how to drill for oil may become meaningless if the world turns to solar or atomic power.

One factor commonly ignored by adolescents is that the range of jobs, the ways in which people can make a living, is almost incredible. There are literally thousands of occupations: Government handbooks list over 25,000, and they do not include them all. With the range of jobs that actually exist, one is foolish to decide to become one specific kind of operator and should certainly consider all the alternatives for which one might be suited. By the time one is 18, he or she should have some notions about his or her repertory of skills compared to those of his or her fellows and should have an idea of the general fields in which they might be useful. Some preliminary experience with a number of different fields might be sought, either in terms of part-time employment or the selection of courses in schools, in order to sample a variety of areas. Basic ability in mathematics and writing skills is a common requirement of nearly all jobs and must, of course, be part of the jobhunter's equipment; it will also set limits to aspirations.

There are other considerations that might be taken. Any job at all may be sufficient if one is not driven by desires for prestige or luxuries. A philosopher can drive a bus for eight hours and enjoy his or her life (even the driving can offer some moments of interest from time to time), and many so-called lowly occupations can provide for necessities as well as leave time for the pursuit of nonremunerative interests. Spinoza ground lenses for a living.

W

WARM-UP   (See READINESS)

Whatever the activity may be in which one is about to engage, it is apparently wise to plan on some initial practice or preparation before one gets down to serious work. The most common example is that of the baseball pitcher who warms up in the bullpen prior to taking his position on the mound. In general, athletes warm up for at least a few minutes before beginning their stints. The interesting feature of *warm-up* is that it also applies to so-called mental work or learning activity. Experimental studies demonstrate that if one is to engage in some learning exercise, such as memorizing a list of words, solving anagrams, or any other kind of intellectual exercise, it also pays off to spend a little time just working over some practice material or activity similar to that in which one will shortly be engaged. Thus, in preparing to write a letter or essay, it will help some to simply scribble away on a sheet of paper, using hand and pen to make wordlike doodles. In taking an examination, it pays to think about the content area and jot down notes about items that might occur to you in relation to the kinds of questions one might anticipate, when the actual questions are presented. The note scribbling might be more directly related to the topic, even though the items thought of do not pertain precisely to the questions. Such notes might remind one of more appropriate answers that might occur to one later. It is assumed that the original notes were somehow sparked by the questions and that some associated answers might occur.

Before getting down to serious reading, it pays to flip pages and glance at topics, examine pictures, and the like. The preparatory activity gets one into the mood for more serious work and brings about a state of readiness. Sometimes, the illumination or noise level of the surroundings takes a bit of getting used to, and the warm-up period helps in this way as well.

WILL AND VOLUNTARY ACTS   (See KINESTHESIS, REWARDS, SELF-CONTROL)

It is one of mankind's vanities to believe that every individual is endowed with some kind of faculty, capacity, function, or feature that somehow comes into play in situations where a decision must be made. Such a capacity is called the *will*. Some people are supposed to have more and others less of this marvelous feature, so that some people can impose their wills on others who must, necessarily, have less. The fact that some are in a position to push others around might be more easily explained if we look at the people involved. If one is stronger, bigger, richer, and has more potent armament, the mystery tends to vanish. To refer to a clash of wills is to recognize that two or more people are disagreeing with each other; adding the reference to will does not clarify anything.

Psychologists do not accept the notion that anyone has anything that would correspond to a will any more than they accept the concept of mind, which is commonly supposed somehow to possess or include the will and other attributes, such as intellect. Instead of concluding that someone weighs things in his or her mind and then makes up his or her mind and wills something, psychologists prefer to work on the assumption that whatever one does, he or she had to do it because of the way he or she is built and because of the way he or she was brought up. The assumption is that if one knew enough about someone else, he or she could predict everything the other would do. Obviously, the assumption is just that, since we can never learn enough about someone else to predict everything that might be done, although sometimes one can do fairly well in prediction when the person involved is known fairly well. Husbands and wives get to know each other quite well and, if wise, act accordingly.

Psychologists assume that every decision is determined by a person's past. Every choice, even such a choice as whether or not to flip a coin, is a function of one's prior history.

It might be accepted that some behavior is habitual, thoughtless, and not involved with choices and decisions, but some of our behavior, at least, seems to be not quite mechanical or automatic. One can choose to raise his or her hand or refrain from doing so, for example. How is such behavior explained? William James, the first American psychologist, suggested, in 1890, that voluntary behavior is a function of thinking about the behavior, with the thought being "father to the act." He had a theory he described as *ideomotor action.* According to this theory, if one thinks of doing something, he or she will do it unless he or she thinks of doing the opposite or of doing something else. Thus, if you think of raising your hand, your arm will begin to move upwards. James did not explain how or why this might come about, but later psychologists suggested that as we grow up and develop, we are always moving our musculature about and that the actions involved generate stimuli in the muscles, tendons, and joints (feedback stimuli). These feedback stimuli always accompany movement, and when a movement is initiated by some external stimulus, the feedback stimuli will soon follow and will tend to occur earlier and earlier in any movement sequence. Eventually, the feedback stimuli will occur before the movement itself, to some degree, and will become conditioned to the movement. Thus, if the feedback stimuli can be associated (conditioned) to any other stimuli—for example, words—they can be aroused and can excite the movement itself. What then looks like a self-initiated movement is really a matter of learning or conditioning—quite mechanical and necessary, with no need for a will in order to account for the action.

In practical matters, the problem of will emerges when we regard someone else as willful, stubborn, recalcitrant, and so on. He or she, of course, considers him- or herself determined, logical, steadfast, justified, and so on. Such terminology does not clarify the issues. Each person reacts according to his or her background, and if you wish to change him or her, you must change that background by making your wishes more attractive to him or her through some reinforcement process. People who use torture rely on making the victim's position less attractive, and they usually succeed, if they are powerful and cruel enough. One can, of course, persist to the death if he or she has been strongly conditioned to value certain positions or principles.

WISHES

The only work in psychology in the area of *wishes* that appears to have any pretense to science is that of the Yale psychologist, Clark Hull, in the 1940s. He described wishes as actual physical responses on a small scale, sometimes too small to be detected. Wishes, according to Hull, are small, preparatory reactions that, like any other reactions, must be stimulated into existence. No one can just have wishes arising out of nothing and, therefore, cannot carry around with him or her, unconsciously or otherwise, some wishes that neither he, she, nor anyone else can know about. We know, for example, that a baby wants to be picked up if he or she stretches his or her arms toward his or her mother in a certain way. We can then say that the baby wishes or has a wish to be picked up. Similarly, if a female puckers her lips in a certain manner, the knowledgeable male will know that she wishes to be kissed. Compressing the lips inwardly similarly indicates a strong wish not to be kissed. Opening the mouth indicates a wish for food, if one is in an eating situation, and anyone can tell when a baby does not wish to be fed some specific food.

According to Hull's treatment of the subject, no one can have a wish if he or she has not already had some prior experience with the wished-for object or action. A person who has never been kissed could not possibly want to be kissed. He or she might want something, but it would not be the kiss as such. The wish derives from the successful and satisfying prior experience. Thus, a baby who is given applesauce for the first time may have to be encouraged or otherwise attracted into opening his or her mouth. Once the applesauce is tasted and liked, the baby can want more and expresses the want by opening his or her mouth. If the profferred food is distasteful, the baby will turn away from the spoon. The wish amounts to a preliminary or preparatory aspect or part of some larger act. Although our examples come from feeding babies, we should appreciate that the principles apply across the board. They amount to these: (1) Wishes are responses. (2) Wishes are responses to stimuli and do not exist in a vacuum. (3) Wishes are learned. (4) You cannot really wish for something you never had, since you do not know how to respond to the object, or whatever, that you have never experienced. Most people will object to this last point, since they believe that they do have wishes for things they have never had—for example, $1,000,000. If they suddenly received that amount of money, they might be quite flustered about what to do with it. Many brides say that they would never have gotten married if they had known what it would be like; clearly, they wished for or wanted something other than what they attained.

Freud made much of *unconscious wishes*. Hull's interpretation leaves little or no room for such, since the wish must have a stimulus, and since there must be some kind of preparatory reaction if there is to be a wish. It is most unlikely, for example, that anyone could have a wish to have sexual intercourse with his mother and not be quite fully aware of it. A baby could, of course, want to be held by his or her mother, but this is a far cry from any sexual operations. In general, we can determine what wishes people have by watching what they do and do not do. If they never travel, they cannot really have travel wishes. If they go bowling frequently, then they obviously have wishes for that activity. In general, we measure the strength of a wish by the amount of preparatory activity. It is easy to tell when one person wants to get going while another takes his or her time and dawdles. Pacing up and down, inquiring "Are you ready?", and taking out the car keys before even going to the garage bespeak a rather strong wish to go someplace. The overeager eater sometimes spills his or her food; his or her wish might thus be thought of as too effective.

WORKING MOTHERS: EFFECTS ON CHILDREN

Increasingly, American mothers are working at paying jobs outside the home: More than half of mothers with children between the ages of 6 and 17 do so. Mothers seek outside employment for many reasons, ranging from financial needs to personal satisfaction—just the same reasons that motivate men. As opportunities for women's employment and vocational development continue to improve, the proportion of working mothers will continue to increase. Women, after all, make up slightly more than half of the adult population, and it is quite reasonable to expect that eventually half of all of the employed positions, from professions to trades, to business, and to unskilled labor, will be filled by women.

At present, our society is in a time of transition as traditional sex-typed roles are changing. One of the concerns that is still raised, as more mothers seek outside employment, is "What are the effects of mothers' employment on the children?" The question itself reflects a traditional expectation of women's roles; we seldom, for example, are too concerned over the effects on children of fathers' employment!

What are the effects on children of mothers holding outside jobs? Are the children lonelier, unhappy, less well adjusted or socialized, more anxious, slower to develop, and so on? According to current psychological research, school-age children of working mothers are, on the whole, no different from children whose mothers stay at home. Many children of working mothers have emotional, academic, and developmental problems; but so do many children of mothers who stay at home. The best available data show that a mother's working outside the home does not, in itself, cause any particular hardships or problems for school-age children.

There are no adequate data on the effects of working mothers on infants and preschoolers. Most child-development researchers believe that there are critical periods in a child's life when a mother's presence and attention are very important and that at those times, a mother should not begin working or start leaving the child for long periods of time without appropriate supervision. For example, in the second half of the infant's first year, close attachments are crucial and should not be disrupted; about the time of the child's second birthday, language development is at an important stage, and, again, the stable presence of a loving caretaker is important. At any time that the child is likely to undergo stress, such as on first entering school, moving to a new home, having a new baby born into the family, or experiencing a divorce or the death

of a parent, the child needs parental support, and it would be harmful for the mother or remaining parent to, at that time, begin leaving the child for the long periods that would be necessary if they begin to work. If possible, the parent should remain at home until the crisis is past, or if that is not at all possible, then arrange for a familiar, competent caretaker who can provide the stable support that is needed.

All in all, it is the quality of the mother-child relationship rather than the amount of time the mother is home that seems most important. Mother's constant presence is generally more important for infants and preschoolers, and at critical periods, than for school-age children. A working mother who provides good attention, love, support, interest, and general care; who avoids being away at critical periods; who carefully selects a competent caretaker for some portion of the time; and who specifically tries to maintain good quality relationships with the child when they are together can be reassured that pursuing her own career need not adversely affect the child. In fact, some psychologists believe that it may even enhance and expand the child's view, particularly a little girl's view of her own opportunities and potentialities.

Probably the best of all situations is a stable, two-parent home in which both parents work to pursue their own vocational and personal satisfactions; the parenting responsibilities are then seen as being equal or even more important than the vocational pursuits and are carefully shared and enjoyed by both parents. Such ideal family settings are rare, if they ever occur, but, perhaps, as society continues its present transitions in sex-role expectations, we might begin seeing this kind of arrangement.

At present, the working mother in a two-parent family will probably still find that, working or not, the major burden of housework and child care remains on her shoulders. A working mother has every right to expect that a responsible husband will assume a large share of parenting and housework.

It should be noted that parent-child relationships are largely socioeconomic class affairs. Wealthy people can employ nurses, governesses, tutors, and other companions. In England, the upper classes send their children away from home to schools at an early age. Children will grow up and become adults. It is still impossible to predict what kinds of parent-child relationships are the most appropriate. We are all too strongly warped by our own parent-child backgrounds to make the perfect decisions.

SUBJECT INDEX

Some topics of interest may not be listed alphabetically in the text but are discussed in connection with other headings. The index also may lead you to other headings where an item of interest is considered.